중급 College

VOCA 5000

■ 이홍배   육군 사관학교 졸업
　　　　　미국 브라운 대학교 석사 · 박사(언어학)
　　　　　서강대학교 교양 영어 주임교수
　　　　　미국 브라운 대학교 객원교수
　　　　　서강대학교 영어영문학과장
　　　　　국제문화교육원 원장
　　　　　한국 영어영문학회 회원
　　　　　한국 언어학회 회원
　　　　　한국 생성문법학회 회원
　　　　　서강대학교 영어영문학과 교수 역임

TOEFL · TOEIC · TEPS · 편입 · 공무원 보카바이블
중급 College VOCA 5000

저 자 이홍배
발행인 고본화
발 행 반석출판사
2021년 5월 10일 초판 2쇄 인쇄
2021년 5월 15일 초판 2쇄 발행
홈페이지 www.bansok.co.kr
이메일 bansok@bansok.co.kr
블로그 blog.naver.com/bansokbooks

07547 서울시 강서구 양천로 583. B동 1007호
(서울시 강서구 염창동 240-21번지 우림블루나인 비즈니스센터 B동 1007호)
대표전화 02) 2093-3399 **팩 스** 02) 2093-3393
출 판 부 02) 2093-3395 **영업부** 02) 2093-3396
등록번호 제315-2008-000033호

Copyright ⓒ 이홍배

ISBN 978-89-7172-853-6 (13740)

■ 교재 관련 문의: bansok@bansok.co.kr을 이용해 주시기 바랍니다.
■ 이 책에 게재된 내용의 일부 또는 전체를 무단으로 복제 및 발췌하는 것을 금합니다.
■ 파본 및 잘못된 제품은 구입처에서 교환해 드립니다.

머리말

어떤 사람의 **영어 실력의 척도**라고 할 수 있을 만큼 영어의 어휘력은 영어학습에 있어서 필수적인 요소이다. 그래서 영어를 배우는 사람이라면 누구나 한번쯤은 **어떻게 하면 어휘력을 향상시킬 수 있을 것인가?** 하는 문제에 부딪치게 된다.

많은 사람들이 이처럼 어휘력 향상 문제에 대하여 깊은 관심을 갖고 있으면서도 이에 대처할 수 있는 마땅한 어휘학습서를 연구·개발 시키는 면에서 여지껏 황무지 상태를 면치 못하고 있음은 어휘학습서의 개발이 영어를 모국어로 하지 않는 어느 한 사람의 힘 만으로 단기간 내에 이루어질 수 없기 때문이다.

이러한 현실로 인하여 몇 권의 한국인용 어휘학습서에 의존하여 각기 나름대로의 해결 방법을 모색하고 있는 실정인데, 그 중에서 Levine이 지은 *VOCABULARY*는 비교적 조직적이면서 과학적인 방법으로 어휘력 증가에 접근하고 있다. 원래 이 책은 약 3,000개의 단어를 근간으로 하여 미국 고등학생들의 어휘력을 향상시키기 위하여 미국인이 쓴 책으로서, 우리나라의 실정으로는 이미 상당한 수준의 어휘력이 있는 사람이 보다 체계적으로 어휘를 정리하는데 적합한 책이 아닌가 하는 것이 필자의 견해이다.

그러나 이 책에 대하여 우리나라 영어 학도들의 입장에서 약간 아쉬운 점이 있다면, 그것은 *VOCABULARY*에서 학습시키는 상당한 수의 단어들이 우리가 흔히 접하는 단어가 아니기 때문에 이 책을 철저히 학습한 사람도 영문서적을 읽는다거나 각종 영어 시험에서 실제로 유익하게 활용할 수 없다는 사실이다. 뿐만 아니라 *VOCABULARY*에서 학습시키는 단어가 실제로 약 3,000개에 지나지 않기 때문에 이를 완전히 습득했다 해도 영어 어휘력을 증가시키는데는 부족한 점이 있다.

여기서 필자는 *VOCABULARY*의 부족한 점을 보충하면서 우리나라 영어 학도들의 현실에 적합한 새로운 어휘 학습의 방법을 제시하고자 일련의 어휘학습서를 내게된 것이다. 이 어휘학습서는 *VOCABULARY*에 나오는 근간단어를 포함하지 않으면서 우리가 중급 또는 고급 영문서적을 읽는데 반드시 알아야 하는 단어 약 8,000개를 정선하여 독자 자신의 어휘력 수준에 맞추어 스스로 학습할 수 있도록

초급 Junior VOCABULARY (3,000개)
중급 College VOCABULARY (5,000개)로 구분하였다.

어휘력이란 단순히 한 단어의 뜻만을 아는 것이 아니기 때문에, 단어의 뜻을 암기하는 것만으로는 효과적인 어휘 학습 방법이 되지 못한다. 그러기에 이 책에서는 정확한 발음과 간결한 정의에 의하여 우선 그 뜻을 안 다음 명쾌한 예문들에 의한 다양한 문제를 통하여 반복·학습 시킴으로써 그 의미와 용법을 완전히 습득하게 되는, 이른바 **인지론적 방법(Cognitive Approach)**을 어휘학습에 시도하였으며 매 과(LESSON)를 시작하기 전에 자신의 어휘력 수준을 진단해 볼 수 있는 **어휘력 측정 시험(Pretest)**을 실시함으로써 지속적인 흥미유지와 문제의 다양성을 기했다.

중급 College VOCABULARY의 구성

Prestudy : 1. 고등학교 영어 교과서 및 중급 수준의 영문서적 독서나 이 수준에 해당하는 각종 영어시험에 나오는 단어들 중 가장 빈도(頻度)수가 많은 3,000개의 단어를 정선(精選)하여 근간(根幹)으로 하였다.
(Lessons 1~16)

2. 총 16개 과(LESSON)로 구성하였으며 매 과(LESSON)마다 동의어(Synonym), 반의어(Antonym), 파생어(Derivative)들을 수록하였다.

3. 매 과(LESSON)마다 근간단어에 대한 이해와 숙달을 돕기 위하여 응용문제를 구성하였으며, 9가지 이상의 상이한 문제형식을 취하였다.

4. 근간단어에 대한 발음은 국제 음성기호로 표시하였고, 우리말 역어(譯語)는 사용빈도가 으뜸이며 가장 대표적인 의미를 일관성있게 달았으며, 그 용례에 있어서 현저한 차이가 있을 경우에는 1, 2로 구분하였고, 이에 대한 명쾌한 예문을 통하여 이해력을 촉진시키고 응용력을 함양할 수 있도록 하였다.

UNIT I : Enlarging Vocabulary through Synonyms (Lessons 17~21)
동의어를 활용하여 다양한 문제를 해결해 나가는 동안 자신도 모르게 어휘력이 증가된다.

UNIT II : Enlarging Vocabulary through Antonyms (Lessons 22~26)
반의어를 통한 어휘 학습으로서 매 단어마다 반대되는 단어를 습득함으로써 일석이조(一石二鳥)의 효과를 거두게 된다.

UNIT III : Enlarging Vocabulary through Derivatives (Lessons 27~31)
각 단어의 주요 파생어를 습득함으로써 새로운 단어를 서로 연관시켜 그 의미를 미루어 생각할 수 있는 연상능력을 증가시킨다.

UNIT IV : Learning Vocabulary through Definitions (Lessons 32~35)
단어에 대한 간결한 정의를 통해서 보다 정확하고 광범위한 어휘에 친숙하게 된다.

UNIT V : Discriminating Troublesome Words (Lessons 36~40)
흔히 골치 아픈 단어라고 부르는 혼동하기 쉬운 단어들을 대조하여 학습함으로써 자주 쓰이면서 혼동을 일으키는 단어들을 명확히 이해한다.

CONTENTS

➤ 머리말 / 3

➤ Prestudy 7
　· Lesson 1 8
　· Lesson 2 20
　· Lesson 3 31
　· Lesson 4 43
　· Lesson 5 54
　· Lesson 6 66
　· Lesson 7 78
　· Lesson 8 90
　· Lesson 9 101
　· Lesson 10 113
　· Lesson 11 124
　· Lesson 12 136
　· Lesson 13 148
　· Lesson 14 159
　· Lesson 15 170
　· Lesson 16 181

➤ UNIT Ⅰ 193
　· Lesson 17 194
　· Lesson 18 207
　· Lesson 19 220
　· Lesson 20 233
　· Lesson 21 246

CONTENTS

▶ UNIT II 259
- Lesson 22 260
- Lesson 23 272
- Lesson 24 284
- Lesson 25 296
- Lesson 26 308

▶ UNIT III 321
- Lesson 27 322
- Lesson 28 333
- Lesson 29 344
- Lesson 30 355
- Lesson 31 366

▶ UNIT IV 377
- Lesson 32 378
- Lesson 33 390
- Lesson 34 402
- Lesson 35 414

▶ UNIT V 427
- Lesson 36 428
- Lesson 37 438
- Lesson 38 449
- Lesson 39 459
- Lesson 40 470

▶ 찾아보기 / 480

Prestudy

(Lessons 1~16)

Lesson 1

PRETEST 1

Insert the *letter* of the best answer in the space provided.

1. The _____ was a *disaster* for the village.
   (A) great fire   (B) new bridge

2. They *coincided* with the answers; they had _____ answers.
   (A) the same   (B) different

3. The news of _____ filled them all with *gloom*.
   (A) victory   (B) defeat

4. We usually _____ the envelope with *paste*.
   (A) open   (B) seal

5. The _____ were called to control the *riot*.
   (A) technicians   (B) policemen

ANSWERS 1.A 2.A 3.B 4.B 5.B

STUDY YOUR NEW WORDS-1

batter
[bǽtər]
beat hard and repeatedly; break to pieces by pounding
v. 계속치다, 두드리다, 쳐부수다
syn. beat
There is someone *battering* at the door. You'd better let him in.

clutch
[klʌtʃ]
seize or grip tightly; hold firmly
v. 꼭 잡다, 꼭 쥐다
syn. grasp
The mother *clutched* her baby in her arms.

contemplate
[kɔ́ntempleit]
think about seriously; consider with continued attention
v. 숙고하다, 주시하다
syn. ponder
The police *contemplated* various kinds of trouble after the football match between the two universities.

garbage
[gá:rbidʒ]

waste; unwanted or spoiled food
n. 쓰레기, 찌꺼기
syn. refuse
Please leave your *garbage* in a can outside the door.

obstacle
[ɔ́bstəkl]

something that blocks or stops progress; obstruction
n. 장애(물), 방해(물)
syn. obstruction
A fallen tree across the road was an *obstacle* to our car.

pious
[páiəs]

showing or feeling deep respect for one's religion; devout
adj. 신앙심이 깊은, 경건한
syn. religious
She is a *pious* woman who goes to church every morning.

regulate
[régjuleit]

1. control by rules or principles
v. 통제하다, 규제하다
The school adopted new rules to *regulate* the behavior of students.

2. put in condition to work properly; adjust
v. 조정하다, 조절하다
syn. control
My watch is losing time; I will have to *regulate* it.

riot
[ráiət]

a wild, violent, public disturbance; disorder; tumult; outbreak
n. 소동, 폭동, 혼잡
syn. uproar
The *riot* during the election was put down by the police.

shovel
[ʃʌ́vl]

a long-handed tool with a broad blade
n. 삽, 부삽
syn. spade
We had better move this tree to our garden. Would you please bring the *shovel*?

stately
[stéitli]

showing great dignity; dignified; grand
adj. 위엄있는, 장중한
syn. majestic
We were much impressed by the general's *stately* appearance.

tow
[tou]

pull along by a rope or chain
v. 끌다, 밧줄로 끌다

Lesson 1

	syn. draw They *towed* the wrecked car to the nearest garage.
upset [ʌpsét]	cause to turn over; tip over; disturb greatly ***v.*** 뒤집어 엎다, 전복시키다 **syn.** overturn Her plans were *upset* by the change of the weather.
vex [veks]	make angry; bother; distress; provoke ***v.*** 성나게 하다, 성가시게 하다 **syn.** annoy His father was *vexed* by the child's impolite behavior.

EXERCISE 1 Fill each blank with the most appropriate word given above.
(Inflect the word if necessary.)

1. The fireman _____ the door down with a heavy ax in order to save the baby in the room.
2. The street was too dirty; it was covered with old tins and other forms of _____.
3. On T.V. we watched the _____ parade of our armed forces.
4. It is good to _____ one's past before making decisions for the future.
5. The _____ old woman made every effort to go to worship each time she could.

STUDY YOUR NEW WORDS-2

communism [kɔ́mjunizəm]	a social system in which property is owned by the community and used for the good of all its members ***n.*** 공산주의 **ant.** democracy *Communism* is expressed in various movements, but Russian sovietism is often referred to as a good sample.
dignify [dígnifai]	cause to seem honorable, worthy, and admirable ***v.*** 위엄을 갖추다, 고귀하게 하다 **ant.** degrade They *dignified* her job by giving her a special title
disaster [dizǽstər]	great or sudden misfortune; terrible accident; calamity ***n.*** 재난, 재해, 재앙

ant. fortune
A great flood, fire, earthquake, or great loss of money is a *disaster*.

gloom
[glu:m]

darkness; deep shadow; deep sadness
n. 어두움, 어둑어둑함, 음울
ant. brightness
The maple shade provided him with a rich *gloom* for sleeping.

hospitable
[hɔ́spitəbl]

giving or liking to give friendly treatment of guests or strangers
adj. 호의적인, 후대하는
ant. hostile
He is *hospitable* to anybody; he likes to give attention to the needs of others.

infant
[ínfənt]

a very young child; a baby
n. 유아, 소아, 아기
ant. adult
The woman was carrying an *infant* in her arms.

mature
[mətjúər]

ripe; arrived at full growth; fully developed
adj. 성숙한, 원숙한, 익은
ant. immature
You mustn't be jealous when your sister gets presents; you must learn to behave in a more *mature* way.

prejudice
[prédʒudis]

unfair and unfavorable feeling or opinion
n. 편견, 선입관
ant. fairness
She has a *prejudice* against popular music.

simplify
[símplifai]

make plainer or easier; make simple
v. 단순하게 하다, 쉽게 하다
ant. complicate
The theory was *simplified* to make it easier to understand.

tranquil
[trǽŋkwil]

peaceful; calm; placid; serene; undisturbed
adj. 평온한, 조용한, 잔잔한
ant. noisy
After he retired, he lived a *tranquil* life in the country.

unworthy
[ʌnwə́:rði]

not worthy; not deserving
adj. 무가치한, 하찮은

ant. valuable

You shouldn't trust him; he is **unworthy** of your trust.

valid
[vǽlid]

having a strong firm base; sound; effective
adj. 타당성 있는, 정당한, 유효한
ant. invalid

His objections to the plan on the basis of cost are *valid*.

EXERCISE 2 Fill each blank with the most appropriate word given above.
(Inflect the word if necessary.)

1. Try to _____ your explanation for the little children.

2. _____ comes from a philosophy based on the writings of Karl Marx and Friedrich Engels in the 1800's.

3. If you can't give me a(n) _____ reason for breaking your promise, I shall not trust you again.

4. _____ descended upon the family when they heard the bad news.

5. Such a silly story is _____ of belief.

STUDY YOUR NEW WORDS-3

ally
[əlái]

join or unite; combine for some special purpose; associate
v. 동맹하다, 연합하다
n. alliance

The workers of the factories *allied* against the big employers and asked them for better wages.

approximate
[əprɔ́ksimit]

1. nearly correct but not exact
adj. 대략적인, 대체적인

The *approximate* length of a meter is 40 inches; the exact length is 39.37 inches.

2. come near to; approach
v. 얼추 ~과 같다, ~에 접근하다
n. approximation

Your account of what happened *approximates* the truth, but there are several small errors.

athlete
[ǽθli:t]

a person trained in a sport that requires strength, speed, and skill
n. 경기자, 운동가
adj. athletic
The young *athlete* was much admired for his speed.

certify
[sə́ːrtifai]

declare true or correct by official statements; attest; affirm
v. 증명하다, 보증하다
n. certificate
This diploma *certifies* that you have completed high school.

coincide
[kouinsáid]

correspond exactly; be in agreement
v. 일치하다, 부합하다
n. coincidence
My religious beliefs and yours do not *coincide*.

convey
[kənvéi]

carry from one place to another
v. 나르다, 운반하다, 전달하다
n. conveyance
A truck *conveyed* my furniture to my new home.

discreet
[diskríːt]

showing good judgment; very careful in speech and action; prudent
adj. 분별 있는, 사려 깊은, 신중한
n. discretion
It wasn't *discreet* of you to call him around midnight.

evolve
[ivɔ́lv]

develop gradually
v. 발전하다, 진화하다
adj. evolutionary
The British political system has *evolved* over several centuries.

identify
[aidéntifai]

1. treat as the same
v. 동일시하다, 같이 취급하다
adj. identical
The good king *identified* the well-being of his people with his own.

2. recognize as being a particular person or thing
v. 식별하다, 확인하다
I could *identify* the coat at once; it was my brother's.

radiate
[réidieit]

send out (light or heat)
v. (빛·열 따위를) 방사하다, 발하다

	adj. radiant
	The sun *radiates* light and heat.
supervise [sjúːpərvaiz]	look after and direct; oversee; superintend
	v. 감독하다, 지휘하다
	n. supervision
	The architect *supervised* the building of the house.
torrent [tɔ́ːrənt]	a violently flowing stream (of water)
	n. 분류(奔流), 억수, 용솟음
	adj. torrential
	A *torrent* of water swept down the valley.

EXERCISE 3

Fill each blank with the most appropriate word given above.
(Inflect the word if necessary.)

1. The rain came down in a(n) _____ during the thunderstorm.
2. Great Britain was _____ with the United States in both World Wars.
3. Do you think a bus can _____ all the guests to the airport? We need at least two buses.
4. The _____ number of students in our school is 800—but remember that 800 is not an exact figure.
5. Your answers are correct; they _____ with the answers in the book.

STUDY YOUR NEW WORDS-4

anniversary [ænivə́ːrsəri]	the yearly return of a special date
	n. 기념일, 기념제
	My parents invited their friends to their 30th wedding *anniversary*.
barracks [bǽrəks]	a building for soldiers to live in
	n. 막사, 병영
	You can't expect soldiers to live in a *barracks* like that!
creed [kriːd]	a statement of the principal beliefs
	n. 신조, 교의, 강령
	"Honesty is the best policy" was his *creed* through his whole life.

drip
[drip]

fall in drops
v. (물방울 등이) 똑똑 떨어지다
We have to fix the roof; water is *dripping* down from the ceiling.

hound
[haund]

a dog used in hunting
n. 사냥개
A good *hound* should have a sharp sense of smell.

jerk
[dʒəːrk]

1. pull or twist suddenly
v. 갑자기 움직이다, 확 당기다
As the water was unexpectedly hot, he *jerked* his hand out.

2. a quick, sharp movement
n. 갑작스런 움직임
As he stopped the car with a *jerk*, we were all thrown to the floor.

mold
[mould]

make or form into a desired shape
v. 만들다, 형성하다
The artist *molded* the clay into a figure of a child.

paste
[peist]

a mixture of flour and water used for making materials stick together
n. 풀, 반죽
The clerk used thick *paste* to put the label on the package.

patron
[péitrən]

1. one who buys regularly at a certain store; a regular customer
n. 단골 손님, 고객
She has been a *patron* of this store for many years.

2. a person who gives his approval and support to a person, art, or cause
n. 후원자, 옹호자, 보호자
The *patrons* of the museum contributed the money for the new museum building.

razor
[réizər]

an instrument for shaving hair from the face
n. 면도칼, 면도기
John shaved off his beard with an electric *razor*.

slap
[slæp]

strike quickly with the open hand; smack
v. 철썩 치다, 철썩 때리다
She *slapped* the boy on the cheek for disobedience, and he began to cry.

suicide
[súːisaid]

the act of killing oneself
n. 자살
The police think that the death was by *suicide*.

telegraph
[téləgræf]

a device or system for sending messages by electric signals

n. 전신, 전보

Mother sent me a message by ***telegraph*** that she would arrive home by afternoon plane.

EXERCISE 4 **Fill each blank with the most appropriate word given above.**
(Inflect the word if necessary.)

1. The new shop across the road has taken away some of my best _____.

2. We usually send an urgent message by _____.

3. More than two hundred soldiers live in this _____.

4. His character has been _____ more by his experiences in life than by the education he got at school.

5. When her husband died of a fever, she committed _____.

EXERCISE 1.	1. battered	2. garbage	3. stately	4. contemplate	5. pious
EXERCISE 2.	1. simplify	2. communism	3. valid	4. gloom	5. unworthy
EXERCISE 3.	1. torrent	2. allied	3. convey	4. approximate	5. coincide
EXERCISE 4.	1. patrons	2. telegraph	3. barracks	4. molded	5. suicide

종합 연습 문제

1 In the space at the left, write the *letter* of the word that has most nearly the SAME MEANING as the italicized word.

_____ 1. a *mature* plant (A) young (B) harmful (C) evergreen (D) full-grown

_____ 2. *clutch* the rope (A) seize (B) throw (C) draw (D) hang

_____ 3. the *discreet* person (A) intelligent (B) violent (C) wealthy (D) prudent

_____ 4. *regulate* the speed of a machine (A) measure (B) increase (C) adjust (D) decrease

_____ 5. a special offer for the regular *patrons* (A) customers (B) travellers (C) visitors (D) followers

2 In the space provided, write the *letter* of the word that most nearly means the OPPOSITE of the italicized word.

_____ 1. *dignify* (A) regulate (B) convey (C) degrade (D) grip

_____ 2. *infant* (A) paste (B) blade (C) creed (D) adult

_____ 3. *hospitable* (A) hostile (B) effective (C) admirable (D) ripe

_____ 4. *disaster* (A) calamity (B) fortune (C) disorder (D) gloom

_____ 5. *prejudice* (A) torrent (B) religion (C) fairness (D) athlete

3 Supply the correct form of the word in italics for the blank space in each sentence.

1. *athlete* The game was played on the _____ field.
2. *supervise* The house was built under the careful _____ of an architect.
3. *ally* The _____ between the two nations strengthened each of them greatly.
4. *approximate* What he had said was a very close _____ to the truth.
5. *coincide* Is there any _____ between his opinion and your own?

4 Fill in the missing *letters* of the word at the right. Each dash stands for one missing letter.

DEFINITION	WORD
1. the yearly return of a special date	A_____ARY
2. treat as the same	I_____FY
3. send out (light or heat)	R___ATE
4. a long-handled tool with a broad blade	SH___L
5. develop gradually	EV___E
6. an instrument for shaving hair from the face	R__OR
7. a statement of the principal beliefs	C___D
8. fall in drops	D__P
9. cause to turn over	UP___
10. a dog used in hunting	H___D

5 In the space provided, write the *letter* of the word NOT RELATED in meaning to the other words in each line.

_____	1.	(A) obstacle	(B) hindrance	(C) obstruction	(D) destruction
_____	2.	(A) ally	(B) slap	(C) beat	(D) smack
_____	3.	(A) pull	(B) upset	(C) draw	(D) tow
_____	4.	(A) supervise	(B) oversee	(C) superintend	(D) overflow
_____	5.	(A) waste	(B) garbage	(C) riot	(D) refuse
_____	6.	(A) ripe	(B) serene	(C) calm	(D) tranquil
_____	7.	(A) contemplate	(B) ponder	(C) consider	(D) evolve
_____	8.	(A) exert	(B) attest	(C) certify	(D) affirm
_____	9.	(A) pious	(B) devout	(C) valid	(D) religious
_____	10.	(A) annoy	(B) coincide	(C) vex	(D) bother

6 Fill each blank with the most appropriate word from the vocabulary list below.

VOCABULARY LIST

molded	jerk	hospitable
torrent	identify	dripping
hound	obstacle	creed
batter	athlete	tranquil

1. He stopped the car with a(n) _____, and we were thrown to the floor.

2. The door is firmly locked. You'll have to _____ it down if you want to get in the room.

3. After he retired, he lived a(n) _____ life in the country.

4. A(n) _____ in the road prevented the cars from moving.

5. The young _____ was much admired for his speed and strength.

6. It was so hot that sweat was _____ from my face.

7. The heavy rains turned the stream into a(n) _____.

8. He is _____ to anybody; he likes to give attention to the needs of others.

9. I could _____ the hat at once; it was my father's.

10. A good _____ should have a sharp sense of smell.

해답

1 1. D 2. A 3. D 4. C 5. A
2 1. C 2. D 3. A 4. B 5. C
3 1. athletic 2. supervision 3. alliance 4. approximation 5. coincidence
4 1. anniversary 2. identify 3. radiate 4. shovel 5. evolve
   6. razor 7. creed 8. drip 9. upset 10. hound
5 1. D 2. A 3. B 4. D 5. C 6. A 7. D 8. A 9. C 10. B
6 1. jerk 2. batter 3. tranquil 4. obstacle 5. athlete
   6. dripping 7. torrent 8. hospitable 9. identify 10. hound

Lesson 1

Lesson 2

PRETEST 2

Insert the *letter* of the best answer in the space provided.

1. She gave me a look of *reproach*; she tried to _____ me.
   (A) praise   (B) blame

2. Cuts become *infected* if they _____ cleaned promptly.
   (A) are   (B) aren't

3. Only a foolish man *dedicates* his _____.
   (A) life to pleasure   (B) health by overworking

4. The girl was _____ and was in *anguish* all that evening.
   (A) very badly hurt   (B) invited to the party

5. My brother is *awkward* with a knife and fork; he _____.
   (A) uses them skillfully   (B) drops food at each meal

ANSWERS 1. B 2. B 3. A 4. A 5. B

STUDY YOUR NEW WORDS-1

abrupt
[əbrʌpt]

1. sudden; unexpected
adj. 갑작스러운, 돌연한, 뜻밖의
syn. sudden
He made an *abrupt* turn to avoid hitting another car.

2. very steep
adj. 가파른, 험준한
The road made an *abrupt* rise up the hill

acknowledge
[əknɔ́lidʒ]

1. agree or admit that something is true; admit as true
v. 인정하다, 승인하다
syn. admit
I am sure that she will soon *acknowledge* her own faults.

2. say that one has received something
v. 접수[수령]를 알리다
We should always *acknowledge* gifts as soon as we receive them.

beware
[biwέər]

be on guard against; be careful
v. 조심하다, 경계하다
syn. heed
You should *beware* of bad companions; they may corrupt you.

dwell
[dwel]

make one's home; live; abide
v. 거주하다, 살다
syn. reside
They *dwell* in the country but work in the city.

endow
[indáu]

1. give money or property to provide an income for
v. 기금을 기부하다, 자산을 증여하다
syn. donate
The rich man *endowed* the college he had attended.

2. provide with some ability, quality or talent
v. 부여하다, (재능을) 주다
syn. donate
Nature *endowed* her with both a good mind and good looks.

pathetic
[pəθétik]

causing a feeling of pity or sorrow
adj. 애처로운, 가련한
syn. pitiable
The lost child I met on the street was very *pathetic*.

reap
[ri:p]

cut and gather in (crops, etc.)
v. 베어들이다, 거둬들이다
syn. harvest
Giant machines *reap* the wheat grown in the field.

reproach
[ripróutʃ]

find fault with; reprove
v. 비난하다, 나무라다
syn. scold
When he came home drunk his wife *reproached* him with a loud angry voice.

rigorous
[rígərəs]

1. severe; painful; stern
adj. 준엄한, 가혹한, 엄격한
Rigorous exercise can damage health instead of improving it.

Lesson 2

2. careful and exact
adj. 엄밀한, 정밀한
syn. rigid
He made a *rigorous* study of the plants in the tropical area.

sustain
[səstéin]

hold up; support the weight of
v. 떠받치다, 버티다, 유지하다
syn. maintain
The large columns *sustained* the weight of the roof.

torment
[tɔ́rmént]

cause great physical or mental suffering; torture
v. 괴롭히다, 고문하다
syn. annoy
She is often *tormented* with violent headaches.

EXERCISE 1 Fill each blank with the most appropriate word given above.
(Inflect the word if necessary.)

1. We could not bear to listen to the sick child's _____ cries from pain.
2. This wooden shelf cannot _____ the weight of all these books.
3. The rich man _____ a new school for special studies in medicine.
4. It took many hands to _____ the cotton crop before the invention of machinery.
5. Teachers are often _____ by the students' stupid questions.

STUDY YOUR NEW WORDS-2

abolish
[əbɔ́liʃ]

put an end to; destroy
v. 폐지하다, 없애다
Slavery was *abolished* in the United States in 1865.

anguish
[ǽŋgwiʃ]

great pain, or suffering of body or mind
n. 고통, 괴로움, 고민
ant. comfort
The injured soldier moaned in *anguish* until the doctor arrived.

awkward
[ɔ́:kwərd]

1. lacking skill in moving parts of body; clumsy
adj. 서투른, 섣부른, 어색한
He needs a great deal of driving practice; he is still *awkward* with his car.

2. causing inconvenience; difficult to deal with; unwilling to agree
adj. 거북한, 곤란한, 불편한
ant. skillful
The meeting was at nine o'clock, which was an *awkward* time for many people.

bliss
[blis]

great happiness joy
n. 기쁨, 즐거움, 희열
ant. misery
What *bliss* it is to be able to lie in bed instead of working!

expenditure
[ikspénditʃər]

spending (money, strength, etc.)
n. 지출, 소비, 비용
ant. income
Such a great work requires the *expenditure* of much money and time.

primitive
[prímitiv]

of early times before recorded history
adj. 원시의, 원시적인
ant. modern
Primitive people lived in caves and made tools from stones and animal bones.

prolong
[prəlɔ́ŋ]

make longer in time; extend
v. 늘리다, 연장하다
ant. reduce
The old woman's life was *prolonged* by the doctor's good care.

rural
[rúːrəl]

of country or village life
adj. 시골의, 전원의
ant. urban
They lived in a small *rural* community.

suspend
[səspénd]

stop for a while
v. 일시 중지시키다, 한때 멈추게 하다, 정학시키다
ant. continue
The hurricane *suspended* all ferry service for three days.

undistinguished
[ʌndistíŋgwiʃt]

not distinguished; common
adj. 두드러지지 않은, 평범한
ant. prominent
The book is very interesting although it was written by an *undistinguished* author.

EXERCISE 2
Fill each blank with the most appropriate word given above.
(Inflect the word if necessary.)

1. She was in _____ until the doctor set her broken leg.

2. Bows and spears are _____ weapons.

3. If war could be _____, armies and navies would be unnecessary.

4. He had many accidents because he was _____ in driving.

5. He was _____ from school for a week for his bad conducts.

STUDY YOUR NEW WORDS-3

concession
[kənséʃən]

the act of yielding or admitting as true
n. 양보, 용인(容認)
v. concede
To reach agreement, both sides must make *concessions*.

deceit
[disíːt]

the act or practice of deceiving or lying
n. 속임, 사기, 기만
v. deceive
The merchant always used *deceit* in his business dealings.

dedicate
[dédikeit]

devote to a special sacred purpose
v. 바치다, 헌납하다, 봉헌하다
n. dedication
The land on which the battle of Gettysburg was fought was *dedicated* to the soldiers who had died there.

dizzy
[dízi]

affected with a spinning or unsteady feeling
adj. 현기증 나는, 어찔어찔한
n. dizziness
When you spin round and round, and stop suddenly, you feel *dizzy*.

economical
[iːkənɔ́mikəl]

avoiding waste; thrifty; saving
adj. 경제적인, 절약하는, 검약한
n. economy
A good manager should be *economical* in the use of his funds.

infect
[infékt]

make ill with something that produces disease
v. 감염시키다, 병독으로 오염시키다

n. infection
She ***infected*** the whole class with her influenza.

intolerant
[intɔ́lərənt]

not willing to let others do and think as they choose
adj. 아량이 없는, 편협한
n. intolerance
The old man did not smoke himself and was so ***intolerant*** that he did not allow his friends to smoke when they visited him.

respective
[rispéktiv]

of or for each individual
adj. 각각의, 각기의
adv. respectively
The party ended and we all went off to our ***respective*** rooms.

scholar
[skɔ́lər]

a person of great learning
n. 학자, 학식이 있는 사람
adj. scholastic
He was respected as a great ***scholar*** of history.

technique
[tekní:k]

technical skill; a method used by an expert
n. 기술, 기교
adj. technical
The pianist's ***technique*** was excellent, though his interpretation of the work was poor.

tedious
[tí:djəs]

tiring; boring
adj. 지루한, 싫증나는
n. tedium
The long wait at the airport was really ***tedious***.

EXERCISE 3 Fill each blank with the most appropriate word given above.
(Inflect the word if necessary.)

1. Anyone with a bad cold may _____ the people around him.
2. A long talk that you cannot understand is _____.
3. This statue is _____ to the memory of soldiers killed in the defense of our country.
4. My husband and I are each going to visit our _____ mothers.
5. As a(n) _____ to public opinion, the government lowered tax on tobacco.

STUDY YOUR NEW WORDS-4

bristle
[brísl]
(have one's hair) stand up straight
v. (털이) 곤두서다, (털을) 곤두세우다
He was so frightened that his hair seemed to *bristle*.

commodity
[kəmɔ́dəti]
anything that is bought and sold; a useful article of trade
n. 상품, 일용품
Prices of household *commodities* have risen since the war began.

dispatch
[dispǽtʃ]
send off quickly for a special purpose
v. 급송하다, 급파하다
The captain *dispatched* a boat to bring a doctor on board ship.

formal
[fɔ́rməl]
according to accepted customs or rules; ceremonial
adj. 공식적인, 형식을 갖춘
You must write a *formal* acceptance to this invitation.

frantic
[frǽntik]
wild with excitement, fear, pain, etc.
adj. 미친 듯이 날뛰는, 대단히 흥분한
Frantic efforts were made to escape the sinking ship.

heave
[hi:v]
raise or lift with great effort
v. 들어 올리다, 높이 올리다
He *heaved* the heavy box into the wagon.

hemisphere
[hémisfiər]
half of a sphere or globe
n. (지구의) 반구(半球)
North America and South America are in the Western *Hemisphere*.

install
[instɔ́:l]
1. place in position for service or use
v. 설치하다, 비치하다
The new owner of the house *installed* a telephone.

2. settle in a place
v. 자리에 앉히다
The cat *installed* itself in a chair near the fireplace.

lash
[læʃ]
a stroke or blow with a whip
n. 채찍질, 매질
I gave my horse a *lash* that sounded through the forest.

pension
[pénʃən]

a regular payment of money to one who is retired
n. 연금(年金)
He will start receiving a *pension* when he retires at sixty.

scope
[skoup]

the field within which an activity takes place
n. 범위, 영역
This book has greater *scope* than others on the same subject.

species
[spíːʃi(ː)z]

a sort; a kind
n. 종(種), 종족, 종류
The wolf and the dog belong to the same *species*.

EXERCISE 4

Fill each blank with the most appropriate word given above.
(Inflect the word if necessary.)

1. I _____ him to his feet so that he could go over the fence.
2. The mother was _____ with grief when she heard that her child was dead.
3. Wine is one of many _____ that France sells abroad.
4. Business letters must always be _____, but we should write in a natural way to friends.
5. A man or woman who makes the armed forces a career may retire with a(n) _____ after serving the required time.

해답

EXERCISE 1.	1. pathetic	2. sustain	3. endowed	4. reap	5. tormented
EXERCISE 2.	1. anguish	2. primitive	3. abolished	4. awkward	5. suspended
EXERCISE 3.	1. infect	2. tedious	3. dedicated	4. respective	5. concession
EXERCISE 4.	1. heaved	2. frantic	3. commodities	4. formal	5. pension

종합 연습 문제

1 In the space provided, write the *letter* of the word NOT RELATED in meaning to the other words in each line.

_____	1.	(A) sudden	(B) abrupt	(C) stale	(D) unexpected
_____	2.	(A) crop	(B) harvest	(C) require	(D) reap
_____	3.	(A) agree	(B) acknowledge	(C) cherish	(D) admit
_____	4.	(A) reprove	(B) interrupt	(C) scold	(D) reproach
_____	5.	(A) pitiable	(B) miserable	(C) pathetic	(D) horrible
_____	6.	(A) take over	(B) beware of	(C) take heed	(D) watch out
_____	7.	(A) sustain	(B) maintain	(C) resist	(D) support
_____	8.	(A) torment	(B) annoy	(C) torture	(D) surrender
_____	9.	(A) habituate	(B) dwell	(C) abide	(D) reside
_____	10.	(A) rigorous	(B) shrewd	(C) rigid	(D) stern

2 In the space before each word in COLUMN I, write the *letter* of its correct meaning in COLUMN II.

	COLUMN I	COLUMN II
_____	1. dispatch	(A) wild with excitement or pain
_____	2. install	(B) (have one's hair) stand up straight
_____	3. heave	(C) the field within which an activity takes place
_____	4. lash	(D) place in a position for service or use
_____	5. bristle	(E) send off quickly
_____	6. scope	(F) a sort; a kind
_____	7. pension	(G) a stroke or blow with a whip
_____	8. commodity	(H) anything that is bought and sold
_____	9. species	(I) a regular payment to a retired man
_____	10. frantic	(J) raise or lift with great effort

3 In the space provided, write the *letter* of the word that most nearly means the OPPOSITE of the italicized word.

_____ 1. *expenditure*   (A) intimacy   (B) income
　　　　　　　　　　　　(C) rest   (D) disappointment

_____ 2. *bliss* (A) fault (B) misery
              (C) mercy (D) deceit

_____ 3. *primitive* (A) modern (B) humble
                  (C) shabby (D) luxurious

_____ 4. *anguish* (A) plea (B) frequence
                (C) compression (D) comfort

_____ 5. *abolish* (A) approve (B) establish
                (C) praise (D) reprove

_____ 6. *rural* (A) rustic (B) disorderly
              (C) abrupt (D) urban

_____ 7. *prolong* (A) erase (B) diffuse
                (C) expand (D) reduce

_____ 8. *suspend* (A) continue (B) believe
                (C) investigate (D) punish

_____ 9. *awkward* (A) courageous (B) hearty
                (C) skillful (D) flat

_____ 10. *undistinguished* (A) prominent (B) common
                    (C) wrong (D) chaotic

4 Complete the following table with the appropriate word forms.

	ADJECTIVE	NOUN	VERB	ADVERB
1.	intolerant	_____	XXXXX	_____
2.	XXXXX	_____	endow	XXXXX
3.	_____	_____	concede	_____
4.	todious	_____	XXXXX	_____
5.	_____	economy	_____	_____
6.	_____	rigor	XXXXX	_____
7.	_____	scholar	XXXXX	XXXXX
8.	_____	_____	dedicate	XXXXX
9.	_____	_____	infect	_____
10.	_____	_____	deceive	_____

5

In the space provided, write the *letter* of the word or expression that has most nearly the SAME MEANING as the italicized word.

_____ 1. Her mother became *frantic* when she heard the news.
   (A) gloomy   (B) mad   (C) animated   (D) delighted

_____ 2. The old man was so *intolerant* that he did not allow his friends to smoke when they visited him.
   (A) hysterical   (B) anxious   (C) ungenerous   (D) angry

_____ 3. No one wishes to *dwell* in such a noisy town.
   (A) live   (B) work   (C) sleep   (D) study

_____ 4. There are many bad customs and laws that ought to be *abolished*.
   (A) reconsidered   (B) destroyed   (C) criticized   (D) amended

_____ 5. I am sure that he will soon *acknowledge* his own faults.
   (A) find   (B) conceal   (C) admit   (D) correct

_____ 6. She was in *anguish* until she knew that her husband's life had been saved.
   (A) suffering   (B) gloom   (C) embarrassment   (D) confusion

_____ 7. His manners are so polite that he will never be *reproached* by anyone.
   (A) despised   (B) scolded   (C) punished   (D) advised

_____ 8. He does more than others because he is *economical* of time and energy.
   (A) thrifty   (B) theoretic   (C) controllable   (D) applicable

_____ 9. These birds belong to the same *species*.
   (A) zoo   (B) owner   (C) sort   (D) animal

_____ 10. The boy's *deceit* made his mother very unhappy.
   (A) dirty clothes   (B) foolish answer   (C) action of lying   (D) cruel treatment

해답

1 1. C   2. C   3. C   4. B   5. D   6. A   7. C   8. D   9. A   10. B
2 1. E   2. D   3. J   4. G   5. B   6. C   7. I   8. H   9. F   10. A
3 1. B   2. B   3. A   4. D   5. B   6. D   7. D   8. A   9. C   10. A

4

ADJECTIVE	NOUN	VERB	ADVERB
1. (intolerant)	intolerance	XXXXX	intolerantly
2. XXXXX	endowment	(endow)	XXXXX
3. concessive	concession	(concede)	concessively
4. (tedious)	tedium	XXXXX	tediously
5. economical	(economy)	economize	economically
6. rigorous	(rigor)	XXXXX	rigorously
7. scholastic	(scholar)	XXXXX	XXXXX
8. dedicatory	dedication	(dedicate)	XXXXX
9. infectious	infection	(infect)	infectiously
10. deceitful	deceit	(deceive)	deceitfully

5 1. B   2. C   3. A   4. B   5. C   6. A   7. B   8. A   9. C   10. C

Lesson 3

PRETEST 3

Insert the *letter* of the best answer in the space provided.

1. As children grow older, they become _____ *rational*.
   (A) more   (B) less

2. Everyone paid *homage* to the _____.
   (A) great leader   (B) strange airplane

3. The *timid* child was very _____ of the big animal.
   (A) fond   (B) afraid

4. *Conservative* people _____ to change their traditions.
   (A) are eager   (B) do not like

5. There are many *vacancies* in _____.
   (A) the river   (B) our office

ANSWERS 1.A 2.A 3.B 4.B 5.B

STUDY YOUR NEW WORDS-1

assail
[əséil]
attack violently, either by words or blows
v. 공격하다, 공박하다
syn. assault
The enemy may *assail* our defense positions tomorrow.

barrier
[bǽriər]
something that stands in the way; obstacle
n. 장벽, 장애, 방벽
syn. hindrance
Countries can no longer depend on mountain *barriers* for protection.

burglar
[bə́ːrɡlər]
a person who beaks into a house or other building to steal; robber
n. 강도, 도둑
syn. thief
A *burglar* broke into my house last night.

Lesson 3   31

devour
[diváuər]

eat up hungrily and quickly
v. 삼켜 버리다, 게걸스레 먹다
syn. gulp
The fire *devoured* twenty square miles of forest.

dreary
[dríəri]

cheerless; depressing; dismal
adj. 음산한, 황량한, 쓸쓸한
syn. gloomy
It was a *dreary* day, cold and without sunshine.

fling
[fliŋ]

throw violently or with force; throw aside
v. 던지다, 팽개치다
syn. cast
Boys like to *fling* stones into water.

homage
[hɔ́midʒ]

respect or honor shown or given to another
n. 존경, 경의
syn. reverence
He bowed in *homage* to the Unknown Soldier.

inescapable
[iniskéipəbl]

not escapable; sure to happen; inevitable
adj. 불가피한, 피할 수 없는
syn. unavoidable
Death is *inescapable*; it comes to everyone.

radical
[rǽdikəl]

1. of the root or base; basic, thorough and complete
adj. 본질적인, 근본적인
syn. fundamental
There are *radical* differences between the two systems.

2. extreme; favoring great changes
adj. 과격한, 급진적인
His ideas are too *radical* to be acceptable to most people.

shiver
[ʃívər]

shake or tremble from cold, excitement, or fear
v. 떨다, 흔들리다
syn. quiver
The boys and girls were *shivering* all over with cold.

sly
[slai]

skillful at tricking; tricky; cunning
adj. 교활한, 간교한
syn. crafty
The *sly* cat stole the meat while the cook's back was turned.

stall [stɔːl]	an indoor enclosure for one animal *n.* 축사, 마굿간 syn. stable Each horse was put in a separate *stall*.
vanquish [vǽŋkwiʃ]	conquer; defeat completely; subdue *v.* 정복하다, 극복하다 syn. overcome At first she shivered from her fear but at last she could *vanquish* it.

EXERCISE 1   Fill each blank with the most appropriate word given above.
(Inflect the word if necessary.)

1. A fox is _____ enough to cross a stream so that dogs can not follow its scent.
2. The desert always has been a(n) _____ to the movement of the people.
3. Don't _____ your clothes on the floor; hang them up.
4. A sudden gust of cold wind made us _____.
5. The horse was missing from its _____, and we spent whole afternoon to find it.

STUDY YOUR NEW WORDS-2

clumsy [klʌ́mzi]	awkward and ungraceful in movement or action *adj.* 서투른, 솜씨 없는, 어색한 ant. skillful He asked me such a *clumsy* question that I did not know what to reply.
conservative [kənsə́ːrvətiv]	opposed to change; wanting to preserve existing conditions *adj.* 보수적인, 보수주의의 ant. progressive Old people are usually more *conservative* than young people.
exhale [ekshéil]	force air out from the lungs; breathe out *v.* 숨을 내쉬다, 내뿜다 ant. inhale He lit his pipe and *exhaled* clouds of smoke.
homely [hóumli]	not good-looking; ugly; plain *adj.* 못난, 못생긴

Lesson 3

ant. pretty
I was very disappointed to see her sister; she was a *homely* girl.

indefinite
[indéfinit]

not clear; not precise; vague; obscure
adj. 불명확한, 막연한, 일정치 않은
ant. definite
"Maybe" or "perhaps" is a very *indefinite* answer.

obedient
[əbí:djənt]

doing what one is ordered to do; willing to obey; docile
adj. 순종하는, 유순한, 고분고분한
ant. disobedient
The *obedient* dog quickly responded to his master's whistle.

precise
[prisáis]

exact; accurate; definite
adj. 정확한, 정밀한, 명확한
ant. approximate
He gave a *precise* account of how much money he had spent.

rational
[rǽʃənəl]

sensible; reasonable; based on reasoning
adj. 이성(理性)적인, 이성이 있는
ant. irrational
When people are very angry, they seldom act in a *rational* way.

rigid
[rídʒid]

not easily bent; stiff; strict
adj. 강직한, 엄격한, 굳은
ant. mild
In our home it is a *rigid* rule to wash one's hands before eating.

timid
[tímid]

fearful; lacking courage; cowardly
adj. 겁 많은, 소심한
ant. bold
A *timid* child is apt to cry when he sees a strange person.

vertical
[və́:rtikəl]

straight up and down; perpendicular; upright
adj. 수직의, 직립의
ant. horizontal
A *vertical* take-off aircraft can rise straight from the ground, without running along for some distance.

wholesome
[hóulsəm]

beneficial; good for the body; healthful
adj. 건전한, 유익한, 건강에 좋은

ant. harmful

Such a movie is not *wholesome* for young children.

> **EXERCISE 2** Fill each blank with the most appropriate word given above.
> (Inflect the word if necessary.)
>
> 1. A(n) _____ woman wouldn't weep just because her husband had forgotten her birthday.
> 2. She bought a cookbook to prepare _____ meals for her family.
> 3. The directions he gave us were so _____ that we found our way easily.
> 4. He does not like his job, but he is too _____ to try to find another.
> 5. I have a very _____ uncle who still thinks that a woman's place is in the home.

STUDY YOUR NEW WORDS-3

abandon
[əbǽndən]

give up entirely; desert; quit
v. 버리다, 그만두다, 단념하다
n. abandonment
He *abandoned* his wife and went away with all their money.

barbarian
[bɑːrbɛ́əriən]

one who is rude and wild in behavior
n. 야만인, 미개인
adj. barbarous
People who behave like *barbarians* are not welcome at this hotel.

essence
[ésəns]

the central or most important quality of a thing
n. 본질, 정수
adj. essential
The *essence* of his religious teaching is love for all men.

harmony
[hάːrməni]

pleasing combination of parts, sounds, or colors
n. 조화, 화합, 일치
v. harmonize
My cat and dog never fight; they live together in perfect *harmony*.

indulge
[indʌ́ldʒ]

give way to one's pleasure; let oneself have, use, or do
v. 충족시키다, ~에 빠지(게 하)다
adj. indulgent
He *indulged* his desire for cigarettes to a harmful extent.

intrude
[intrú:d]

come in without being asked or wanted
v. 침입하다, 밀고 들어가다
n. intrusion
I was unwilling to *intrude* upon them so late at night.

modify
[mɔ́difai]

1. make partial changes in; change slightly
v. 수정하다, 고치다
n. modification
The company *modified* the design of the automobile in order to make it more attractive.

2. limit the meaning of; qualify
v. 수식하다, 제한하다
n. modification
In the phrase, "a green hat," the adjective "green" *modifies* the noun "hat."

oppress
[əprés]

control or rule by the use of unjust and cruel force
v. 억압하다, 압박하다
adj. oppressive
A good government will not *oppress* the people.

proficient
[prəfíʃənt]

thoroughly skilled; expert
adj. 숙달된, 능숙한
n. proficiency
His mother is very *proficient* in music.

sequence
[sí:kwəns]

the act of coming one after another; succession
n. 연속, 계속
adj. sequent
The books should be arranged in *sequence* according to author.

suburb
[sʌ́bə:rb]

an outer area of a town or city, where people live; outskirt
n. 교외, 시외, 근교
adj. suburban
They would rather live in the *suburbs* than in the city.

summary
[sʌ́məri]

a brief statement giving the main points of a matter; abstract; abridgement
n. 요약, 적요
v. summarize
This history book has a *summary* at the end of each chapter.

vacancy
[véikənsi]

empty space; unfilled position; emptiness
n. 공백, 공석, 공허
adj. vacant
There are many *vacancies* in the parking lot when the stores are closed.

EXERCISE 3 Fill each blank with the most appropriate word given above.
(Inflect the word if necessary.)

1. The industrial revolution _____ the whole structure of English society.
2. In our factory we've got a(n) _____ for metal worker; all the other positions are filled.
3. Please keep the numbered cards in _____; don't mix them up.
4. Many people who work in the city live in the _____.
5. The search was _____ when night came, even though the child had not been found.

STUDY YOUR NEW WORDS-4

alley
[æli]

a narrow street between or behind buildings
n. 골목, 소로(小路)
The truck was too large to pass through the *alley*.

apologize
[əpɔ́lədʒaiz]

express regret, as for a fault or causing pain
v. 사과하다, 사죄하다
I *apologized* to her for stepping on her foot.

dairy
[déəri]

a place where milk and cream are made and kept
n. 낙농장, 낙농실, 우유점
We could see lots of milk products in the *dairy*.

discern
[disə́ːrn]

see clearly; perceive; distinguish; recognize
v. 식별하다, 분간하다, 알아보다
I was not able to *discern* the road in the dark.

jaw
[dʒɔː]

the lower part of a face
n. 턱, (*pl.*) 입 부분
The meat was so tough that his *jaws* hurt from chewing it.

limp
[limp]

walk unevenly because of an injured leg
v. 절뚝거리다, 다리를 절다
After falling down the stairs, he *limped* for several days.

pillar
[pílər]

a slender, upright structure used as a support
n. 기둥, 표주(標柱)
The roof of the porch was supported by brick *pillars*.

potential
[pouténʃəl]

possible, though not yet actually existing or fully in use
adj. 잠재적인, 장래 가능성이 있는
He is regarded as a *potential* leader of our political party.

refrigerator
[rifrídʒəreitər]

a cabinet or room which is kept very cold to prevent food from spoiling
n. 냉장고, 냉장실
In summer we have to keep milk and meat in the *refrigerator*.

skull
[skʌl]

the bone frame of the head which encloses the brain
n. 두개골, 머리
He was knocked unconscious by a sudden blow on the *skull*.

strategy
[strǽtidʒi]

the art of planning movements of armies or forces in war
n. 전략, 병법
Tactics refers to the disposition of armed forces in combat whereas *strategy* refers to the overall plan of a nation at war.

trench
[trentʃ]

a long, narrow ditch dug in the ground as a protection for soldiers
n. 참호
The soldiers dug *trenches* to protect themselves against enemy fire or attack.

undertake
[ʌndərtéik]

1. take up (a position); agree to do
v. 떠맡다, 약속하다
I will *undertake* the responsibility of feeding your dogs while you are away.

2. try; attempt
v. 시도하다, 기도하다
He always *undertakes* more than he can do.

EXERCISE 4 Fill each blank with the most appropriate word given above.
(Inflect the word if necessary.)

1. When there are many conflicting opinions, it is hard to _____ the truth.

2. I cannot _____ what you ask, but will do the best for your interests.

3. Let me _____ for my being so late in writing to you.

4. The education of the elementary school often develops one's _____ abilities.

5. His strong square _____ is a sign of his firm character.

EXERCISE 1.	1. sly	2. barrier	3. fling	4. shiver	5. stall
EXERCISE 2.	1. rational	2. wholesome	3. precise	4. timid	5. conservative
EXERCISE 3.	1. modified	2. vacancy	3. sequence	4. suburbs	5. abandoned
EXERCISE 4.	1. discern	2. undertake	3. apologize	4. potential	5. jaw

종합 연습 문제

1 In the space at the left, write the *letter* of the word that has most nearly the SAME MEANING as the italicized word.

_____ 1. *discerned* a car coming to me
    (A) perceived   (B) watched
    (C) photographed   (D) pushed

_____ 2. made her *dreary*
    (A) angry   (B) rich
    (C) happy   (D) gloomy

_____ 3. the *homely* woman
    (A) diligent   (B) lazy
    (C) beautiful   (D) ugly

_____ 4. the *timid* soldier
    (A) faithful   (B) strong
    (C) fearful   (D) brave

_____ 5. *radical* difference between the two systems
    (A) slight   (B) fundamental
    (C) well-known   (D) possible

2 In the space provided, write the *letter* of the word that most nearly means the OPPOSITE of the italicized word.

_____ 1. *clumsy*
    (A) awkward   (B) skillful
    (C) ungraceful   (D) plain

_____ 2. *wholesome*
    (A) beneficial   (B) obscure
    (C) harmful   (D) healthful

_____ 3. *rigid*
    (A) bold   (B) cowardly
    (C) vacant   (D) mild

_____ 4. *conservative*
    (A) obedient   (B) progressive
    (C) rational   (D) suburban

_____ 5. *vertical*
    (A) horizontal   (B) accurate
    (C) upright   (D) precise

3 Supply the correct form of the word in italics for the blank space in each sentence.

1. *modify*   The law, in its present form, is unjust; it needs _____.
2. *harmony*   The colors of the picture don't seem to _____ at all.
3. *proficient*   The job requires a good _____ in English and French.
4. *essence*   We can live without clothes, but food and drink are _____ to life.
5. *indulge*   The _____ mother brought her little son everything he wanted.

4 Fill in the missing letters of the word at the right. Each dash stands for one missing letter.

DEFINITION	WORD
1. the bone frame of the head	S _ _ _ L
2. a place where milk and cream are made	D _ _ _ Y
3. eat up hungrily and quickly	DE _ _ _ R
4. a narrow street between buildings	A _ _ _ Y
5. come in without being asked or wanted	IN _ _ _ _ E
6. a slender, upright structure used as a support	P _ _ _ AR
7. not clear; vague	IN _ _ _ _ _ ITE
8. the art of planning movements of the armed forces	ST _ _ _ _ GY
9. walk unevenly	L _ _ P
10. one who is rude and wild in behavior	BAR _ _ _ _ AN

5 In the space provided, write the *letter* of the word NOT RELATED in meaning to the other words in each line.

_____	1.	(A) quit	(B) conquer	(C) vanquish	(D) overcome
_____	2.	(A) accurate	(B) precise	(C) definite	(D) dismal
_____	3.	(A) tremble	(B) fling	(C) throw	(D) cast
_____	4.	(A) strict	(B) thorough	(C) rigid	(D) stiff
_____	5.	(A) barbarian	(B) thief	(C) robber	(D) burglar
_____	6.	(A) assail	(B) attack	(C) assault	(D) assert
_____	7.	(A) sly	(B) tricky	(C) vague	(D) crafty
_____	8.	(A) abandon	(B) desert	(C) devour	(D) quit
_____	9.	(A) summary	(B) docile	(C) abstract	(D) abridgement
_____	10.	(A) inescapable	(B) unavoidable	(C) inevitable	(D) unfavorable

Lesson 3

6 Fill each with the most appropriate word from the vocabulary list below.

> **VOCABULARY LIST**
>
> | | | |
> |---|---|---|
> | discern | modified | apologize |
> | obedient | limped | vertical |
> | exhaled | harmony | indulged |
> | abandoned | trench | pillar |

1. The _____ boy did his homework as his mother had ordered, though his friends wanted him to go swimming.

2. John came to London to study law, but _____ it for art.

3. These plans must be _____ if they are to be carried out successfully.

4. I _____ my interest in flowers for several years by planting tulips in the garden.

5. We have to dig a(n) _____ to protect ourselves against enemy fire or attack.

6. Telegraph poles must be set in the ground so that they are _____.

7. He held his breath for a moment before he _____.

8. Through the thick fog I could just _____ a car coming toward me.

9. After falling down the stairs, he _____ for several days.

10. In a beautiful landscape there is a(n) _____ of different colors.

해답

1 1. A   2. D   3. D   4. C   5. B
2 1. B   2. C   3. D   4. B   5. A
3 1. modification   2. harmonize   3. proficiency   4. essential   5. indulgent
4 1. skull   2. dairy   3. devour   4. alley   5. intrude
    6. pillar   7. indefinite   8. strategy   9. limp   10. barbarian
5 1. A   2. D   3. A   4. B   5. A   6. D   7. C   8. C   9. B   10. D
6 1. obedient   2. abandoned   3. modified   4. indulged   5. trench
    6. vertical   7. exhaled   8. discern   9. limped   10. harmony

Lesson 4

PRETEST 4

Insert the *letter* of the best answer in the space provided.

1. A _____ should be placed where it is *conspicuous*.
   (A) traffic sign   (B) secret document

2. The President tried to *liberate* _____.
   (A) farmers   (B) slaves

3. Those are the two _____ that will appear in the main *bout*.
   (A) articles   (B) boxers

4. It is _____ for a *temperate* man to get angry.
   (A) rare   (B) usual

5. The child is a real *pest*; she is a(n) _____ girl.
   (A) obedient   (B) troublesome

ANSWERS 1.A 2.B 3.B 4.A 5.B

STUDY YOUR NEW WORDS-1

adore
[ədɔ́ːr]

regard with the greatest love and respect
v. 숭배하다, 흠모하다
syn. worship
All the girls in our school *adore* the handsome mathematics teacher who happens to be a bachelor.

blend
[blend]

1. mix together or become mixed
v. 섞다, 섞이다
syn. mix
A grocer must know how to *blend* different kinds of tea.

2. go well together; harmonize
v. 어울리다, 조화되다
syn. mix
These houses seem to *blend* well with the trees and the countryside.

breadth
[bredθ]

distance from side to side
n. 폭, 나비, 넓이
syn. width
The wise man has a great *breadth* of understanding.

commend
[kəménd]

speak favorably of; acclaim
v. 칭찬하다, 갈채를 보내다
syn. praise
Many children were *commended* for their good deeds on Children's Day.

conspicuous
[kənspíkjuəs]

easily seen; clearly visible
adj. 눈에 띄는, 뚜렷이 보이는, 두드러진
syn. noticeable
There are several *conspicuous* errors in your composition.

delusion
[dilú:ʒən]

a false belief or idea; fallacy
n. 망상, 잘못된 생각
syn. illusion
She is under the *delusion* that I'm going to give her a lot of money.

impatient
[impéiʃənt]

not patient; unwilling to wait or delay
adj. 조급한, 성급한, 참을성 없는
syn. hasty
As she was *impatient* to start to school, she forgot to take her homework.

miracle
[mírəkl]

any remarkable or wonderful happening
n. 기적, 경이
syn. prodigy
According to the Bible, Christ worked many *miracles*.

provisional
[prəvíʒənəl]

for the time being; intended to serve for a short time
adj. 잠정적인, 임시의, 일시적인
syn. tentative
Let's arrange the *provisional* meeting for next Tuesday, even though we may have to change it.

restrain
[ristréin]

hold under control; limit actions; prevent from doing something
v. 제지하다, 억누르다, 금하다
syn. suppress
She could not *restrain* the children from running into the street.

stroll
[stroul]

walk slowly or idly
v. 산책하다, 어슬렁어슬렁 걷다
syn. ramble
The old couple were *strolling* under the trees arm in arm.

EXERCISE 1 — **Fill each blank with the most appropriate word given above.**
(Inflect the word if necessary.)

1. A tree standing alone on the top of a hill is _____.
2. That sickman is under the _____ that he is Napoleon.
3. Oil does not _____ with water.
4. If you can't _____ your dog from biting the milkman, you must lock him up.
5. Doctors do their best to treat the sick, but they can't perform a(n) _____.

STUDY YOUR NEW WORDS-2

cradle
[kréidl]

a baby's bed
n. 요람, 유아용 침대
ant. grave
The frightened baby refused to sleep in his *cradle*.

deny
[dinái]

say that something is not true
v. 부정하다, 부인하다
ant. admit
Justice must not be *denied* to anyone, however poor he may be.

disperse
[dispə́rs]

scatter; cause to break apart and go different ways
v. 흩어지다, 흩뜨리다
ant. gather
The crowd *dispersed* when the rain fell suddenly.

endanger
[indéindʒər]

cause danger; expose to loss or injury
v. 위태롭게 하다, 위험에 빠뜨리다
ant. secure
You will *endanger* your health if you work so hard every night.

Lesson 4   45

fiction
[fíkʃən]

a piece of writing about imaginary persons or events
n. 소설, 창작, 꾸며낸 이야기
ant. fact
Works of *fiction* are reviewed in the Sunday papers in England.

initial
[iníʃəl]

first; of the beginning
adj. 처음의, 시작의
ant. last
His *initial* effort at skating was failure, but he succeeded the second time that he tried.

intimacy
[íntiməsi]

close friendship or relationship
n. 친교, 친밀감, 밀접함
ant. unfamiliarity
The *intimacy* with which the two friends talked showed how fond they were of one another.

invade
[invéid]

enter in order to seize or conquer
v. 침략하다, 침입하다
ant. defend
At the beginning of World War Ⅱ, Hitler *invaded* Poland without a declaration of war.

selfish
[sélfiʃ]

caring only for oneself; egoistic
adj. 이기적인, 이기주의의
ant. altruistic
He was too *selfish* to share his candy with his little brother.

thrifty
[θrífti]

careful in spending; frugal; saving
adj. 검소한, 절약하는, 알뜰한
ant. wasteful
Mr. Thompson is so *thrifty* that he is able to save more than half of his weekly salary.

voluntary
[vɔ́ləntəri]

acting, done, of one's own free will
adj. 자발적인, 자진해서 하는, 지원의
ant. compulsory
Voluntary workers built a road to the boys' camp.

EXERCISE 2
Fill each blank with the most appropriate word given above.
(Inflect the word if necessary.)

1. He is an honest man; I don't _____ the truth of his statement.

2. In the 16th century, Japan _____ Korea, but failed to conquer it.

3. "From the _____ to the grave, man is the most unfortunate of all creatures," a philosopher said.

4. Groups of police were _____ all along the street where the President was to pass.

5. A(n) _____ person always puts his own interest first.

STUDY YOUR NEW WORDS-3

absorb
[əbsɔ́ːrb]

1. take in or suck up (liquid or gas)
v. 흡수하다, 빨아들이다
Anything black *absorbs* most of the light rays that fall on it.

2. take up all the attention of; interest very much
v. 열중케하다
adj. absorbent
He was so *absorbed* in his reading that he did not hear the telephone ring.

accuse
[əkjúːz]

charge with a crime
v. 고발하다, 고소하다
n. accusation
It is wrong to *accuse* a person of crime unless you have proof that he is guilty.

adjust
[ədʒʌ́st]

change something to make fit; make suitable
v. 조정하다, 조절하다
n. adjustment
You can *adjust* your chair to make it more comfortable.

erroneous
[iróuniəs]

incorrect; mistaken
adj. 잘못된, 틀린
n. error
Years ago many people held the *erroneous* belief that the earth was flat.

expend
[ikspénd]

spend; use up
v. (시간·노력을) 들이다, 소비하다
n. expenditure
He had *expended* much time and energy on that experiment.\

Lesson 4

fury
[fjúəri]

violent excitement or anger; fierce passion
n. 격노, 격분
adj. furious
It's no use trying to argue with you when you fly into a *fury*.

liberate
[líbəreit]

set free; release
v. 해방하다, 자유롭게 하다
n. liberation
Abraham Lincoln is the President who tried to *liberate* slaves.

perplex
[pərpléks]

make a person uncertain or unsure; confuse
v. 당혹케하다, 어리둥절케하다
n. perplexity
He was so *perplexed* that he asked many persons for advice.

sovereign
[sɔ́vrin]

independent of control of another government
adj. 자주적인, 주권이 있는
n. sovereignty
When the thirteen colonies won the Revolutionary War, America became a *sovereign* nation.

temperate
[témpərit]

not very hot, and not very cold; moderate
adj. 온난한, 온화한, 온건한
n. temperance
The *temperate* areas of the world are found to the north and south of the tropics.

EXERCISE 3 Fill each blank with the most appropriate word given above.
(Inflect the word if necessary.)

1. The United Nations is an assembly of _____ states.
2. The old farmer was _____ by the crowds and traffic in the big city.
3. I was _____ in a book and didn't hear my mother call.
4. You can't see through a telescope until it has been _____ to your eyes.
5. They _____ all their strength in trying to climb out of the deep hole.

STUDY YOUR NEW WORDS-4

bout
[baut]

a trial of strength or skill; contest
n. 한판 승부, 한차례의 일
Those are the two boxers who will appear in the main *bout* tonight.

category
[kǽtigəri]

a group of division
n. 범주, 부류, 종류
The selfish man places all people in two *categories*: those he likes and those he dislikes.

choir
[kwáiər]

a group of persons trained to sing together
n. 성가대, 합창대
As the *choir* rose to sing, the people joined in, filling the church with the music of the first hymn.

compact
[kəmpǽkt]

closely, firmly or tightly packed or fitted together
adj. 빽빽하게 찬, 밀접한
The salesman tied the customer's purchases into a *compact* bundle.

concentrate
[kɔ́nsentreit]

bring or come together to one place
v. (주의·노력을) 집중하다, 한곳에 모으다
The defeated troops were ordered to scatter and then *concentrate* fifty miles to the south.

emigrate
[émigreit]

leave one's own country to settle in another
v. (타국으로) 이주하다, 이민가다
In the 19th century many Europeans *emigrated* to America.

navigate
[nǽvigeit]

sail or direct a ship or other vessel
v. 항행하다, 조종하다
He *navigated* the ship across the Atlantic Ocean.

pane
[pein]

a piece of glass in a window or door
n. 창유리
The broken *pane* in the window was replaced by a man whose son threw a stone and broke it.

pest
[pest]

any troublesome or destructive creature or thing
n. 해충, 유해물, 골칫덩어리
We have to get rid of *pests* in the garden.

Lesson 4

salute
[səlúːt]

greet in a way that shows honor
v. ~에 경례하다, ~에게 인사하다
The soldiers **saluted** the flag by raising the right hand to the forehead as they passed it.

severe
[sivíər]

stern; strict; not lenient
adj. 엄중한, 모진, 호된
The students who cheat in examinations will be given a **severe** punishment.

EXERCISE 4 Fill each blank with the most appropriate word given above.
(Inflect the word if necessary.)

1. A large magnifying glass can _____ enough sunlight to burn paper.
2. Last night, strong and sudden gusts of wind broke several _____ of window.
3. He _____ to Brazil from Korea where he had lived for twenty years.
4. The captain safely _____ the ship across the ocean.
5. The leaves of cabbage are folded into a _____ head.

해답

EXERCISE 1.   1. conspicuous   2. delusion   3. blend   4. restrain   5. miracle
EXERCISE 2.   1. deny   2. invaded   3. cradle   4. dispersed 5. selfish
EXERCISE 3.   1. sovereign   2. perplexed 3. absorbed   4. adjusted   5. expended
EXERCISE 4.   1. concentrate   2. panes   3. emigrated 4. navigated 5. compact

종합 연습 문제

1 In the space provided, write the *letter* of the word NOT RELATED in meaning to the other words in each line.

_____ 1. (A) marked   (B) noticeable   (C) conspicuous (D) spreading
_____ 2. (A) mix   (B) allay   (C) blend   (D) compound
_____ 3. (A) incorrect   (B) erroneous   (C) inquisitive (D) mistaken
_____ 4. (A) fury   (B) anger   (C) rage   (D) fallacy
_____ 5. (A) myriad   (B) marvel   (C) miracle   (D) prodigy
_____ 6. (A) worship   (B) adore   (C) grant   (D) revere
_____ 7. (A) acclaim   (B) persist   (C) praise   (D) commend
_____ 8. (A) strangle   (B) stroll   (C) ramble   (D) saunter
_____ 9. (A) width   (B) grace   (C) range   (D) breadth
_____ 10. (A) suppress   (B) prevent   (C) restrain   (D) stagger

2 In the space before each word in COLUMN I, write the *letter* of its correct meaning in COLUMN II.

COLUMN I   COLUMN II

_____ 1. category   (A) a group of persons who sing together
_____ 2. navigate   (B) a trial of strength or skill
_____ 3. concentrate   (C) firmly or tightly packed
_____ 4. pest   (D) greet in a way that shows honor
_____ 5. bout   (E) sail or direct a ship
_____ 6. severe   (F) any troublesome creature
_____ 7. pane   (G) a group of division
_____ 8. choir   (H) not lenient; stern
_____ 9. salute   (I) a piece of glass in a window
_____ 10. compact   (J) bring together to one place

3 In the space provided, write the *letter* of the word that most nearly means the OPPOSITE of the italicized word.

_____ 1. *invade*   (A) offend   (B) defend
                            (C) finish   (D) cover

Lesson 4   51

_____ 2. *endanger*   (A) float   (B) guide
                            (C) pretend   (D) secure

_____ 3. *thrifty*   (A) fresh   (B) ambiguous
                            (C) wasteful   (D) strict

_____ 4. *cradle*   (A) tranquility (B) peace
                            (C) grave   (D) order

_____ 5. *voluntary* (A) compulsory   (B) entire
                            (C) coward   (D) pleasant

_____ 6. *initial*   (A) obedient   (B) foreign
                            (C) external   (D) last

_____ 7. *disperse*   (A) allow   (B) gather
                            (C) frighten   (D) perform

_____ 8. *selfish*   (A) gregarious   (B) gullible
                            (C) altruistic   (D) egoistic

_____ 9. *intimacy*   (A) unfamiliarity (B) testimony
                            (C) absurdity   (D) disruption

_____ 10. *fiction*   (A) fact   (B) invention
                            (C) novel   (D) drama

4 Complete the following table with the appropriate word forms.

ADJECTIVE	NOUN	VERB	ADVERB
1. _____	error	_____	_____
2. adjustable	_____	_____	XXXXX
3. _____	_____	perplex	_____
4. sovereign	_____	XXXXX	XXXXX
5. liberal	_____	_____	_____
6. _____	_____	absorb	_____
7. _____	temperance	_____	_____
8. _____	fury	XXXXX	_____
9. expensive	_____	_____	_____
10. accusing	_____	_____	_____

5 In the space provided, write the *letter* of the word or expression that has most nearly the SAME MEANING as the italicized word.

_____ 1. I have traveled through the length and *breadth* of this country.
  (A) extent   (B) border   (C) width   (D) center

_____ 2. As the old gentleman walked along the avenue, all the children *saluted* him.
 (A) greeted (B) tricked (C) called (D) followed

_____ 3. If a thing is *conspicuous* by its absence, it is something that everyone expects to be there.
 (A) noticeable (B) necessary (C) regrettable (D) indifferent

_____ 4. Let's arrange the *provisional* meeting for next Wednesday, even though we may have to change it.
 (A) tentative (B) practical (C) local (D) commercial

_____ 5. He spoke in a *temperate* manner, not favoring either side especially.
 (A) respectable (B) moderate (C) polite (D) prudent

_____ 6. She is under the *delusion* that I'm going to give her a lot of money.
 (A) hypothesis (B) miracle (C) condition (D) fallacy

_____ 7. *Blend* the sugar, flour, and eggs together.
 (A) bring (B) mix (C) take (D) buy

_____ 8. The defeated troops were ordered to scatter and then *concentrate* fifty miles to the south.
 (A) rally (B) attack (C) march (D) retreat

_____ 9. The doctors performed a heart operation that was a *miracle* of medical skill.
 (A) climax (B) prodigy (C) mirage (D) acme

_____ 10. He flew into a *fury* when I said I couldn't help any more.
 (A) anger (B) pool (C) boat (D) crowd

해답

1 1. D 2. B 3. C 4. D 5. A 6. C 7. B 8. A 9. B 10. D
2 1. G 2. E 3. j 4. F 5. B 6. H 7. I 8. A 9. D 10. C
3 1. B 2. D 3. C 4. C 5. A 6. D 7. B 8. C 9. A 10. A
4

ADJECTIVE	NOUN	VERB	ADVERB
1. erroneous	(error)	err	erroneously
2. (adjustable)	adjustment	adjust	XXXXX
3. perplexed	perplexity	(perplex)	perplexedly
4. (sovereign)	sovereignty	XXXXX	XXXXX
5. (liberal)	liberation, liberty	liberate	liberally
6. absorbing, absorbent	absorption	(absorb)	absorbingly
7. temperate	(temperance)	temper	temperately
8. furious	(fury)	XXXXX	furiously
9. (expensive)	expense, expenditure	expend	expensively
10. (accusing)	accusation	accuse	accusingly

5 1. C 2. A 3. A 4. A 5. B 6. D 7. B 8. A 9. B 10. A

Lesson 5

PRETEST 5

Insert the *letter* of the best answer in the space provided.

1. Don't be too *sullen* when you are _____ by your parents.
   (A) praised　　　　　　(B) punished

2. They decided to *exile* him to the _____.
   (A) island　　　　　　(B) chairman

3. We felt *humiliated* by our _____.
   (A) success　　　　　　(B) failure

4. I live in the *vicinity* of the school; it takes _____ to go to school on foot.
   (A) only five minutes　　(B) more than one hour

5. Millions of _____ are *slaughtered* every year in the country.
   (A) pigs　　　　　　(B) cars

ANSWERS　1.B 2.A 3.B 4.A 5.A

STUDY YOUR NEW WORDS-1

abode　　home; a place where one lives; dwelling
[əbóud]　　*n.* 주거, 거주지, 집
　　　　　syn. residence
　　　　　The woodcutter's *abode* was a house in the forest.

annual　　appearing every year; coming once a year
[ǽnjuəl]　　*adj.* 일년마다의, 일년에 한번씩의
　　　　　syn. yearly
　　　　　The company allows us an *annual* vacation of two weeks.

coax　　ask gently and repeatedly for something
[kouks]　　*v.* 감언으로 설복하다, 살살 어르다

syn. cajole
The mother *coaxed* the boy to take the medicine, but he refused to take it.

colleague
[kɔ́li:g]

a fellow member of a profession or organization
n. 동료
syn. associate
The teacher's *colleagues* taught his classes while he was ill.

dispense
[dispéns]

give out in portions; allot
v. 분배하다, 나누어주다
syn. distribute
The Red Cross *dispensed* food and clothing to the flood victims.

gingerly
[dʒíndʒərli]

with great care or caution; warily
adv. 조심스럽게, 신중하게
syn. cautiously
In the darkness, he turned to the left, stepping *gingerly*.

hug
[hʌg]

hold someone or something tightly in the arms
v. 껴안다, 품다
syn. embrace
The mother *hugged* her lost child and kissed him.

humiliate
[hju:mílieit]

cause to lose pride and self-respect; make ashamed; mortify
v. 창피를 주다, 굴욕을 주다
syn. disgrace
The boys *humiliated* their parents by behaving badly in front of the guests.

obstruct
[əbstrʌ́kt]

make hard to pass through; close up
v. 가로막다, 차단하다, 방해하다
syn. impede
The mountain roads were *obstructed* by falls of rock.

overthrow
[ouvərθróu]

cause to fall; defeat; overturn
v. 뒤엎다, 쓰러뜨리다, 전복시키다
syn. upset
The government was *overthrown* by the hands of communists.

recapture
[ri:kǽptʃər]

get into one's power again; capture again
v. 되찾다, 탈환하다
syn. retake
The soldiers *recaptured* the city lost to the enemy.

slim
[slim]

very thin; not fat
adj. 가느다란, 홀쭉한
syn. slender
He was very *slim*, being six feet tall and weighing only 130 pounds.

vicinity
[vísínəti]

1. the region near or about a place
n. 근처, 부근, 근방
There are no houses for sale in this *vicinity*.

2. nearness in place; being close
n. 가까움, 근접함
syn. neighborhood
The *vicinity* of the apartment to his office was an advantage on rainy days.

EXERCISE 1 Fill each blank with the most appropriate word given above. (Inflect the word if necessary.)

1. After the terrible storm, many fallen trees _____ the road.
2. "Are there any shops in this _____ ?" "Not really; the nearest is 10 miles away from here."
3. One's birthday is a(n) _____ event; it comes once a year.
4. His _____ of the office gave him a gift when he retired.
5. He is a(n) _____ boy, but he may fill out as he becomes older.

STUDY YOUR NEW WORDS-2

arctic
[á:rktik]

the most northern part of the world
n., adj. 북극(의)
ant. antarctic
The *Arctic* has an extremely cold winter.

attic
[ǽtik]

the space in a house just below the roof
n. 다락
ant. basement
We store trunks in the *attic* of the house.

diminish
[dimíniʃ]

make smaller in size or amount; lessen; reduce; decrease
v. 줄이다, 감소시키다

ant. enlarge
Poor crops so *diminished* the food supply that people were starving.

dishonest
[disɔ́nist]

showing lack of homesty; deceiving; insincere
adj. 부정직한, 불성실한
ant. candid
A person who lies, cheats, or steals is *dishonest*.

drunken
[drʌ́ŋkən]

resulting from too much drinking of alcohol; drunk
adj. 술취한, 술고래의
ant. sober
The noisy *drunken* man on the street was soon arrested by the police.

foe
[fou]

a hostile person or group; enemy; opponent
n. 적, 적군, 원수
ant. friend
The person who holds ill feelings against you is your *foe*.

foresee
[fɔːrsíː]

see or know in advance; expect; anticipate
v. 예견하다, 예측하다
ant. retrospect
He *foresaw* that his journey would be delayed by bad weather.

jolly
[dʒɔ́li]

very cheerful; full of fun; joyful; gay; merry; nice
adj. 유쾌한, 즐거운, 명랑한
ant. gloomy
Everyone at the party was very *jolly*, and didn't want to leave the party.

maximum
[mǽksiməm]

the largest amount; the highest degree
n. 최대, 최대수, 극대
ant. minimum
Sixteen miles in a day was the *maximum* distance we could walk.

mistress
[místris]

the woman who is at the head of a household
n. 여주인
ant. master
She felt she was no longer *mistress* in her own house when her husband's mother came to stay.

prefix
[príːfiks]

word or syllable placed in front of a word
n. 접두사

Lesson 5

	ant. suffix
	"Under-" in underline, "dis-" in disappear, and "pre-" in prepaid are *prefixes*.
relax [rilǽks]	cause to become less tight, strict, or rigid; lessen in force ***v.*** 늦추다, 경감하다, 쉬다 **ant.** strain Discipline cannot be *relaxed* until the last day of school has passed.
superficial [su:pərfíʃəl]	of the surface; not thorough; shallow ***adj.*** 외면의, 표면적인, 피상적인 **ant.** internal The speaker had only a *superficial* knowledge of the subject.

EXERCISE 2   Fill each blank with the most appropriate word given above.
(Inflect the word if necessary.)

1. The medical bills during my long sickness have _____ my savings.

2. Drivers must not exceed a(n) _____ of 60 miles an hour on this road.

3. The cut is not deep. It is a(n) _____ cut.

4. Let's stop working and _____ for an hour.

5. We didn't take our bathing suits, because we could _____ that the water would be cold.

STUDY YOUR NEW WORDS-3

allege [əlédʒ]	state or declare without proof; assert ***v.*** 주장하다, 우겨대다 **adv.** allegedly The storekeeper *alleged* that the boy had stolen some fruit.
current [kʌ́rənt]	of the present time; belonging to the present day ***adj.*** 현재의, 현행의 **n.** currency We read the daily newspaper to keep up with the *current* situation.
exalt [igzɔ́:lt]	raise in honor or rank; elevate; ennoble; praise ***v.*** 높이다, 올리다, 고양하다 **n.** exaltation They were *exalted* by their son's success.

expand
[ikspǽnd]

make or grow larger; enlarge; swell
v. 부풀(리)다, 팽창하(게 하)다
n. expansion
The balloon *expanded* as it was filled with air.

industrialize
[indʌ́striəlaiz]

make industrial; develop large industries as an important feature
v. 산업화하다, 공업화하다
n. industrialization
We have to make our every effort to *industrialize* our country.

justify
[dʒʌ́stifai]

give a good reason for; show to be just or right
v. 정당화하다, 정당성을 부여하다
n. justification
Your wish to go for a walk does not *justify* your leaving the baby alone in the house.

prescribe
[priskráib]

1. order as medicine or treatment
v. 처방하다
n. prescription
The doctor *prescribed* a new medicine for the pain in my joints.

2. lay down as a rule to be followed; direct
v. 규정하다, 지시하다
n. prescription
Good citizens do what the laws *prescribe*.

presume
[prizjú:m]

take something as true or as a fact without proving; suppose; assume
v. 추정하다, 추측하다
n. presumption
John didn't say when he would return, but I *presume* he'll be back for dinner.

slaughter
[slɔ́:tər]

killing of animals for food
n., v. 학살(하다), 도살(하다)
adj. slaughterous
The cattle were sent to the city for *slaughter*.

statistics
[stətístiks]

numbers arranged to express facts; the science of arranging such facts
n. 통계(표), 통계학
adj. statistical
These *statistics* show that the population of the country will be doubled in ten years.

supplement
[sʌ́plimənt]

something added to complete a thing, or to make it better
n. 부록, 보충, 추가

Lesson 5

adj. supplementary

Today's newspaper has a **supplement** on the new automobile models.

trifle
[tráifl]

a thing that is of little value; trivial affair

n. 사소한 일, 하찮은 물건

adj. trifling

You will not succeed if you waste your time on **trifles** such as movies and dances.

withdraw
[wiðdrɔ́]

draw back; take back; draw away

v. 움츠리다, 철수하다, 취하하다

n. withdrawal

He quickly **withdrew** his hand from the hot stove.

EXERCISE 3
Fill each blank with the most appropriate word given above.
(Inflect the word if necessary.)

1. The fine quality of the clothes _____ its high price.

2. _____ is a rather modern branch of mathematics.

3. Iron _____ when it is heated.

4. What punishment does the law _____ for this crime?

5. The newspaper reporters _____ that the man was murdered, though they have no proof.

STUDY YOUR NEW WORDS-4

armor
[áːrmər]

a protective covering for the body, made of metal

n. 장갑, 기갑, 갑옷

Nothing could break through the **armor** of the new tank.

buzz
[bʌz]

make a long, low sound like that made by bees

v. 윙윙거리다, 윙하고 울리다

The radio should be fixed; it **buzzes** whenever I turn it on.

cancer
[kǽnsər]

a dangerous disease which often causes death

n. 암

A great many **cancers** can be cured, but only if properly treated before they have begun to spread.

collapse
[kəlǽps]

1. fall down or inwards suddenly
v. 붕괴되다, 와해되다, 무너지다
The roof *collapsed* as a result of the fire.

2. fold into a shape that takes up less space
v. (기구나 가구 등을) 접다
This table can be *collapsed*, so I can store it easily when I'm not using it.

contemporary
[kəntémpərèri]

1. belonging to the same period of time
adj. 동시대의, 그 당시의
In 1066 William landed in England, and a *contemporary* Englishman wrote the report of his landing.

2. belonging to the present; modern
adj. 현대의, 현재의
Our teacher reads the books of many *contemporary* authors to us.

exile
[iɡzáil]

make a person leave his home or country; expel; banish
v. 추방하다, 귀양보내다
The political leaders were *exiled* to an island far away from the country.

infantry
[ínfəntri]

soldiers who fight on foot
n. 보병 (步兵)
Men in the *infantry* often march long distances.

monk
[mʌŋk]

a member of a religious organization devoting his life to religious exercises
n. 수도승, 수도사
He left his successful business and life of luxury to become a *monk*.

orchard
[ɔ́ːrtʃərd]

a large area of ground on which fruit trees are grown
n. 과수원
These apples and pears come from an *orchard* near Incheon.

pirate
[páiərit]

robber on the seas; a ship used by pirates
n. 해적, 해적선
The terrible *pirates* attacked a merchant ship again.

sullen
[sʌ́lən]

silent and unpleasant; gloomy; dismal
adj. 시무룩한, 기분이 언짢은, 음울한
That boy became *sullen* if he was punished by his teacher.

telescope
[téləskòup]

an instrument for making distant objects appear nearer and larger
n. 망원경
He was studying the stars through a *telescope*.

usher
[ʌ́ʃər]

a person who shows people to their seats
n. (극장·식장 따위의) 안내원, 수위
The *usher* of the theater helped us find our seats.

EXERCISE 4 Fill each blank with the most appropriate word given above. (Inflect the word if necessary.)

1. Her father died of _____; he had been a heavy smoker.
2. They _____ Napoleon to the island of St. Helena.
3. You'd better _____ the telescope to half its size so that you can carry it easily.
4. He was so disappointed with the world that he decided to be a(n) _____.
5. It is disagreeable to have to sit at the breakfast table with a(n) _____ person.

해답

EXERCISE 1.	1. obstructed	2. vicinity	3. annual	4. colleagues	5. slim
EXERCISE 2.	1. diminished	2. maximum	3. superficial	4. relax	5. foresee
EXERCISE 3.	1. justifies	2. statistics	3. expands	4. prescribe	5. allege
EXERCISE 4.	1. cancer	2. exiled	3. collapse	4. monk	5. sullen

종합 연습 문제

1 In the space provided, write the *letter* of the word that has most nearly the SAME MEANING as the italicized word.

_____ 1. a *jolly* holiday
  (A) nice (B) cloudy (C) short (D) regular

_____ 2. *superficial* knowledge
  (A) deep (B) shallow (C) useless (D) thorough

_____ 3. *contemporary* art
  (A) classic (B) modern (C) primitive (D) industrial

_____ 4. *withdraw* the troops
  (A) send (B) organize (C) break up (D) take back

_____ 5. the word in *current* use
  (A) frequent (B) local (C) ancient (D) present

2 In the space provided, write the *letter* of the word that most nearly means the OPPOSITE of the italicized word.

_____ 1. *attic*
  (A) porch (B) basement
  (C) roof (D) backyard

_____ 2. *drunken*
  (A) sober (B) joyful
  (C) slender (D) shallow

_____ 3. *foe*
  (A) opponent (B) pirate
  (C) soldier (D) friend

_____ 4. *relax*
  (A) lessen (B) defeat
  (C) strain (D) capture

_____ 5. *diminish*
  (A) enlarge (B) waste
  (C) praise (D) fold

3 Supply the correct form of the word in italics for the blank space in each sentence.

1. *industrialize*   Korea is experiencing a rapid _____ of every economic field.
2. *exalt*   The news of the victory filled them with _____.
3. *presume*   As his face was pale, the _____ was that he had been ill.
4. *supplement*   The new members of the class received _____ instruction.
5. *expand*   The _____ of the factory made room for more machines.

Lesson 5

4 Fill in the missing letters of the word at the right. Each dash stands for one missing letter.

DEFINITION	WORD
1. a thing that is of little value	T _ _ FLE
2. the most northern part of the world	AR _ _ _ C
3. soldiers who fight on foot	IN _ _ _ _ RY
4. get into one's power again	RE _ _ _ TURE
5. home; residence	AB _ _ E
6. a person who shows people to their seats	U _ _ ER
7. hold tightly in the arms	H _ G
8. killing of animals for food	SL _ _ _ _ TER
9. fall down suddenly	CO _ _ _ _ SE
10. cause to fall; defeat	OVER _ _ _ _ _

5 In the space provided, write the *letter* of the word NOT RELATED in meaning to the other words in each line.

_____	1.	(A) cautiously	(B) notably	(C) warily	(D) gingerly
_____	2.	(A) allege	(B) humiliate	(C) mortify	(D) disgrace
_____	3.	(A) colleague	(B) abode	(C) fellow	(D) associate
_____	4.	(A) banish	(B) exile	(C) coax	(D) expel
_____	5.	(A) dismal	(B) sullen	(C) gloomy	(D) current
_____	6.	(A) dispense	(B) allot	(C) distribute	(D) overthrow
_____	7.	(A) ennoble	(B) evaluate	(C) elevate	(D) exalt
_____	8.	(A) withdraw	(B) expand	(C) swell	(D) enlarge
_____	9.	(A) prevent	(B) obstruct	(C) justify	(D) impede
_____	10.	(A) repose	(B) presume	(C) suppose	(D) assume

TOEFL·TOEIC·TEPS 중급 College Vocabulary

6 Fill each blank with the most appropriate word from the vocabulary list below.

VOCABULARY LIST

vicinity	cancer	prescribe
hugged	buzzes	armor
usher	foes	presume
statistics	supplement	dishonest

1. The radio should be fixed; it always _____ when I turn it on.

2. Steve didn't say when he would return, but I _____ he will be back for dinner.

3. _____ show that the population of the world is ever increasing.

4. The _____ of the apartment to his office was an advantage on rainy days.

5. Someone who behaves as foolishly as you has no right to _____ how others should behave.

6. That history book has a(n) _____ containing an account of what has happened since 1950.

7. _____ is a change in the normal growth of cells, but the causes have not yet been fully determined.

8. The mother _____ her lost child and kissed him.

9. A person who lies, cheats, or steals is _____.

10. The _____ of the theater helped us find our seats.

해답

1 1. A   2. B   3. B   4. D   5. D

2 1. B   2. A   3. D   4. C   5. A

3 1. industrialization 2. exaltation 3. presumption 4. supplementary 5. expansion

4 1. trifle   2. arctic   3. infantry   4. recapture   5. abode
    6. usher   7. hug   8. slaughter   9. collapse   10. overthrow

5 1. B   2. A   3. B   4. C   5. D   6. D   7. B   8. A   9. C   10. A

6 1. buzzes   2. presume   3. statistics   4. vicinity   5. prescribe
    6. supplement   7. cancer   8. hugged   9. dishonest   10. usher

Lesson 6

PRETEST 6

Insert the *letter* of the best answer in the space provided.

1. The baby likes to *splash* _____.
   (A) water in his tub   (B) toys in his cradle

2. _____, all efforts to rescue the survivors were *futile*.
   (A) Unfortunately   (B) Fortunately

3. It is *prudent* to wear light shirt when the weather is _____.
   (A) cold   (B) hot

4. The little baby was _____ by his mother's *caresses*.
   (A) walking   (B) pleased

5. The two *simultaneous* shots sounded _____.
   (A) at the same time   (B) one after another.

ANSWERS 1.A 2.A 3.B 4.B 5.A

STUDY YOUR NEW WORDS-1

appropriate
[əpróupriit]

1. fit or suitable
adj. 적당한, 적절한, 알맞는
syn. proper
Thick, woolen clothes would not be *appropriate* for a hot summer day.

[əpróuprieit]

2. take (a thing) and treat it as if it were one's own; steal
v. 착복하다, 사유(私有)하다, 훔치다
syn. embezzle
You should not *appropriate* other people's belongings without their permission

coarse
[kɔːrs]

of poor quality or appearance; rough
adj. 조잡한, 상스런, 거친

syn. vulgar

You mustn't use such *coarse* language when talking to innocent young girls.

legend
[lédʒənd]

an old tale of marvellous events, probably untrue
n. 전설, 전해 오는 이야기
syn. tradition
The stories about King Arthur and his Knights of the Round Table are *legends*, not history.

mischief
[místʃif]

harm; injury; damage
n. 해악, 해, 손해
syn. harm
He apologized the *mischief* his false story had caused.

persist
[pərsíst]

1. continue steadily, despite difficulties or resistance
v. 고집하다, 주장하다
syn. insist
If you *persist* in breaking the law you will go to prison.

2. continue to exist
v. 지속하다, 존속하다
syn. remain
In spite of washing, many stains *persisted* on the table cloth.

prudent
[prú:dənt]

cautious; discreet
adj. 세심한, 신중한, 분별 있는
syn. careful
In order to make a *prudent* decision, you must consider all of the possibilities carefully.

simultaneous
[siməltéinjəs]

happening or done at the same time
adj. 동시의, 동시에 일어나는
syn. coincident
Everyone in the audience burst into *simultaneous* applause.

splash
[splǽʃ]

cause liquid to scatter in all directions by striking it
v. (물·흙탕을) 튀기다, 튀기어 적시다
syn. spatter
The children were *splashing* water on each other in the swimming pool.

stubborn
[stʌ́bərn]

determined; resolute
adj. 완고한, 고집센

Lesson 6

	syn. obstinate The ***stubborn*** boy refused to listen to reasons for not going out in the rain.
symptom [símptəm]	an evidence or a sign of the existence of something ***n.*** 징후, 조짐, 증상 **syn.** token A cough is sometimes a ***symptom*** of serious disease.
trait [treit]	a particular quality of someone or something; a distinguishing mark. ***n.*** 특색, 특성, 특질 **syn.** characteristic The chief ***traits*** in the American character are generosity and energy.
vile [vail]	morally bad; degraded; shameful ***adj.*** 부도덕한, 타락한, 천한 **syn.** evil She has a ***vile*** temper; it's impossible to live with her.

EXERCISE 1 Fill each blank with the most appropriate word given above.
(Inflect the word if necessary.)

1. Courage, sincerity, and kindness are desirable _____.

2. His _____ speech and manners show that he is not accustomed to polite society.

3. Plain and simple clothes are _____ for the elementary school wear.

4. The monkey did a lot of _____ before it was caught and put back in its cage; it broke a number of things.

5. The doctor made his diagnosis after studying the patient's _____.

STUDY YOUR NEW WORDS-2

adequate [ǽdikwit]	equal to or enough for (what is needed) ***adj.*** 충분한, 흡족한 **ant.** insufficient His wages are not ***adequate*** to support his wife and children.
careless [kέərlis]	1. not taking care; thoughtless; not paying attention ***adj.*** 부주의한, 조심성 없는 A boy who is ***careless*** in what he does will never succeed.

2. not caring; indifferent
adj. 개의치 않는, 무관심한
ant. attentive
The brave soldiers did their duty, *careless* of dangers and discomforts.

chaos
[kéiɔs]

complete disorder; confusion
n. 대혼란, 무질서, 혼돈
ant. order
His room was in state of *chaos* after the burglar had left.

eminent
[éminənt]

famous; distinguished; of high position; outstanding
adj. 유명한, 저명한, 뛰어난
ant. common
The most *eminent* doctors treated the king in his illness.

enlarge
[inlá:rdʒ]

make larger; increase in size
v. 크게 하다, 확장하다
ant. reduce
The factory was *enlarged* to make room for more machinery.

fertile
[fə́:rtail]

producing plentiful crops; rich
adj. 비옥한, 기름진
ant. sterile
This land is *fertile*; it is rich in material needed to sustain plant growth.

futile
[fjú:tail]

having no effect; useless; unsuccessful
adj. 쓸데없는, 무익한, 소용없는
ant. useful
All his attempts to unlock the door were *futile*, because he was using the wrong key.

grim
[grim]

stern, harsh or fierce; without mercy
adj. 엄격한, 냉혹한, 무자비한
ant. mild
The judge's expression was *grim* when he told them they were to be shot.

impolite
[impəláit]

not polite; discourteous; rude
adj. 무례한, 버릇없는
ant. courteous
It is *impolite* behavior to smoke in a crowded bus.

vague
[veig]

not clear in shape or form; indistinct; ambiguous
adj. 막연한, 애매한, 모호한
ant. distinct
The directions were so *vague* that it was impossible to complete the assignment.

EXERCISE 2 — Fill each blank with the most appropriate word given above. (Inflect the word if necessary.)

1. After the failure of electricity supplies the city was in complete _____.
2. Many people have made _____ attempts to swim from England to France.
3. She is so _____ that I can never understand what she is trying to say.
4. If the driver of a car is _____, there will probably be an accident.
5. Washington was _____ as general and as President.

STUDY YOUR NEW WORDS-3

astronomy
[əstrɔ́nəmi]

the science of the heavenly bodies
n. 천문학, 성학(星學)
adj. astronomical
Astronomy deals with the motion of the sun, moon, and stars.

controversy
[kɔ́ntrəvəːrsi]

a dispute or argument
n. 논쟁, 논전, 논의
v. controvert
There was a *controversy* about the location of the new school.

hazard
[hǽzərd]

danger; peril; risk
n. 위험, 모험
adj. hazardous
The ice on the roads is a *hazard* for driving and walking

magnify
[mǽgnifai]

cause to appear larger
v. 확대하다, 크게 보이게 하다
n. magnificence
A lens *magnifies* the size of the words on the paper.

nominate
[nɔ́mineit]

put forward the name of a person for election to an office or position
v. 지명하다, 임명하다, 지정하다

n. nomination

Three times we ***nominated*** Tom for president of our club, but he was never elected.

provoke
[prəvóuk]

1. cause to feel anger; bother
v. 성나게 하다, 분개시키다
n. provocation

The dog is very dangerous when it is ***provoked***.

2. bring into being; cause; bring about
v. 일으키다, 유발시키다
n. provocation

Don't throw one bone to two dogs; you'll only ***provoke*** a fight between them.

recite
[risáit]

repeat or say aloud from memory
v. 암송하다, (청중 앞에서) 낭음하다
n. recital

My daughter is going to ***recite*** a poem at the Mother's Day program.

restore
[ristɔ́:r]

1. return; give back (what has been lost, stolen, etc.)
v. 반환하다, 반송하다
n. restoration

The honest boy ***restored*** the money he had found to its owner.

2. put back into a former form; bring back into use; renew
v. 복구하다, 회복하다, 재흥시키다
n. restoration

It took more than a year to ***restore*** the ancient castle.

tension
[ténʃən]

1. the act of stretching or straining
n. 팽팽함, 장력
adj. tense

If you increase the ***tension*** of that violin string it will break.

2. mental or emotional strain
n. 긴장, 흥분
adj. tense

The doctor said I was suffering from nervous ***tension***.

tyrant
[táiərənt]

a cruel or unjust ruler or master
n. 폭군, 압제자, 전제 군주
v. tyranize

There is no tyrant who admits that he is a ***tyrant***.

vigor
[vígər]

strength and force; energy; vitality
n. 정력, 활력, 체력
adj. vigorous
The ***vigor*** of a person's body lessens as he grows old.

> **EXERCISE 3** Fill each blank with the most appropriate word given above.
> (Inflect the word if necessary.)
>
> 1. The President _____ me as his representative at the National Security Council.
> 2. The _____ of the bow gives speed to the arrow.
> 3. He is well over sixty, but works with young men with great _____.
> 4. The _____ between the company and the union ended after the strike was settled.
> 5. He is always calm and never becomes nervous; it is very difficult to _____ him.

STUDY YOUR NEW WORDS-4

blot
[blɔt]

1. a spot or mark, especially of ink on paper
n. 얼룩, 더러움
The spilled ink left a ***blot*** on the letter paper.

2. a fault; a disgrace
n. 흠, 오점
The ugly advertisement is a ***blot*** on the beautiful landscape.

caress
[kərés]

a touch showing affection; tender embrace of kiss
n. 애무, 쓰다듬기
His mother's ***caress*** calmed the frightened child.

chuckle
[tʃʌ́kl]

laugh quietly to oneself
v. 낄낄 웃다, 혼자서 웃다
He was ***chuckling*** to himself as he read that funny story.

claw
[klɔː]

a sharp nail on animal's foot
n. (고양이·매 등의) 발톱
The cat usually catches a mouse with its ***claws***.

craft
[kræft]

1. any kind of skilled work done with the hands
n. 기교, 솜씨, 기술
The art and ***crafts*** of the people are an important part of their culture.

2. boat, ship, aircraft
n. 선박, 항공기
All kinds of *crafts* come into New York harbor every day.

dainty
[déinti]

having delicate beauty; fresh and pretty
adj. 우미한, 고상한, 미려한
The violet and the dandelion are *dainty* spring flowers which could be seen in early March.

hermit
[hə́rmit]

a person who goes away from other people and lives alone
n. 은자(隱者), 속세를 떠난 사람
He lives in that forest alone; he is enjoying the *hermit*'s life.

panel
[pǽnəl]

a group formed for discussion
n. (청중 앞에서 하는) 토론회
Professor Kim participated in a *panel* to discuss the energy crisis.

phenomenon
[finɔ́minən]

a fact, event, or circumstance that can be observed
n. 현상(現象), 사상(事象)
Snow in Egypt is an almost unknown *phenomenon* of nature.

spectator
[spektéitər]

a person who looks on without taking part in
n. 구경꾼, 관객
There were many *spectators* at the National Football League.

thrash
[θræʃ]

beat as punishment; flog; whip
v. 때리다, 채찍질하다
The host of the market *thrashed* the little boy for stealing apples.

EXERCISE 4   **Fill each blank with the most appropriate word given above.**
(Inflect the word if necessary.)

1. The carpenter shaped and fitted the wood into a cabinet with great _____.
2. A(n) _____ of experts gave its opinions on ways to solve traffic problems.
3. Father always _____ when he reads the funny magazines.
4. The cat's _____ stuck out and scratched my arm.
5. Lightning is an electrical _____.

EXERCISE 1.	1. traits	2. coarse	3. appropriate	4. mischief	5. symptoms
EXERCISE 2.	1. chaos	2. futile	3. vague	4. careless	5. eminent
EXERCISE 3.	1. nominated	2. tension	3. vigor	4. controversy	5. provoke
EXERCISE 4.	1. craft	2. panel	3. chuckles	4. claws	5. phenomenon

종합 연습 문제

1 In the space provided, write the *letter* of the word NOT RELATED in meaning to the other words in each line.

_____	1.	(A) proper	(B) appropriate	(C) intimate	(D) suitable
_____	2.	(A) discreet	(B) frugal	(C) cautious	(D) prudent
_____	3.	(A) harm	(B) mischief	(C) illusion	(D) injury
_____	4.	(A) splash	(B) spatter	(C) splatter	(D) slash
_____	5.	(A) legend	(B) tradition	(C) miracle	(D) folklore
_____	6.	(A) symptom	(B) mark	(C) token	(D) hazard
_____	7.	(A) persist	(B) thrash	(C) whip	(D) flog
_____	8.	(A) vile	(B) virtuous	(C) evil	(D) vicious
_____	9.	(A) trait	(B) garment	(C) quality	(D) characteristic
_____	10.	(A) coarse	(B) humble	(C) vulgar	(D) rough

2 In the space before each word in COLUMN I, write the *letter* of its correct meaning in COLUMN II.

	COLUMN I	COLUMN II
_____	1. claw	(A) laugh quietly to oneself
_____	2. panel	(B) having delicate beauty
_____	3. hermit	(C) any kind of skilled work done with the hands
_____	4. chuckle	(D) a touch showing affection
_____	5. phenomenon	(E) a person who looks on without taking part in
_____	6. thrash	(F) a group formed for discussion
_____	7. caress	(G) a person who lives alone
_____	8. spectator	(H) a sharp nail on animal's foot
_____	9. craft	(I) a fact or event that can be observed
_____	10. dainty	(J) beat as punishment.

Lesson 6

3 In the space provided, write the *letter* of the word that most nearly means the OPPOSITE of the italicized word.

_____ 1. *eminent*	(A) noble	(B) vain	
	(C) common	(D) haughty	
_____ 2. *careless*	(A) heedless	(B) attentive	
	(C) hateful	(D) favorable	
_____ 3. *fertile*	(A) sterile	(B) narrow	
	(C) passionate	(D) fantastic	
_____ 4. *adequate*	(A) immature	(B) crude	
	(C) insufficient	(D) abundant	
_____ 5. *vague*	(A) full	(B) distinct	
	(C) strong	(D) dense	
_____ 6. *enlarge*	(A) reduce	(B) misguide	
	(C) duplicate	(D) expand	
_____ 7. *impolite*	(A) proper	(B) eloquent	
	(C) courteous	(D) passive	
_____ 8. *futile*	(A) useful	(B) profuse	
	(C) social	(D) grand	
_____ 9. *grim*	(A) thorough	(B) calm	
	(C) famous	(D) mild	
_____ 10. *chaos*	(A) honesty	(B) fitness	
	(C) formality	(D) order	

4 Complete the following table with the appropriate word forms.

	ADJECTIVE	NOUN	VERB	ADVERB
1.	_____	_____	controvert	_____
2.	_____	mischief	___XXXXX___	_____
3.	_____	_____	recite	___XXXXX___
4.	_____	hazard	_____	_____
5.	___XXXXX___	_____	restore	___XXXXX___
6.	_____	adequacy	___XXXXX___	_____
7.	provocative	_____	_____	_____
8.	___XXXXX___	_____	nominate	___XXXXX___
9.	_____	astronomy	___XXXXX___	_____
10.	magnificent	_____	_____	_____

5 In the space provided, write the *letter* of the word or expression that has most nearly the SAME MEANING as the italicized word.

_____ 1. Everyone in the audience burst into *simultaneous* applause.
(A) coincident (B) continuous (C) loud (D) unanimous

_____ 2. He *chuckled* at the amusing way things were happening.
(A) laughed (B) looked (C) doubted (D) complained

_____ 3. When I entered the room, it was in a state of *chaos*.
(A) order (B) disorder (C) calmness (D) noisiness

_____ 4. His clothes were made of *coarse* materials.
(A) rough (B) expensive (C) calmness (D) noisiness

_____ 5. All kinds of *crafts* come into the harbor every day.
(A) passengers (B) ships (C) foreigners (D) cargos

_____ 6. The honest boy *restored* the money he had found to its owner.
(A) gathered (B) spent (C) saved (D) returned

_____ 7. The minister was found to have *appropriated* a great deal of government money.
(A) donated (B) saved (C) stolen (D) borrowed

_____ 8. He had a *vague* memory of having read the magazine a few months ago.
(A) unpleasant (B) unforgettable (C) marvellous (D) indistinct

_____ 9. The *stubborn* boy refused to listen to reasons for not going out in the heavy rain.
(A) shabby (B) obstinate (C) irreparable (C) indiscreet

_____ 10. The girl wore a *dainty* dress.
(A) pretty and delicate   (B) small and tight
(C) shabby and ragged   (D) cheap and showy

해답

1 1. C 2. B 3. C 4. D 5. C 6. D 7. A 8. B 9. B 10. B
2 1. H 2. F 3. G 4. A 5. I 6. J 7. D 8. E 9. C 10. B
3 1. C 2. B 3. A 4. C 5. B 6. A 7. C 8. A 9. D 10. D

4
ADJECTIVE	NOUN	VERB	ADVERB
1. controversial	controversy	(controvert)	controversially
2. mischievous	(mischief)	XXXXX	mischievously
3. recitable	recitation	(recite)	XXXXX
4. hazardous	(hazard)	hazard	hazardously
5. XXXXX	restoration	(restore)	XXXXX
6. adequate	(adequacy)	XXXXX	adequately
7. (provocative)	provocation	provoke	provocatively
8. XXXXX	nomination	(nominate)	XXXXX
9. astronomical	(astronomy)	XXXXX	astronomically
10. (magnificent)	magnificence magnification	magnify	magnificently

5 1. A 2. A 3. B 4. A 5. B 6. D 7. C 8. D 9. B 10. A

Lesson 7

PRETEST 7

Insert the *letter* of the best answer in the space provided.

1. An argument was *inevitable* because they _____ each other so much.
   (A) liked   (B) disliked

2. Sugar is one of the *ingredients* _____.
   (A) sold in supermarkets   (B) needed to make cakes

3. He *consumed* all his money _____.
   (A) on women and drinking   (B) through hard working

4. _____ *grunt* as they eat.
   (A) Pigs   (B) Hens

5. Every country needs *allegiance* of its _____.
   (A) citizens   (B) ruler

Answers 1. B 2. B 3. A 4. A 5. A

STUDY YOUR NEW WORDS-1

appeal
[əpíːl]

1. ask earnestly; make an earnest request
v. 간청하다, 애원하다
syn. implore
The government is *appealing* to everyone to save water.

2. be attractive, interesting, or enjoyable
v. 마음에 들다, 마음에 호소하다
syn. implore
The music is too old-fashioned to *appeal* to people any longer.

bustle
[bʌ́sl]

noise or activity; ado; commotion
n. 혼잡, 분주함, 떠들썩함
syn. fuss
There was a great *bustle* as the children got ready for the party.

crave
[kreiv]

long for; desire very much
v. 갈망하다, 열망하다
syn. covet
I'm *craving* for a cup of tea. I've not had one all day.

discord
[diskɔ́ːrd]

difference of opinion; conflict; dispute
n. 불화, 알력, 불일치
syn. disagreement
Various *discords* have arisen in the university over this question.

drill
[dril]

thorough training by practical experiences with much repetition
n. 훈련, 교련
syn. training
The English teacher gave the class plenty of *drill* in pronunciation.

eventually
[ivéntʃuəli]

in the end; finally
adv. 결국은, 마침내, 최후에
syn. ultimately
We waited more than an hour for him, but *eventually* we had to leave without him.

futile
[fjúːtail]

of no use; useless; ineffectual
adj. 쓸데없는, 무익한
syn. vain
Please don't waste time by asking such *futile* questions.

ingredient
[ingríːdjənt]

one of the parts of a mixture; constituent; element
n. 성분, 원료, 요소
syn. component
The *ingredients* of a cake usually include eggs, sugar, and flour.

predict
[pridíkt]

announce or tell beforehand; forecast; prophesy
v. 예언하다, 예보하다
syn. foretell
The weather service *predicts* heavy rain for tomorrow.

raid
[reid]

a quick or sudden attack
n., v. 급습(하다), 습격(하다)
syn. attack
During their *raid* on the house, the police found a lot of dangerous drugs.

repel
[ripél]

drive or force back; drive away
v. 격퇴시키다, 쫓아버리다

Lesson 7

syn. repulse
The enemy in the city was **repelled** by our troops.

rouse
[rauz]
wake up; stir up; arouse
v. 깨우다, 일깨우다, 분기시키다
syn. awaken
The speaker tried to **rouse** the masses from their lack of interest.

tolerate
[tɔ́lərèit]
suffer something without complaining; bear; put up with
v. 참다, 관대히 봐주다, 묵인하다
syn. endure
I can't **tolerate** your bad manners any longer.

utmost
[ʌ́tmoust]
of the greatest degree; highest; farthest
adj. 극단의, 극도의, 최대한의
syn. extreme
She was standing at the **utmost** edge of the cliff to kill herself.

EXERCISE 1
Fill each blank with the most appropriate word given above. (Inflect the word if necessary.)

1. All his attempts to unlock the door were _____, because he was using the wrong key.
2. The ring of the telephone _____ me out of a deep sleep.
3. Blue and red _____ to me, but I don't like gray or yellow.
4. The principal would not _____ smoking or drinking in the school building.
5. The radio station was destroyed in the air _____.

STUDY YOUR NEW WORDS-2

assault
[əsɔ́lt]
a violent attack with weapons or blows
n. 강습, 공격, 돌격
ant. defense
We are ready to meet the enemy's **assault** on our fort.

hostile
[hɔ́stail]
showing dislike; unfriendly; of an enemy
adj. 적의(敵意)에 찬, 적대하는, 적(敵)의
ant. hospitable
Their **hostile** looks showed that I was unwelcome.

independent
[indipéndənt]

needing no help from others; not depending on others
adj. 독립한, 자립의
ant. dependent
Since she inherited her father's fortune, she is completely *independent* of her husband.

inevitable
[inévitəbl]

not to be avoided; sure to happen; unavoidable
adj. 불가피한, 피할 수 없는
ant. avoidable
They ran short of money during the tour, and their return was *inevitable*.

link
[liŋk]

join; connect
v. 잇다, 연결하다
ant. separate
The new road *links* all the towns in the state.

obscure
[əbskjúər]

not easily noticed; not clear; not prominent
adj. 어두컴컴한, 불명료한, 눈에 띄지 않는
ant. distinct
We had difficulty in finding the *obscure* path through the forest.

optimism
[ɔ́ptimizəm]

a tendency to look on the bright side of things
n. 낙천주의, 낙관론
ant. pessimism
The candidate's *optimism* about his chances of winning encouraged his supporters.

serene
[sirí:n]

completely peaceful without trouble; calm; tranquil
adj. 고요한, 잠잠한, 평화로운
ant. agitated
He kept *serene* and calm, knowing nothing of the dangers which surrounded him.

submit
[səbmít]

agree to obey; yield to the power; surrender
v. 굴복하다, 항복하다, 복종하다
ant. conquer
No one would *submit* silently to such an insult.

summit
[sʌ́mit]

the top; the highest point; peak; zenith
n. 정상, 정점, 절정
ant. bottom
At last the mountain climbers reached the *summit* of the mountain.

unique
[ju:ní:k]

single in kind; being the only one of its sort; sole
adj. 유일한, 단 하나의

ant. common

This proposal seems to be the *unique* solution to our problem.

vacuum　an empty space without even air in it; void; emptiness
[vǽkjuəm]　*n.* 진공, 공허, 공백
　　　　　　ant. fullness
　　　　　　For that experiment you need a complete *vacuum*.

veteran　one who has had much experience in a profession or service
[vétərən]　*n.* 노련가, 고참병
　　　　　　ant. apprentice
　　　　　　At the age of 12 the boy was already a *veteran* traveller, having flown all over the world with his father.

EXERCISE 2　**Fill each blank with the most appropriate word given above.**
　　　　　　(Inflect the word if necessary.)

1. Death is _____; it comes to everyone.
2. This stamp is _____ in the world; all others like it have been lost or destroyed.
3. The two villages were _____ together by a tunnel built recently.
4. The mountain is so high that we can see its _____ twenty miles away.
5. It was such a(n) _____ summer night that we went out for a walk around the peaceful lake.

STUDY YOUR NEW WORDS-3

abide　1. put up with; endure; tolerate
[əbáid]　*v.* 참다, 견디다
　　　　　n. abidance
　　　　　A good housekeeper can't *abide* dust.

　　　　　2. be faithful to; keep
　　　　　v. 준수하다, 지키다 (항상 by가 따름)
　　　　　n. abidance
　　　　　If you join the club you must *abide* by its rules.

allegiance　the loyalty owed by a citizen to his country or government
[əlí:dʒəns]　*n.* 충성, 충절

adj. allegiant
His *allegiance* to his country lasted all his life.

analyze
[ǽnəlaiz]

divide a mixture into its separate parts
v. 분석하다, 분해하다
n. analysis
The food was *analyzed* and found to contain small amounts of poison.

consume
[kənsjú:m]

use up; spend; waste away; expend; exhaust
v. 소비하다, 소모하다
n. consumption
He *consumed* almost all the money he earned last summer.

dictate
[díktéit]

1. read aloud for another person to write down
v. 받아쓰게 하다, 구술(口述)하다
n. dictation
The president of the company *dictated* a letter to his secretary.

2. command with authority; order in clear terms
v. 명령하다, 지령하다
n. dictation
The country that won the war *dictated* the terms of peace to the conquered country.

fluent
[flú:ənt]

flowing smoothly or easily
adj. 유창한, 막힘 없는, 능변의
n. fluency
He is very *fluent* in English, but not in French.

friction
[fríkʃən]

rubbing of one object against another; difference of opinion; disagreement; conflict
n. 마찰, 불화, 알력
adj. frictional
Friction against the rock, combined with the weight of the climber, caused his rope to break.

miser
[máizər]

a person who loves money and hates spending it
n. 구두쇠, 수전노
n. misery
A *miser* lives poorly in order to save money and keep it.

monarch
[mɔ́nərk]

a sole ruler, such as an emperor, queen, king, etc.
n. 군주, 제왕
n. monarchy
The national band played for the visiting *monarch*.

Lesson 7

partition
[pɑːrtíʃən]

division into parts, sections, or shares; apportionment
n., v. 분할(하다), 구분(하다)
adj. partitive
The *partition* of the country into two parts caused many problems.

qualify
[kwɔ́lifai]

make fit or competent; furnish with legal power
v. 자격을 부여하다, 적격하게 하다
n. qualification
Being the son of a member of parliament doesn't *qualify* him to talk about politics.

succession
[səkséʃən]

a series of things or persons coming one after another
n. 연속, 계승
adj. successive
After a *succession* of warm days, the weather became cold.

tribute
[tríbjuːt]

1. forced payment by one nation to another for peace or protection
n. 공물(貢物)
adj. tributary
Many conquered nations had to pay *tribute* to the rulers of ancient Rome.

2. something said or given to show respect or admiration for someone
n. 찬양의 표시, 감사의 표시
By erecting this statue we have paid a *tribute* to the memory of the founder of our college.

EXERCISE 3   Fill each blank with the most appropriate word given above.
(Inflect the word if necessary.)

1. We can _____ water into two colorless gases, hydrogen and oxygen.

2. Mary is neat and Jane is careless; if they have to share a room there will probably be _____.

3. Arguing about unimportant affairs _____ many hours of the committee's valuable time.

4. When the king dies, his oldest son will be first in _____ to the throne.

5. A(n) _____ dislikes to spend money for anything, except to gain more money.

STUDY YOUR NEW WORDS-4

clue
[kluː]

a fact or object which aids in solving a mystery or problem
n. 실마리, 단서
The police could find no fingerprints or other *clues* to help them in solving the robbery.

cluster
[klʌ́stər]

similar things growing or grouped together; bunch; clump
n. 송이, 떼, 떨기
She bought two *clusters* of grapes for her little son.

flush
[flʌʃ]

1. become red suddenly; blush; glow
v. 붉어지다, 홍조를 띠다
Her face *flushed* when she could not answer the easy question.

2. flow suddenly and freely; rush rapidly
v. 왈칵 흐르다, 좍 흐르다
The steam was *flushing* after the heavy rain.

germ
[dʒəːrm]

a very tiny animal or plant, especially one that causes disease
n. 세균, 병균
The wound must be kept clean so that *germs* do not infect it.

grunt
[grʌnt]

make deep rough sounds in the throat
v. 투덜대다, (돼지 따위가) 꿀꿀거리다
"I'm too tired," he *grunted*, and then fell asleep again.

junction
[dʒʌ́ŋkʃən]

the state of being joined
n. 접합, 연접, 합체(合體)
The two rivers make their *junction* near the sea.

pinch
[pintʃ]

squeeze between the thumb and forefinger; nip
v. 꼬집다, 집다, 죄다
He *pinched* fruit to see if it was soft.

prairie
[prɛ́əri]

a wide treeless grassy plain
n. 대초원
The *prairie* was ideal for growing wheat.

rim
[rim]

an edge, margin, or border of something rounded or curved
n. 가장자리, 테
The basketball hit the *rim* of the basket and bounced off.

shove
[ʃʌv]

push along by applying force
v. 밀치다, 떠밀다, 밀어젖히다
There was a lot of pushing and *shoving* to get on the bus.

stammer
[stǽmər]

speak with pauses and repeated sounds; stutter
v. 말을 더듬다, 더듬으며 말하다
"Th-th-thank you v-v-very much," he *stammered*.

technical
[téknikəl]

concerning the mechanical or practical arts or skills
adj. 공업의, 기술의, 기술적인
He is studying automobile repairs at a *technical* school.

tint
[tint]

slight degree of a color
n. 색조, 빛깔
The picture was painted in several *tints* of blue.

EXERCISE 4 — Fill each blank with the most appropriate word given above.
(Inflect the word if necessary.)

1. The shy girl _____ when a strange man spoke to her.
2. Have any _____ been found that can help the police find the criminal?
3. A(n) _____ is so tiny that it cannot be seen by the eye alone.
4. She _____ the heavy table against the wall to sweep the room.
5. There was a band of blue around the _____ of the cup.

해답					
EXERCISE 1.	1. futile	2. roused	3. appeal	4. tolerate	5. raid
EXERCISE 2.	1. inevitable	2. unique	3. linked	4. summit	5. serene
EXERCISE 3.	1. analyze	2. friction	3. consumed	4. succession	5. miser
EXERCISE 4.	1. flushed	2. clues	3. germ	4. shoved	5. rim

종합 연습 문제

1 In the space at the left, write the *letter* of the word that has most nearly the SAME MEANING as the italicize word.

_____ 1. a *futile* attempt   (A) effective   (B) indirect
                                                 (C) useless   (D) necessary

_____ 2. the *ingredients* of the cake   (A) components   (B) prices
                                                 (C) tastes   (D) qualities

_____ 3. an *obscure* poet   (A) famous   (B) undistinguished
                                              (C) imaginative   (D) foreign

_____ 4. the *utmost* danger   (A) unexpected   (B) sudden
                                              (C) greatest   (D) slight

_____ 5. many *discords* over the question   (A) conflicts   (B) solutions
                                                           (C) trials   (C) mistakes

2 In the space provided, write the *letter* of the word that most nearly means the OPPOSITE of the italicized word.

_____ 1. *hostile*   (A) serene   (B) unique
                               (C) hospitable   (D) vain

_____ 2. *optimism*   (A) pessimism   (B) communism
                               (C) idealism   (D) realism

_____ 3. *veteran*   (A) expert   (B) raid
                               (C) germ   (D) apprentice

_____ 4. *vacuum*   (A) friction   (B) fullness
                               (C) summit   (D) tribute

_____ 5. *submit*   (A) assault   (B) conquer
                               (C) rouse   (D) surrender

3 Supply the correct form of the word in italics for the blank space in each sentence.

1. *analyze*   A careful _____ of the substance was made in the laboratory.
2. *qualify*   What are the _____ for the job?
3. *consume*   There is too great _____ of alcohol in Korea.
4. *succession*   It has rained for five _____ days.
5. *fluent*   She speaks both Spanish and English with _____.

Lesson 7   87

4 Fill in the missing letters of the word at the right. Each dash stands for one missing letter.

DEFINITION	WORD
1. of the greatest degree; highest	__MOST
2. a wild treeless grassy plain	P___RIE
3. drive or force back	RE__L
4. a violent attack with weapons or blows	ASS___T
5. slight degree of a color	T__T
6. make fit or competent	Q____FY
7. the state of being joined	J___TION
8. a sole ruler such as an emperor or king	M____CH
9. become red suddenly	F___H
10. speak with pauses and repeated sounds	ST___ER

5 In the space provided, write the *letter* of the word NOT RELATED in meaning to the other words in each line.

_____	1.	(A) cluster	(B) bustle	(C) bunch	(D) clump
_____	2.	(A) peak	(B) summit	(C) zenith	(D) clue
_____	3.	(A) monarch	(B) partition	(C) division	(D) apportionment
_____	4.	(A) link	(B) join	(C) dictate	(D) connect
_____	5.	(A) rim	(B) germ	(C) margin	(D) edge
_____	6.	(A) forecast	(B) predict	(C) prophesy	(D) shove
_____	7.	(A) crave	(B) desire	(C) repel	(D) covet
_____	8.	(A) squeeze	(B) nip	(C) pinch	(D) rouse
_____	9.	(A) distinctly	(B) finally	(C) eventually	(D) ultimately
_____	10.	(A) serene	(B) calm	(C) prominent	(D) tranquil

6 Fill each blank with the most appropriate word from the vocabulary list below.

> **VOCABULARY LIST**
>
> friction   tint   junction
> dictated   repelled tolerate
> clues   appeal   clusters
> obscure   abide   tribute

1. He pushed the box very hard down the slope, but _____ gradually caused it to slow down and stop.
2. That music is too old-fashioned to _____ to people any longer.
3. Many conquered nations had to pay _____ to the rulers of ancient Rome.
4. The police could not find any _____ to help them in solving the robbery.
5. The enemy in the city was _____ by our troops.
6. If you join the club you must _____ by its rules.
7. The two rivers make their _____ near the sea.
8. We had difficulty in finding the _____ path through the forest.
9. She bought two _____ of grapes for her little son.
10. The president of the company _____ a letter to his secretary.

해답

1 1. C	2. A	3. B	4. C	5. A
2 1. C	2. A	3. D	4. B	5. B
3 1. analysis	2. qualifications	3. consumption	4. successive	5. fluency
4 1. utmost	2. prairie	3. repel	4. assault	5. tint
6. qualify	7. junction	8. monarch	9. flush	10. stammer
5 1. B 2. D	3. A 4. C	5. B 6. D	7. C 8. D	9. A 10. C
6 1. friction	2. appeal	3. tribute	4. clues	5. repelled
6. abide	7. junction	8. obscure	9. clusters	10. dictated

Lesson 7

Lesson 8

PRETEST 8

Insert the *letter* of the best answer in the space provided.

1. Hundreds of people *besieged* the _____.
   (A) famous actress   (B) radical idea

2. Usually domestic *fowls* can fly _____ distance.
   (A) short   (B) long

3. The farmer *breeds* _____ for market.
   (A) cattle and horse   (B) wheat and barley

4. He worked as an *apprentice* until he became _____.
   (A) successful   (B) skillful

5. An employee is *reliable* if he always does his work _____.
   (A) responsibly   (B) neglectfully

ANSWERS   1.A 2.A 3.A 4.B 5.A

STUDY YOUR NEW WORDS-1

amaze
[əméiz]

astonish greatly
v. 깜짝 놀라게 하다, 아연케 하다
syn. surprise
They were all *amazed* at the mighty power of God.

bargain
[bá:ɾgin]

1. an agreement to trade or exchange.
n. 매매, 계약, 거래
syn. contract
The boys made a *bargain* with one another to exchange base ball gloves.

2. something that can be or has been bought for less than its real value
n. 싼 물건, 떨이
These good shoes are a real *bargain* at such a low price.

belongings
[bilɔ́ŋiŋz]

things that belong to a person; one's property
n. 소지품, 소유물
syn. possessions
She packed all her *belongings* in a box and took them with her.

besiege
[bisíːdʒ]

1. surround with armed forces
v. 포위공격하다, 에워싸다
syn. attack
Troy was *besieged* by the Greeks for ten years.

2. crowd round in order to do or get something
v. 몰려들다, 쇄도하다
syn. congregate
The teacher was *besieged* with the questions and requests from pupils.

fowl
[faul]

birds, especially farm birds; chicken raised for eating
n. 새, 조류 (특히 가금(家禽), 닭)
syn. poultry
I prefer the taste of chicken to that of other kinds of *fowl*.

harsh
[háːrʃ]

rough and disagreeable to the senses
adj. 거친, 껄껄한, 거슬리는
syn. coarse
At the end of the football game, the cheer leader's voice became *harsh*.

menace
[ménəs]

a threat; something that could cause harm
n. 위협, 협박, 위험
syn. intimidation
The cross road in front of the school is a *menace* to the children's safety.

rapture
[ræptʃər]

a feeling of great joy; extreme pleasure
n. 환희, 황홀, 큰 기쁨
syn. ecstasy
The beauty of the sunset filled everybody with *rapture*.

renowned
[rináund]

famous; noted; eminent
adj. 유명한, 명성이 있는
syn. famous
Ladies and gentlemen, now I will introduce to you the *renowned* star of the stage and screen John Wayne.

stool
[stuːl]

a chair without arms or a back
n. (등받이가 없는) 의자, 걸상

syn. chair

I pulled the *stool* near the wall to hang a picture.

verify confirm; prove the truth of
[vérifai] ***v.*** 확증하다, 입증하다, 증명하다
         syn. certify
         We will repeat the experiment twice in order to *verify* the results.

EXERCISE 1 Fill each blank with the most appropriate word given above.
(Inflect the word if necessary.)

1. The crowd _____ the minister with questions about their increased taxes.
2. The boys went hunting for pheasant and other wild _____.
3. She was so _____ by the surprise party that she could not think of a thing to say.
4. Communist' aggressive nature is a great _____ to world peace.
5. The young mother gazed at the newborn baby with _____.

STUDY YOUR NEW WORDS-2

abnormal   not usual; odd; different from what is ordinary or expected
[æbnɔ́rməl] ***adj.*** 비정상적인, 변칙의, 이상한
            ant. normal
            His *abnormal* behavior shows that something is wrong.

abundance a great quantity; plenty; affluence
[əbʌ́ndəns]   ***n.*** 풍부, 많음, 부유
             ant. shortage
             At the party there was food and drink in *abundance*.

apprentice a person learning a trade or art; a beginner
[əpréntis]   ***n.*** 도제(徒弟), 견습공, 초심자
              ant. expert
              He worked seven years at the printing company as an *apprentice*.

bearable   that can be endured; tolerable
[bɛ́ərəbl]   ***adj.*** 견딜 수 있는, 감내할 수 있는
              ant. intolerable
              She said to the doctor that her pain would be just *bearable*.

immortal
[imɔ́ːrtl]

not mortal; never dying; everlasting
adj. 죽지 않는, 불후(不朽)의, 영원한
ant. dying
Most people believe that a man's body dies but his soul is *immortal*.

innumerable
[injúːmərəbl]

too many to be counted; countless
adj. 무수한, 셀 수 없는, 대단히 많은
ant. countable
The sun is one of the *innumerable* stars in the universe.

preliminary
[prilímənəri]

coming before and preparing for something more important; preparatory
adj. 예비의, 준비의
ant. consequent
The chairman made a *preliminary* statement before beginning the main business meeting.

remote
[rimóut]

far away; distant in space or time
adj. 먼, 멀리 떨어진
ant. near
Some of your statements are rather *remote* from the subject we are discussing.

repose
[ripóuz]

rest; sleep
n. 휴식, 안면(安眠)
ant. work
His brief *repose* was interrupted by her sudden arrival.

shrewd
[ʃruːd]

having keen insight; astute; clever
adj. 빈틈없는, 기민한
ant. stupid
Although he had no formal education, he is one of the *shrewd* businessmen in the steel company.

temporary
[témpərəri]

lasting for a short time only
adj. 일시의, 임시의
ant. permanent
He has a *temporary* job which ends in two weeks.

EXERCISE 2 **Fill each blank with the most appropriate word given above.**
(Inflect the word if necessary.)

1. There is such a(n) _____ of apples this year that many are not picked.

Lesson 8 93

2. All members of the family except _____ relatives were invited to his birthday party.

3. Many students find _____ jobs during their summer holidays.

4. The lawyer knows all the tricks; he is very _____.

5. It is _____ for a baby to have teeth at the age of two months.

STUDY YOUR NEW WORDS-3

automatic
[ɔ:təmǽtik]

having the power of moving by itself
adj. 자동의, 자동적인
n. automation
An *automatic* timer turns the street light on at night and off in the morning.

comprehend
[kɔmprihénd]

understand fully and completely
v. 이해하다, 파악하다
adj. comprehensive
The child read the story but did not *comprehend* its meaning.

cordial
[kɔ́:rdjəl]

warm; friendly; hearty
adj. 성심성의의, 충심으로부터의
n. cordiality
When one of his former students visited him the teacher gave him a *cordial* welcome.

elaborate
[ilǽbərit]

1. full of detail
adj. 공들인, 정교한
n. elaboration
The scientists made an *elaborate* plan for landing a man on the moon.

[ilǽbəreit]

2. work out with great care; add details to
v. 정성들여 만들다, 공들여 완성하다
n. elaboration
The inventor *elaborated* his plans for a new engine, spending several months in his laboratory.

expire
[ikspáiər]

cease; terminate; die
v. 끝나다, 만기가 되다
n. expiration
His term of office as President will *expire* next year.

external
[ikstə́ːrnəl]

1. on the outside; outward; exterior
adj. 외부의, 밖의, 표면의
He judges people by mere *external* clothes rather than internal character.

2. foreign
adj. 국외의, 외국의
adv. externally
This newspaper doesn't pay enough attention to *external* affairs.

glorify
[glɔ́ːrifai]

give praise and thanks to; worship
v. 찬미하다, 칭송하다
n. glory
Singing hymns is one of the ways to *glorify* God.

priority
[praiɔ́rəti]

being prior or earlier in time or order
n. (시간, 순서가) 앞임, 우선권
adj. prior
The badly wounded take *priority* for medical attention over those slightly hurt.

reliable
[riláiəbl]

worthy of trust; dependable
adj. 믿을 만한, 확실한
v. rely
Send the boy to the bank for money; he is a *reliable* boy.

repetition
[repítiʃən]

the act of repeating
n. 반복, 되풀이
v. repeat
Repetition of the sentence helped him to memorize it.

survive
[sə(ː)rváiv]

remain alive; continue to live
v. 살아남다, ~후까지 살아남다
n. survival
Only three of the fifty passengers *survived* the shipwreck.

EXERCISE 3 Fill each blank with the most appropriate word given above.
(Inflect the word if necessary.)

1. If you know how to use a word correctly, you _____ it.

2. You must obtain a new automobile license when your old one _____.

3. Fire engines and ambulances have _____ over other vehicles.

4. I believe whatever he says because he is very _____.

5. We _____ although others died in the traffic accident.

STUDY YOUR NEW WORDS-4

behalf
[bihǽːf]

on someone's behalf = in (on) behalf of someone = for someone
(아무)를 대신하여, (아무)를 위하여
My husband can't be here today, so I'm going to speak on his *behalf*.

breed
[briːd]

raise animals; bring up; produce young
v. 기르다, 사육하다, 번식시키다
The farmer *breeds* cattle and horse for market.

disguise
[disgáiz]

1. hide the true nature or character of; change the usual appearance
v. 변장하다, 가장하다
She *disguised* her writing by writing with her left hand.

2. something that is worn to hide who one really is
n. 변장, 가장
The thief wore a false beard and glasses as a *disguise*.

domain
[dəméin]

1. a territory under the rule of one ruler or government; an estate
n. 영역, 영토
The king is respected throughout his *domain*.

2. a field of action or knowledge
n. (연구, 활동의) 분야, 범위
I can't answer your question about photography; it's not in my *domain*.

morsel
[mɔ́ːrsəl]

a small amount of food
n. (음식의) 한입, 조각, 소량
The dinner must have been good because there is not even a *morsel* of it left over.

routine
[ruːtíːn]

a way of working or doing things regularly
n. 판에 박힌 일, 일상적인 과정
Getting up and going to bed are parts of your daily *routine*.

transform
[trænsfɔ́ːrm]

change in appearance or form
v. 변형시키다, 바꾸다
That dress *transforms* her from a little girl into a young lady.

transit
[trǽnsit]

a passage from one place to another
n. 통로, 통과, 통행
The points of *transit* from one country to another are carefully guarded.

ultimate
[ʌ́ltimit]

final; coming at the end
adj. 최후의, 마지막의, 궁극의
Her *ultimate* goal is to receive her degree and return to her country to work as a teacher.

warily
[wɛ́ərili]

cautiously; with care
adv. 주의깊게, 조심스럽게
The hikers climbed *warily* up the dangerous path.

EXERCISE 4

Fill each blank with the most appropriate word given above.
(Inflect the word if necessary.)

1. Great Britain is a large island _____ under the Crown of England.

2. She was alone, so she opened the door _____, leaving the chain lock fastened.

3. He went among the enemy in the _____ of an enemy soldier.

4. Most people who drive too fast never consider that the _____ result of their action might be a serious accident.

5. The professor was writing a letter of recommendation on _____ of his former student who wanted to apply for a foreign university.

해답

EXERCISE 1.	1. besieged	2. fowls	3. amazed	4. menace	5. rapture
EXERCISE 2.	1. abundance	2. remote	3. temporary	4. shrewd	5. abnormal
EXERCISE 3.	1. comprehend	2. expires	3. priority	4. reliable	5. survived
EXERCISE 4.	1. domain	2. warily	3. disguise	4. ultimate	5. behalf

종합 연습 문제

1 In the space provided, write the *letter* of the word NOT RELATED in meaning to the other words in each line.

_____	1.	(A) fowl	(B) poultry	(C) chicken	(D) fault
_____	2.	(A) belongings	(B) property	(C) desire	(D) possessions
_____	3.	(A) eminent	(B) active	(C) famous	(D) renowned
_____	4.	(A) harsh	(B) shrewd	(C) coarse	(D) rough
_____	5.	(A) astound	(B) astonish	(C) ascribe	(D) amaze
_____	6.	(A) trust	(B) certify	(C) verify	(D) confirm
_____	7.	(A) intimidation	(B) threat	(C) menace	(D) jail
_____	8.	(A) ecstasy	(B) bliss	(C) favor	(D) rapture
_____	9.	(A) promotion	(B) bargain	(C) pact	(D) contract
_____	10.	(A) terminate	(B) surrender	(C) cease	(D) expire

2 In the space before each word in COLUMN I, write the *letter* of its correct meaning in COLUMN II.

	COLUMN I	COLUMN II
_____	1. ultimate	(A) change in appearance or form
_____	2. breed	(B) a regular way of doing things
_____	3. transit	(C) warm; friendly; hearty
_____	4. warily	(D) raise animals; produce young
_____	5. morsel	(E) hide the true nature or characteristic of
_____	6. domain	(F) final; coming to an end
_____	7. cordial	(G) a territory under the rule of one government
_____	8. transform	(H) a passage from one place to another
_____	9. disguise	(I) cautiously; with care
_____	10. routine	(J) a small amount of food

3 In the space provided, write the *letter* of the word that most nearly means the OPPOSITE of the italicized word.

_____ 1. *repose*   (A) despise   (B) loneliness
                                           (C) work   (D) agreement

TOEFL·TOEIC·TEPS 중급 College Vocabulary

_____ 2. *immortal*   (A) fresh   (B) literal
                           (C) patient   (D) dying

_____ 3. *temporary*   (A) permanent   (B) cool
                           (C) ugly   (D) wild

_____ 4. *shrewd*   (A) tranquil   (B) stupid
                           (C) moderate   (D) comfortable

_____ 5. *abnormal*   (A) informal   (B) private
                           (C) normal   (D) personal

_____ 6. *remote*   (A) future   (B) similar
                           (C) near   (D) fluent

_____ 7. *bearable*   (A) impossible   (B) intolerable
                           (C) sterile   (D) pensive

_____ 8. *preliminary* (A) consequent   (B) insufficient
                           (C) postal   (D) direct

_____ 9. *abundance*   (A) obeyance   (B) royalty
                           (C) priority   (D) shortage

_____ 10. *apprentice* (A) expert   (B) rejection
                           (C) proof   (D) coincidence

4 Complete the following table with the appropriate word forms.

	ADJECTIVE	NOUN	VERB	ADVERB
1.	cordial	_____	XXXXX	_____
2.	prior	_____	XXXXX	XXXXX
3.	_____	_____	comprehend	_____
4.	_____	_____	repeat	_____
5.	_____	abundance	XXXXX	_____
6.	_____	_____	elaborate	_____
7.	XXXXX	_____	survive	XXXXX
8.	reliable	_____	_____	_____
9.	automatic	_____	_____	_____
10.	_____	_____	glorify	_____

Lesson 8

5 In the space provided, write the *letter* of the word or expression that has most nearly the SAME MEANING as the italicized word.

_____ 1. After the *preliminary* exercises of pray and song, the speaker of the day gave an address.
(A) preparatory (B) religious (C) sympathetic (D) thorough

_____ 2. He *comprehends* the theory of relativity.
(A) teaches (B) learns (C) investigates (D) understands

_____ 3. I hope you have left none of your *belongings* in the hotel.
(A) documents (B) possessions (C) children (D) clothes

_____ 4. You can *verify* the spelling of the word by looking in a dictionary.
(A) correct (B) investigate (C) confirm (D) find

_____ 5. They muttered prayers to themselves for the *repose* of the soul of their dead friend.
(A) purpose (B) return (C) blessing (D) rest

_____ 6. She was alone, so she opened the door *warily*, leaving the chain lock fastened.
(A) quietly (B) hesitantly (C) cautiously (D) slowly

_____ 7. The boys made a *bargain* with one another to exchange their baseball gloves.
(A) contract (B) joke (C) order (D) plan

_____ 8. The trade agreement between the two countries will *expire* in three years.
(A) cease (B) negotiate (C) amend (D) adopt

_____ 9. There is such an *abundance* of apples this year that many of them are not picked.
(A) disease (B) plenty (C) deflation (D) harvest

_____ 10. He was *renowned* as a doctor who found a cure for the disease.
(A) assigned (B) famous (C) designated (D) praised

해답

1 1. D 2. C 3. B 4. B 5. C 6. A 7. D 8. C 9. A 10. B
2 1. F 2. D 3. H 4. I 5. J 6. G 7. C 8. A 9. E 10. B
3 1. C 2. D 3. A 4. B 5. C 6. C 7. B 8. A 9. D 10. A
4

ADJECTIVE	NOUN	VERB	ADVERB
1. (cordial)	cordiality	XXXXX	cordially
2. (prior)	priority	XXXXX	XXXXX
3. comprehensive	comprehension	(comprehend)	comprehensively
4. repetitious	repetition	(repeat)	repetitiously
5. abundant	(abundance)	XXXXX	abundantly
6. elaborate	elaboration	(elaborate)	elaborately
7. XXXXX	survival	(survive)	XXXXX
8. (reliable)	reliability	rely	reliably
9. (automatic)	automation	automatize	automatically
10. glorious	glory	(glorify)	gloriously

5 1. A 2. D 3. B 4. C 5. D 6. C 7. A 8. A 9. B 10. B

Lesson 9

PRETEST 9

Insert the *letter* of the best answer in the space provided.

1. The little girl *moaned* in _____.
   (A) delight   (B) pain

2. *Architecture* deals with the designing and planning of various _____.
   (A) buildings   (B) ships

3. The _____ hand is *dominant* in most people.
   (A) right   (B) left

4. _____ is *transparent*.
   (A) Gold or silver   (B) Window glass

5. This is the *site* for a new _____.
   (A) hospital   (B) student

ANSWERS 1. B 2. A 3. A 4. B 5. A

STUDY YOUR NEW WORDS-1

allot
[əlɔ́t]

give as a share, task or duty; assign; distribute
v. 할당하다, 배분하다
syn. allocate
The profits from the candy sale have been *allotted* equally to the Boy Scouts and the Girl Scouts.

banner
[bǽnər]

flag of a country, state, or organization
n. 기, 깃발
syn. flag
The *banners* of many countries fly outside of the headquarters of the United Nations.

cliff
[klif]

a very steep slope of rock or clay; precipice
n. 절벽, 벼랑, 낭떠러지

Lesson 9 101

syn. bluff
Standing at the edge of the *cliff*, she could see the waves below.

crook
[kruk]
make a curve or hook
v. 갈고리 모양으로 하다, 구부리다
syn. bend
I *crooked* my leg around the branch to keep from falling.

ensue
[insjúː]
come afterwards (as a result); succeed
v. 계속해서 일어나다, 결과로 일어나다
syn. follow
In his anger he hit the man, and a fight *ensued*.

gap
[gæp]
a vacant space or interval; empty part
n. 틈, 빈틈, 간격
syn. opening
The cows ran away through a *gap* in the fence.

hoard
[hɔrd]
1. what is saved and stored; things stored
n. 축적, 저장(물)
syn. stock
They have a *hoard* of food in the basement.

2. save in large amounts; pile up; keep for future use
v. 축적하다, 저장하다
syn. stock
When sugar, coffee, and other foods were scarce, many people *hoarded* them.

marsh
[mɑːrʃ]
soft wet land
n. 늪, 소택(沼澤), 습지
syn. swamp
It is not easy to cross the *marsh* on foot; we'd better go round it.

moan
[moun]
1. a long, low sound indicating pain or sorrow
n. 신음, 끙끙대기
syn. groan
From time to time, during the night, there was a *moan* of pain from the sick man.

2. make the sound of moans
v. 신음하다, 끙끙거리다
syn. groan
The sick child *moaned* a little, and then fell asleep.

notorious
[noutɔ́:riəs]

well known because of something bad
adj. (나쁜 의미로) 소문난, 악명 높은
syn. infamous
The *notorious* thief was finally caught and put to prison for his many crimes.

sermon
[sə́:rmən]

a talk on a religious subject; a serious talk about conduct, morals, or duty
n. 설교, 잔소리, 장광설
syn. preach
After the guests left, father gave a *sermon* on table manners to the children.

site
[sait]

place where something was, is, or will be built
n. 위치, 집터, 부지
syn. location
The big house on the hill has one of the best *sites* in town.

suppress
[səprés]

stop by force; put down; keep in; hold back; restrain
v. 진압하다, 억누르다, 가라앉히다
syn. subdue
The police *suppressed* the riot by firing over the heads of the crowd.

EXERCISE 1   Fill each blank with the most appropriate word given above.
(Inflect the word if necessary.)

1. The boy was severly hurt in a fall from a(n) _____.
2. A lasting friendship _____ from our working together during the war.
3. The tired horse _____ under the heavy load.
4. A(n) _____ is all or partly soft and wet, because of its low position.
5. The teacher _____ each boy a part in the Christmas play.

STUDY YOUR NEW WORDS-2

agony
[ǽgəni]

very great pain of mind or body; suffering
n. 고뇌, 고민, 고통
ant. joy
He has suffered *agonies* from his broken arm.

desolate
[désəlit]

sad and without people in it; deserted; forlorn; lonely
adj. 쓸쓸한, 황량한, 황폐한

Lesson 9

ant. cozy
I was very *desolate* when my mother died last year.

everlasting
[evərlǽstiŋ]
lasting forever; never stopping; eternal; perpetual; permanent;
adj. 영원한, 영구적인
ant. transient
We do not want to be involved in any war; we wish for *everlasting* peace.

excess
[ékses]
more than necessary; extra amount surplus; superfluity
n., adj. 초과(의), 과잉(의), 과도(의)
ant. deficiency
Passengers must pay for *excess* baggage on an airplane.

gross
[grous]
with nothing taken out; total; entire; whole
adj. 총체의, 전체의, 총량의
ant. net
The *gross* weight of the sack of flour is more than the net weight of the flour alone.

idiot
[ídiət]
a very foolish or stupid person
n. 백치, 천치, 바보
ant. genius
He is intelligent, but sometimes he behaves like an *idiot*.

infinite
[ínfinit]
without limits or end; boundless; unlimited; vast
adj. 무한한, 무수한, 막대한
ant. finite
Teaching little children usually requires *infinite* patience.

integrate
[íntigreit]
make into a whole; put or bring together
v. 통합하다, 완전하게 하다
ant. disintegrate
The committee will try to *integrate* the different ideas into one uniform plan.

liable
[láiəbl]
1. responsible; required by law to pay
adj. 책임이 있는, 의무가 있는
ant. irresponsible
He stated that he was not *liable* for his wife's debts.

2. likely to happen with unpleasant results
adj. ~하기 쉬운, 자칫하면 ~하는
ant. irresponsible
You are *liable* to catch a cold if you go out without an overcoat.

miscellaneous
[misəléinjəs]

of several kinds; various; many sided
adj. 잡다한, 가지가지의
ant. sole
The boy had a *miscellaneous* collection of stamps, stones, and many other things.

revenue
[révənju]

income, especially the total annual income of a state
n. 세입, 세수, 수입
ant. expenditure
The government got much *revenue* from taxes last year.

trifling
[tráifliŋ]

of little value; not important; insignificant; trivial
adj. 하찮은, 보잘것없는, 사소한
ant. important
The friends treated their quarrel as only a *trifling* matter.

EXERCISE 2 Fill each blank with the most appropriate word given above.
(Inflect the word if necessary.)

1. The loss of her husband filled her with _____.
2. His _____ monthly income is ＄2,000, but his net income is less than ＄1,500.
3. The Postal Service is not _____ for damage to a parcel unless it is insured.
4. It's not a(n) _____ matter; we can't pass it by.
5. This _____ of imports over exports will ruin the nation.

STUDY YOUR NEW WORDS-3

amend
[əménd]

change the form of; improve; make better; correct
v. 수정하다, 개정하다, 정정하다
n. amendment
The Constitution of the United States was *amended* so that women could vote.

architecture
[á:rkitektʃər]

The art of designing building; the style of building
n. 건축술, 건축학
adj. architectural
Greek *architecture* was quite different from modern architecture.

Lesson 9

clarify [klǽrifai]	make clearer; explain; purify ***v.*** 명료하게 하다, 맑게 하다 **n.** clarification The teacher's explanation ***clarified*** the puzzling problems.
concept [kɔ́nsept]	general idea, thought, or notion ***n.*** 개념(概念) **adj.** conceptual Some people still believe in the old ***concept*** that the sun moves round the earth.
dominant [dɔ́minənt]	most powerful or influential; stronger or higher than the others ***adj.*** 지배적인, 우세한, 우뚝 솟은 **v.** dominate John had a very ***dominant*** nature; we all did what he wanted.
edit [édit]	prepare another person's writings for publication ***v.*** 편집하다 **n.** edition The teacher is ***editing*** famous speeches for use in school books.
portrait [pɔ́ːrtreit]	painting, drawing, or photograph of a real person ***n.*** 초상화 **v.** portray She had her ***portrait*** painted by a famous artist.
precaution [prikɔ́ːʃən]	care taken beforehand to avoid a risk ***n.*** 예방, 예방책, 경계 **adj.** precautionary They took heavy coats as a ***precaution*** against the possibility of cold weather.
pulse [pʌls]	the regular beating of blood in the main blood vessels ***n.*** 맥박, 고동 **v.** pulsate The doctor began to measure my ***pulse*** rate per minute.
renew [rinjúː]	make new again; restore; begin again ***v.*** 새롭게 하다, 갱신하다, 회복하다 **n.** renewal I came back from by holiday with ***renewed*** strength.
transparent [trænspɛ́ərənt]	allowing light to pass through; thin enough to be seen through ***adj.*** 투명한, 들여다 보이는, 명료한

	n. transparency
	Her silk dress she was wearing in the party was almost *transparent*.
universal [juːnivə́rsəl]	belonging to all; shared by all; existing everywhere *adj.* 일반적인, 보편적인, 만인의 n. universality It is a subject of *universal* interest; everyone is interested in it.

> **EXERCISE 3** **Fill each blank with the most appropriate word given above.**
> (Inflect the word if necessary.)
>
> 1. Locking doors is a good _____ against thieves.
> 2. The incorrect spelling in my theme was _____ by the teacher.
> 3. You have to _____ your library ticket before it expires.
> 4. The painting that hung in the hall was the _____ of George Washington.
> 5. The tower was built in a(n) _____ position on a hill where everyone could see it.

STUDY YOUR NEW WORDS-4

bullet [búlit]	a type of shoot fired from a rifle or pistol *n.* 탄환, 총탄 The captain was killed in the battle by an enemy's *bullet*.
congressman [kɔ́ŋgresmən]	a member of the United States Congress *n.* 국회의원 (특히 하원의원) Mary is very proud of her father; he is a *congressman*.
flake [fleik]	a very small, thin piece *n.* 조각, 박편, 눈송이 The snow was falling on the ground in large *flakes*.
index [índeks]	a list of what is in a book, telling on what pages to find each thing *n.* 색인, 찾아보기 The teacher taught the pupils how to use the *index* of their textbook.
nuisance [njúːsns]	an act, thing, or person that causes trouble *n.* 폐되는 행위, 불법 방해 Don't make a *nuisance* of yourself; sit down and be quiet!

panic
[pǽnik]

sudden uncontrollable quick spreading fear or terror
n. 공포, 당황, 낭패
When the theater caught fire, there was *panic* in the audience.

scramble
[skrǽmbl]

1. climb or crawl quickly, using hands and feet
v. 기어오르다, 타고 오르다
We *scrambled* up the rock for a better look at the sea.

2. struggle with others for something
v. 다투어 빼앗다, 쟁탈하다
When the money fell on the floor, everyone *scrambled* to get some.

squeeze
[skwi:z]

press together; get or force out by pressure; compress
v. 죄다, 짜내다, 압박을 가하다
She *squeezed* the juice out of several oranges.

strait
[streit]

a narrow passage of water connecting two large bodies of water
n. 해협
This ship sails through the *Strait* of Gibraltar, where the water is often rough.

submarine
[sʌ́bməri:n]

a ship that travels under water
n. 잠수함
The *submarine* will soon rise to the surface of water.

vehicle
[ví:ikl]

any conveyance for goods or passengers on land
n. 차량
The Main Street is crowed with *vehicles* every morning.

weave
[wi:v]

make something out of threads or strips
v. 짜다, 뜨다
My mother is *weaving* a winter sweater for me.

zinc
[ziŋk]

a hard, bluish-white, metallic chemical element
n. 아연
Zinc is combined with copper to make brass.

EXERCISE 4   Fill each blank with the most appropriate word given above.
(Inflect the word if necessary.)

1. A(n) _____ is usually put at the end of a book and arranged in alphabetical order.

2. The rapid rise of flood water caused _____ among the people in the city.

3. The bad king tried to _____ more money out of the people by increasing taxes.

4. _____ are often used in warfare for attacking enemy ships.

5. The children _____ to get the coins that were thrown to them.

EXERCISE 1.	1. cliff	2. ensued	3. moaned	4. marsh	5. allotted
EXERCISE 2.	1. agony	2. gross	3. liable	4. trifling	5. excess
EXERCISE 3.	1. precaution	2. amended	3. renew	4. portrait	5. dominant
EXERCISE 4.	1. index	2. panic	3. squeeze	4. submarines	5. scrambled

종합 연습 문제

1 In the space at the left, write the letter of the word that has most nearly the SAME MEANING as the italicized word.

_____ 1. the *notorious* robber   (A) terrible   (B) skilled
                                                              (C) poor   (D) well-known

_____ 2. *amend* your table manners   (A) improve   (B) learn
                                                              (C) show   (D) repeat

_____ 3. *everlasting* complaint   (A) useless   (B) angry
                                                              (C) continual   (D) severe

_____ 4. *miscellaneous* collection of goods   (A) careful   (B) various
                                                              (C) foolish   (D) interesting

_____ 5. the *desolate* old house   (A) beautiful   (B) peaceful
                                                              (C) historic   (D) deserted

2 In the space provided, write the *letter* of the word that most nearly means the OPPOSITE of the italicized word.

_____ 1. *idiot*   (A) scholar   (B) genius
                              (C) bullet   (D) fool

_____ 2. *revenue*   (A) extra   (B) result
                              (C) strait   (D) expenditure

_____ 3. *agony*   (A) joy   (B) excess
                              (C) flake   (D) zinc

_____ 4. *liable*   (A) infinite   (B) cozy
                              (C) irresponsible   (D) whole

_____ 5. *gross*   (A) total   (B) grand
                              (C) net   (D) sole

3 Supply the correct from of the word in italics for the blank space in each sentence.

1. *clarify*   We need more _____ of your plans before we can promise to support you.

2. *amend*   So many _____ were made to the rule that its original meaning was completely changed.

3. *portrait*   In his book, the writer _____ the king as a cruel man.

4. *concept*   The result is due to the _____ difference.

5. *dominant*   The strong usually _____ over the weak.

4 Fill in the missing *letters* of the word at the right. Each dash stands for one missing letter.

DEFINITION	WORD
1. a ship that travels under water	SUB _ _ _ _ _ _
2. a talk on a religious subject	S _ _ MON
3. care taken beforehand to avoid a risk	_ _ _ CAUTION
4. soft wet land	M _ _ SH
5. make clearer; purify	C _ _ _ _ FY
6. a very small, thin piece	F _ _ KE
7. the art of designing building	AR _ _ _ _ _ _ TURE
8. lasting forever; eternal	_ _ _ _ LASTING
9. a very foolish person	I _ _ OT
10. belonging to all; shared by all	U _ _ _ _ _ SAL

5 In the space provided, write the *letter* of the word NOT RELATED in meaning to the other words in each line.

_____	1.	(A) allot	(B) amend	(C) assign	(D) allocate
_____	2.	(A) notorious	(B) everlasting	(C) perpetual	(D) eternal
_____	3.	(A) excess	(B) surplus	(C) superfluity	(D) crook
_____	4.	(A) infinite	(B) boundless	(C) unlimited	(D) distrustful
_____	5.	(A) cliff	(B) marsh	(C) bluff	(D) precipice
_____	6.	(A) crawl	(B) climb	(C) squeeze	(D) scramble
_____	7.	(A) universal	(B) various	(C) many-sided	(D) miscellaneous
_____	8.	(A) suppress	(B) restrain	(C) weave	(D) subdue
_____	9.	(A) edit	(B) ensue	(C) follow	(D) succeed
_____	10.	(A) trifling	(B) insignificant	(C) trivial	(D) dominant

6 Fill each blank with the most appropriate word from the vocabulary list below.

VOCABULARY LIST

site	nuisance	miscellaneous
gap	flakes	bullet
excess	weaving	moaning
pulse	integrate	banners

1. The fat woman went on a diet to get rid of her _____ weight.
2. Jack's father was killed in the battle by an enemy's _____.
3. The committee will try to _____ the different ideas into one uniform plan.
4. Don't make a(n) _____ of yourself; sit down and be quiet!
5. The doctor began to measure my _____ rate per minute.
6. A new school is to be built on the _____ of the old town hall.
7. The _____ of many countries fly outside of the headquarters of the United Nations.
8. Mary is _____ a winter sweater for me.
9. The gate was locked, but we went through a(n) _____ in the fence.
10. Bryan has a(n) _____ collection of stamps, stones, and many other things.

해답

1 1. D   2. A   3. C   4. B   5. D
2 1. B   2. D   3. A   4. C   5. C
3 1. clarification   2. amendments   3. portrayed   4. conceptual   5. dominate
4 1. submarine   2. sermon   3. precaution   4. marsh   5. clarify
    6. flake   7. architecture   8. everlasting   9. idiot   10. universal
5 1. B   2. A   3. D   4. D   5. B   6. C   7. A   8. C   9. A   10. D
6 1. excess   2. bullet   3. integrate   4. nuisance   5. pulse
    6. site   7. banners   8. weaving   9. gap   10. miscellaneous

Lesson 10

PRETEST 10

Insert the *letter* of the best answer in the space provided.

1. His brother *scolded* him for _____ the baseball bat.
   (A) finding　　　　(B) breaking

2. An agreement signed by _____, to repay borrowed money, is *void*.
   (A) an adult　　　　(B) a child

3. They used the *chips* of wood to _____.
   (A) start a fire　　　(B) build a house

4. The child *tugged* _____ round the garden.
   (A) the big dog　　(B) small flowers

5. The little chair was too *frail* to _____.
   (A) take a man's weight　　(B) be broken easily

ANSWERS　1. B　2. A　3. A　4. A　5. A

STUDY YOUR NEW WORDS-1

attain
[ətéin]

succeed in doing or getting; gain
v. 이루다, 달성하다, 얻다
syn. achieve
They fought against the tyranny to *attain* freedom.

awe
[ɔː]

a feeling of respect mixed with fear and wonder
n. 경외, 두려움
syn. dread
We feel *awe* when we stand near vast mountains or when we think of God's power and glory.

commence
[kəméns]

start; come into existence
v. 시작하다, 개시하다

syn. begin
The ceremony will *commence* as soon as the minister arrives.

conceit
[kənsít]

too much pride in oneself; vanity
n. 자만, 자기 과대 평가
syn. pride
Her *conceit* about her beauty angered many people.

dismiss
[dismís]

release from office, service, or employment
v. 해고하다, 떠나게 하다
syn. discharge
He was *dismissed* from the company because he was always late for work.

glisten
[glísn]

shine with a sparkling light; spark
v. 빛나다, 반짝이다
syn. glitter
Her eyes *glistened* with tears as she struggled to control her emotions.

grab
[græb]

take hold suddenly; snatch
v. 움켜잡다, 잡아채다
syn. seize
The dog *grabbed* the bone and ran off with it in his mouth.

hearty
[há:rti]

warm hearted or friendly; sincere; genial
adj. 진심으로부터의, 정성어린, 친절한
syn. cordial
We gave our old friends a *hearty* welcome.

kin
[kin]

family or relatives; kinsfolk
n. 친족, 친척, 일가
syn. kindred
All our *kin* came to the family reunion.

peep
[pí:p]

look through a narrow opening; peer
v. 엿보다, 훔쳐보다
syn. peek
The girl *peeped* at the guests through the partly opened door.

realm
[relm]

a country ruled by a king or queen; region
n. 왕국, 영역
syn. kingdom
The queen visited every town in her *realm*.

EXERCISE 1
Fill each blank with the most appropriate word given above.
(Inflect the word if necessary.)

1. The servant was _____ for being dishonest.
2. Your mother is my mother's sister, so you are _____ to me.
3. Looking up at the vast mountains, they were filled with _____.
4. The committee gave its _____ support to the plan.
5. The champion thought that no one could defeat him; he was full of _____.

STUDY YOUR NEW WORDS-2

accurate
[ǽkjurit]

exactly right; free from error
adj. 정확한, 정밀한
ant. incorrect
Her report is always *accurate* and well written.

ancestor
[ǽnsestər]

a person from whom one is directly descended; forebear
n. 선조, 조상
ant. descendant
His *ancestors* came to America on the Mayflower.

dwarf
[dwɔːrf]

a person, animal or plant that is much smaller than usual size
n. 난쟁이, 꼬마둥이
ant. giant
Children of the world love to read the story of Snow White and the Seven *Dwarfs*.

emerge
[imə́ːrdʒ]

come into view; appear; become known
v. 나타나다, 출현하다
ant. disappear
After the rain, the sun *emerged* from behind the clouds.

illusion
[ilúːʒən]

an appearance or feeling that is not real
n. 환영(幻影), 환상
ant. reality
It was an *illusion* that made me think I saw a man in the shadow.

injustice
[indʒʌ́stis]

lack of justice; being unjust; wrong
n. 불의, 불공평, 부정

ant. fairness
It is an *injustice* to send an innocent person to jail.

multitude
[mʌ́ltitjuːd]

a great number; a crowd
n. 다수, 수가 많음, 군중
ant. minority
A *multitude* of European plants have been naturalized in America.

soothe
[suːð]

1. lessen or relieve pain, anxiety, etc.
v. (고통을) 덜다, 완화하다
A hot cloth pressed against your jaw will usually *soothe* a toothache.

2. comfort; make quiet or calm
v. 달래다, 위로하다, 진정시키다
ant. aggravate
The mother *soothed* her crying baby by ringing a bell in front of his face.

vicious
[víʃəs]

cruel; evil; immoral
adj. 잔인한, 사악한, 악덕한
ant. virtuous
He gave the dog a *vicious* blow with his long stick.

void
[vɔid]

1. invalid; without force; having no value or effect
adj. 무효의
ant. valid
An agreement signed by a child, to repay borrowed money, is *void*.

2. empty; without; lacking
adj. 텅 빈, ~이 없는
That part of the town is completely *void* of interest for visitors.

EXERCISE 2 Fill each blank with the most appropriate word given above.
(Inflect the word if necessary.)

1. The agreement, not having been signed officially, was _____.

2. As the moon _____ from behind the clouds, we could see all things clearly.

3. He doesn't make any mistakes; he is _____ in his work.

4. At night a white rock often produces a(n) _____ which seems to be a man standing there.

5. We should _____ those who are in sorrow and mischief.

STUDY YOUR NEW WORDS-3

debate
[dibéit]

give arguments for or against something; discuss
v. 토론하다, 논쟁하다
adj. debatable
We were *debating* whether to go to the mountains or to the seaside for our summer holidays.

extract
[ikstrǽkt]

1. take out from a book, speech, or play, etc.; pull out with effort
v. 발췌하다, 인용하다
n. extraction
He *extracted* several paragraphs from the newspaper article to read at the meeting.

2. get; obtain
v. 얻어내다, 획득하다
n. extraction
Did you manage to *extract* any information from him?

facilitate
[fəsíliteit]

make easy or easier; help
v. 쉽게 하다, 돕다, 촉진하다
n. facility
The broken lock *facilitated* my entrance into the empty house.

frail
[freil]

weak in body or health; not strongly made
adj. 연약한, 무른, 부서지기 쉬운
n. frailty
The sick woman's *frail* hands could hardly hold a cup.

insignificant
[insignífikənt]

having little influence or importance; trivial
adj. 하찮은, 무의미한, 무가치한
n. insignificance
The ideas of an *insignificant* person have no influence.

inspect
[inspékt]

view closely; examine; scan
v. 조사하다, 검사하다
n. inspection
In this state, every car must be *inspected* annually by the high way patrol.

prohibit
[prəhíbit]

forbid; stop; prevent
v. 금지하다, 금하다
n. prohibition
Smoking is *prohibited* in public buildings or in the crowded bus.

Lesson 10

repent
[ripént]

be or feel sorry for wrongdoing; regret
v. 후회하다, 회개하다
n. repentance
The criminal *repented* his crimes before the priest.

resolute
[rézəljuːt]

having an unchanging purpose; constant
adj. 굳은, 확고한, 단호한
n. resolution
Despite the opposition from his family, he remained *resolute* in his decision.

suspend
[səspénd]

1. cause to stop for a time
v. 일시 중지하다, 보류하다
n. suspension
The train schedule was *suspended* until the railroad tracks were repaired.

2. hang down by attaching to something else.
v. 매달다, 걸다
n. suspension
The swing was *suspended* from a branch of tree.

| **EXERCISE 3** | **Fill each blank with the most appropriate word given above. (Inflect the word if necessary.)** |

1. Mother's vacuum cleaner _____ her house work.

2. A tenth of a cent is a(n) _____ amount of money.

3. The question of whether war can be abolished has often been _____.

4. Government officials _____ all factories and mines to make sure that they are safe for workers.

5. Don't you _____ of having wasted your money so foolishly?

STUDY YOUR NEW WORDS-4

bleak
[bli:k]

bare, cold, and cheerless
adj. 황량한, 쓸쓸한, 차가운
In winter, when the trees are bare and snow covers the ground, the landscape is very *bleak*.

brisk
[brisk]

quick and active; lively
adj. 팔팔한, 활발한, 기운찬
A *brisk* walk brings him home from work in a short time.

chip
[tʃip]

a small, thin piece of wood
n. (나무) 쪼가리, (자잘한) 부스러기
When you sharpen a pencil, you make *chips*.

hearth
[ha:rθ]

the floor of a fireplace, usually made of brick or stone
n. 난로, 노변, 노(爐)
We talked about his death all night, sitting around the *hearth*.

laundry
[lɔ́:ndri]

a place where clothes are washed or dried; clothes that are washed
n. 세탁소, 세탁물
They sent their dirty clothes to the *laundry*.

overwhelm
[ouvərhwélm]

1. defeat or make powerless by much greater force; overcome
v. 압도하다, 제압하다
At the beginning of the Korean War, the weapons that the enemy had *overwhelmed* ours.

2. flow over or cover completely
v. (물결 따위가) 덮치다, 휩싸다
The village was *overwhelmed* when the floods came.

prevalent
[prévələnt]

existing commonly, generally, or widely
adj. 널리 퍼진, 유행하는
The habit of travelling by aircraft is becoming more *prevalent* each year.

rumor
[rú:mər]

a report or information which may or may not be true
n. 소문, 풍문
I heard a *rumor* that there would be a change in the Cabinet.

scold
[skould]

speak in an angry and complaining way; blame
v. 꾸짖다, 잔소리하다
His parents *scolded* him for staying out so late at night.

shrug
[ʃrʌg]

raise the shoulder as an expression of doubt or lack of interest
v. (어깨를) 으쓱하다 (의문·무관심을 나타낼 때)
When I asked him about his plans, he only *shrugged* his shoulders.

streak
[stríːk]

1. a line or mark different from what surrounds it.
n. 줄, 선, 줄무늬
There are *streaks* of grey appearing in his black hair.

2. move very fast
v. 쏜살같이 달리다, 질주하다
The cat *streaked* across the road with the dog behind it.

tug
[tʌg]

pull with an effort or with force
v. 잡아끌다, 잡아당기다
The small child *tugged* the table across the room and broke the milk bottle on it.

EXERCISE 4   **Fill each blank with the most appropriate word given above.**
(Inflect the word if necessary.)

1. As soon as he came into the room, he warmed himself at the _____.

2. Malaria is still _____ in some tropical countries.

3. He merely _____ his shoulders in answer to our request for help.

4. The weather in early December is _____ and unpleasant.

5. The old woman doesn't like children; she is always _____ any children in our neighborhood.

해답

EXERCISE 1.	1. dismissed	2. kin	3. awe	4. hearty	5. conceit
EXERCISE 2.	1. void	2. emerged	3. accurate	4. illusion	5. soothe
EXERCISE 3.	1. facilitates	2. insignificant	3. debated	4. inspect	5. repent
EXERCISE 4.	1. hearth	2. prevalent	3. shrugged	4. bleak	5. scolding

종합 연습 문제

1 In the space provided, write the *letter* of the word NOT RELATED in meaning to the other words in each line.

_____	1.	(A) glitter	(B) scatter	(C) glisten	(D) spark
_____	2.	(A) realm	(B) sanction	(C) region	(D) kingdom
_____	3.	(A) dread	(B) awe	(C) bliss	(D) fear
_____	4.	(A) grab	(B) snatch	(C) dig	(D) seize
_____	5.	(A) peer	(B) peek	(C) peel	(D) peep
_____	6.	(A) attain	(B) grant	(C) gain	(D) achieve
_____	7.	(A) frugal	(B) hearty	(C) cordial	(D) genial
_____	8.	(A) conceit	(B) pride	(C) vanity	(D) deceit
_____	9.	(A) kin	(B) kindle	(C) kindred	(D) kinsfolk
_____	10.	(A) commence	(B) discharge	(C) release	(D) dismiss

2 In the space before each word in COLUMN I, write the *letter* of its correct meaning in COLUMN II.

COLUMN I	COLUMN II
_____ 1. chip	(A) existing commonly, generally, or widely
_____ 2. tug	(B) bare, cold, and cheerless
_____ 3. brisk	(C) speak in anger and complaining way
_____ 4. rumor	(D) raise the shoulder as an expression of doubt
_____ 5. laundry	(E) the floor of a fireplace
_____ 6. bleak	(F) quick and active; lively
_____ 7. prevalent	(G) a place where clothes are washed and dried
_____ 8. scold	(H) a small, thin piece of wood
_____ 9. hearth	(I) pull with an effort or force
_____ 10. shrug	(J) a report which may or may not be true

3 In the space provided, write the *letter* of the word that most nearly means the OPPOSITE of the italicized word.

_____ 1. *soothe*   (A) criticize   (B) aggravate
            (C) revere   (D) illuminate

_____ 2. *emerge* (A) decrease (B) ascend
                        (C) disappear (D) draw

_____ 3. *accurate* (A) friendly (B) cool
                         (C) incorrect (D) impolite

_____ 4. *injustice* (A) reproof   (B) fairness
                          (C) reputation (D) necessity

_____ 5. *dwarf* (A) giant (B) valor
                       (C) pigmy (D) miser

_____ 6. *vicious* (A) practical (B) public
                        (C) virtuous (D) agreeable

_____ 7. *multitude* (A) minority (B) magnitude
                          (C) detail   (D) apathy

_____ 8. *ancestor* (A) dependant (B) relative
                         (C) forebear (D) descendant

_____ 9. *void* (A) valid   (B) continual
                      (C) preliminary (D) affirmative

_____ 10. *illusion* (A) allusion (B) reality
                          (C) objection (D) vividness

4 Complete the following table with the appropriate word forms.

	ADJECTIVE	NOUN	VERB	ADVERB
1.	_____	_____	debate	XXXXX
2.	XXXXX	_____	inspect	XXXXX
3.	_____	facility	_____	_____
4.	_____	_____	attain	XXXXX
5.	frail	_____	XXXXX	_____
6.	_____	_____	repent	_____
7.	_____	_____	extract	XXXXX
8.	_____	prohibition	_____	_____
9.	resolute	_____	_____	_____
10.	suspensive	_____	_____	_____

5 In the space provided, write the *letter* of the word or expression that has most nearly the SAME MEANING as the italicized word.

_____ 1. She bought the red hat and has *repented* her choice.
  (A) regretted (B) changed (C) returned (D) determined

_____ 2. The fireman's *brisk* action could bring the fire under control.
  (A) brave (B) constant (C) quick (D) proper

_____ 3. Let us *suspend* judgment until we know all the facts.
  (A) be through (B) put off (C) announce (D) conclude

_____ 4. The monkey was sitting on a *frail* branch of the tree.
  (A) small (B) long (C) weak (D) dead

_____ 5. The climbers reached a *bleak* mountain top covered with snow.
  (A) desolate (B) high (C) steep (D) white

_____ 6. Our neighbors are always making a noise, *scolding* their children.
  (A) calling (B) gathering (C) hitting (D) blaming

_____ 7. He was *resolute* in his attempt to climb up the top of the mountain.
  (A) disgusted (B) determined (C) tired (D) disappointed

_____ 8. After the election the government *commenced* to develop the new highway.
  (A) agreed (B) planned (C) decided (D) started

_____ 9. He had a feeling of *awe* as he was taken in front of the Emperor.
  (A) surprise (B) dread (C) pride (D) sorrow

_____ 10. It was an *illusion* that made me think that I saw a man in the shadow.
  (A) allusion (B) dream (C) delusion (D) reflection

해답

1	1. B	2. B	3. C	4. C	5. C	6. B	7. A	8. D	9. B	10. A
2	1. H	2. I	3. F	4. J	5. G	6. B	7. A	8. C	9. E	10. D
3	1. B	2. C	3. C	4. B	5. A	6. C	7. A	8. D	9. A	10. B

4	ADJECTIVE	NOUN	VERB	ADVERB
1.	debatable	debate	(debate)	XXXXX
2.	XXXXX	inspection	(inspect)	XXXXX
3.	facile	(facility)	facilitate	facilely
4.	attainable	attainment	(attain)	XXXXX
5.	(frail)	frailty	XXXXX	frailly
6.	repentant	repentance	(repent)	repentantly
7.	extractive	extraction	(extract)	XXXXX
8.	prohibitive	(prohibition)	prohibit	prohibitively
9.	(resolute)	resolution	resolve	resolutely
10.	(suspensive)	suspension	suspend	suspensively

5 1. A   2. C   3. B   4. C   5. A   6. D   7. B   8. D   9. B   10. C

Lesson 10

Lesson 11

PRETEST 11

Insert the *letter* of the best answer in the space provided.

1. The speaker was very *gratified* by the _____ audience.
   (A) large (B) small

2. He is always *punctual* in keeping appointments, and we _____ him.
   (A) like (B) dislike

3. The _____ is a *tropical* animal.
   (A) penguin (B) lion

4. The hunter was *trampled* to death by _____.
   (A) the forest fire (B) a wild elephant

5. She was *expelled* from school because of her _____.
   (A) excellent grades (B) recent scandal

ANSWERS 1.A 2.A 3.B 4.B 5.B

STUDY YOUR NEW WORDS-1

blunder
[blʌ́ndər]

a stupid or careless mistake
n. 실수, 실책
syn. mistake
It was his great **blunder** to have ordered the soldiers to attack the enemy in the daytime.

brink
[briŋk]

the edge at the top of a steep place
n. 가장자리, 끝, 가
syn. verge
He fell over the **brink** of the cliff, but was slightly hurt.

cab
[kæb]

an automobile that can be hired with driver; taxicab
n. 택시, 승합 마차

	syn. taxi
	It is very hard to catch a *cab* in the rush hour.
cast [kæst]	throw away, out, or down; hurl *v.* 던지다, 내던지다 syn. fling The fishermen *cast* their nets into the sea.
component [kəmpóunənt]	one of the parts that make up a whole *n.* 성분, 구성 요소 syn. ingredient A chemist can separate a medicine into its *components*.
convention [kənvénʃən]	1. a custom or rule approved by general agreement *n.* 인습, 풍습 syn. custom It is a matter of *convention* that men should open doors for ladies. 2. a large meeting for a particular purpose *n.* 집회, 회의 Businessmen attend *conventions* to learn of new developments and products.
expel [ikspél]	drive or force out; put a person out; dismiss permanently *v.* 내쫓다, 추방하다, 제명하다 syn. banish A pupil who cheats or steals may be *expelled* from school.
notable [nóutəbl]	worthy of notice or attention; important; outstanding *adj.* 주목할 만한, 괄목할 만한 syn. remarkable Korea has made a *notable* progress in industry since 1960.
spectacle [spéktəkl]	1. a grand public show or scene; a thing to look at *n.* 장관, 구경거리, 볼만한 광경 syn. sight The sunrise as seen from the top of the mountain was a great *spectacle*. 2. (*pl.*) eyeglasses *n.* 안경 The old man bought a new pair of *spectacles*.
tackle [tǽkl]	1. equipment used for a particular sport or activity *n.* 도구, 기구, 연장

syn. equipment

He bought some fishing *tackles* in the store.

2. seize and attack

v. 달라붙다, 붙들다, 태클하다

The robber tried to run away, but a brave man ran and *tackled* him.

throng
[θrɔːŋ]

a large gathering of people

n. 군중, 사람 떼

syn. crowd

At the railroad station I saw *throngs* of passengers waiting for their trains.

waver
[wéivər]

move one way and then the other; be unsteady; hesitate

v. 흔들리다, 동요하다, 머뭇거리다

syn. sway

As I opened the window, the flame *wavered* and then went out.

EXERCISE 1   **Fill each blank with the most appropriate word given above.**
(Inflect the word if necessary.)

1. He _____ a stone into the pond, and it formed many small waves.
2. His failure to lock the door was a serious _____.
3. It is a(n) _____ in many countries for people to shake hands when they meet.
4. Just before Christmas there are _____ of people in the streets.
5. We'd better take a(n) _____ to the airport; we have only thirty minutes left.

STUDY YOUR NEW WORDS-2

affirmative
[əfə́ːrmətiv]

saying that some statement is a fact; answering "yes"

adj. 긍정의, 긍정적인, 승낙의

ant. negative

Her final answer to my question would be *affirmative*.

amid
[əmíd]

surrounded by; in the middle of; among

adv. ~의 한가운데, ~의 사이에

ant. around

The woman teacher stood *amid* the crowd of the little children.

appease
[əpíːz]

make quiet; calm; pacify
v. 가라앉히다, 진정시키다, 달래다
ant. stir
The angry man was not *appeased* until I said I was sorry.

eternal
[i(ː)tə́ːrnəl]

going on forever; permanent; perpetual; everlasting
adj. 영원한, 영구의, 불멸의
ant. momentary
Most religions in the world promise *eternal* life after one's death.

gallant
[gǽlənt]

1. brave; high-spirited; heroic
adj. 용감한, 씩씩한
ant. timid
Mr. Johnson was one of the most *gallant* soldiers in our unit during World War Ⅱ.

2. splendid; beautiful; fine
adj. 화려한, 호사스러운
Our garden was made *gallant* with roses and tulips.

gratify
[grǽtifai]

give pleasure to; satisfy; indulge
v. 만족시키다, 기쁘게하다
ant. disappoint
Now that she has a job in France, she can *gratify* her desire to see Paris.

petty
[péti]

small; of little worth; unimportant; trifling; trivial
adj. 대단찮은, 하찮은, 사소한
ant. significant
The children's quarrels usually concern a *petty* problem.

sturdy
[stə́ːrdi]

strong and firm; stout
adj. 튼튼한, 건장한, 굳건한
ant. weak
Children need *sturdy* clothes, because they like to play so violently.

tropical
[trɑ́pikəl]

related to the tropics; living in the tropics; very hot
adj. 열대의, 열대적인, 무더운
ant. polar
It is very hard to work in such *tropical* weather.

zoology
[zouɑ́lədʒi]

the science of animals
n. 동물학
ant. botany
Zoology and botany are the two main branches of biology.

EXERCISE 2 Fill each blank with the most appropriate word given above. (Inflect the word if necessary.)

1. The nurse tried to _____ the crying child by giving him candy.
2. Put these books in a(n) _____ box so that I can easily carry them.
3. We were all _____ to learn that you had passed the examination.
4. Bananas are _____ fruit; apples are not.
5. A ship with all its sails spread is a(n) _____ sight.

STUDY YOUR NEW WORDS-3

administer
[ədmínistər]

manage; control; look after
v. 관리하다, 통치하다, 돌보다
n. administration
In the United States, the Secretary of State *administers* foreign affairs.

coordinate
[kouɔ́ːrdinit]

work together for greater effectiveness; adjust; harmonize
v. 통합하다, 종합하다, 조정하다
n. coordination
If we *coordinate* our efforts we should be able to defeat the enemy.

deprive
[dipráiv]

take away from; prevent from using
v. 빼앗다, 박탈하다
n. deprivation
They *deprived* the criminal of his right to vote.

heritage
[héritidʒ]

what is handed on to a person from his ancestors; inheritance
n. 유산, 상속 재산, 전통
adj. heritable
Many foreigners say that Koreans have a great cultural *heritage*.

insert
[insə́ːrt]

put in; set in; put something inside
v. 끼워 넣다, 삽입하다
n. insertion
He *inserted* the key into the lock, but found it was a wrong key.

irritate
[íriteit]

make angry or impatient; annoy; provoke; vex
v. 화나게 하다, 자극하다
n. irritation
When she has a headache, the slightest noise *irritates* her.

legitimate
[lidʒítimit]

allowed or admitted by law; lawful; rightful
adj. 합법적인, 적법의, 정당한
n. legitimacy
The boy couldn't give a *legitimate* reason for being absent from school.

margin
[má:rdʒin]

1. blank space around the writing or printing on a page
n. 여백, 난외(欄外)
adj. marginal
He made some important notes in the *margin* of the book.

2. an amount allowed beyond what is necessary
n. 여유, 여지
adj. marginal
Allow a *margin* of money for unexpected expenses.

punctual
[pʌ́ŋktʃuəl]

on time; doing something at the exact time; prompt
adj. 시간을 엄수하는, 시간에 정확한
n. punctuality
She's never *punctual* in answering letters; she's always late.

restrain
[ristréin]

hold back; keep down; keep under control
v. 억누르다, 억제하다, 금하다
n. restraint
She could not *restrain* her curiosity to see what was in the box.

sensitive
[sénsitiv]

easily or quickly affected by the senses; quick to notice
adj. 민감한, 감도가 좋은
n. sensitivity
The girl is very *sensitive* about her ugly appearance.

significant
[signífikənt]

having a special or suggestive meaning; important
adj. 의미심장한, 의의 있는
n. significance
August 15, 1945, was a *significant* day for Koreans.

Lesson 11

> **EXERCISE 3** Fill each blank with the most appropriate word given above.
> (Inflect the word if necessary.)
>
> 1. A(n) _____ skin is easily hurt by too much sunshine.
> 2. A swimmer should _____ the movements of his arms and legs.
> 3. The people _____ the cruel king of his power, and drove him out of the country.
> 4. His wife has a(n) _____ claim to her husband's property, for they have no children.
> 5. Leave a(n) _____ of one inch on the left side of your paper.

STUDY YOUR NEW WORDS-4

altar
[ɔ́:ltər]

a raised place on which offerings are made to God
n. 제단(祭壇), 제대(祭臺)
The *altar* is the most sacred part of a church or temple.

bounce
[bauns]

the action of bouncing; springing back
n. 되튐, 튀어오름, 반발력
I caught the ball on the first *bounce*.

bugle
[bjú:gl]

a brass musical instrument like a small trumpet
n. 나팔
Bugles have been used in military forces for sounding calls and orders.

charcoal
[tʃá:rkoul]

the black substance made by burning wood
n. 숯, 목탄
We cooked our food over burning *charcoal*.

crisis
[kráisis]

the turning point in illness, life, or history; time of difficulty
n. 고비, 위기, 갈림길
The patient passed the *crisis*, and began to regain his strength.

deputy
[dépjuti]

a person who has the power to act for another
n. 대리인, 대리관, 부관
John will be my *deputy* while I am away.

grind
[graind]

crush into small pieces or powder
v. 갈다, 가루로 만들다, 분쇄하다
The mill *grinds* corn into meal and wheat into flour.

missionary
[míʃənəri]

a person sent on a religious mission
n. 선교사, 전도사
The *missionary* will be sent to Africa to teach and spread Christianity there.

premier
[prémjər]

a prime minister; the chief official of a government
n. 수상, 국무총리
Winston Churchill is one of the well-known *premiers* of Great Britain.

recruit
[rikrúːt]

a new member, especially of the armed forces
n. 신병, 신입 회원, 신참자
The *recruits* were already given their uniforms, and now they are being drilled on the parade ground.

salvation
[sælvéiʃən]

the act of saving from danger, difficulty, or evil
n. 구원, 구제, 구조
He proposed government loans for the *salvation* of several shaky business companies.

standstill
[stǽndstil]

a complete stop; halt; pause
n. 정지, 멈춤
When I was walking along the street, a car came to a *standstill* near me.

trample
[trǽmpl]

step heavily with the feet; crush; tramp
v. 짓밟다, 유린하다
The herd of wild cattle *trampled* the farmer's crops.

yoke
[jouk]

a wooden frame to fasten two animals together; bond
n. 멍에, 굴레, 속박
Slaves are under the *yoke* of their masters.

EXERCISE 4 **Fill each blank with the most appropriate word given above.**
(Inflect the word if necessary.)

1. The ball has a plenty of _____, and goes up very high after it hits the ground.
2. I must find someone to act as a(n) _____ for me during my absence.
3. New _____ to our music club are always welcome.
4. They _____ the eggshells to powder and give it to the hens with their food.
5. The Battle of Waterloo was a(n) _____ in Napoleon's career.

EXERCISE 1.	1. cast	2. blunder	3. convention	4. throngs	5. cab
EXERCISE 2.	1. appease	2. sturdy	3. gratified	4. tropical	5. gallant
EXERCISE 3.	1. sensitive	3. coordinate	3. deprived	4. legitimate	5. margin
EXERCISE 4.	1. bounce	2. deputy	3. recruits	4. grind	5. crisis

종합 연습 문제

1 In the space left, write the *letter* of the word that has most nearly the SAME MEANING as the italicized word.

_____ 1. *notable* events in 1979   (A) several   (B) unknown
                                                   (C) funny   (D) important

_____ 2. running on his *sturdy* legs   (A) weak   (B) strong
                                                   (C) short   (D) long

_____ 3. *eternal* life   (A) happy   (B) short
                                  (C) unhappy   (D) everlasting

_____ 4. the *recruits* of the club   (A) activities   (B) funds
                                           (C) new members   (D) main goals

_____ 5. a *significant* smile   (A) childish   (B) meaningful
                                     (C) happy   (D) false

2 In the space provided, write the *letter* of the word that most nearly means the OPPOSITE of the italicized word.

_____ 1. *gallant*   (A) stupid   (B) exact
                          (C) timid   (D) difficult

_____ 2. *affirmative*   (A) negative   (B) unsteady
                               (C) sensitive   (D) important

_____ 3. *zoology*   (A) biology   (B) botany
                         (C) ecology   (D) physics

_____ 4. *tropical*   (A) effective   (B) special
                        (C) polar   (D) patient

_____ 5. *eternal*   (A) momentary   (B) splendid
                       (C) notable   (D) complete

3 Supply the correct from of the word in italics for the blank space in each sentence.

1. *insert*   The _____ of one word can change the meaning of a whole sentence.

2. *punctual*   The old professor is famous for _____ for his lecture.

3. *restrain*   He was very angry but he spoke with _____ .

4. *administer*   The _____ of a big business requires skill in dealing with people.

5. *significant*   She didn't understand the _____ of my words.

Lesson 11

4 Fill in the missing letters of the word at the right. Each dash stands for one missing letter.

DEFINITION	WORD
1. drive or force but	EX_ _ _
2. step heavily with the feet	TR_ _ _ LE
3. in the middle of	A_ _ D
4. a new member of the armed forces	RE_ _ _ _ T
5. work together for great effectiveness	CO_ _ _ _ _ ATE
6. a brass musical instrument like a trumpet	B_ _ _ E
7. one of the parts that make up a whole	COM_ _ _ ENT
8. manage; control; look after	AD_ _ _ _ _ TER
9. a prime minister	P_ _ _ _ ER
10. a complete stop; halt	STAND_ _ _ _ _

5 In the space provided, write the *letter* of the NOT RELATED in meaning to the other words in each line.

_____	1.	(A) adjust	(B) appease	(C) calm	(D) pacify
_____	2.	(A) edge	(B) throng	(C) brink	(D) verge
_____	3.	(A) prompt	(B) sturdy	(C) firm	(D) stout
_____	4.	(A) notable	(B) remarkable	(C) outstanding	(D) vague
_____	5.	(A) pause	(B) standstill	(C) bounce	(D) halt
_____	6.	(A) cast	(B) seize	(C) fling	(D) hurl
_____	7.	(A) gratify	(B) satisfy	(C) indulge	(D) deprive
_____	8.	(A) illegal	(B) legitimate	(C) rightful	(D) lawful
_____	9.	(A) irritate	(B) provoke	(C) hesitate	(D) vex
_____	10.	(A) petty	(B) trivial	(C) punctual	(D) insignificant

6 Fill each blank with the most appropriate word from the vocabulary list below.

VOCABULARY LIST

sturdy	convention	heritage
spectacle	yoke	altar
punctual	charcoal	expelled
cab	wavered	legitimate

1. Does _____ allow women to smoke in public in your country?

2. The sunrise as seen from the top of the mountain was a great _____.

3. The _____ is the most sacred part of a church or temple.

4. The traffic accident that delayed our bus gave us a(n) _____ reason for being late.

5. As I opened the window, the flame _____ and then went out.

6. Shall we go by bus or take a(n) _____?

7. Many foreigners say that Koreans have a great cultural _____.

8. We cooked our food over burning _____.

9. The teacher is very _____ for his lecture; he always enters the classroom on time.

10. Slaves are under the _____ of their masters.

해답

1 1. D   2. B   3. D   4. C   5. B
2 1. C   2. A   3. B   4. C   5. A
3 1. insertion   2. punctuality   3. restraint   4. administration 5. significance
4 1. expel   2. trample   3. amid   4. recruit   5. coordinate
     6. bugle   7. component   8. administer 9. premier   10. standstill
5 1. A   2. B   3. A   4. D   5. C   6. B   7. D   8. A   9. C   10. C
6 1. convention   2. spectacle   3. altar   4. legitimate   5. wavered
     6. cab   7. heritage   8. charcoal   9. punctual   10. yoke

Lesson 11   135

Lesson 12

PRETEST 12

Insert the *letter* of the best answer in the space provided.

1. If you wish to be a member, you must *conform* to the _____ of our club.
   (A) rules (B) fund

2. The little boy had no *appetite*; so his mother had to persuade him to _____.
   (A) eat (B) study

3. We decided to *defer* our departure _____.
   (A) without delay (B) until tomorrow

4. In olden times, the conquered country was *plundered* by _____.
   (A) the invading soldiers (B) its citizens

5. Try to *pacify* the baby; he has been _____ for hours.
   (A) sleeping (B) crying

ANSWERS 1.A 2.A 3.B 4.A 5.B

STUDY YOUR NEW WORDS-1

adorn
[ədɔ́ːrn]

add beauty or ornament to; beautify
v. 꾸미다, 장식하다, 치장하다
syn. decorate
He *adorned* his story with all sorts of adventures that never happened.

baggage
[bǽgidʒ]

suitcase, boxes, etc. used in travel
n. 수하물, 짐
syn. luggage
I need a man to carry my *baggage* to the train.

bunch
[bʌntʃ]

a group of things of the same kind fastened or placed together
n. 다발, 송이

	syn. cluster
	We sent him a *bunch* of flowers on his birthday.
clap [klæp]	strike together sharply, esp. the hands *v.* 손뼉을 치다, 박수치다 syn. applaud The children *clapped* when he finished his speech on Children's Day.
deliberate [dilíbərit]	1. slow and careful in movement, action, speech, etc. *adj.* 신중한, 생각이 깊은 syn. considerate A statesman should be *deliberate* in his political speeches.
[dilíbəreit]	2. consider carefully; think about thoroughly *v.* 숙고하다, 심의하다 syn. reflect We were *deliberating* whether we should buy a new motorcar.
enclose [inklóuz]	1. put a wall or fence around; encircle; encompass *v.* 울을 치다, 둘러싸다, 에워싸다 We are going to *enclose* our back yard to keep dogs out. 2. put something inside *v.* 동봉하다, 봉해 넣다 syn. surround I *enclosed* a check for $10 with the letter.
frontier [frʌ́ntíər]	the limit or edge of the land of one country *n.* 국경, 변경 syn. border There were many guards and soldiers along the *frontier*.
implement [ímplimənt]	an instrument used in performing work *n.* 도구, 기구, 용구 syn. tool Plows and threshing machines are farm *implements*.
leap [li:p]	a jump or spring; bound *n.* 깡충 뜀, 도약(跳躍) syn. jump He went over the fence with a single *leap*.

luster
[lʌ́stər]

a bright shine on the surface
n. 광택, 윤
syn. brilliance
This shampoo adds more *luster* to your hair than any other brand.

perfume
[pə́rfju:m]

a sweet or pleasant smell; scent
n. 향기, 방향(芳香)
syn. fragrance
We enjoyed the *perfume* of the flowers in the garden.

swear
[swɛə́r]

promise formally or by an oath
v. 맹세하다, 선서하다
syn. pledge
Will you *swear* to the truth of your statement?

EXERCISE 1   Fill each blank with the most appropriate word given above.
(Inflect the word if necessary.)

1. A(n) _____ person takes enough time to make up his mind.
2. He polished the metal until it had a fine _____.
3. When the violinist finished playing, the audience _____ for two minutes.
4. An axe is a useful _____ to cut trees.
5. The witness _____ the oath in the court with the right hand on the Bible before giving evidence.

STUDY YOUR NEW WORDS-2

acquire
[əkwáiər]

get by one's own efforts or action; gain; attain
v. 손에 넣다, 획득하다, 습득하다
ant. lose
You must work hard to *acquire* a good command of a foreign language.

benevolent
[binévələnt]

kindly; charitable; intended to do good
adj. 자비심 많은, 인정 많은, 자선의
ant. malevolent
The free food was given to a beggar by a *benevolent* person.

compliment
[kɔ́mplimənt]

an expression of praise or admiration
n. 칭찬, 치하, 경의

ant. reprimand
The famous actress was used to hearing audience's *compliments*.

courtesy
[kə́ːrtisi]

polite behavior; good manners
n. 예의, 공손, 정중
ant. impoliteness
Giving one's seat to a lady in a crowded bus is a sign of *courtesy*.

equivalent
[ikwívələnt]

equal or same in quality, value, or meaning
adj. 동등한, 같은
ant. different
He changed his pounds for the *equivalent* amount of dollars.

ingenious
[indʒíːnjəs]

clever and skillful
adj. 재간있는, 영리한
ant. clumsy
My brother is so *ingenious* that he will think of a way to do the work more easily.

internal
[intə́ːrnəl]

of or for the interior; inner
adj. 내부의, 내면의
ant. external
An accident often causes *internal* injuries as well as cuts and wounds.

irresponsible
[irispɔ́nsəbl]

unreliable; not responsible
adj. 무책임한, 책임이 없는
ant. reliable
An *irresponsible* person deserves to be blamed and punished.

miserable
[mízərəbl]

very unhappy; causing unhappiness
adj. 불쌍한, 비참한, 가련한
ant. happy
The child is cold, hungry, and tired, so of course he is *miserable*.

respond
[rispɔ́nd]

answer; make reply
v. 응답하다, 반응하다
ant. ask
When John insulted Tom, he *responded* with a kick.

tentative
[téntətiv]

made or done only as a suggestion; not certain; experimental
adj. 시험적인, 시험 삼아하는, 잠정적인
ant. decisive
We've made *tentative* plans for a holiday but haven't decided anything certain yet.

EXERCISE 2 Fill each blank with the most appropriate word given above.
(Inflect the word if necessary.)

1. Giving money to help the Red Cross is a(n) _____ act.
2. This program for my birthday party is just a(n) _____ one; it may be changed sooner or later.
3. Nodding your head is _____ to saying yes.
4. It is against _____ to smoke in the crowded bus or in the theater.
5. With the money he had won, he was able to _____ some property.

STUDY YOUR NEW WORDS-3

appetite
[ǽpitait]

a desire to eat or drink
n. 식욕, 욕구
n. appetizer
The little boy had no *appetite*; so his mother had to persuade him to eat.

assume
[əsjúːm]

1. take as a fact or as true without proof; suppose
v. 가정하다, 억측하다
n. assumption
They *assumed* that the war would end in six months, but it proved wrong in a short time.

2. take upon oneself; undertake
v. (임무·책임을) 떠맡다
n. assumption
He *assumed* the responsibility for planning and preparing the picnic.

conform
[kənfɔ́ːrm]

be in agreement with what is required
v. 따르(게 하)다, 순응(하게) 하다
n. conformation
A citizen is expected to *conform* to the law of his country.

defer
[difə́r]

1. put off to a later time; postpone
v. 늦추다, 연기하다
n. deferment
The ship *deferred* its sailing because of bad weather.

	2. give way; yield; submit *v.* 승복하다, 복종하다 n. deference Do you always *defer* to your parents' wishes?
distract [distrǽkt]	draw away (the mind or attention) *v.* (마음, 주의를) 전환하다, 흩뜨리다 n. distraction What can we do to *distract* her mind from sorrow?
mutual [mjú:tʃuəl]	common to two or more persons; reciprocal *adj.* 서로의, 상호간의 n. mutuality A family has a *mutual* affection when each person likes the others and is liked by them.
pacify [pǽsifai]	make calm, quiet, and satisfied; appease *v.* 달래다, 가라앉히다, 진정시키다 adj. pacific She *pacified* the crying child by giving him milk.
prominent [prɔ́minənt]	1. easily seen; conspicuous *adj.* 눈에 잘 띄는, 뚜렷이 보이는 She hung the picture in a *prominent* position in the living room. 2. well-known or important; distinguished *adj.* 저명한, 탁월한 n. prominence Several *prominent* people were present at the meeting.
receipt [risí:t]	1. a written statement that one has received money *n.* 영수증, 인수증 Ask the shop for a *receipt* when you pay the bill. 2. the act of receiving *n.* 수령(受領), 수취(受取) v. receive Please notify me upon *receipt* of the package.
variable [vɛ́əriəbl]	changeable; not staying the same; unsteady *adj.* 가변성의, 일정치 않은, 변하는 v. vary The amount of heat produced by this electrical apparatus is *variable* by turning a small handle.

EXERCISE 3   **Fill each blank with the most appropriate word given above.**
(Inflect the word if necessary.)

1. He _____ that the train would be on time; but it left the platform twenty minutes later.

2. His military service was _____ until he finished college.

3. The noise of the radio _____ me from my reading.

4. His long walk for three hours gave him a good _____.

5. Most people willingly _____ to the customs of society.

STUDY YOUR NEW WORDS-4

associate
[əsóuʃieit]

1. make a companion of; keep company with
v. 교제하다, 사귀다
Don't *associate* with bad and dishonest boys.

[əsóuʃiit]

2. a partner; a friend; a companion
n. 동료, 한패
He has been my *associate* in several business enterprises.

chauffeur
[ʃóufər]

a person whose work is driving an automobile
n. 운전수
They rented a car with a *chauffeur* for the winter trip.

dump
[dʌmp]

throw down; unload; empty out
v. (쓰레기를) 내버리다, (짐을) 내쏟다
Don't *dump* that trash in the middle of the path.

dye
[dai]

give a color to something
v. 물들이다, 염색하다
Many women like to *dye* their hair blonde.

feat
[fiːt]

a great deed; act showing great courage, skill, or strength
n. 위업(偉業), 공적, 공훈
The first flight into space was a brilliant *feat*.

nasty
[nǽsti]

1. very dirty and unpleasant; causing disgust
adj. 불쾌한, 싫은
The medicine has a *nasty* smell and *nastier* taste.

2. showing ill-will; ill-natured
adj. 사나운, 성질이 나쁜
Be tactful when you tell him because he has a very *nasty* temper.

plunder
[plʌ́ndər]

rob or take by force
v. 약탈하다, 노략질하다
The pirates entered the harbor and began to *plunder* the town.

speck
[spek]

a small spot or stain
n. 반점, 얼룩, 오점
I found a few *specks* of dirt on the wallpaper.

strife
[straif]

quarrelling; struggle; conflict
n. 투쟁, 싸움, 다툼
There has always been *strife* between the two countries.

strip
[strip]

take off the covering of
v. (껍질을) 벗기다, 까다
The monkey *stripped* the banana by taking off the skin.

tutor
[tjúːtər]

a private teacher
n. 가정 교사
Her father employed a *tutor* for her during her long illness.

twinkle
[twiŋkl]

shine with quick little gleams; sparkle
v. 반짝반짝 빛나다, 반짝이다
His eyes *twinkled* with delight when he heard the news that he had passed the entrance examination.

EXERCISE 4 Fill each blank with the most appropriate word given above.
(Inflect the word if necessary.)

1. He rapidly _____ his clothes and jumped into the pool.
2. Some children had a _____ instead of going to school.
3. The truck backed up to the hole and _____ the dirt in it.
4. A great many stars _____ like diamonds in the night sky.
5. Most high school students want to _____ with foreign students to learn their languages.

EXERCISE 1.	1. deliberate	2. luster	3. clapped	4. implement	5. swore
EXERCISE 2.	1. benevolent	2. tentative	3. equivalent	4. courtesy	5. acquire
EXERCISE 3.	1. assumed	2. deferred	3. distracted	4. appetite	5. conform
EXERCISE 4.	1. stripped	2. tutor	3. dumped	4. twinkled	5. associate

종합 연습 문제

1 In the space provided, write the *letter* of the word NOT RELATED in meaning to the other words in each line.

_____ 1.   (A) deliberate   (B) inflate   (C) reflect   (D) consider

_____ 2.   (A) bound   (B) descend   (C) jump   (D) leap

_____ 3.   (A) clap   (B) applaud   (C) grasp   (D) praise

_____ 4.   (A) vow   (B) swear   (C) pledge   (D) provoke

_____ 5.   (A) tool   (B) panel   (C) instrument   (D) implement

_____ 6.   (A) craft   (B) cluster   (C) bundle   (D) bunch

_____ 7.   (A) decorate   (B) adore   (C) beautify   (D) adorn

_____ 8.   (A) scent   (B) perfume   (C) fragrance   (D) speck

_____ 9.   (A) laundry   (B) frontier   (C) border   (D) boundary

_____ 10.   (A) encircle   (B) surround   (C) enclose   (D) fasten

2 In the space before each word in COLUMN I, write the *letter* of its correct meaning in COLUMN II.

	COLUMN I	COLUMN II
_____	1. feat	(A) give a color to something
_____	2. strife	(B) a private teacher
_____	3. plunder	(C) very dirty and unpleasant
_____	4. associate	(D) a small spot or stain
_____	5. dye	(E) throw down; unload; empty out
_____	6. strip	(F) quarrelling; struggle; conflict
_____	7. nasty	(G) act showing great courage, skill, or strength
_____	8. dump	(H) make a companion of; keep company with
_____	9. tutor	(I) take off the covering of
_____	10. speck	(J) rob or take by force

3 In the space provided, write the *letter* of the word that most nearly means the OPPOSITE of the italicized word.

_____ 1. respond   (A) require   (B) peel
                               (C) influence   (D) ask

Lesson 12

_____ 2. ingenious   (A) false   (B) clumsy
                                                  (C) ugly   (D) genius

_____ 3. tentative   (A) harsh   (B) reluctant
                                                  (C) decisive   (D) fragile

_____ 4. acquire   (A) answer   (B) lose
                                                  (C) praise   (D) restore

_____ 5. compliment   (A) citation   (B) interruption
                                                  (C) reprimand   (D) appendix

_____ 6. miserable   (A) certain   (B) enough
                                                  (C) trustful   (D) happy

_____ 7. benevolent   (A) futile   (B) prevalent
                                                  (C) eminent   (D) malevolent

_____ 8. equivalent   (A) different   (B) definite
                                                  (C) dual   (D) dubious

_____ 9. internal   (A) contrast   (B) lofty
                                                  (C) narrow   (D) external

_____10. irresponsible   (A) reliable   (B) relevant
                                                  (C) responsive   (D) relative

4 Complete the following table with the appropriate word forms.

	ADJECTIVE	NOUN	VERB	ADVERB
1.	_____	deference	_____	_____
2.	mutual	_____	XXXXX	_____
3.	_____	prominence	XXXXX	_____
4.	_____	_____	assume	_____
5.	_____	variety	_____	_____
6.	_____	_____	_____	distractedly
7.	XXXXX	_____	receive	XXXXX
8.	_____	_____	conform	_____
9.	XXXXX	_____	associate	XXXXX
10.	pacific	_____	_____	_____

5 In the space provided, write the *letter* of the word or expression that has most nearly the SAME MEANING as the italicized word.

_____ 1. That young man is always ready to pay *compliments* to a pretty young lady.
  (A) attention   (B) politeness   (C) tributes   (D) greetings

_____ 2. Examinations were *deferred* because so many students were sick.
  (A) canceled   (B) objected   (C) impossible   (D) postponed

_____ 3. The statesman was very *deliberate* in his political speeches.
  (A) considerate   (B) polite   (C) careless   (D) rough

_____ 4. Cut a piece of lead or zinc, and observe the *luster* of its fresh surface.
  (A) fragment   (B) particle   (C) brilliance   (D) width

_____ 5. There has always been *strife* between the two countries for a long time.
  (A) relationship   (B) conflict   (C) gap   (D) intimacy

_____ 6. The weather bureau has announced *variable* winds for tomorrow.
  (A) mild   (B) strong   (C) frequent   (D) unsteady

_____ 7. Do you think a wife should *conform* her habits and tastes to those of her husband?
  (A) compare   (B) adjust   (C) prefer   (D) devote

_____ 8. He *adorned* his story with all sorts of adventures that never happened.
  (A) narrated   (B) added   (C) beautified   (D) created

_____ 9. This medicine has a *nasty* smell.
  (A) strong   (B) natural   (C) unpleasant   (D) sweet

_____ 10. Our house is the most *prominent* one in street; it's painted red.
  (A) beautiful   (B) expensive   (C) noticeable   (D) vivid

해답

1 1. B   2. B   3. C   4. D   5. B   6. A   7. B   8. D   9. A   10. D
2 1. G   2. F   3. J   4. H   5. A   6. I   7. C   8. E   9. B   10. D
3 1. D   2. B   3. C   4. B   5. C   6. D   7. D   8. A   9. D   10. A

4

ADJECTIVE	NOUN	VERB	ADVERB
1. deferential	(deference)	defer	deferentially
2. (mutual)	mutuality	XXXXX	mutually
3. prominent	(prominence)	XXXXX	prominently
4. assumptive	assumption	(assume)	assumably
5. variable, various	(variety)	vary	variably, variously
6. distracted	distraction	distract	(distractedly)
7. XXXXX	receipt	(receive)	XXXXX
8. conformable	conformation	(conform)	conformably
9. XXXXX	association	(associate)	XXXXX
10. (pacific)	pacification	pacify	pacifically

5 1. C   2. D   3. A   4. C   5. B   6. D   7. B   8. C   9. C   10. C

Lesson 13

PRETEST 13

Insert the *letter* of the best answer in the space provided.

1. Jane is a *cripple*; she _____.
   (A) can run very fast
   (B) walks on a wooden leg.

2. A *traitor* is _____ to his country.
   (A) loyal
   (B) disloyal

3. It is so *flexible* that we _____ easily bend it.
   (A) can
   (B) cannot

4. Mr. Kim is *sane*; he is _____ in mind.
   (A) healthy
   (B) unhealthy

5. The couple had severely quarrelled _____ were soon *reconciled*.
   (A) and
   (B) but

ANSWERS 1.B 2.B 3.A 4.A 5.B

STUDY YOUR NEW WORDS-1

cite
[sait]

give or mention as an example
v. 인용하다, 인증하다
syn. quote
He *cited* a paragraph from the book to prove his statement.

esteem
[istí:m]

high regard; very favorable opinion
n. 존경, 존중
syn. respect
All his friends held him in high *esteem*, for he was very sincere and diligent.

grumble
[grʌ́mbl]

complain in a low unpleasant voice; show dissatisfaction
v. 투덜대다, 푸념하다

syn. mutter
He was always *grumbling* about his low salary.

hideous
[hídiəs]

very ugly; filling the mind with horror; frightful
adj. 섬뜩한, 끔찍한, 소름끼치는
syn. horrible
The old woman had such a *hideous* face that the girls couldn't even get close to her.

loiter
[lɔ́itər]

move slowly with frequent stops
v. 어슬렁거리다, 빈들거리다
syn. linger
She *loitered* along the street, looking into all the show windows.

rip
[rip]

cut something roughly; tear off; pull apart by force
v. 홱 찢다, 잡아찢다, 뜯어내다
syn. tear
She *ripped* her stocking on a sharp nail.

specs
[speks]

(informal) spectacles
n. (口語) 안경
syn. eyeglasses
She has very poor eyesight; she can read nothing without her *specs*.

threshold
[θréʃhould]

the entering or beginning point of something; entrance
n. 입구, 문간, 문지방
syn. doorway
Scientists are now on the *threshold* of a better understanding of how the human brain works.

token
[tóukən]

a mark or sign; something that represents some fact of feeling
n. 표시, 징표
syn. symbol
All the family wore black as a *token* of their grief.

traitor
[tréitər]

a person who betrays his country or ruler
n. 반역자, 배반자
syn. betrayer
The *traitor* sold our important military secrets to the enemy.

uphold
[ʌphóuld]

support or approve; give aid; agree with
v. 지지하다, 떠받치다, 격려하다

Lesson 13

	syn. support The judge *upheld* the decision of the lower court.
yawn [jɔːn]	open the mouth wide when one is tired or sleepy *v.* 하품하다 syn. gape He *yawned* several times during the lecture; he was not interested in it.

> **EXERCISE 1**   **Fill each blank with the most appropriate word given above.**
> **(Inflect the word if necessary.)**
>
> 1. It is useless to _____ the Bible to someone who doesn't believe in God.
> 2. My husband gave me a ring as a(n) _____ of our first meeting.
> 3. The _____ who had helped the enemy during the war was killed by the people.
> 4. The new government will be _____ by the majority of its people.
> 5. She is very obedient to her boss, but often _____ about him when he is out.

STUDY YOUR NEW WORDS-2

advocate [ǽdvəkeit]	1. speak or write in favor of *v.* 옹호하다, 주창하다 ant. object The professor *advocates* building more schools than roads. 2. a person who speaks or writes in favor of; supporter *n.* 주창자, 변론자, 옹호자 Many scientists who supported the production of atomic bombs are *advocates* of peace.
denial [dináiəl]	a statement that something is not true; refusal of a request *n.* 부인, 거부, 거절 ant. acceptance The minister asked the newspaper to print a *denial* of the untrue story.
depart [dipáːrt]	go away; leave *v.* 출발하다, 떠나다 ant. arrive We arrived in the village in the morning, and *departed* that night.

flexible
[fléksəbl]

easily bent without breaking; easily changed to suit new conditions
adj. 잘 휘는, 유연한, 융통성 있는
ant. stiff
Leather and rubber are *flexible*; glass and iron are not.

formidable
[fɔ́ːrmidəbl]

hard to overcome; hard to deal with; frightening
adj. 만만치 않은, 대단한, 무서운
ant. feeble
The enemy's attack was more *formidable* than we had expected.

gale
[geil]

a strong and violent wind
n. 강풍, 질풍
ant. breeze
The old tree at the top of the hill was blown down in the *gale*.

sane
[sein]

having a healthy mind; sound; not mad
adj. 정신이 건전한, 제 정신의, 온건한
ant. crazy
The court judged the man *sane* and therefore responsible for his acts.

underworld
[ʌ́ndərwəːrld]

the lower world; hell
n. 하계(下界), 지하계, 지옥
ant. heaven
Those who live by vice and crime would go to the *underworld* after death.

vanity
[vǽnəti]

1. too much pride in one's appearance, possessions, etc.
n. 허영, 허식, 허영심
ant. humbleness
The girl's *vanity* made her look in the mirror often.

2. worthlessness; useless or worthless thing or act; lack of effect
n. 공허, 헛됨, 무익
Fame, power, wealth—all is *vanity* before death.

EXERCISE 2
Fill each blank with the most appropriate word given above.
(Inflect the word if necessary.)

1. Your _____ is of no use; we have proof.

2. I do not _____ building large factories in our town, for they may be a source of pollution.

3. He suffered from mental disorder last year, but is now _____ enough to do the work.

4. Her _____ caused her to spend more money on clothes than she could afford.

5. The examination paper contained several _____ questions, which I failed to solve.

STUDY YOUR NEW WORDS-3

convict
[kənvíkt]

1. prove or declare guilty after trial
v. 유죄로 하다, 유죄를 선언하다
n. conviction
The judge *convicted* the accused man of theft.

[kɔ́nvikt]

2. a person who has been found guilty and sent to prison
n. 죄수
The policeman was chasing a *convict* who escaped from prison last night.

employee
[implɔ́ií:]

a person who works for some person or firm for pay
n. 고용인, 종업원
n. employment
That large factory has more than 1,000 *employees* who make cars.

envy
[énvi]

discontent and ill will at another's better fortune
n. 시샘, 부러움, 질투
adj. envious
Some boys were full of *envy* when they saw my new bicycle.

impose
[impóuz]

lay or place a tax, burden, or duty on
v. 부과하다, 과(課)하다, 지우다
n. imposition
The judge *imposed* a fine of $500 on the guilty man.

invest
[invést]

use money to buy something that will produce a profit
v. 투자하다
n. investment
If I had any money, I would *invest* it in land.

legislate
[lédʒisleit]

make laws
v. 법률을 제정하다
adj. legislative
In the United States the Congress has the power to *legislate*.

maintain
[meintéin]

keep; preserve; continue; support
v. 유지하다, 지속하다
n. maintenance
He *maintained* a speed of 60 miles an hour on the highway.

petition
[pitíʃən]

a formal request prepared by a number of people
n. 탄원(서), 진정(서), 청원(서)
adj. petitionary
The people signed a *petition* to stop destruction of the historic buildings.

reconcile
[rékənsail]

cause to be friendly again; bring into agreement
v. 화해시키다, 분쟁을 조정하다
n. reconciliation
They quarrelled last week but now they are completely *reconciled*.

sensation
[senséiʃən]

1. any feeling coming from the senses
n. 느낌, 지각, 감각
adj. sensational
I knew the train had stopped, but I had the *sensation* that it was moving backwards.

2. a state of excited interest
n. 평판거리, 대사건
adj. sensational
The show was a great *sensation* for several weeks.

sociable
[sóuʃəbl]

fond of company; enjoying social life; friendly
adj. 사교적인, 사교를 좋아하는
n. sociability
The secretary doesn't seem *sociable*; she likes to be left in the office alone.

EXERCISE 3 Fill each blank with the most appropriate word given above.
(Inflect the word if necessary.)

1. Their beautiful garden is an object of _____ to all the neighbors.

2. It is difficult to _____ your family on $100 a week.

3. A new tax will be _____ on wine.

4. He had no _____ in his fingers after he had burned them.

5. He _____ most of his money in stocks.

Lesson 13   153

STUDY YOUR NEW WORDS-4

all-out
[ɔ́ːláut]
greatest possible; complete; total
adj. 전력을 다하는, 전면적인, 전적인
He made an *all-out* effort to be the best student in his class.

aptitude
[ǽptitjuːd]
natural ability or skill
n. 적성, 소질, 재능
The student shows a great *aptitude* for languages; he can learn a foreign language much faster than others.

axis
[ǽksis]
the real or imaginary line around which something turns
n. 축(軸), 축선, 굴대
It takes 24 hours for the earth to make one rotation on its *axis*.

budget
[bʌ́dʒit]
estimate of probable future income and expenditure
n. 예산, 예산안
They planned a monthly *budget* for their family.

cargo
[káːrgou]
the load of goods carried by a ship or plane; freight
n. 선하(船荷), 뱃짐, 화물
A *cargo* of coal has arrived from Pusan.

clergy
[klə́ːrdʒi]
the men who serve a church as ministers or priests
n. 목사, 성직자 (집합적 의미)
Members of the *clergy* are serious students of religion.

cripple
[krípl]
a person unable to use one or more of his limbs
n. 불구자, 신체 장애자
He became a *cripple* as a result of the accident.

dodge
[dɔdʒ]
move quickly to oneside
v. 살짝 피하다, 홱 몸을 비키다
The man jumped aside to *dodge* the speeding truck.

grin
[grin]
smile broadly (showing one's teeth)
v. 싱글벙글 웃다, 이를 보이고 웃다
The boy *grinned* with pleasure when I gave him candy.

headquarters
[hédkwɔːrtərs]
any center from which orders are issued
n. 본부, 본사, 사령부
The policeman was ordered to report to the police *headquarters*.

retort
[ritɔ́ːrt]

answer quickly in a sharp or clever way
v. 말대꾸하다, 응수하다
"Your question is not worth answering," he *retorted*.

textile
[tékstail]

cloth made by weaving
n. 직물(織物), 옷감
We need to produce more *textiles*, especially silk and cotton.

thigh
[θai]

the upper part of the leg above the knee
n. 넓적다리
The fisherman's boots came up to his *thighs*.

toilet
[tɔ́ilit]

a bowl with a seat and lid for the disposal of body waste
n. 변기, 변소
The youngest child has not yet learned how to use the *toilet*.

EXERCISE 4
Fill each blank with the most appropriate word given above.
(Inflect the word if necessary.)

1. Edison had a remarkable _____ for inventing new things.
2. He _____ quickly when I threw my shoe at him.
3. A(n) _____ is not able to move or walk properly.
4. "It's none of your business," she _____.
5. He failed in the examination though he had made a(n) _____ effort for it.

해답					
EXERCISE 1.	1. cite	2. token	3. traitor	4. upheld	5. grumbles
EXERCISE 2.	1. denial	2. advocate	3. sane	4. sensation	5. formidable
EXERCISE 3.	1. envy	2. maintain	3. imposed	4. sensation	5. invested
EXERCISE 4.	1. aptitude	2. dodged	3. cripple	4. retorted	5. all-out

종합 연습 문제

1 In the space at the left, write the *letter* of the word that has most nearly the SAME MEANING as the italicized word.

_____ 1. *grinned* with pleasure   (A) sang   (B) jumped
                                                                        (C) smiled   (D) cried

_____ 2. a *formidable* question   (A) easy   (B) difficult
                                                                        (C) interesting   (D) foolish

_____ 3. *ripped* the curtain   (A) washed   (B) made
                                                                        (C) tore   (D) opened

_____ 4. the *hideous* noise   (A) sudden   (B) horrible
                                                                        (C) slight   (D) long

_____ 5. *maintain* one's family   (A) support   (B) desert
                                                                        (C) meet   (D) kill

2 In the space provided, write the *letter* of the word that most nearly means the OPPOSITE of the italicized word.

_____ 1. *flexible*   (A) mad   (B) feeble
                                        (C) stiff   (D) unpleasant

_____ 2. *gale*   (A) breeze   (B) exit
                                        (C) profit   (D) expenditure

_____ 3. *sane*   (A) shy   (B) worthless
                                        (C) favorable   (D) crazy

_____ 4. *denial*   (A) refusal   (B) esteem
                                        (C) disposal   (D) acceptance

_____ 5. *vanity*   (A) guilt   (B) humbleness
                                        (C) aptitude   (D) fortune

3 Supply the correct form of the word in italics for the blank space in each sentence.

1. *employ*   A large office requires the _____ of many people.
2. *invest*   Getting an education is a wise _____ of time and money.
3. *envy*   She was very _____ of her sister's beauty.
4. *convict*   The _____ of the accused man surprised all of us.
5. *maintain*   Travelers pay tolls for the _____ of roads.

4 Fill in the missing letters of the word at the right. Each dash stands for one missing letter.

DEFINITION	WORD
1. move slowly with frequent stops	LO___R
2. enjoying social life; friendly	____ABLE
3. the lower world; hell	_____WORLD
4. prove or declare guilty after trial	CON___T
5. natural ability or skill	A___TUDE
6. a formal request signed by a number of people	P___TION
7. open the mouth wide when one is tired	Y__N
8. the upper part of the leg	T__GH
9. a person who betrays his country	T____OR
10. make laws	LE____ATE

5 In the space provided, write the *letter* of the word NOT RELATED in meaning to the other words in each line.

_____ 1. (A) complain (B) uphold (C) grumble (D) mutter

_____ 2. (A) sane (B) vicious (C) sound (D) healthy

_____ 3. (A) cripple (B) priest (C) clergy (D) minister

_____ 4. (A) preserve (B) maintain (C) continue (D) impose

_____ 5. (A) respect (B) yawn (C) esteem (D) regard

_____ 6. (A) hideous (B) frightful (C) rough (D) horrible

_____ 7. (A) partial (B) whole (C) total (D) all-out

_____ 8. (A) cargo (B) freight (C) load (D) axis

_____ 9. (A) threshold (B) doorway (C) budget (D) entrance

_____ 10. (A) tear (B) cut (C) rip (D) cite

6 Fill each blank with the most appropriate word from the vocabulary list below.

VOCABULARY LIST

petition	flexible	maintain
grumble	token	formidable
gale	advocate	specs
textiles	dodged	retorted

1. A white flag is used as a(n) _____ of surrender.

2. Many old trees on the street were blown down in the _____.

3. A person who has poor eyesight needs _____.

4. It is difficult to _____ law and order in an emergency.

5. The people on our street signed a(n) _____ asking the city council for a new sidewalk.

6. In the United States many women _____ equal pay for men and women.

7. Rubber is _____; it can be easily bent without breaking.

8. I _____ behind a tree so that she could not see me.

9. Wool and silk are very good _____.

10. John has everything he needs; he has nothing to _____ about.

해답

1 1. C 2. B 3. C 4. B 5. A

2 1. C 2. A 3. D 4. D 5. B

3 1. employment 2. investment 3. envious 4. conviction 5. maintenance

4 1. oiter 2. sociable 3. underworld 4. convict 5. aptitude
    6. petition 7. yawn 8. thigh 9. traitor 10. legislate

5 1. B 2. B 3. A 4. D 5. B 6. C 7. A 8. D 9. C 10. D

6 1. token 2. gale 3. specs 4. maintain 5. petition
    6. advocate 7. flexible 8. dodged 9. textiles 10. grumble

PRETEST 14

Insert the *letter* of the best answer in the space provided.

1. If you always *exaggerate*, people will no longer _____.
   (A) doubt you (B) believe you

2. Foreigners who have entered Korea _____ may be *banished*.
   (A) legally (B) illegally

3. Several villages were *isolated* by the lack of _____.
   (A) food (B) buses

4. The little boy was as *meek* as a (an) _____.
   (A) lamb (B) tiger

5. _____ began, but it was difficult to decide which side was guilty of *aggression*.
   (A) War (B) Game

ANSWERS 1.B 2.B 3.A 4.A 5.A

STUDY YOUR NEW WORDS-1

attribute
[ətríbju(ː)t]

1. say or think that something is caused by; assign
   v. (～에) 돌리다, (～의) 탓으로 하다
   syn. ascribe
   We *attribute* Edison's success to intelligence and hard work.

[ǽtribjuːt]

2. a quality considered as belonging to a person or thing
   n. 속성, 특질
   syn. characteristic
   Politeness and kindness are *attributes* of a gentleman.

banish
[bǽniʃ]

send (a person) away from his home or out of his country
v. 추방하다, 쫓아내다
syn. exile
England once *banished* many criminals to Australia.

Lesson 14   159

barrier
[bǽriər]

anything that prevents people from going forward or getting near
n. 장벽, 장애(물), 방벽
syn. hindrance
The Sahara desert is a natural *barrier* that separates North and Central Africas.

code
[koud]

1. a collection of laws arranged in a clear and practical manner
n. 법규, 법전, 규약
syn. rule
The city building *code* limits the height of new buildings.

2. system of secret writing
n. 암호법, 약호
The enemy could not understand the *code* in which the general's letter was written.

hinder
[híndər]

stop someone from dong something
v. 방해하다, 훼방하다
syn. prevent
You're *hindering* me in my work by talking all the time.

isolate
[áisəleit]

place apart; separate from others
v. 고립시키다, 격리시키다
syn. separate
Several villages in the North have been *isolated* by heavy snowfall.

mist
[mist]

a cloud of very fine drops of water in the air
n. 안개, 연무
syn. fog
During the autumn the mountain top is always covered in *mist*.

porter
[pɔ́ːrtər]

one employed to carry traveler's bags
n. 운반인, 짐꾼
syn. carrier
The hotel *porter* carried their suitcases to their room.

subdue
[səbdjúː]

overcome by superior force; bring under control
v. 정복하다, 진압하다, 가라앉히다
syn. conquer
They *subdued* the enemy and captured the city after a long battle.

tempest
[témpist]

a violent windstorm usually accompanied by rain
n. 폭풍우
syn. storm
The *tempest* forced the ship onto the rocks.

transform
[trænsfɔ́ːrm]

change the shape or nature of
v. 변형시키다, 바꾸다
syn. change
The beautiful dress *transformed* the girl into a pretty young lady.

> **EXERCISE 1** Fill each blank with the most appropriate word given above.
> (Inflect the word if necessary.)
>
> 1. Deserts and high mountains have always been _____ to the movement of people.
>
> 2. The constant ringing of telephone _____ my work.
>
> 3. When a person has an infectious disease, he is usually _____.
>
> 4. One who has entered a foreign country illegally may be _____.
>
> 5. The punishments of robbery and murder are prescribed in the criminal _____.

STUDY YOUR NEW WORDS-2

amenable
[əmíːnəbl]

willing to obey or take advice or suggestion
adj. 복종하는, 순종하는
ant. disobedient
People living in a country are *amenable* to its laws.

casual
[kǽʒuəl]

happening by chance; not planned; informal
adj. 우연한, 무심결의, 평시의
ant. intentional
Our long friendship began with a *casual* meeting at a Christmas party.

condense
[kəndéns]

put into a smaller or shortened form; say briefly
v. 압축하다, 요약하다
ant. expand
A long story can sometimes be *condensed* into a few sentences.

detach
[ditǽtʃ]

1. part; separate; unfasten or remove from
v. 떼다, 떨어지게 하다, 분리하다
ant. attach
The engine was *detached* from the body of the train.

2. send away on special duty
v. 파견하다, 분견하다
One squad of soldiers was *detached* to guard the important road and bridge.

Lesson 14

exaggerate
[igzǽdʒəreit]

make too large; say or think (something) greater than it is
v. 과장하다, 과대하게 보이다
ant. underestimate
He *exaggerated* the dangers of the trip in order to frighten them into not going.

inadequate
[inǽdikwit]

not enough; not sufficient; not equal to what is necessary
adj. 불충분한, 부적당한
ant. sufficient
He was tired because he had had *inadequate* sleep last night.

literate
[lítərit]

able to read and write; educated
adj. 읽고 쓸 수 있는, 학식 있는, 교양 있는
ant. uneducated
A *literate* person can get knowledge through reading many books.

mansion
[mǽnʃən]

a very large house, usually that of a wealthy family
n. 대저택, 귀인의 저택
ant. hut
That old *mansion* has more than twenty rooms.

meek
[mi:k]

mild and gentle; not easily angered
adj. 온순한, 유순한
ant. violent
He isn't bad-tempered; he is as *meek* as a lamb.

zeal
[zi:l]

strong and active interest; enthusiasm
n. 열의, 열심, 열성
ant. negligence
A good citizen works with *zeal* for his country's interests.

EXERCISE 2 **Fill each blank with the most appropriate word given above.**
(Inflect the word if necessary.)

1. _____ preparation caused the boy to fail in his final examination.

2. Your request was too mild. If you had done with more _____ it would have been accepted.

3. He _____ the lock from the door in order to repair it.

4. The little boy _____ when he said there was a lion in the backyard.

5. The school's main goal is to make people _____.

STUDY YOUR NEW WORDS-3

aggression
[əgréʃən]

the first step in an attack or a quarrel
n. 침략, 침범, 공략
adj. aggressive
We need the self-defense posture to deter the possible *aggression* from North Korea.

agitate
[ǽdʒiteit]

1. excite; move violently
v. 흥분시키다, 동요시키다, 들먹이다
n. agitation
We thought that the bad news would upset Tom, but it didn't seem to *agitate* him.

2. move or shake vigorously
v. 심히 흔들어대다
n. agitation
The slightest wind *agitates* the leaves of the trees.

architect
[á:rkitekt]

builder; planner; constructor
n. 건축가, 건축 기사
adj. architectural
We employed an *architect* to design our summer house.

bond
[bɔnd]

1. anything that joins or keeps together
n. 유대, 결속, 결합력
n. bondage
There is a close *bond* of affection between the two sisters.

2. a written agreement or promise, usually about money
n. 증서, 약정서
He is so honest that his spoken promise is as good as a *bond*.

dominate
[dɔ́mineit]

control, govern, or rule; have authority or influence over
v. 지배하다, 권세를 부리다
adj. dominant
The chairman's strong will *dominated* the committee, which did what he wanted without arguing.

integrate
[íntəgreit]

bring together to form a whole
v. 통합하다, 완전하게 하다
adj. integral
He *integrated* ideas from several philosophers into his own philosophy.

Lesson 14

publicity
[pʌblísiti]

the state of fact of being known to the public
n. 널리 알려짐, 명성, 평판
v. publicize
His rescue of the child from the burning house brought him much *publicity*.

rely
[rilái]

trust; confide in; depend on
v. 신뢰하다, 의지하다
n. reliance
Send the boy to the bank for money; we can *rely* on him.

retract
[ritrǽkt]

1. draw in; draw back
v. 쑥 들어가게 하다, 수축시키다
adj. retractive
A cat can *retract* its claws, but a dog can't.

2. take back; withdraw
v. 철회하다, 취소하다
adj. retractive
You can depend on Frank. Once he has given his promise, he will not *retract* it.

unify
[júnifai]

make into one
v. 통일하다, 통합하다
n. unification
We should make every effort to *unify* the divided Korean peninsula.

EXERCISE 3 Fill each blank with the most appropriate word given above.
(Inflect the word if necessary.)

1. The committee try to _____ the different ideas into one uniform plan.

2. The film actress' marriage got a lot of _____, though she tried to keep it secret.

3. A country that sends its army to occupy another country is guilty of _____.

4. A great man _____ others by force of character.

5. She was _____ with grief when she heard the news that her husband's ship had sunk.

STUDY YOUR NEW WORDS-4

broil
[brɔil]

1. cook or be cooked by direct contact with fire
v. (고기를) 불에 굽다, 불에 쬐다
Flames flared as he *broiled* the meat over fire in the backyard.

2. fight; quarrel
v. 싸움하다, 말다툼하다
When I left, two women were quarreling noisily; when I returned an hour later, they were still *broiling*.

desolate
[désəlit]

1. not lived in; deserted; ruined
adj. 사는 사람이 없는, 황폐한, 황량한
A few *desolate* houses stood in the former mining town.

2. unhappy; miserable; lonely
adj. 쓸쓸한, 외로운, 고독한
She has led a *desolate* life since her husband's death.

gamble
[gǽmbl]

play games of chance for more money; bet; risk
v. 도박을 하다, 도박으로 날리다
A reckless young man *gambled* his fortune on a turn of cards in one night.

improve
[imprúːv]

make better; increase the value or usefulness of
v. 개선하다, 향상시키다, 증진시키다
I'll *improve* the shape of the handle so that it's easier to use.

incense
[inséns,
ínsens]

1. make very angry; fill with rage
v. 성나게 하다, 격앙시키다
The official was *incensed* at the lack of respect shown to him.

2. substance producing a sweet smell when burning
n. 향, 향료, 향냄새
Incense is burnt in some religious services.

marine
[məríːn]

of the sea; formed in the sea
adj. 바다의, 해양의, 바다에서 사는
Many kinds of *marine* life are found in this ocean.

nourish
[nʌ́riʃ]

give food to; help to grow; support
v. 먹여살리다, 기르다, 육성하다
There are hundreds of children in the slums who need to be *nourished*.

phase
[feiz]

a stage of development
n. (발달·변화 과정의) 단계, 국면
The old man overcame the critical *phase* of his illness.

spur
[spəːr]

an instrument fitted to a rider's heel to prick a horse to make it run faster
n. 박차(拍車)
The horse leaped over the fence at the touch of the *spur*.

thaw
[θɔː]

1. melt; become liquid or soft
v. (눈·서리·얼음이) 녹다, 녹이다
Exposed to the warm air, the frozen meat *thawed* rapidly.

2. become more friendly; become less stiff
v. (감정·날씨가) 누그러지다, 풀리다
At first the visitors were shy, but after drinking a glass of wine they *thawed*.

EXERCISE 4
Fill each blank with the most appropriate word given above.
(Inflect the word if necessary.)

1. My handwriting is very poor; I want to _____ it.

2. Some of the members were so _____ by the way Jack opened the meeting that they walked right out.

3. After a big fire, the forest land became _____.

4. Milk is all we need to _____ our small baby.

5. The sun at noon _____ the ice on the roads very quickly.

EXERCISE 1.	1. barriers	2. hinders	3. isolated	4. banished	5. code
EXERCISE 2.	1. inadequate	2. zeal	3. detached	4. exaggerated	5. literate
EXERCISE 3.	1. integrate	2. publicity	3. aggression	4. dominates	5. agitated
EXERCISE 4.	1. improve	2. incensed	3. desolate	4. nourish	5. thaws

종합 연습 문제

1 In the space provided, write the *letter* of the word NOT RELATED in meaning to the other words in each line.

_____ 1.　(A) hinder　(B) conceal　(C) prevent　(D) interrupt

_____ 2.　(A) fog　(B) mist　(C) veil　(D) haze

_____ 3.　(A) aspire　(B) banish　(C) exile　(D) expel

_____ 4.　(A) rule　(B) code　(C) law　(D) morale

_____ 5.　(A) separate　(B) isolate　(C) specify　(D) segregate

_____ 6.　(A) attribute　(B) achieve　(C) ascribe　(D) assign

_____ 7.　(A) verify　(B) transform　(C) alter　(D) change

_____ 8.　(A) gale　(B) storm　(C) blot　(D) tempest

_____ 9.　(A) barrier　(B) obstruction　(C) hindrance　(D) friction

_____ 10.　(A) subdue　(B) destruct　(C) conquer　(D) overcome

2 In the space before each word in COLUMN I, write the letter of its correct meaning in COLUMN II.

	COLUMN I	COLUMN II
_____	1. improve	(A) make very angry; fill with rage
_____	2. nourish	(B) deserted; ruined; not lived in
_____	3. broil	(C) become liquid or soft; melt
_____	4. gamble	(D) give food to; help to grow
_____	5. marine	(E) a stage of development
_____	6. spur	(F) cook by a direct contact with fire
_____	7. incense	(G) play games of chance for more money
_____	8. phase	(H) make better; increase the usefulness of
_____	9. desolate	(I) an instrument fitted to rider's heel
_____	10. thaw	(J) of the sea; found in the sea

3 In the space provided, write the *letter* of the word that most nearly means the OPPOSITE of the italicized word.

_____ 1. *inadequate*　(A) disagreeable　(B) rough
　　　　　　　　　　　(C) supreme　(D) sufficient

Lesson 14　167

_____ 2. *mansion*   (A) hut   (B) lad
                             (C) sack   (D) pot

_____ 3. *condense*   (A) object   (B) expand
                             (C) dismiss   (D) disguise

_____ 4. *detach*   (A) clutch   (B) attach
                             (C) search   (D) scratch

_____ 5. *meek*   (A) healthy   (B) perfect
                             (C) secret   (D) violent

_____ 6. *amenable*   (A) strict   (B) inflexible
                             (C) disobedient (D) permanent

_____ 7. *zeal*   (A) respect   (B) negligence
                             (C) suppression (D) illusion

_____ 8. *exaggerate*   (A) underestimate (B) shriek
                             (C) prevail   (D) assume

_____ 9. *literate*   (A) restrained   (B) uneducated
                             (C) prudent   (D) compact

_____ 10. *casual*   (A) usual   (B) provisional
                             (C) practical   (D) intentional

Complete the following table with the appropriate word forms.

	ADJECTIVE	NOUN	VERB	ADVERB
1.	integral	_____	_____	_____
2.	public	_____	_____	_____
3.	_____	_____	unify	___XXXXX___
4.	reliable	_____	_____	_____
5.	_____	_____	aggress	_____
6.	_____	retraction	_____	___XXXXX___
7.	_____	zeal	___XXXXX___	_____
8.	_____	architect	___XXXXX___	_____
9.	_____	_____	dominate	_____
10.	_____	_____	agitate	_____

5 In the space provided, write the *letter* of the word or expression that has most nearly the SAME MEANING as the italicized word.

_____ 1. The boy was disciplined for being *amenable* to his elders.
   (A) gentle   (B) obedient   (C) kind   (D) courteous

_____ 2. It was not a business appointment, but just a *casual* meeting with a friend.
   (A) popular   (B) intentional   (C) regular   (D) informal

_____ 3. On my way back home from school, I found two little boys *broiling*.
   (A) wandering   (B) walking   (C) crying   (D) fighting

_____ 4. The color of one's skin should be no *barrier* to success in life.
   (A) influence   (B) advantage   (C) obstruction   (D) connection

_____ 5. It was difficult to decide which side was guilty of *aggression*.
   (A) murder   (B) defeat   (C) attack   (D) destruction

_____ 6. She could hardly recognize him through the thick *mist*.
   (A) fog   (B) curtain   (C) wood   (D) glass

_____ 7. She was much *agitated* by the unexpected news of her brother's sudden death.
   (A) surprised   (B) excited   (C) embarrassed   (D) disappointed

_____ 8. The weather service said it would probably *thaw* tomorrow.
   (A) be cloudy   (B) be warm   (C) be snowing   (D) be rainy

_____ 9. The attacking forces quickly *subdued* the country.
   (A) captured   (B) observed   (C) surrounded   (D) conquered

_____ 10. I am sure he will not *retract* his promise.
   (A) withdraw   (B) change   (C) forget   (D) fulfill

해답

1 1. B   2. C   3. A   4. D   5. C   6. B   7. A   8. C   9. D   10. B
2 1. H   2. D   3. F   4. G   5. J   6. I   7. A   8. E   9. B   10. C
3 1. D   2. A   3. B   4. B   5. D   6. C   7. B   8. A   9. B   10. D

4

ADJECTIVE	NOUN	VERB	ADVERB
1. (integral)	integration	integrate	integrally
2. (public)	publicity	publicize	publicly
3. unifiable	unification	(unify)	XXXXX
4. (reliable)	reliance	rely	reliably
5. aggressive	aggression	(aggress)	aggressively
6. retractive	(retraction)	retract	XXXXX
7. zealous	(zeal)	XXXXX	zealously
8. architectural	(architect)	XXXXX	architecturally
9. dominant	domination	(dominate)	dominantly
10. agitative, agitated	agitation	(agitate)	agitatively, agitatedly

5 1. B   2. D   3. D   4. C   5. C   6. A   7. B   8. B   9. D   10. A

Lesson 15

PRETEST 15

Insert the *letter* of the best answer in the space provided.

1. We saw many _____ in the *meadow*.
   (A) cows (B) cars

2. The purpose of this *tariff* is to protect our _____.
   (A) troops (B) markets

3. He _____ at the *banquet*.
   (A) made a speech (B) bought a hat

4. _____ is a *plural* noun.
   (A) "Sugar" (B) "Oxen"

5. The girl was _____ to see a *corpse* near the rock.
   (A) pleased (B) surprised

ANSWERS 1.A 2.B 3.A 4.B 5.B

STUDY YOUR NEW WORDS-1

allure
[əljúr]

attract very strongly; tempt; charm
v. 꾀다, 유혹하다
syn. fascinate
The beautiful beaches of Hawaii *allure* many tourists from the mainland of the United States.

anew
[ənjú]

once more; in a new or different way
adv. 다시, 새로
syn. again
He made so many mistakes that he had to begin his work *anew*.

banquet
[bǽŋkwit]

a formal dinner in honor of a special occasion
n. 연회, 향연

syn. feast
A *banquet* was given to honor the retiring president.

crouch
[krautʃ]

lower the body close to the ground by bending the knees and back
v. 쭈그리다, 웅크리다, 몸을 구부리다
syn. squat
The cat saw the bird and *crouched* down ready to jump.

flank
[flæŋk]

the right or left side of anything
n. 측면, 옆구리
syn. side
The enemy may attack us on the left *flank*.

indignant
[indígnənt]

angry at something unjust or unfair
adj. 노한, 분개한
syn. wrathful
I was very *indignant* at the man, for he had treated me so badly.

meadow
[médou]

a piece of grassy land; grassland
n. 초원, 목초지
syn. pasture
They raise many cows and sheep in the *meadow*.

mobile
[móubi:l]

moving; able to be moved; easy to move
adj. 움직이는, 이동성이 있는, 유동하는
syn. movable
Many workmen aren't *mobile*; if they move to new employment they have difficulties in moving their families.

reverse
[rivə́:rs]

1. turned backward; opposite in position or direction
adj. 뒤의, 반대의 거꾸로의
Would you play the *reverse* side of that phonograph record, please?

2. turn the other way; turn inside out or upside down
v. 뒤집다, 반대로 하다, 거꾸로하다
syn. contrary
Reverse your sweater or you will put it on wrong side out.

roam
[roum]

go about with no special plan
v. 배회하다, 돌아다니다, 거닐다
syn. wander
The lovers *roamed* around the fields in complete forgetfulness of the time.

withstand
[wiðstǽnd]

stand against; endure; oppose
v. ~에 잘 견디다, 버티다, 저항하다
syn. resist
Children's furniture must *withstand* kicks and blows.

> **EXERCISE 1** Fill each blank with the most appropriate word given above.
> (Inflect the word if necessary.)
>
> 1. The tall man had to _____ to get into the small car.
> 2. She is much more _____ now that she has bought a car.
> 3. The general said, "Soldiers have to _____ hardships."
> 4. His name is written on the _____ side of the medal.
> 5. The king celebrated the birth of his son with a(n) _____.

STUDY YOUR NEW WORDS-2

concrete
[kɑnkríːt]

existing in material form; real; specific
adj. 구체적인, 실재적인, 유형의
ant. abstract
Do you have any *concrete* ideas on how to deal with this difficulty?

exclude
[iksklúːd]

keep out; shut out; refuse to consider
v. 제외하다, 배제하다
ant. include
The committee decided to *exclude* all foreigners from joining the club.

incomplete
[inkəmplíːt]

not complete; unfinished; imperfect
adj. 불완전한, 불충분한
ant. perfect
My homework is *incomplete*, but I'll finish it by 3 o'clock this afternoon.

intellectual
[intəléktʃuəl]

needing or using the power of the mind
adj. 지적인, 지성있는, 지력의
ant. physical
Teaching or counseling is an *intellectual* occupation.

plural
[plúərəl]

more than one in number
adj. 복수(複數)의, 둘 이상의

	ant. singular "Dog" is a singular noun; "dogs" is a *plural* noun.
quaint [kweint]	attractive or pleasing because it is unusual or old-fashioned ***adj.*** 색다른, 기묘한, 이상한 *ant.* common American visitors to Korea admire our *quaint* traditions and customs.
savory [séivəri]	pleasing in taste or smell; tasty ***adj.*** 맛좋은, 풍미 있는, 기분좋은 *ant.* unsavory The *savory* smell of cooking pleased us when we entered the house.
submerge [səbmə́:rdʒ]	(cause to) go down into water; sink ***v.*** (물 속에) 가라앉히다, 가라앉다 *ant.* float The flooded river *submerged* most of the farmland in the valley.
ultimate [ʌ́ltimit]	happening in the end; final; last ***adj.*** 최후의, 최종의, 종국의 *ant.* primary After many defeats, the war ended for us in *ultimate* victory.
violate [váiəleit]	break; fail to obey; act against ***v.*** 위반하다, 어기다, 범하다 *ant.* observe He *violated* the law and was arrested by the police.

EXERCISE 2 Fill each blank with the most appropriate word given above.
(Inflect the word if necessary.)

1. The _____ form of a word in English often ends in "s" or "es."

2. The teacher gave _____ examples to show the meanings of hope, faith and honor.

3. We can't see the small islet at high tide, for it is _____ under water.

4. The government _____ immigrants who have certain diseases.

5. We considered all their plans, but the _____ decision was to follow our own.

STUDY YOUR NEW WORDS-3

array
[əréi]

1. place in order; line up; arrange
v. 정렬시키다, 배열하다
n. arrayal
The soldiers were *arrayed* for battle in front of the general.

2. dress splendidly; clothe in fine clothes; adorn
v. 차려입히다, 성장(盛裝)시키다
n. arrayal
She was *arrayed* like a queen in her colorful dress.

bald
[bɔːld]

with little or no hair on the head; hairless
adj. 대머리의, 털이 없는
n. baldness
The old man's *bald* head glistened in the sun.

classify
[klǽsifai]

arrange in classes or groups; divide according to classes
v. 분류하다, 유별하다
n. classification
In a library, books are usually *classified* by subjects.

context
[kɔ́ntekst]

the parts of a sentence which influence the meaning of a word
n. 문맥, 전후 관계, 배경
adj. contextual
In some *contexts* "mad" means "crazy", but in others it may mean "angry" or "foolish."

destine
[déstin]

intend by fate; decide in advance
v. 운명을 결정짓다, 장래를 정하다
n. destiny
I never thought I would marry her, but I suppose it was *destined*.

formulate
[fɔ́ːrmjuleit]

express in a short clear form; state definitely or systematically
v. 공식화하다, 체계화하다, 형식화하다
n. formulation
Formulate your ideas before you begin to write.

hoarse
[hɔːrs]

rough and deep in sound; having a rough sound
adj. 쉰, 목쉰 소리의
n. hoarseness
A person with a bad cold usually has a *hoarse* voice.

inaugurate
[inɔ́:gjureit]

place in office with ceremony; make a formal beginning of
v. 취임시키다, (신시대를) 시작하다
adj. inaugural
The new President of the United States will be *inaugurated* on January 20.

psychology
[saikɔ́lədʒi]

the science concerned with the study of the mind
n. 심리학
adj. psychological
Child *psychology* is a required course in teacher training.

refine
[rifáin]

make pure; free from other substances
v. 정제하다, 순화하다, 다듬다
n. refinement
Sugar, oil, metals are *refined* before being used.

vengeance
[véndʒəns]

punishment in return for a wrong; revenge
n. 복수, 원수 갚기, 앙갚음
adj. vengeful
He took *vengeance* on the men who had killed his father.

EXERCISE 3   **Fill each blank with the most appropriate word given above.**
(Inflect the word if necessary.)

1. You can often tell the meaning of a word from its _____ though you are not familiar with the word itself.

2. The prince was _____ from his birth to be a king.

3. The invention of the airplane _____ a new era in transportation.

4. _____ tries to explain why people act, think, and feel as they do.

5. Employees in the post office _____ mail according to the places where it is to go.

STUDY YOUR NEW WORDS-4

aisle
[ail]
a passage for walking between rows of seats
n. (극장·열차 내부의) 통로
The *aisle* was wide enough for only one person.

booth
[bu:θ]
a small enclosed space used for a special purpose
n. 칸막이 시설 (매점, 투표소, 공중 전화 박스 등)
He went into the telephone *booth* to call his wife.

bulletin
[búlitin]
a short statement of news
n. 공보, 고시, 보도, 회보
Sports *bulletins* and weather bulletins are published in most newspapers.

corpse
[kɔ:rps]
a dead body (of a person)
n. 시체, 송장
A man has reported to the police that he saw a *corpse* under the bridge.

extracurricular
[ekstrəkəríkjulər]
outside the regular course of study
adj. 과외 (課外)의, 정규 과목 이외의
Swimming and skating are popular *extracurricular* activities in our high school.

garage
[gərá:dʒ]
a place where automobiles are kept or repaired
n. (자동차) 차고, 자동차 수리소
You'd better keep your car in a *garage* while it's snowing.

knob
[nɔb]
a rounded handle of a door, radio, etc.
n. (원형) 손잡이, 쥐는 곳, 혹
He turned the door *knob* to open the door.

license
[láisəns]
legal written permission to do something
n. 면허(증), 특허(장), 인가
While driving a car, you have to carry your driver's *license* with you.

parallel
[pǽrəlel]
(of lines) continuing at the same distance from one another
adj. 평행의, 나란히 있는
Parallel lines run side by side, but never get nearer to or farther away from each other.

skeleton
[skélətn]
the framework of all the bones of a body
n. 골격, 뼈대, 골자
The *skeleton* of the missing man was discovered in the cave.

tariff
[tǽrif]

a system of taxes placed by government on imports or exports
n. 관세, 관세율
There is a very high *tariff* on imported jewelry.

tickle
[tíkl]

touch lightly on the body, causing thrills
v. 간질이다, 간질거리다
She *tickled* the baby's feet and made him laugh.

tray
[trei]

a flat holder or container with slightly raised edges
n. 쟁반
The waiter carried the dishes on a *tray*.

EXERCISE 4   Fill each blank with the most appropriate word given above.
(Inflect the word if necessary.)

1. I'll have to go there by bus; my car is in the _____ for repairs.
2. There are fifty listening _____ in the language laboratory.
3. A(n) _____ on the radio warned of the spread of the forest fire.
4. He pulled the _____ of the drawer to get some pencils in it.
5. I've written the _____ of my report, but I have to fill in the details.

EXERCISE 1.	1. crouch	2. mobile	3. withstand	4. reverse	5. banquet
EXERCISE 2.	1. plural	2. concrete	3. submerged	4. excludes	5. ultimate
EXERCISE 3.	1. context	2. destined	3. inaugurated	4. psychology	5. classify
EXERCISE 4.	1. garage	2. booths	3. bulletin	4. knob	5. skeleton

종합 연습 문제

1 In the space at the left, write the *letter* of the word that has most nearly the SAME MEANING as the italicized word.

_____ 1. the *skeleton* of a building   (A) frame   (B) construction
                                                                                  (C) blueprint   (D) basement

_____ 2. a *mobile* library   (A) private   (B) convenient
                                           (C) quiet   (D) movable

_____ 3. to *formulate* her thought   (A) insist upon   (B) object to
                                                            (C) express clearly   (D) change suddenly

_____ 4. the *ultimate* goal   (A) common   (B) final
                                    (C) great   (D) impossible

_____ 5. her grandmother's *quaint* dress   (A) very colorful   (B) very long
                                                                           (C) luxurious and expensive
                                                                           (D) old-fashioned but attractive

2 In the space provided, write the *letter* of the word that most nearly means the OPPOSITE of the italicized word.

_____ 1. *intellectual*   (A) mental   (B) spiritual
                             (C) physical   (D) ideal

_____ 2. *concrete*   (A) abstract   (B) flat
                         (C) splendid   (D) primary

_____ 3. *plural*   (A) formal   (B) unfair
                   (C) material   (D) singular

_____ 4. *submerge*   (A) tickle   (B) float
                       (C) refuse   (D) tempt

_____ 5. *exclude*   (A) refine   (B) observe
                   (C) raise   (D) include

3 Supply the correct form of the word in italics for the blank space in each sentence.

1. *inaugurate*   The President gave an impressive _____ address when he took office.
2. *context*   This word has a special _____ meaning here.
3. *hoarse*   The actor did not perform because of _____.
4. *psychology*   _____ tests may be used to find out a person's character.
5. *refine*   Good manners and correct speech are marks of _____.

4 Fill in the missing letters of the word at the right. Each dash stands for one missing letter.

DEFINITION	WORD
1. a dead body (of a person)	CO_ _SE
2. the right or left side of anything	FL_ _K
3. a short statement of news	BU_ _ _ _IN
4. legal written permission to do something	L_ _ _ _SE
5. place in order; arrange	A_ _ _Y
6. outside the regular course of study	EXTRA_ _ _ _ _ _ _ _AR
7. once more; again	_NEW
8. touch lightly on the body, causing thrills	TI_ _ _E
9. go about with no special plan	R_ _M
10. (of lines) continuing at the same distance from one another.	PA_ _ _ _EL

5 In the space provided, write the *letter* of the word NOT RELATED in meaning to the other words in each line.

_____	1.	(A) meadow	(B) aisle	(C) pasture	(D) grassland
_____	2.	(A) delicious	(B) tasty	(C) tough	(D) savory
_____	3.	(A) array	(B) violate	(C) disobey	(D) commit
_____	4.	(A) allure	(B) refine	(C) attract	(D) fascinate
_____	5.	(A) quaint	(B) strange	(C) queer	(D) bald
_____	6.	(A) wrathful	(B) indignant	(C) angry	(D) parallel
_____	7.	(A) indefinite	(B) incomplete	(C) unfinished	(D) imperfect
_____	8.	(A) withstand	(B) resist	(C) roam	(D) oppose
_____	9.	(A) reverse	(B) legal	(C) contrary	(D) opposite
_____	10.	(A) final	(B) ultimate	(C) hoarse	(D) last

6 Fill each blank with the most appropriate word from the vocabulary list below.

VOCABULARY LIST

parallel	hoarse	meadow
tray	knob	vengeance
intellectual	license	savory
allured	crouched	destined

1. She opened the door by turning the _____.
2. The cat _____ in the corner waiting for the mouse to come out of its hole.
3. Teaching or counseling is a(n) _____ occupation.
4. They raise many cows and sheep in the _____.
5. A person with a bad cold usually has a(n) _____ voice.
6. The _____ smell of cooking pleased us when we entered the house.
7. The waiter carried the dishes on a(n) _____.
8. My brother passed the tests and got a(n) _____ to drive a car.
9. He took _____ on the men who had killed his brother.
10. _____ lines never get nearer to or farther away from each other.

해답

1 1. A   2. D   3. C   4. B   5. D
2 1. C   2. A   3. D   4. B   5. D
3 1. inaugural   2. contextual   3. hoarseness   4. psychological   5. refinement
4 1. corpse   2. flank   3. bulletin   4. license   5. array
   6. extracurricular   7. anew   8. tickle   9. roam   10. parallel
5 1. B   2. C   3. A   4. B   5. D   6. D   7. A   8. C   9. B   10. C
6 1. knob   2. crouched   3. intellectual   4. meadow   5. hoarse
   6. savory   7. tray   8. license   9. vengeance   10. parallel

180 TOEFL·TOEIC·TEPS 중급 College Vocabulary

Lesson 16

PRETEST 16

Insert the *letter* of the best answer in the space provided.

1. She was *attired* in a beautiful _____ for the dance party.
   (A) carriage   (B) garment

2. The summer flowers *withered* _____.
   (A) after the rain   (B) under the hot sun

3. *Applause* for the performance rang out from the _____.
   (A) audience   (B) orchestra

4. Old people find it difficult to *adapt* themselves _____.
   (A) to modern life   (B) from their old habits

5. If a soldier acts in *defiance* of _____, he is severely punished.
   (A) order   (B) enemy

ANSWERS 1.B 2.B 3.A 4.A 5.A

STUDY YOUR NEW WORDS-1

adjourn
[ədʒə́ːrn]

put off until a last time; suspend
v. 연기하다, 미루다, 휴회하다
syn. postpone
The members of the club voted to *adjourn* their meeting until 5 p.m.

astonish
[əstóniʃ]

surprise greatly; fill with wonder
v. 놀라게 하다, 경악시키다
syn. astound
She was *astonished* to hear the news that she had won the first prize in the speech contest.

attire
[ətáiər]

put on clothes; clothe or dress
v. 차려입히다, 치장시키다

syn. array

The queen was *attired* in blue for her birthday party.

candidate
[kǽndidit]

one who wants to get a position, enter a school, etc.
n. 후보자, 지원자
syn. applicant
There are three *candidates* for president of the club.

discipline
[dísiplin]

1. training of the mind and character
n. 훈련, 단련, 수양
The *discipline* of his early hardships contributed to his success.

2. order among pupils, soldiers or members of any group
n. 규율, 풍기, 군기
syn. training
Military schools are known for their strict *discipline*.

interpret
[intə́rprit]

tell or explain the meaning of something hard to understand
v. 해설하다, 통역하다
syn. translate
Please *interpret* the meaning of this foreign word that I've never heard.

lounge
[laundʒ]

stroll, stand, sit or lie in a lazy way
v. 어슬렁어슬렁거리다, 빈둥거리다
syn. loiter
There were some men and women who were *lounging* along the beach.

secure
[sikjúər]

1. make safe against loss, attack, or danger
v. 안전하게 하다, 굳게 지키다
By strengthening the river banks, the city *secured* itself against floods.

2. free from anxiety; confident
adj. 걱정없는, 안심되는, 안전한
syn. protect
Are you worried about passing the final exam, or do you feel *secure*?

siege
[si:dʒ]

the act of surrounding a fortified place by an army trying to capture it
n. 포위, 공위(攻圍)
syn. besiegement
The country was in a state of *siege*, and tanks were lined up in front of the Presidential palace.

strive
[stráiv]

work hard; make a great effort
v. 노력하다, 애쓰다
syn. endeavor
Korea is *striving* to establish self-reliant defense posture.

vocation
[voukéiʃən]

a profession for which one is best suited by talent and interest
n. 직업, 천직, 일
syn. profession
Teaching children ought to be a *vocation* as well as a way of earning money.

> **EXERCISE 1** Fill each blank with the most appropriate word given above.
> (Inflect the word if necessary.)
>
> 1. The gift of ten dollars _____ the little child.
> 2. Children who have had no _____ are often hard to teach.
> 3. The judge decided to _____ the court to the following Monday.
> 4. You cannot _____ yourself against all risks and dangers.
> 5. My friend is going to be a nurse, I, however, have not yet chosen a _____.

STUDY YOUR NEW WORDS-2

amiable
[éimiəbl]

lovable; good-natured; pleasant and agreeable
adj. 호감을 주는, 귀염성 있는
ant. unpleasant
Charlotte is an *amiable* child; everybody loves her.

capture
[kǽptʃər]

1. make a prisoner of; catch (by force, skill, or a trick)
v. 붙잡다, 생포하다
ant. release
The traitor was *captured* trying to escape from the country.

2. attract; catch and keep
v. 끌다, 매혹시키다, 사로잡다
ant. release
Her beauty *captured* him and he swore to stay with her forever.

congregate
[kɔ́ŋgrigeit]

gather together; assemble; collect
v. 모이다, 집합하다

ant. disperse

The crowds **congregated** in the square in front of the palace when they heard the news of the king's death.

cowardly
[káuərdli]

without courage; faint-hearted
adj. 겁많은, 소심한, 비겁한
ant. brave
When I was a boy, I was too *cowardly* to go out at night.

feeble
[fí:bl]

weak; without strength; frail
adj. 연약한, 약한, 힘없는
ant. robust
The old lady's *feeble* hands could hardly hold a small cup.

identical
[aidéntikəl]

the same; exactly alike
adj. 동일한, 일치하는
ant. different
It is the *identical* coat that I lost a month ago.

perpetual
[pərpétjuəl]

continuing forever; for an unlimited time
adj. 영구의, 영속하는, 종신의
ant. temporary
Bathing in the Fountain of Youth is supposed to assure *perpetual* beauty.

twilight
[twáilait]

the faint light of the sun remaining after the sun sets
n. 황혼, 땅거미, 박명(薄明)
ant. dawn
The old man likes to take a walk in the *twilight*.

unfair
[ʌnfɛ́ər]

not fair or equitable; unjust
adj. 공정치 못한, 편파적인
ant. just
The spectators were disappointed at the *unfair* decision by the umpire.

vacant
[véikənt]

empty; unoccupied
adj. 비어 있는, 공허한
ant. occupied
She had a few *vacant* rooms to rent for the students.

veracity
[vəræsəti]

truthfulness (of a person)
n. 진실, 정직
ant. falsehood
Since you have lied to us in the past, you should not wonder that we doubt your *veracity*.

EXERCISE 2 Fill each blank with the most appropriate word given above.
(Inflect the word if necessary.)

1. The police have not _____ the murderer yet.
2. Eddie was quite _____ until the age of 12, but then he developed into a robust youth.
3. She is a(n) _____ girl and gets along with everyone without any trouble.
4. You may believe this statement; it comes from a person of unquestionable _____.
5. The fingerprints of two persons are never _____.

STUDY YOUR NEW WORDS-3

applause
[əplɔ́:z]

handclapping, shouting or other outward expressions of approval
n. 박수 갈채, 칭찬
v. applaud
When the singer ended his song on the stage, there was a great *applause* in the concert hall.

brutal
[brú:tl]

cruel; savage; inhuman
adj. 잔인한, 야수적인
n. brutality
The murder was so *brutal* that the jury was not allowed to see the police photographs.

defiance
[difáiəns]

standing up against authority and refusing to obey it
n. 반항, 도전, 무시
v. defy
He shouted in *defiance* of the policeman's warning to be quiet.

demonstrate
[démənstreit]

prove by facts; show clearly
v. 증명하다, 실물로 입증하다
adj. demonstrative
How can you *demonstrate* that the world is round?

eloquence
[éləkwəns]

fluent forceful speaking; the act of speaking so as to stir the feelings
n. 능변, 웅변
adj. eloquent
The *eloquence* of the President moved all hearts who listened to him.

exclusive
[iksklú:siv]

1. shutting out all or almost all others
adj. 비개방적인, 폐쇄적인
v. exclude
He donated a lot of money to join the *exclusive* club.

2. limited or belonging to a particular individual or group
adj. 독점적인, 유일의
v. exclude
I have the *exclusive* rights for the sale of Ford cars in this town.

initiative
[iníʃətiv]

the first movement or act which starts something happening
n. 주도(권), 발의, 솔선
v. initiate
She took the *initiative* in getting acquainted with her neighbors.

reluctant
[rilʌ́ktənt]

showing unwillingness; hesitant
adj. 마음내키지 않는, 꺼리는
n. reluctance
He was very *reluctant* to give his money away.

risky
[ríski]

full of risk; dangerous; perilous
adj. 위험한, 모험적인
n. risk
Because of advances in medical technology, heart surgery is not as *risky* as it formerly was.

terminate
[tə́:rmineit]

bring to an end; put an end to
v. 끝내다, 그만두다, 종결시키다
adj. terminal
The policeman *terminated* the quarrel by sending the boys home.

typify
[típifai]

be a symbol of; represent
v. 전형이 되다, 대표하다
adj. typical
Abraham Lincoln *typifies* the politician who rises from humble origins to a position of power and influence.

EXERCISE 3 Fill each blank with the most appropriate word given above.
(Inflect the word if necessary.)

1. The science teacher _____ that the magnet attracts a piece of iron.
2. That school is very _____ and only the wealthy send their children.
3. She is shy and does not take the _____ in making acquaintances.
4. Talking and _____ are not the same; to talk and to talk well are two different things.
5. The thief pulled out a knife and bade _____ to the police officer.

STUDY YOUR NEW WORDS-4

adapt
[ədǽpt]

make fit or suitable
v. 적응시키다, 적합시키다
When you go to a foreign country, you must *adapt* yourself to new manners and customs.

clash
[klæʃ]

1. make a loud, confused noise by striking one thing to another
v. (소리내어) 충돌시키다, 부딪치다
She *clashed* the tow pans together to wake us up.

2. a strong disagreement or conflict
n. (의견·이해의) 충돌, 불일치
There are many *clashes* of opinion in that family, for no two of them think alike.

compromise
[kɔ́mprəmaiz]

negotiation; adjustment
n. 타협, 절충
The disagreement about the boundary between the two countries was settled by *compromise*.

era
[íərə]

historical period; an age in history; epoch
n. 연대, 시대, 기원
The years from 1817 to 1824 in the United States history are often called the *Era* of Good Feeling.

gulp
[gʌlp]

swallow greedily or too quickly
v. 꿀꺽꿀꺽 마시다, 삼켜버리다
After running 1,000 meters, the runner became thirsty and *gulped* a bowl of water.

Lesson 16

proprietor
[prəpráiətər]

an owner (of business, or invention, etc.)
n. 소유주, 경영주
I wasn't satisfied with our treatment at that hotel; I shall write and complain to the *proprietor*.

revise
[riváiz]

change or correct because of new information or more thought; alter
v. 개정하다, 교정하다, 수정하다
When you know the facts, you may *revise* your opinion.

superstition
[su:pərstíʃən]

unreasonable belief in the supernatural
n. 미신(迷信)
She has a *superstition* that breaking a mirror brings bad luck.

tract
[trækt]

an area of land; a region
n. 토지, 지역
During last summer's flood, a large *tract* of farmland was under water.

wail
[weil]

cry long and loud because of grief or pain
v. 울부짖다, 목놓아 울다
The little baby *wailed* until his mother entered the room.

wither
[wíðər]

(cause to) become dry and faded
v. 시들(게 하다), 말라죽(게 하)다
The grass *withered* and died for lack of water under the hot sun.

EXERCISE 4
Fill each blank with the most appropriate word given above.
(Inflect the word if necessary.)

1. They both wanted the apple; their _____ was to cut it into two pieces and share it.
2. The Christian _____ counted from the birth of Christ.
3. The heat of the summer day _____ the leaves of the sunflowers in the garden.
4. Cats can _____ themselves very well to indoor life.
5. The goods are too expensive; I would like to speak to the _____ of this store.

해답

EXERCISE 1.	1. astonished	2. discipline	3. adjourn	4. secure	5. vocation
EXERCISE 2.	1. captured	2. feeble	3. amiable	4. veracity	5. identical
EXERCISE 3.	1. demonstrated	2. exclusive	3. initiative	4. eloquence	5. defiance
EXERCISE 4.	1. compromise	2. era	3. withered	4. adapt	5. proprietor

종합 연습 문제

1 In the space provided, write the *letter* of the word NOT RELATED in meaning to the other words in each line.

_____ 1. (A) weep (B) sob (C) defy (D) wail

_____ 2. (A) guard (B) clash (C) secure (D) protect

_____ 3. (A) occupation (B) profession (C) regulation (D) vocation

_____ 4. (A) postpone (B) adjourn (C) deter (D) suspend

_____ 5. (A) compose (B) interpret (C) explain (D) translate

_____ 6. (A) struggle (B) endeavor (C) strive (D) perish

_____ 7. (A) array (B) dress (C) attire (D) assess

_____ 8. (A) brutal (B) cruel (C) savage (D) benevolent

_____ 9. (A) capture (B) revise (C) alter (D) correct

_____ 10. (A) lounge (B) streak (C) loiter (D) stroll

2 In the space before each word in COLUMN I, write the letter of its correct meaning in COLUMN II.

COLUMN I   COLUMN II

_____ 1. superstition   (A) historical period; an age in history

_____ 2. compromise   (B) an area of land; a region

_____ 3. tract   (C) make fit or suitable

_____ 4. revise   (D) swallow greedily or too quickly

_____ 5. wither   (E) unreasonable belief in the supernatural

_____ 6. adapt   (F) a strong disagreement or conflict

_____ 7. wail   (G) become dry and faded

_____ 8. era   (H) change or correct because of more information

_____ 9. gulp   (I) negotiation; adjustment

_____ 10. clash   (J) cry long and loud

3 In the space provided, write the *letter* of the word that most nearly means the OPPOSITE of the italicized word.

_____ 1. *cowardly*   (A) courageous   (B) direct
                              (C) fluent   (D) sufficient

Lesson 16

_____ 2. *perpetual* (A) near (B) terminal
  (C) temporary (D) incomplete

_____ 3. *capture* (A) assemble (B) respond
  (C) broil (D) release

_____ 4. *identical* (A) relative (B) different
  (C) natural (D) righteous

_____ 5. *twilight* (A) dawn (B) shade
  (C) dusk (D) darkness

_____ 6. *amiable* (A) cold (B) nominal
  (C) unpleasant (D) partial

_____ 7. *vacant* (A) occupied (B) dominant
  (C) imposing (D) heavy

_____ 8. *feeble* (A) multiple (B) robust
  (C) frail (D) wide

_____ 9. *unfair* (A) gloomy (B) just
  (C) poor (D) wise

_____ 10. *congregate* (A) disperse (B) participate
  (C) flee (D) concentrate

4 Complete the following table with the appropriate word forms.

	ADJECTIVE	NOUN	VERB	ADVERB
1.	_____	_____	demonstrate	_____
2.	brutal	_____	_____	_____
3.	_____	risk	_____	_____
4.	_____	eloquence	XXXXX	_____
5.	_____	_____	terminate	_____
6.	initial	_____	_____	_____
7.	_____	_____	applaud	_____
8.	reluctant	_____	XXXXX	_____
9.	_____	exclusion	_____	_____
10.	_____	defiance	_____	_____

5 In the space provided, write the *letter* of the word or expression that has most nearly the SAME MEANING as the italicized word.

_____ 1. At that *identical* time, he was looking out for a young man.
　　　　(A) specified　(B) free　　(C) critical　(D) same

_____ 2. Don't ask him to do so much just after his illness, when he is still *feeble*.
　　　　(A) sick　　　(B) weak　　(C) nervous　(D) young

_____ 3. An inventor has an *exclusive* right for a certain number of years to make what he has invented.
　　　　(A) great　　　(B) formal　(C) substantial　(D) sole

_____ 4. We must *secure* ourselves against the dangers of the coming storm.
　　　　(A) rescue　　(B) protect　(C) prepare　(D) avoid

_____ 5. The *compromise* satisfied neither the workers nor the employer.
　　　　(A) negotiation (B) regulation　(C) promise　(D) suggestion

_____ 6. This advertisement will surely *capture* the public attention.
　　　　(A) arise　　　(B) attract　(C) demand　(D) influence

_____ 7. The teacher led the *reluctant* student to the principal.
　　　　(A) lazy　　　(B) troublesome (C) unwilling　(D) wrongdoing

_____ 8. We have a few *vacant* rooms to rent for the students.
　　　　(A) beautiful　(B) unoccupied　(C) small　(D) furnished

_____ 9. He could not sleep well last night, because of the *perpetual* noise of the machines.
　　　　(A) continuing (B) strange　(C) high-pitched (D) disgusting

_____ 10. When the fire broke out, the students showed good *discipline*.
　　　　(A) effort　　(B) order　　(C) courage　(D) service

해답

1	1. C	2. B	3. C	4. C	5. A	6. D	7. D	8. D	9. A	10. B
2	1. E	2. I	3. B	4. H	5. G	6. C	7. J	8. A	9. D	10. F
3	1. A	2. C	3. D	4. B	5. A	6. C	7. A	8. B	9. B	10. A

4	ADJECTIVE	NOUN	VERB	ADVERB
1.	demonstrative	demonstration	(demonstrate)	demonstratively
2.	(brutal)	brutality	brutalize	brutally
3.	risky	(risk)	risk	riskily
4.	eloquent	(eloquence)	XXXXX	eloquently
5.	terminal	termination	(terminate)	terminally
6.	(initial)	initiative	initiate	initially
7.	applausive	applause	(applaud)	applausively
8.	(reluctant)	reluctance	XXXXX	reluctantly
9.	exclusive	(exclusion)	exclude	exclusively
10.	defiant	(defiance)	defy	defiantly

5　1. D　2. B　3. D　4. B　5. A　6. B　7. C　8. B　9. A　10. B

UNIT 1
(Lessons 17~21)

- **Enlarging Vocabulary through SYNONYMS** •

Lesson 17

PRETEST 17

Insert the *letter* of the best answer in the space provided.

1. A monument was built to *commemorate* the _____.
   (A) caution   (B) victory   (C) building

2. The children *huddled* together for _____.
   (A) warmth   (B) travel   (C) expenditure

3. *Censure* is sometimes harder to bear than _____.
   (A) fortitude   (B) praise   (C) punishment

4. The new vaccine *eradicated* all traces of the _____ within three months.
   (A) wealth   (B) disease   (C) crime

5. The barbarians *defiled* the church by using it as a _____.
   (A) stable   (B) temple   (C) shrine

ANSWERS   1.B 2.A 3.C 4.B 5.A

STUDY YOUR NEW WORDS-1

abdomen
[æbdóumən]

the middle part of the body containing the stomach and bowels
n. 배, 복부
syn. belly
The pregnant woman has an enlarged *abdomen*.

bereave
[birí:v]

1. deprive ruthlessly; rob; take away
v. 빼앗다, 잃게 하다, 앗아가다
syn. deprive
The lost hikers were *bereft* of hope when the rescue plane did not see them.

2. leave desolate and alone
v. 외롭고 쓸쓸히 남게 되다
The children were *bereaved* by the death of their parents.

consecrate
[kónsikreit]

devote to some special use; make holy or sacred
v. 바치다, 봉헌하다, 신성하게 하다

syn. devote
This battlefield is *consecrated* to the memory of the soldiers who died here.

evoke
[ivóuk]

bring out; call forth; cause to appear
v. 불러일으키다, 자아내다
syn. invoke
A good joke does not necessarily *evoke* a heartily laugh.

groove
[gru:v]

a long narrow channel or furrow; corrugation; rut
n. (파인) 홈, 바큇 자국
syn. furrow
Wheels left *grooves* in a muddy dirt road.

jolt
[dʒoult]

shake roughly; shake with sudden jerks
v. 동요하다, 덜컹거리다
syn. joggle
The old car *jolted* its passengers badly as it went over the rough road.

obsolete
[ɔ́bsəli:t]

no longer in use; out of date
adj. 못쓰게 된, 시대에 뒤진, 구식의
syn. antiquated
Bowing to greet a lady is now an *obsolete* custom.

prowl
[prául]

wander about quietly and secretly in search of something; stroll
v. 찾아 헤매다, 배회하다
syn. rove
Many wild animals *prowl* at night looking for something to eat.

scoop
[sku:p]

dig out; hollow out
v. 파다, 푸다
syn. shovel
The children *scooped* holes in the sand.

status
[stéitəs]

state or condition of affairs; position; standing; stage
n. 상태, 지위, 신분
syn. situation
Diplomats are interested in the *status* of world affairs.

sue
[sju:, su:]

start a law case against; appeal to; charge; impeach
v. 고소하다, ~에게 소송을 제기하다
syn. indict
The farmer *sued* the railroad station because his cow was killed by the train.

EXERCISE 1
Fill each blank with the most appropriate word given above.
(Inflect the word if necessary.)

1. The counter of the sink has many _____ along which the water will run off.
2. The cat _____ around the cellar looking for mice.
3. We all sympathized with the husband who was _____ of his beloved wife.
4. Her singing _____ admiration from the public.
5. We still use this machine though it is _____.

STUDY YOUR NEW WORDS-2

bandit
[bǽndit]

a highway man or robber, especially one of a gang; outlaw
n. 산적, 노상 강도, 도둑, 악당
syn. brigand
The *bandit* in a typical Western movie rides a horse and goes armed, either alone or in a group.

commemorate
[kəmémərèit]

honor the memory of; observe
v. 기념하다, 축하하다
syn. celebrate
Christmas *commemorates* the birth of Jesus Christ.

defile
[difáil]

make dirty or impure; pollute; sully
v. 더럽히다, 모독하다
syn. infect
The children's muddy shoes *defiled* all the rugs in hotel.

deviation
[dì:viéiʃən]

turning aside; divergence; detour
n. 탈선, 벗어남
syn. divergence
Running in the hall is a *deviation* from the school rules and will not be allowed.

fortitude
[fɔ́:rtitjùːd]

courage in facing pain, danger, or trouble; firmness of spirit
n. 불굴의 정신, 꿋꿋함, 강한 참을성
syn. endurance
She could bear the disappointments of other people with tolerable *fortitude*.

inconsolable
[inkənsóuləbl]

not to be comforted; broken-hearted
adj. 위로할 길 없는, 슬픔에 잠긴
syn. depressed
The little girl was *inconsolable* at the loss of her kitten.

nibble
[níbl]

eat away with quick, small bites as a rabbit or a mouse does
v. (짐승, 물고기가) 조금씩 물어 뜯다
syn. bite
Aren't you hungry? You are only *nibbling* your food.

pageant
[pǽdʒənt]

an elaborate spectacle; exposition
n. 장관, 구경거리
syn. exhibition
The coronation of the new king was a splendid *pageant*.

scourge
[skəːrdʒ]

something or person which causes great trouble or misfortune
n. 재앙, (하늘의) 응징, 천벌
syn. disaster
After the *scourge* of flood usually comes the *scourge* of disease.

tumble
[tʌ́mbl]

fall to the ground; fall suddenly and violently
v. 넘어지다, 굴러 떨어지다
syn. fall
The crippled child *tumbled* down the stairs and was badly hurt.

EXERCISE 2 Fill each blank with the most appropriate word given above.
(Inflect the word if necessary.)

1. The iron in the ship caused a(n) _____ of the magnetic needle of the compass.
2. A marathon runner must have great _____ to run such a long distance.
3. The pretty girl's reputation was _____ by malicious gossips.
4. The boy is just learning to walk; she is always _____ over the floor.
5. The inauguration ceremony of the new President was a splendid _____.

STUDY YOUR NEW WORDS-3

afflict
[əflíkt]

cause pain to; trouble very much; sicken; ail
v. 괴롭히다
syn. distress
There are many illnesses which *afflict* old people.

censure
[sénʃər]

express an unfavorable opinion; reprove; reproach
v. 비난하다, 혹평하다, 나무라다
syn. blame
His employer *censured* him for neglecting his work.

dissimulation
[disimjuléiʃən]

the act of deceit; hypocrisy; pretention; make believe
n. 시치미 뗌, (감정을) 감춤, 위선
syn. deception
The thief intruded into the house with caution and *dissimulation*.

flog
[flɔg]

beat or whip hard; paddle; cane
v. 매질〔채찍질〕하다, 징계〔징벌〕하다
syn. spank
Nowadays, it is an inhumane punishment to *flog* the disobedient soldiers or sailors.

inscription
[inskrípʃən]

something written on a monument, coin, etc.; heading; epigraph
n. 새긴 문자, 명각
syn. caption
According to the *inscription* on its cornerstone, this building was erected in 1919.

meddle
[médl]

touch unnecessarily; interfere; butt in
v. 쓸데없이 참견〔간섭〕하다
syn. intervene
The gifts of charity *meddled* with a gentlemen's private affair.

posture
[pɔ́stʃər]

the position of the body; way of holding the body; demeanor
n. 자세, 태세, 마음 가짐
syn. attitude
He doesn't sit straight; his *posture* is very bad.

rummage
[rʌ́midʒ]

search thoroughly by moving things about; search
v. 샅샅이 조사하다, 뒤적거리다
syn. ransack
John *rummaged* all the drawers to find his gloves.

spout
[spáut]

come or send out suddenly in a stream; eject; exude
v. 내뿜다, 분출하다
syn. pour
The water *spouted* out when the pipe was broken.

traverse
[trævə́:rs]

pass across, over, or through; cut across; bisect
v. 가로지르다, 횡단하다
syn. intersect
The climber *traversed* a long horizontal crack in the face of the mountain slope.

wistful
[wístfəl]

wishful; longing; desirous; wishful
adj. 동경하는, 탐내는
syn. yearning
A child stood looking with *wistful* eyes at the toys in the shop window.

EXERCISE 3 Fill each blank with the most appropriate word given above.
(Inflect the word if necessary.)

1. He was _____ his horse in a very cruel way.
2. She _____ change from the bottom of her purse.
3. The law does not _____ unduly with a person's private life.
4. The lights _____ the sky searching for enemy planes.
5. The _____ on the ancient monument was very hard to read.

STUDY YOUR NEW WORDS-4

amicable
[ǽmikəbl]

having or showing a friendly attitude; affable; agreeable
adj. 우호[친화]적인, 유쾌한
syn. amiable
The *amicable* flash of her white teeth was very impressive.

blizzard
[blízərd]

a long severe snowfall
n. 눈보라
syn. snowstorm
The soldiers are very exhausted, for they have advanced forward without rest in a *blizzard*.

cruise
[kru:z]

sail or travel about from place to place on pleasure or business
v. 순항하다, 바다 위를 떠돌아다니다
syn. voyage
If I were rich, I would like to *cruise* in the Southern Pacific for six months in a private yacht.

eradicate
[irǽdikeit]

get rid of entirely; destroy completely; annihilate; uproot
v. 뿌리채 뽑다, 일소하다
syn. extirpate
Yellow fever has been *eradicated* in the United States but it still exists in some countries.

glimmer
[glímər]

a faint, unsteady light; glow; flicker
n. 희미한[가물거리는] 빛
syn. gleam
The doctor's report gave us only a *glimmer* of hope.

lump
[lʌmp]

a mass of something solid without a special size or shape; bump
n. 덩어리
syn. block
On his desk, many articles and documents are always piled in a great *lump*.

ransack
[rǽnsæk]

search thoroughly through; scour
v. 샅샅이 찾다, 뒤지다
syn. rummage
The woman *ransacked* the house for her lost jewelry.

slash
[slæʃ]

make long, quick cuts with something sharp
v. 베다, 내리쳐 베다
syn. gash
He *slashed* a path through the high grass with a long knife.

slump
[slʌmp]

drop or fall heavily or suddenly
v. 푹[쑥] 떨어지다, 빠지다
syn. depress
Our feet *slumped* repeatedly through the melting ice.

vogue
[voug]

popularity or acceptance; mode
n. 유행, 인기
syn. fashion
That pop song had a great *vogue* at one time.

EXERCISE 4 Fill each blank with the most appropriate word given above. (Inflect the word if necessary.)

1. Enemy soldiers _____ the city and carried off its treasures.
2. Tired from his long walk, he _____ into a chair.
3. We saw the _____ of a distant light through the trees.
4. He used to have a great _____ as a film actor, but no one goes to the cinema to see him now.
5. What the Ice Age did was to _____ the abundant mammalian life in the northern hemisphere.

STUDY YOUR NEW WORDS-5

ascribe (to) [əskráib]
think as caused or coming from; assign (to)
v. (원인, 동기를) ~의 탓으로 돌리다
syn. attribute
He *ascribes* his success to skill and hard work.

bulwark [búlwərk]
a person, thing, or idea that is a defense or a protection; support
n. 보루, 방벽
syn. safeguard
The soldiers kept their heads down behind the *bulwark*.

dubious [djúbiəs]
uncertain; ambiguous; not very good or reliable
adj. 의심스러운, 모호한
syn. doubtful
She looked around this way and that in a *dubious* manner.

facet [fæsit]
any of the many parts of subject to be considered; phase
n. 양상, 국면
syn. aspect
Selfishness was a *facet* of his character that we seldom saw before.

heed [hi:d]
give careful attention to; take notice of; mind
v. 주의하다, 유의하다
syn. attention
For the first time he had to pay *heed* to his appearance, and in fact he became very well-dressed from then on.

huddle
[hʌ́dl]

crowd close; press in a mass or heap
v. (떼지어) 몰리다, 왁시글거리다
syn. gather
The boys *huddled* together under the rock to keep warm out of the wind.

mumble
[mʌ́mbl]

speak unclearly; speak in a low tone; mutter; whisper
v. 웅얼거리다, 중얼거리다
syn. murmur
The old man *mumbled* something to me, but I could not understand him.

relic
[rélik]

a thing, custom, or the remains left from the past
n. 유물, 유적
syn. remainder
This ruined bridge is a *relic* of the Korean War in 1950.

smog
[smɔg]

a combination of smoke and fog in the air
n. 연무 (연기 섞인 안개)
syn. fume
Automobile exhaust fumes are one of the major causes of *smog*.

wayfarer
[wéifɛərər]

a tourist, especially one who travels on foot; journeyer
n. (도보) 여행자, 나그네
syn. traveller
The thirsty *wayfarer* was glad to find a fresh spring near the road.

wont
[wount]

habitude; rule; practice; custom
n. 습관, 풍습
syn. habit
He always speaks with his mouth full of food; it is his *wont*.

EXERCISE 5
Fill each blank with the most appropriate word given above.
(Inflect the word if necessary.)

1. Four people were _____ under one umbrella to avoid the sudden shower.

2. I'm feeling better than yesterday, but it is _____ that I can go to school tomorrow.

3. No one knows who wrote that play, but it is usually _____ to Cyril Tourneur.

4. We believe that a free press and a free speech are _____ of democracy.

5. Take _____ of what I say, or you will fail in the final examination.

EXERCISE 1.	1. grooves	2. prowled	3. bereaved	4. evoked	5. obsolete
EXERCISE 2.	1. deviation	2. fortitude	3. defiled	4. tumbling	5. pageant
EXERCISE 3.	1. flogging	2. rummaged	3. meddle	4. traversed	5. inscription
EXERCISE 4.	1. ransacked	2. slumped	3. glimmer	4. vogue	5. eradicate
EXERCISE 5.	1. huddled	2. dubious	3. ascribed	4. bulwarks	5. heed

종합 연습 문제

1 In the space provided, write the *letter* of the word NOT RELATED to the other words on the line.

_____ 1. (A) abdomen   (B) intuition   (C) belly   (D) paunch
_____ 2. (A) contaminate (B) defile   (C) inflect   (D) pollute
_____ 3. (A) torment   (B) distress   (C) afflict   (D) cheat
_____ 4. (A) hurricane (B) blizzard   (C) draught   (D) tempest
_____ 5. (A) out-of-date (B) antiquated (C) obsolete   (D) impolite
_____ 6. (A) burglar   (B) outlaw   (C) bandit   (D) chisel
_____ 7. (A) bereave   (B) deprive   (C) nibble   (D) rob
_____ 8. (A) discharge (B) blame   (C) reprove   (D) censure
_____ 9. (A) endurance (B) resolution   (C) fortitude   (D) emphasis
_____10. (A) rummage   (B) explore   (C) ransack   (D) search

2 Read the following sentence and write the *letter* of the meaning of the italicized word in the space provided.

_____ 1. At one time, criminals were *flogged* as a punishment.
   (A) confined   (B) killed
   (C) buried   (D) whipped

_____ 2. The value of the jewelry was very *dubious*.
   (A) uncertain   (B) tremendous
   (C) trifling   (D) various

_____ 3. Roman emperors built arches to *commemorate* their victories.
   (A) encourage   (B) record in history
   (C) celebrate   (D) publicize widely

_____ 4. A doctor's life is *consecrated* to curing poor and sick people.
   (A) limited   (B) dedicated
   (C) subjected   (D) depended

_____ 5. You must not *censure* him until you know the whole story about his mistakes.
   (A) reprove   (B) insult
   (C) doubt   (D) despise

_____ 6. The police *ascribed* the automobile accident to fast driving.
   (A) supposed   (B) attributed
   (C) described   (D) illustrated

_____ 7. Instead of fighting, the two nations settled the quarrel in an *amicable* way.
   (A) natural   (B) negotiative
   (C) peaceable   (D) reasonable

_____ 8. Most science books written 20 years ago are now *obsolete*.
      (A) antiquated   (B) more useful
      (C) studied again   (D) very expensive

_____ 9. There seems to be a *vogue* for sailing small boats this summer.
      (A) difficulty   (B) utility
      (C) fashion   (D) request

_____ 10. Rain runs down a *spout* from the roof to the ground.
      (A) flow   (B) dust
      (C) seed   (D) filth

3 In the space provided, write the *letter* of the word that has most nearly the SAME MEANING as the italicized word.

_____ 1. good *posture*   (A) attitude   (B) personality
                                         (C) placard   (D) profession

_____ 2. insect's *abdomen*   (A) harm   (B) instinct
                                         (C) characteristic   (D) belly

_____ 3. *bulwark* of freedom   (A) definition   (B) tyranny
                                         (C) protection   (D) disturbance

_____ 4. the mounted *bandit*   (A) knight   (B) robber
                                         (C) instrument   (D) urn

_____ 5. the *scourge* of Heaven   (A) bliss   (B) delusion
                                         (C) expectation   (D) punishment

4 Fill each blank with the most appropriate word from the vocabulary list below.

VOCABULARY LIST

censure	consecrated	defiled
inconsolable	obsolete	rummaged
huddle	spout	eradicate
groove	meddle	heed

1. One country should not _____ with the internal affairs of another.

2. The police officers _____ the ship in search of drugs.

3. He _____ his whole life to the service of his country's welfare.

4. No tyrant can hope to _____ the love of liberty, which is strongly embedded in men's heart.

Lesson 17

5. The death penalty for theft has long been _____.

6. No one will defend them if they incur public _____.

7. The river was _____ by the wastes poured out of the many factories.

8. He cut a(n) _____ in the wood with a chisel to make the water run off along it.

9. They were warned repeatedly, but they were careless and did not give a(n) _____.

10. The mother cat was _____ because her kitten died a few days ago.

해답

1 1. B   2. C   3. D   4. C   5. D   6. D   7. C   8. A   9. D   10. B
2 1. D   2. A   3. C   4. B   5. A   6. B   7. C   8. A   9. C   10. A
3 1. A   2. D   3. C   4. B   5. D
4 1. meddle   2. rummaged   3. consecrated   4. eradicate   5. obsolete
   6. censure   7. defiled   8. groove   9. heed   10. inconsolable

Lesson 18

PRETEST 18

Insert the *letter* of the best answer in the space provided.

1. The crossroad in front of the school is a *menace* to the _____.
   (A) children's safety (B) traffic rules (C) construction of buildings

2. The girl's dresses showed most of the *hues* of the _____.
   (A) admiration   (B) rainbow   (C) fashion

3. My brother was *absolved* of _____ for the automobile accident.
   (A) cause   (B) prediction   (C) blame

4. The _____ was standing in the *pulpit* to give sermon.
   (A) pastor   (B) shadow   (C) pillar

5. He _____ numerous *fractures* in his fox hunting days.
   (A) captured   (B) suffered   (C) wished

ANSWERS 1. A 2. B 3. C 4. A 5. B

STUDY YOUR NEW WORDS-1

absolve
[əbzɔ́lv]

free from sin, guilt, responsibility; exculpate; clear
v. 면제하다, 해제하다, 용서하다
syn. exonerate
The judge *absolved* the man of the crime.

bias
[báiəs]

leaning of the mind; inclination; preconception
n. 편견, 선입관
syn. prejudice
The umpire should have no *bias* in favor of either side.

contend
[kənténd]

struggle against; fight; argue; contest
v. 다투다, 경쟁하다
syn. compete
Our baseball team is *contending* for the championship.

Lesson 18   207

deplore
[diplɔ́:r]

be very sorry about; regret deeply; mourn; grieve
v. 한탄〔개탄〕하다, 애도하다
syn. lament
We *deplore* the terrible traffic accident, by which 30 persons were killed and 50 injured.

fracture
[fræktʃər]

a break or creck, especially of a bone; split; splinter
n. 골절, 분열
syn. shatter
The boy fell from a tree and suffered *fractures* of his right arm and leg.

magnitude
[mǽgnitju:d]

greatness of size, or importance; extent; mass
n. 크기, 중대(성)
syn. bulk
A crowd of great *magnitude* attended the President's inaugration.

pith
[piθ]

the important or essential part; point; marrow
n. 요점, 심(心)
syn. essence
The *pith* of his speech was focused on the importance of education.

relish
[réliʃ]

a good favor; pleasure; taste; appetite; savor; flavor
n. 흥미, 풍미, 맛
syn. zest
I have no *relish* for seeing people being whipped.

sneak
[sni:k]

move silently and secretly, usually for a bad purpose; go stealthily
v. 몰래 움직이다, 몰래 ~ 하다
syn. lurk
Trying not to be seen, they quietly *sneaked* into the room.

tidings
[táidiŋz]

a message; news; intelligence
n. 통지, 기별, 소식
syn. information
The messenger brought *tidings* from the battlefield.

EXERCISE 1 Fill each blank with the most appropriate word given above.
(Inflect the word if necessary.)

1. The first settlers in America had to _____ with unfriendly Indians, sickness, coldness, and lack of food.

2. _____ of the leg can be very serious in old people.

3. Most newspapers try not to show _____ in their reporting.

4. They say that hunger is the best _____ for food.

5. The book was a work of such _____ that it took 10 years to write.

STUDY YOUR NEW WORDS-2

aghast
[əgǽːst]

filled with surprise, horror, or terror; surprised
adj. 깜짝 놀라서, 소스라치게 놀라서
syn. astonished
Many people would be *aghast* at the thought of another war.

cumber
[kʌ́mbər]

trouble or burden with something useless or unnecessary
v. 방해하다, 괴롭히다, 압박하다
syn. hinder
We shall not *cumber* our thought with his reproaches.

decree
[dikríː]

give an order; order or settle by authority; decide
v. 포고(布告)하다, 판결하다
syn. determine
The city government *decreed* that all dogs must be licensed.

frolic
[frɔ́lik]

play in gay and lively manner; play about joyously
v. 들떠서 떠들다, 야단법석하다, 장난치다
syn. frisk
The children were *frolicking* with the puppy in the backyard.

intercourse
[íntərkɔːrs]

connection; communication; transactions
n. 교제, 교섭, 왕래
syn. relations
There was much commercial *intercourse* between the two countries before World War II.

menace
[ménis]

something that threatens; threat
n., v. 위협(하다), 협박(하다)
syn. intimidation
In dry weather forest fires are great *menace*.

Lesson 18

precipice
[présipis]

a very steep cliff or slope; crag or steep mountainside
n. 절벽, 벼랑
syn. cliff
I was standing on the very edge of a bank, a *precipice* not less than fifty feet deep.

sanctuary
[sǽŋktjuəri]

a sacred place; a temple
n. 성당, 신전
syn. shrine
The church is generally considered as a *sanctuary*.

sprout
[spraut]

begin to grow; shoot forth
v. 싹이 트다(나게 하다)
syn. grow
After a light spring rain, leaves began to *sprout* from trees.

tread
[tred]

set the foot down; walk or step on
v. 밟다, 걷다
syn. trample
She *trod* lightly in order not to wake the sleeping baby.

EXERCISE 2 Fill each blank with the most appropriate word given above. (Inflect the word if necessary.)

1. They have _____ that all the conflict between countries should end.
2. After a shower a meadow _____ with the yellow buds of dandelion.
3. The gunman _____ him with weapons and forced him to give up his money.
4. My friend's suggestion that we should run away from home left my sister _____.
5. Airplanes, good roads and telephones make _____ with different parts of the country far easier than it was 50 years ago.

STUDY YOUR NEW WORDS-3

ammunition
[æmjuníʃən]

supplies of what is needed for firing guns; cartridge
n. 탄약
syn. bullets
The soldiers still had their guns but they were out of *ammunition*.

doting
[dóutiŋ]

foolishly fond; too fond; loving blindly
adj. 사랑에 빠져 있는
syn. fond
A *doting* mother alienates her husband by lavishing too much love on their child.

engross
[ingróus]

occupy wholly; fill up completely; take up attention of
v. 빼앗다, 몰두시키다, 열중하다
syn. absorb
The artist was so *engrossed* in his painting that he didn't notice the people watching him.

gush
[gʌʃ]

a rush of water or other liquid from an enclosed place; stream
n. 내뿜음, 분출
syn. flow
If you got a deep cut in your arm, there's usually a *gush* of flood.

insuperable
[insjú:pərəbl]

too difficult to be conquered or passed; unbeatable
adj. 이겨낼 수 없는, 극복할 수 없는
syn. unconquerable
The deep river was an *insuperable* barrier to those who could not swim.

ordeal
[ɔːrdíːl]

a severe test or experience; tribulation
n. 호된 시련, 고된 체험
syn. trial
Her life has been full of *ordeals*; sickness, poverty, and loss of her beloved son.

pouch
[pautʃ]

a bag; a small bag attached in the pocket; poke
n. 주머니, 쌈지
syn. sack
He kept his tobacco in a leather *pouch* fastened to the belt.

screech
[skriːtʃ]

give a sharp, high scream; cry; shrill
n., v. 날카로운 소리(를 내다)
syn. shriek
The brakes *screeched* and the car suddenly stopped with a jerk.

stature
[stǽtʃər]

the height of a person or thing; elevation; altitude
n. 키, 신장
syn. height
A man who is six feet tall is above the average *stature* in Korea.

undermine [ʌndərmáin]	1. weaken by secret or deceitful means; corrode *v.* 모르는 사이에 해치다 The President's enemies are spreading ill rumors to **undermine** his authority. 2. dig beneath; to wear away the earth beneath, removing support *v.* 밑을 파다, ~의 토대를 침식하다 syn. erode, dig The house is unsafe since the foundations were **undermined** by floods.

EXERCISE 3   Fill each blank with the most appropriate word given above.
(Inflect the word if necessary.)

1. Some people tried to _____ the chairman's influence by spreading ill rumors about him.
2. He heard a(n) _____ of anger from the old woman's room.
3. He was so _____ in his work that he completely forgot the time.
4. The boy was so courageous that he overcame every _____ difficulty and became the leader of his tribe.
5. After the Korean War, the Koreans passed through terrible _____.

STUDY YOUR NEW WORDS-4

assess [əsés]	estimate the value of property; value (at) *v.* 평가하다, 액수를 정하다 syn. appraise Damages from last week's flood have been **assessed** at $50,000.
chamber [tʃéimbər]	1. a room (in a house); a bed room *n.* 방, 침실 syn. room The children searched each and every **chamber** of the house for the cat. 2. a group of lawmakers *n.* 입법자, (국회·의회의) 의원 The Congress of the United States has two **chambers**; the Senate and the House of Representatives.
disdain [disdéin]	treat with contempt; look down on; scorn; contempt *v.* 경멸하다, 멸시하다

syn. despise
Now that she is rich, she *disdains* to speak to her old friends.

espy
[ispái]

catch sight of; see at a distance
v. 찾아내다, 발견하다
syn. perceive
One day Robinson Crusoe *espied* a foot print on the sand.

glossy
[glɔ́si]

smooth and shiny; polished; slick; burnished; sheeny
adj. 광택 있는, 번들번들한
syn. sleek
The beautiful *glossy* coat of the cat shone as it lay in sunlight.

janitor
[dʒǽnitər]

a doorkeeper or porter; caretaker; gatekeeper
n. 청소부, 수위, 문지기, 관리인
syn. doorman
The *janitor* swept the floors and locked up the building every night.

packet
[pǽkit]

a small bundle; package
n. 묶음, 꾸러미
syn. parcel
She bought a *packet* of envelope at the stationary.

pulpit
[pʌ́lpit]

a platform or raised structure in a church from which the minister preaches; desk
n. 설교단
syn. lectern
The eloquent and ornate carving on a church *pulpit* was done by Indian hands.

scorch
[sɔːrtʃ]

1. burn the surface of; parch
v. ~을 눋게 하다, 그슬리다
syn. singe
The meat was black and *scorched* outside but still raw inside.

2. dry up; wither
v. 마르다, 시들어지다
The grass is *scorched* by so much hot sunshine in summer.

surge
[səːrdʒ]

rise and fall as a ship does on the waves
v. 파동치다, 들끓다
syn. rise
The ship *surged* in the stormy seas, rolling and pitching with each wave.

utensil
[ju(ː)ténsil]

an instrument; anything useful for a particular purpose; tool
n. 기구, 도구
syn. implement
Pots, pans and kettles are useful kitchen *utensils*.

> **EXERCISE 4** Fill each blank with the most appropriate word given above.
> (Inflect the word if necessary.)
>
> 1. It is wrong to _____ a man merely because he has no money.
> 2. This is the death _____ where murderers wait to be put to death.
> 3. The committee met to _____ the idea of establishing a new college school.
> 4. She _____ my shirt by setting iron too high for the fabric.
> 5. She turned around just in time to _____ an old friend disappear in the crowd.

STUDY YOUR NEW WORDS-5

bayonet
[béiənit]

a knife or dagger that may be fixed to the end of a rifle; dirk
n. 대검, 총검
syn. dagger
When the soldiers ran out of ammunition, they fixed *bayonets* to their rifles.

compassion
[kəmpǽʃən]

sorrow for the suffering of others; pity; mercy; clemency
n. 동정, 불쌍히 여김
syn. sympathy
Compassion for the orphans caused him to give money for their support.

detain
[ditéin]

1. prevent a person from going away; delay
v. 붙들다, 기다리게 하다, 지체시키다
syn. retard
Lazy boys sometimes are *detained* at school to do extra work after ordinary lessons are finished.

2. hold as a prisoner; confine
v. 구류하다, 억류하다
The police *detained* the suspected thief for more questioning.

faction
[fǽkʃən]

a group or party within a large group; part; side
n. 당파, 도당

syn. clique
A *faction* in our club tried to make the president resign.

hue
[hju:]

ton; tint; a shade of color
n. 색조, 빛깔
syn. color
The diamond shone with every *hue* under the bright sun.

luster
[lÁstər]

1. a bright shine on the surface
n. 광택, 윤
syn. shimmer
He polished the metal until it had a fine *luster*.

2. glory; fame; splendor
n. 영광, 영예
syn. honor
The deeds of heroes add *luster* to a nation's history.

persevere
[pə:rsivíər]

continue steadily in doing something hard; be stubborn; hold on
v. 꾸준히 노력하다, 견디다, 버티다
syn. persist
He *persevered* in his study until he succeeded.

rave
[reiv]

talk wildly; speak in a confused manner
v. 고함치다, 헛소리하다
syn. effervesce
Because of his high fever, the sick man *raved* all night.

slay
[slei]

kill violently; put to death
v. 죽이다, 살해하다
syn. kill
He intended to *slay* his father's murderer.

tablet
[tǽblit]

a small piece of medicine pressed into a flat, round cake; capsule
n. 정제(錠劑)
syn. pill
The doctor told her to take three *tablets* a day.

voluptuous
[vəlÁptjuəs]

delighting in sensual pleasure; fleshly; carnal
adj. 육감적인, 관능적인
syn. sensuous
Nowadays an actress with *voluptuous* beauty seems to be more popular than the one with intelligent look.

EXERCISE 5 Fill each blank with the most appropriate word given above.
(Inflect the word if necessary.)

1. I was _____, partly by the rain, and partly by company that I liked very much.

2. After all ammunition ran out, the soldiers fought with their _____.

3. He belongs to the liberal _____ of the political party.

4. The dancer's movements were slow and _____.

5. The world's main religions all teach us to have _____ for the poor, and those in need.

해답

EXERCISE 1.	1. contend	2. fracture	3. bias	4. relish	5. magnitude
EXERCISE 2.	1. decreed	2. sprouts	3. menaced	4. aghast	5. intercourse
EXERCISE 3.	1. undermine	2. screech	3. engrossed	4. insuperable	5. ordeals
EXERCISE 4.	1. disdain	2. chamber	3. assess	4. scorched	5. espy
EXERCISE 5.	1. detained	2. bayonets	3. faction	4. voluptuous	5. compassion

종합 연습 문제

1 In the space provided, write the *letter* of the word NOT RELATED to the other words on the line.

_____ 1. (A) preoccupied (B) engrossed (C) absorbed (D) supplemented

_____ 2. (A) bereave (B) deplore (C) lament (D) bemoan

_____ 3. (A) instrument (B) utensil (C) facility (D) implement

_____ 4. (A) trial (B) rebuke (C) ordeal (D) tribulation

_____ 5. (A) bias (B) torment (C) prejudice (D) inclination

_____ 6. (A) estimate (B) compensate (C) appraise (D) assess

_____ 7. (A) tablet (B) lump (C) pill (D) capsule

_____ 8. (A) despise (B) reprove (C) disdain (D) scorn

_____ 9. (A) escarpment (B) cliff (C) crack (D) precipice

_____ 10. (A) glory (B) luster (C) desire (D) splendor

2 Read the following sentence and write the *letter* of the MEANING of the italicized word in the space provided.

_____ 1. When the soldiers has used all their *ammunition*, they went on fighting with their swords.
(A) ration (B) weapons
(C) strength (D) bullets

_____ 2. Public tranquility was disturbed by a discontented *faction*.
(A) reality (B) throng
(C) accident (D) clique

_____ 3. Her heart was filled with *compassion* for the motherless children.
(A) sympathy (B) regret
(C) wistfulness (D) sorrow

_____ 4. The priest *absolved* the boy when he confessed he had stolen some money from his father's desk drawer.
(A) exonerated (B) consoled
(C) reproved (D) blamed

_____ 5. Many innocent people were *slain* by the communist during the Korean War.
(A) imprisoned (B) killed
(C) menaced (D) protested

_____ 6. The boy did not reach the *stature* of his father; he was always under his arm.
(A) feature (B) independence
(C) height (D) position

Lesson 18

_____ 7. This matter is not very important, and shouldn't *detain* us long time.
(A) retard (B) embarrass
(C) disdain (D) deplore

_____ 8. Farmers in 1930's had to *contend* against drought and dust.
(A) prevent (B) conquer
(C) struggle (D) censure

_____ 9. In 1845 Daewonkoon *decreed* the expulsion of the Jesuits.
(A) prohibited (B) practised
(C) prescribed (D) proclaimed

_____ 10. Cut a piece of lead or zinc, and observe the *luster* of its fresh surface.
(A) brilliance (B) fraction
(C) pureness (D) groove

3 In the space provided, write the *letter* of the word that has most nearly the SAME MEANING as the italicized word.

_____ 1. *glossy* fur
(A) heavy (B) shaggy
(C) lustrous (D) comfortable

_____ 2. firm *tread*
(A) body (B) footstep
(C) position (D) resolution

_____ 3. gorgeous *hue*
(A) color (B) costume
(C) implement (D) appearance

_____ 4. *pith* of speech
(A) essence (B) manner
(C) necessity (D) divergence

_____ 5. *insuperable* difficulties
(A) not extreme (B) ordinary
(C) unconquerable (D) imaginary

4 Fill each blank with the most appropriate word from the vocabulary list below.

VOCABULARY LIST

surged	deploring	gush
undermine	packet	persevered
bias	hues	sneaked
disdained	detained	faction

1. The honest official _____ the offer of a bribe from the citizen.

2. She _____ in typing assignment despite her exhaustion and her loss of accuracy.

3. He liked old-fashioned ways and had a _____ against progress.

4. The room was decorated in various _____ of blue ranging from light to dark.
5. She tied a ribbon around the _____ of letters.
6. The man _____ about the barn watching for a chance to steal the cow.
7. He got home two hours late and said he had been _____ in the office by some special business.
8. There was a _____ of blood as the wound reopened.
9. The little girl was _____ the loss of her doll.
10. A big crowd _____ out of the baseball stadium.

해답

1 1. D   2. A   3. C   4. B   5. B   6. B   7. B   8. B   9. C   10. C
2 1. D   2. D   3. A   4. A   5. B   6. C   7. A   8. C   9. D   10. A
3 1. C   2. B   3. A   4. A   5. C
4 1. disdained   2. persevered   3. bias   4. hues   5. packet
   6. sneaked   7. detained   8. gush   9. deploring 10. surged

Lesson 18

Lesson 19

PRETEST 19

Insert the *letter* of the best answer in the space provided.

1. Too strong a sense of _____ *hampered* him from enjoying life.
   (A) pleasure   (B) humor   (C) duty

2. They *denounced* him to the police as a(n) _____.
   (A) observer   (B) criminal   (C) witness

3. A strange _____ *pervaded* the garden, like the hush before a storm.
   (A) stillness   (B) odor   (C) feeling

4. They *despoiled* the villagers of their _____.
   (A) diseases   (B) visitors   (C) belongings

5. A(n) _____ provided the only *access* to the attic.
   (A) bandit   (B) ladder   (C) soldier

ANSWERS 1. C 2. B 3. A 4. C 5. B

STUDY YOUR NEW WORDS-1

access
[ǽkses]

1. a way of getting to a place
n. 접근로
syn. approach
The only *access* to the farm house is across the rice fields.

2. the right or privilege to approach
n. 면접, 출입
Only high officials had *access* to the emperor.

beckon
[békən]

sign by a motion of the head or hand
v. 손짓(몸짓)으로 부르다
syn. signal
The guide for visitors *beckoned* us to follow him.

concur
[kənkə́:r]

1. agree; be of the same opinion
v. 일치하다, 의견이 같다
syn. agree
I *concur* with the speaker in condemning every criminal.

2. happen at the same time; come together
v. 동시에〔일시에〕일어나다
This summer two weeks of rain *concurred* with our vacation.

denounce
[dináuns]

speak against in public; accuse; denunciate; damn
v. 공공연히 비난하다, 고발〔적발〕하다
syn. accuse
He was *denounced* as a coward and traitor.

fray
[frei]

1. noisy quarrel; fight
n. 소동, 싸움, 다툼질
syn. combat
The first blow makes the anger, but the second makes the *fray*.

2. make ragged or worn along the edge
v. 닳(게 하)다, 해지(게 하)다
syn. shred
Long wear had *frayed* the collar and cuffs of his old shirts.

hamper
[hǽmpər]

get in the way of; hold back; impede; interfere with
v. 방해〔훼방〕하다, 곤란하게 하다
syn. hinder
Heavy clothing *hampered* the movements of the climbers.

malady
[mǽlədi]

disease; sickness; illness; affliction; complaint
n. 병, 질병
syn. ailment
Cancer and tuberculosis are serious *maladies* in every country.

plod
[plɔd]

walk heavily or slowly
v. 터벅터벅 걷다, 힘들게 걷다
syn. trudge
The old man was *plodding* wearily along the bank of the river.

remnant
[rémnənt]

a small part left; rest; remains
n. 나머지, 잔여
syn. residue
Since the factory moved, this town has only a *remnant* of its former population.

snore
[snɔːr]

breathe noisily when sleeping
v. 코를 골다
syn. wheeze
The child with a cold in his nose *snored* all night.

tinge
[tindʒ]

color slightly; tint; stain
v. 물들이다, 착색하다
syn. tincture
Blood *tinged* the water as he washed his wound.

EXERCISE 1
Fill each blank with the most appropriate word given above.
(Inflect the word if necessary.)

1. The two scientists, working separately and unknown to each other, had reached conclusions that _____.
2. Poor health and lack of money _____ his efforts to get college education.
3. _____ to the mountain towns is often difficult because of poor roads.
4. The preacher _____ war, calling it immoral destruction.
5. _____ of the meal lay on the table when he had finished eating.

STUDY YOUR NEW WORDS-2

ailment
[éilmənt]

pain or disease; trouble; distress
n. 고통, 병
syn. malady
It was necessary for them to have remedies for their *ailments*.

bicker
[bíkər]

quarrel, especially about small matters; argue
n., v. 말다툼(하다), 언쟁(하다)
syn. wrangle
The children are *bickering* with each other about who is the tallest among them.

contrive
[kəntráiv]

plan with cleverness or skill; invent; project
v. 연구하다, 고안(발명)하다, 꾀하다
syn. hatch
The inventor *contrived* a new kind of engine with fewer moving parts.

dazzle
[dǽzl]

hurt (the eyes) with too bright or quick moving light; daze
v. ~의 눈을 부시게 하다, 현혹시키다
syn. glare
The bright light of the motor car on the dark country road *dazzled* my eyes.

fumble
[fʌ́mbl]

move fingers or hands awkwardly in search of something
v. 더듬(어 찾)다, 만지작거리다
syn. grope
She *fumbled* about in her handbag for a pen to write a memorandum.

impair
[impɛ́ər]

make worse; weaken; harm
v. 해치다, 손상하다
syn. damage
Poor food and hard work *impaired* her health and she became thin.

mortify
[mɔ́ːrtifai]

wound (a person's feelings); degrade
v. (기분을) 상하게 하다, 모욕을 주다
syn. humiliate
His parents were *mortified* by their children's bad behavior before the guests.

predominant
[pridɔ́minənt]

having more power, authority, or influence than others; salient
adj. 우세한, 탁월한
syn. outstanding
The United States became the *predominant* nation in the Western Hemisphere.

sanitary
[sǽnitəri]

having to do with health; healthful
adj. 위생적인, 청결한
syn. hygienic
He worked to improve the *sanitary* conditions of slums.

wallet
[wɔ́lit]

a folding pocketbook, usually of leather
n. 지갑
syn. purse
He always keeps a lot of money in his *wallet*.

warrant
[wɔ́rənt]

proper reason for action; guarantee; permit; authority; right
n., v. 근거, 정당한 이유; 보증하다
syn. assurance
Do you consider the wild behavior of the crowd was *warrant* enough for the police to use force?

Lesson 19

EXERCISE 2   Fill each blank with the most appropriate word given above. (Inflect the word if necessary.)

1. The outlaws _____ a robbery of the cargo train.
2. The doctor made sure that the injection needle was _____.
3. Two children ended their _____ and became friendly again.
4. A mother is _____ when her child behaves badly in the church.
5. Coming out of the dark theatre, we were _____ by the bright sunlight.

STUDY YOUR NEW WORDS-3

allocate
[ǽləkeit]

divide and give as shares; assign
v. 할당하다, 배분하다
syn. apportion
The Ford Foundation *allocates* millions of dollars for cancer research.

brawl
[brɔːl]

a noisy and disorderly quarrel; bicker; wrangle
n. 말다툼, 대소동
syn. fight
The *brawl* in the street could be heard in the house nearby.

cynical
[sínikəl]

contemptuous; sneering; unbelieving; suspicious
adj. 냉소적인, 비꼬는
syn. sarcastic
The boys made several *cynical* remarks to cover up their disappointment at being left out of the play.

embellish
[imbéliʃ]

add beauty to; decorate; ornament; beautify
v. 아름답게 하다, 꾸미다
syn. adorn
She *embellished* the simple dress with colorful laces and ribbons.

gallant
[gǽlənt]

brave and high-spirited; courageous; grand
adj. 씩씩한, 용감한, 화려한
syn. splendid
The defense of the Alamo was a heroic action of *gallant* men.

immerse
[imə́:rs]

dip or lower into a liquid until covered by it; merge; immerge
v. 잠기다, 적시다, 가라앉히다
syn. plunge
He *immersed* his aching feet in a bucket of cold water.

ostentatious
[ɔstentéiʃəs]

done for display; intended to attract notice; pretentious
adj. 과시하는, 겉보기로 꾸미는
syn. showy
He rode his new bicycle up and down in front of our house in an *ostentatious* way.

presentiment
[prizéntimənt]

a feeling that something is about to happen
n. 예감, 육감
syn. foreboding
Soapy followed the man with a *presentiment* that luck would again run against him.

satiate
[séiʃieit]

feed fully; satisfy fully; supply with too much; saturate
v. 물릴 정도로 주다, 충분히 만족시키다
syn. surfeit
She was so *satiated* with bananas that she would not even look at one.

undulate
[ʌ́ndjuleit]

move in waves; rise and fall with a wavelike motion; billow; swing
v. 물결치다, 굽이치다, 진동하다
syn. wave
The field of wheat was *undulating* in the breeze.

EXERCISE 3 Fill each blank with the most appropriate word given above.
(Inflect the word if necessary.)

1. It is difficult to make friends with a person who is _____ about friendship.
2. He welcomed his friend in a(n) _____ manner, though he didn't like their visiting really.
3. I felt strong _____ that my belief would finally give way.
4. That space has already been _____ for building a new hospital.
5. The grass was _____ like waves in the field.

STUDY YOUR NEW WORDS-4

apparel
[əpǽrəl]

a person's outer clothing; suit; dress
n. 의복, 옷차림
syn. garment
A shop selling woman's *apparel* is at the corner of this street.

cajole
[kədʒóul]

persuade by pleasant words or flattery; urge
v. 구워삶다, 감언으로 속이다
syn. coax
He *cajoled* his friends into deciding in his favor.

discard
[diskά:rd]

give up as useless, or worn out; throw aside.
v. 버리다, 폐기하다
syn. reject
You can *discord* your old coat but not your old friends.

effete
[efí:t]

no longer able to produce; worn out
adj. 쇠약한, 지친, 무능하게 된
syn. exhausted
During the middle ages, Greek civilization declined and became *effete*.

grudge
[grʌdʒ]

ill will; sullen feeling (against)
n. 적의, 원한, 유감
syn. resentment
She has had a *grudge* against me ever since I disagreed with her.

kidnap
[kídnæp]

steal or carry off a person (child) by force; take away; ravish
v. 유괴하다
syn. abduct
Four men *kidnapped* the little girl, but the police soon caught them and rescued the girl.

pact
[pækt]

a solemn agreement; compact; contract; bargain
n. 협정, 조약, 계약
syn. treaty
There is some hope that a peace *pact* will be signed between the two countries.

pry
[prai]

examine closely and curiously; spy; investigate; snoop
v. 엿보다, 동정을 살피다
syn. peep
She *pries* too closely into the private life of ther friends.

scour
[skáuər]

1. move quickly over in order to search something
v. 찾아다니다, 헤매다
syn. ransack
Men *scoured* the whole country looking for the lost child.

2. clean or polish by hard rubbing; scrub
v. 문질러 닦다, 활보하다
The servant *scoured* the frying pan until it shone like silver.

swagger
[swǽgər]

walk with a swinging movement, as if proud
v. 뽐내며 걷다, 활보하다
syn. strut
He *swaggered* down the street after winning the fight.

vagary
[véigəri]

an unusual, purposeless, or unexpected idea, act or thought; humor
n. 기발한 행동, 엉뚱한 행동
syn. fancy
The building of this house in the shape of the temple was a rich man's *vagary*.

EXERCISE 4
Fill each blank with the most appropriate word given above.
(Inflect the word if necessary.)

1. My father repaired the toy that I had _____ as a useless thing.
2. She was always _____ into other people's affairs.
3. He _____ the town looking for the lost child, but he couldn't find him.
4. My outgoing friends were able to _____ the shy newcomer into attending the party.
5. I always feel she has a(n) _____ against me, although I do not know what wrong I've done to her.

STUDY YOUR NEW WORDS-5

asset
[ǽset]

something that has value; possession; belonging
n. 자산, 재산
syn. property
Ability to get along with people is an *asset* in business.

chasm
[kǽzəm]

a deep opening or crack in the earth; yawn; crater
n. 간격, 갈라진 틈, 깊은 구렁

Lesson 19 | 227

syn. gap
There was a deep political *chasm* between the two countries which nearly led to a war.

despoil
[dispɔ́il]
rob; steal from; spoil
v. 탈취하다, 약탈하다
syn. depredate
The cities of Greece and Asia were *despoiled* of their most valuable ornaments.

facetious
[fəsíːʃəs]
slyly; joking; said in fun; jocular
adj. 익살맞은, 우스운
syn. humorous
I became angry with the little boy at his *facetious* remarks.

hurtle
[hə́ːrtl]
move or rush with great speed; lunge; crash
v. 돌진하다, 부딪치다
syn. dash
The wing of the airplane came off and the machine *hurtled* to the ground.

larceny
[láːrsni]
theft; stealing; the unlawful take or carrying away of the property
n. 절도, 절도죄
syn. robbery
He want to be accused of *larceny*, because he felt comfortable in prison.

pervade
[pə(ː)rvéid]
go or spread throughout; penetrate; diffuse; impregnate
v. 널리 퍼지다, 고루 미치다
syn. spread
He worked so hard that the weariness *pervaded* his whole body.

recant
[rikǽnt]
take back formally or publicly; withdraw.
v. 취소하다, 철회하다
syn. retract
Though he was tortured to make him change his religion, the prisoner would not *recant*.

shambles
[ʃǽmblz]
general disorder; babel; bedlam
n. 수라장, 혼란 상태
syn. confusion
He left his affairs in a complete *shambles* when he died.

taboo
[təbúː]
prohibition; interdiction; restriction
n. 금기, 금지

	syn. prohibition	
	Eating human flesh is a *taboo* in civilized countries.	
trappings [trǽpiŋz]	ornamental coverings for a house; fittings ***n.*** 장식, 치장, 말 장식 **syn.** decorations He wore all the *trappings* of high office.	

EXERCISE 5

Fill each blank with the most appropriate word given above. (Inflect the word if necessary.)

1. The enemy troops _____ the villages of their belongings.

2. The violent wind caused chimney pots and roof tiles to _____ down to the ground.

3. The radio voice was a _____ of several different operator's speaking at once.

4. Many questions and problems that were once _____ are now discussed openly.

5. The subversive ideas that _____ all these periodicals may do great harm.

해답

EXERCISE 1.	1. concurred	2. hampered	3. access	4. denounced	5. remnants
EXERCISE 2.	1. contrived	2. sanitary	3. bicker	4. mortified	5. dazzled
EXERCISE 3.	1. cynical	2. ostentatious	3. presentiment	4. allocated	5. undulating
EXERCISE 4.	1. discarded	2. prying	3. scoured	4. cajole	5. grudge
EXERCISE 5.	1. despoiled	2. hurtle	3. shambles	4. taboos	5. pervade

종합 연습 문제

1 In the space provided, write the *letter* of the word NOT RELATED to the other words on the line

_____ 1. (A) impair   (B) weaken   (C) invalid   (D) injure
_____ 2. (A) cynical   (B) contemptuous (C) effete   (D) sneering
_____ 3. (A) infirmity   (B) ailment   (C) malady   (D) scourge
_____ 4. (A) healthful   (B) consecrated (C) hygienic   (D) sanitary
_____ 5. (A) submerge   (B) plunge   (C) absolve   (D) immerse
_____ 6. (A) hinder   (B) impede   (C) slash   (D) hamper
_____ 7. (A) humorous   (B) facetious   (C) obstinate   (D) waggish
_____ 8. (A) assign   (B) allocate   (C) apportion   (D) allay
_____ 9. (A) contrive   (B) scheme   (C) implore   (D) hatch
_____ 10. (A) ostentatious (B) gaudy   (C) pretentious (D) prominent

2 Read the following sentences and write the *letter* of the MEANING of the italicized words in the space provided.

_____ 1. The teacher was *mortified* by his own inability to answer such a simple question.
   (A) distressed   (B) humiliated
   (C) surprised   (D) satisfied

_____ 2. He is suffering from a strange *malady* for a long time.
   (A) screech   (B) pageant
   (C) sound   (D) ailment

_____ 3. I am not about to *cajole* you into the reception of my opinion.
   (A) beseech   (B) coax
   (C) imply   (D) request

_____ 4. She was *cynical* about her husband's vow to quit smoking.
   (A) distrustful   (B) commenting
   (C) complaining   (D) critical

_____ 5. Whoever violates the *taboo* will be stricken to death by unseen beings.
   (A) regulation   (B) ceremony
   (C) feast   (D) prohibition

_____ 6. The electric wire is *fraying* and could be dangerous to handle.
   (A) worn   (B) burning
   (C) watering   (D) magnetic

_____ 7. He had all the *trappings* of a cowboy, but he couldn't even ride a horse.
   (A) technics   (B) conditions
   (C) ornaments   (D) qualities

_____ 8. The storekeeper *warranted* the quality of the eggs.
    (A) doubted   (B) guaranteed
    (C) examined   (D) worried

_____ 9. She *embellished* her white hat with black belt and pink roses.
    (A) filled   (B) ornamented
    (C) added   (D) exchanged

_____ 10. The *chasm* between England and the American colonies grew wider and wider until it finally resulted in the American Revolution.
    (A) struggle   (B) distance
    (C) gap   (D) difference

3 In the space provided, write the *letter* of the word that has most nearly the SAME MEANING as the italicized word.

_____ 1. *gallant* ship   (A) splendid   (B) floating
    (C) fast   (D) heavy

_____ 2. a street *brawl*   (A) quarrel   (B) accident
    (C) passage   (D) ornament

_____ 3. a trade *pact*   (A) exchange   (B) policy
    (C) relation   (D) agreement

_____ 4. *sanitary* place   (A) sacred   (B) clean
    (C) lonesome   (D) vacant

_____ 5. *pry* about the affairs   (A) wander   (B) creep
    (C) peep   (D) trudge

4 Fill each blank with the most appropriate word from the vocabulary list below.

VOCABULARY LIST

fray	dazzles	beckoned
effete	gallant	mortified
access	pervade	despoil
hurtle	plodded	predominent

1. The only _____ to that building is along that muddy track.

2. The fleet of warships, gaily decorated with flags for the review, made a(n) _____ show.

3. To look straight at the headlights _____ the eyes.

4. His old shirt was beginning to _____ at the cuffs.

Lesson 19

5. In the eyes of priest, God seemed to _____ all of creation in the world.

6. The teacher was _____ by his pupil's poor answer.

7. He stood waiting until policeman _____ him on.

8. The Roman Empire was once strong, but it grew _____ when there were not enough slaves to do all the work.

9. The _____ feature of his character is pride.

10. The old man _____ along the road, hardly able to lift each foot.

해답

1	1. C	2. C	3. D	4. B	5. C	6. C	7. C	8. D	9. C	10. D
2	1. B	2. D	3. B	4. A	5. D	6. A	7. C	8. B	9. B	10. C
3	1. A	2. A	3. D	4. B	5. C					
4	1. access	2. gallant	3. dazzles	4. fray	5. pervade					
	6. mortified	7. beckoned	8. effete	9. predominant	10. plodded					

PRETEST 20

Insert the *letter* of the best answer in the space provided.

1. The fun of playing the game was a greater *incentive* than the _____.
   (A) fighting   (B) participation   (C) prize

2. The spy went in the *guise* of _____ and was not recognized by the enemy.
   (A) monk   (B) sanitary   (C) pretention

3. He *dissipated* his large fortune in a few years of heavy _____.
   (A) working   (B) trial   (C) spending

4. You are always *badgering* me with such a(n) _____.
   (A) amicable greeting   (B) silly question   (C) sincere praise

5. He got too near the _____ and *singed* his long beard.
   (A) door   (B) water   (C) fire

ANSWERS 1.C 2.A 3.C 4.B 5.C

STUDY YOUR NEW WORDS-1

abdicate
[ǽbdikeit]
give up (office, power, or authority); surrender
v. 버리다, 포기하다, 양위[퇴임]하다
syn. relinquish
When the king *abdicated* his throne, his brother succeeded him.

accrue
[əkrúː]
come as a natural product or result; add up; be received; amass
v. (결과로서) 생기다, 발생하다, (이자가) 붙다
syn. accumulate
Ability to think clearly will *accrue* to you from good habits of study.

badger
[bǽdʒər]
keep on annoying or teasing; bother or question persistently
v. 지분거리다, 못살게 굴다, 괴롭히다

Lesson 20   233

syn. tease
That salesman has been *badgering* my father for two weeks to buy a new car.

baffle
[bǽfl]

make effective action impossible by confusing; hinder; thwart
v. 곤란케하다, 당황케하다, 방해하다
syn. bewilder
They succeeded in *baffling* the enemy's attack plans.

conjecture
[kəndʒéktʃər]

guess; speculate; suspect
n., v. 추측(하다), 짐작(하다)
syn. surmise
He *conjectured* that his new stocks would rise on the stock market.

derange
[diréindʒ]

disturb the order or arrangement of; throw into confusion
v. 혼란시키다, 교란시키다, 어지럽히다
syn. upset
The poor woman's mind has been *deranged* for many years.

fiend
[fi:nd]

an evil spirit; a very wicked person; witch
n. 악령, 마귀, 악마
syn. devil
The natives thought the explorer was possessed by a *fiend*.

pine
[pain]

long eagerly; waste away through sorrow or disease; wither
v. 연모〔갈망〕하다, 파리〔수척〕해지다
syn. yearn
The mother was *pining* to see her son and daughter.

smother
[smʌ́ðər]

prevent from breathing freely; kill by depriving of air; throttle
v. 숨막히게 하다, 질식시키다
syn. choke
The gas almost *smothered* the coal miners but they got out in time.

throb
[θrɔb]

beat rapidly or strongly; flutter; palpiate
v. 고동치다, 두근거리다
syn. pulse
The long climb up the mountain made her heart *throb* rapidly.

EXERCISE 1
Fill each blank with the most appropriate word given above.
(Inflect the word if necessary.)

1. The dead man had been _____ by smoke from the chimney.

2. Your heart will _____ when you are excited with terror.

3. The thief _____ our pursuit by locking us in the house before escaping.

4. If you put your money in the bank, interest _____.

5. The origin of the human race is a matter for pure _____.

STUDY YOUR NEW WORDS-2

broth
[brɔ(:)θ]

a thin soup made from water in which meat, fish or vegetables have been boiled
n. 묽은 수프, 고깃국
syn. soup
Many people usually drink hot *broth* when they are sick.

crevice
[krévis]

a narrow split or cut; cranny
n. 갈라진 틈, 균열
syn. crack
Some tiny plants grow in the *crevice* of the stone wall.

demean
[dimíːn]

lower in dignity or standing; humble; debase
v. 품위를 떨어뜨리다, 천하게 하다
syn. degrade
The duke's son *demeaned* himself by doing manual labor with his servants.

foster
[fɔ́stər]

bring up; care for fondly; rear; cherish
v. 양육하다, 기르다, 소중히 간직하다
syn. nurse
We *fostered* the young girl while her mother was in hospital.

incentive
[inséntiv]

a thing that urges a person on; a cause of action or effort; motive
n., adj. 자극(적인), 유발(적인), 동기
syn. stimulus
Our country has prospered by various *incentive* systems.

maze
[meiz]

a network of path through which it is hard to find one's way
n. 미로, 미궁, 혼란
syn. labyrinth
A guide led us through the *maze* of tunnels in the cave.

pore
[pɔːr]

1. gaze earnestly or steadily; study or give close attention to; ponder
v. 자세히 보다, 주시하다
syn. speculate
She *pored* over the picture book in silence enjoying the various colors.

2. a very small opening
n. 세공(細孔), 털구멍
Like human skin, soil has holes that are called *pores*.

rubbish
[rʌ́biʃ]

waste material to be thrown away; garbage; junk
n. 쓰레기, 폐물, 잡동사니
syn. trash
Pick up the *rubbish* and throw it in the garbage can.

speculate
[spékjuleit]

think long and carefully about some subject; consider; reflect
v. 숙고하다, 사색하다
syn. meditate
We don't need to *speculate* about the possible winner in the game.

transfix
[trænsfíks]

fasten or fix by piercing through with something pointed
v. 오금을 못쓰게 하다, 꼼짝 못하게 하다
syn. petrify
Sweet music caught and held him *transfixed* against the iron fence.

EXERCISE 2
Fill each blank with the most appropriate word given above.
(Inflect the word if necessary.)

1. Many books and magazines are filled with cheap, sensational and vulgar _____.
2. After waiting a long time, I opened a little _____ in the door.
3. His interest about my scholastic records gave me a(n) _____ and I worked twice as hard.
4. They _____ about the author's hidden meaning.
5. She was lost in a(n) _____ of narrow winding streets.

STUDY YOUR NEW WORDS-3

anomaly
[ənɔ́məli]

something abnormal; unusual irregularity
n. 변칙, 이례, 이상
syn. abnormality
A bird that cannot fly is an *anomaly*.

converge
[kənvə́ːrdʒ]

tend to meet in a point; be directed towards a single point
v. 한 점에 모이다[모으다]
syn. focus
If you look at the end of your nose, your eyes *converge*.

duplicate
[djúːplikit]

same, selfsame; alike; twofold
adj. 이중의, 한 쌍의, 동일한
syn. double
We have a *duplicate* key to the front door.

epoch
[íːpɔk]

a period of historical time; the starting point of such a period
n. 시대, 새시대, 신기원
syn. age
There were few peaceful *epoches* in the history of our country.

gaunt
[gɔːnt]

very thin and bony; with hollow eyes and starved look; lean
adj. 수척한, 몹시 여윈
syn. haggard
Hunger and suffering from cold had made the lost hikers *gaunt*.

incessant
[insésnt]

never stopping; unceasing; interminable; unending; timeless
adj. 끊임없는, 그칠 새 없는
syn. continuous
The *incessant* barking of the dog kept him awake through all night.

mute
[mjuːt]

without speech; making no sound; dumb; unable to speak
adj. 무언의, 말이 없는
syn. silent
Though the teacher asked a simple question about her parents, the little girl stood *mute* with embarrassment.

partisan
[pɑːrtizǽn]

a strong supporter of a person, party, or cause; zealot
n. 도당, 일당, 열성적인 지지자
syn. defender
He was a passionate *partisan* of these people and had organized a Worker's Union.

scan
[skæn]
v.

1. examine carefully and closely; regard; pore over
(얼굴 따위를) 자세히 쳐다보다
syn. contemplate
The parents of the sick boy **scanned** the doctor's face for a sign of hope.

2. glance at quickly; read hurriedly; skim
v. (신문 따위를) 대충 훑어보다
syn. overlook
She **scanned** the news paper in a few minutes.

stab
[stæb]

pierce or wound with a pointed weapon
v. 찌르다, 꿰뚫다
syn. pierce
He **stabbed** a piece of meat from the plate with his fork.

EXERCISE 3 Fill each blank with the most appropriate word given above.
(Inflect the word if necessary.)

1. Railway lines seem to _____ when one looks at them from a distance.

2. A person's lungs are _____, but he has only one heart.

3. The _____ of his position is that he is very famous, but still doesn't make much money.

4. They _____ the mountain side for any sign of the climbers.

5. The invention of the steam engine marks a(n) _____ in the growth of history.

STUDY YOUR NEW WORDS-4

botch
[bɔtʃ]

spoil by poor work; do something badly
v. (실수하여) 망쳐버리다, (일을) 그르치다
syn. ruin
I tried to cook a nice dinner, but I'm afraid I've rather **botched** it.

chafe
[tʃeif]

make sore by rubbings or scraping; rub to make warm
v. 쓸려서 벗겨지게 하다, 비벼서 따뜻하게 하다
syn. abrade
Her new shoes **chafed** the skin on her both feet.

dissipate
[dísipeit]

1. spread in different directions
v. 소산시키다, 흩뜨리다

syn. scatter

After a brisk morning wind *dissipated* the clouds, the sky was clear all day.

2. spend foolishly; waste on things of little value

v. 낭비하다, 다 써버리다

syn. waste

The foolish son *dissipated* his father's fortune spending in drinking and gambling.

efface
[iféis]

rub out; do away with; wipe out; destroy

v. 지우다, 삭제하다, 소멸시키다

syn. erase

The inscriptions on the ancient monuments have been *effaced* by time.

glint
[glint]

a gleam; sparkle; glitter

n. 섬광, 반짝임

syn. flash

There was a *glint* in her eye that showed she was angry.

iterate
[ítəreit]

say again or repeatedly; reiterate

v. 되풀이하여 말하다

syn. repeat

The girl did not move though the policeman *iterated* his command that she go.

onerous
[ónərəs]

hard to take or carry; oppressive; troublesome; burdensome

adj. 귀찮은, 무거운 짐이 되는, 성가신

syn. arduous

Overtime work is often *onerous*, though it is well paid.

propensity
[prəpénsəti]

a natural inclination or bent; leaning

n. 경향, 성질, 성벽

syn. tendency

Most boys have a *propensity* of playing with machinery.

singe
[sindʒ]

burn a little; sear; scald

v. 태워 그스르다

syn. scorch

Mother *singed* chicken to get rid of hairs.

strut
[strʌt]

walk in a vain, important, or affected manner; parade; prance

v. 점잖빼며 걷다

syn. swagger

The little boy put on his father's medals and *strutted* around the room.

unravel

[ʌnrǽvəl]

solve; make clear

v. 해결하다, (문제를) 풀다

syn. solve

There are many kinds of diseases that medical science is yet to *unravel*.

EXERCISE 4 Fill each blank with the most appropriate word given above. (Inflect the word if necessary.)

1. It takes many years to _____ the terrible memories of war.
2. He is engaged in the _____ job of correcting hundreds of themes a week.
3. The careless boy made so many mistakes making his model airplane that he completely _____ the job.
4. She _____ the meat over a high flame.
5. The candidate _____ about the room like a latter-day Napoleon.

STUDY YOUR NEW WORDS-5

bellow

[bélou]

shout loudly, with anger, or with pain; roar

v. 울부짖다, 울다

syn. shout

He *bellowed* in pain when the hammer came down on his finger.

cloak

[klouk]

1. a loose outer garment with or without sleeves

n. (보통 소매가 없는) 외투, 망토

syn. mantle

The horseback rider drew his *cloak* tightly around him in the rain.

2. something which covers, hides or keeps secret

n. 은폐하는 수단, 가면, 구실

His friendly behavior was a *cloak* for his evil intention.

devout

[diváut]

paying attention to religious duties; devoted to religion

adj. 독실한, 경건한

syn. pious

The ministry was a very *devout* man and devoted his while life to Christian mission work.

guise
[gaiz]

style of dress; outward appearance
n. 옷차림, 모습, 외양
syn. appearance
A man appeared at the castle gate in the *guise* of a woodcutter.

latent
[léitənt]

present but not active; hidden; covert
adj. 잠재적인, 숨어 있는, 보이지 않는
syn. concealed
The power of a grain of wheat to grow into a plant remains *latent* if it is not planted.

pawn
[pɔːn]

leave something with another person as security that borrowed money will be repaid; pledge
n., v. 전당(잡히다), 인질(로 하다)
syn. gage
He *pawned* his watch to buy food until he could get a job.

quake
[kweik]

shake or tremble; violate
v. 흔들리다, 진동하다, 떨다
syn. shudder
When the cannon was fired, the earth *quaked* under his feet.

salvage
[sǽlvidʒ]

the act of saving a ship or its cargo from wreck or capture
n. 해난 구조, 난파선 화물 구조
syn. rescue
After the ship sank, *salvage* of its cargo was impossible.

sequel
[síːkwəl]

that which follows; continuation
n. 계속, 후편, 귀추, 결과
syn. result
Famine has often been the *sequel* of war.

virtual
[və́ːrtjuəl]

being something in effect though not in name; real
adj. 실질적인, 사실상의
syn. actual
The battle was won with so great a loss of soldiers that it was a *virtual* defeat.

wizard
[wízərd]

a man supposed to have magic power; enchanter
n. 요술쟁이, 마술사
syn. magician
He does things that are marvellous or apparently impossible; he is a *wizard*.

EXERCISE 5 Fill each blank with the most appropriate word given above.
(Inflect the word if necessary.)

1. One of the most important aims of education is to develop students' _____ abilities to the utmost extent.

2. His television set is in _____ to pay his room rent.

3. He _____ with pain when the tooth was pulled out.

4. She referred to the expected decease of her mother, and the gloomy _____ of funeral rites.

5. There is nothing new here; just the same old ideas in a different _____.

EXERCISE 1.	1. smothered	2. throb	3. baffled	4. accrues	5. conjecture
EXERCISE 2.	1. rubbish	2. crevice	3. incentive	4. speculated	5. maze
EXERCISE 3.	1. converge	2. duplicate	3. anomaly	4. scanned	5. epoch
EXERCISE 4.	1. efface	2. onerous	3. botched	4. singed	5. strutted
EXERCISE 5.	1. latent	2. pawn	3. bellowed	4. sequel	5. guise

종합 연습 문제

1 In the space provided, write the *letter* of the word NOT RELATED to the other words on the line.

_____ 1. (A) demon (B) witch (C) fiend (D) devil

_____ 2. (A) prediction (B) inclination (C) propensity (D) tendency

_____ 3. (A) stroll (B) strut (C) swagger (D) stutter

_____ 4. (A) relinquish (B) abdicate (C) debase (D) surrender

_____ 5. (A) virtual (B) righteous (C) real (D) actual

_____ 6. (A) surge (B) scorch (C) singe (D) sear

_____ 7. (A) baffle (B) dissemble (C) mystify (D) perplex

_____ 8. (A) quake (B) sting (C) shiver (D) shudder

_____ 9. (A) labyrinth (B) tyro (C) maze (D) perplexity

_____ 10. (A) temporary (B) covert (C) latent (D) potential

2 Read the following sentence and write the *letter* of the MEANING of the italicized word in the space provided.

_____ 1. Sudden illness *deranged* our plan for a trip.
    (A) delayed   (B) amended
    (C) disturbed   (D) influenced

_____ 2. The boy *iterated* his assurances that he would be very careful with my bicycle.
    (A) proclaimed   (B) urged
    (C) stressed   (D) repeated

_____ 3. Tom has been *badgering* his big brother to buy him a new bicycle.
    (A) teasing   (B) demanding
    (C) suggesting   (D) forcing

_____ 4. *Salvage* of the furniture was hampered by the heat of the flames.
    (A) protection   (B) rescue
    (C) alignment   (D) concealment

_____ 5. His mother *scanned* his face to see if he was telling the truth.
    (A) indicated   (B) scrutinized
    (C) carassed   (D) penetrated

_____ 6. Among the *sequels* of party were many stomachaches.
    (A) diseases   (B) expectations
    (C) consequences   (D) foods

Lesson 20

_____ 7. The odd noises and flashes of light in the empty house completely *baffled* him.
    (A) horrified   (B) surrounded
    (C) perplexed   (D) surprised

_____ 8. A young woman of modest *guise* was standing before a shop window.
    (A) appearance   (B) height
    (C) age   (D) behavior

_____ 9. The *incessant* noise from the factory kept me awake all night.
    (A) irritating   (B) shrill
    (C) continuous   (D) uncomfortable

_____ 10. The male bird *strutted* in front of the female bird.
    (A) swaggered   (B) stopped
    (C) crouched   (D) screeched

3 In the space provided, write the *letter* of the word that has most nearly the SAME MEANING as the italicized word.

_____ 1. *mute* letter   (A) capital   (B) last
    (C) silent   (D) small

_____ 2. *latent* period   (A) sluggish   (B) hidden
    (C) facetious   (D) tardy

_____ 3. *gaunt* face   (A) lean   (B) fat
    (C) large   (D) bright

_____ 4. *sequel* of drama   (A) development   (B) performance
    (C) continuation   (D) semblance

_____ 5. *onerous* duty   (A) unique   (B) honorable
    (C) common   (D) arduous

4 Fill each blank with the most appropriate word from the vocabulary list below.

VOCABULARY LIST

conjecturing	pined	converged
demean	efface	baffled
sequel	propensity	cloak
dissipate	transfixed	scanned

1. The attention of all the audience _____ on the screen as soon as the motion picture started.

2. Day and night she _____ for her departed mother.

3. She would never _____ the memory of her dead child.

4. Don't _____ yourself by doing such a dishonorable things.

5. Famine and disease are sometimes the _____ of flood or war.

6. The examination _____ me completely and I couldn't answer it.

7. She looks more attractive in a(n) _____ than in a coat.

8. He had a(n) _____ to blame everything on his little brother.

9. I don't agree with his _____ that the government will lose the next election.

10. He was _____ to the spot when I told him the terrible news.

해답

1 1. B   2. A   3. D   4. C   5. B   6. A   7. B   8. B   9. B   10. A
2 1. C   2. D   3. A   4. B   5. B   6. C   7. C   8. A   9. C   10. A
3 1. C   2. B   3. A   4. C   5. D
4 1. converged   2. pined   3. efface   4. demean   5. sequel
   6. baffled   7. cloak   8. propensity   9. conjecturing   10. transfixed

Lesson 20

Lesson 21

PRETEST 21

Insert the *letter* of the best answer in the space provided.

1. The _____ man was *appeased* when they said they were sorry.
   (A) coward   (B) angry   (C) great

2. More than a thousand people were _____ in the *massacre*.
   (A) gathered   (B) captured   (C) killed

3. She worked herself up into a *frenzy* because she thought she'd miss her _____.
   (A) job   (B) train   (C) baby

4. At last she *surmised* from his _____ from school that there's something wrong with him.
   (A) friend   (B) absence   (C) compliment

5. A leader must take _____ unless he is *incapacitated*.
   (A) example   (B) prestige   (C) command

ANSWERS 1.B 2.C 3.B 4.B 5.C

STUDY YOUR NEW WORDS-1

admonish
[ədmɔ́niʃ]

warn of a fault; advise against doing something; forewarn
v. 훈계하다, 타이르다, 충고하다
syn. advise
He *admonished* his friend not to be late for his work.

bide
[baid]

wait for a long time until the right moment; wait
v. 기다리다, 머무르다
syn. remain
He seems to be doing nothing, but really he's just *biding* his time.

condone
[kəndóun]

forgive (wrong action or behavior); overlook; pass over
v. 용서하다, 너그럽게 보아주다

syn. excuse

A man who cheats on his income tax and on his expense account tends to *condone* these practices in his friends.

designate
[dézigneit]

mark out; point out; select for duty or other position
v. 지정하다, 임명하다, 가리키다
syn. appoint
I *designate* you to act for me while I am away.

fend
[fend]

defend oneself from; take care of; provide for
v. 자신을 지키다[돌보다], 스스로 생계를 유지하다
syn. defend
Most animals let their young *fend* for themselves at an early age.

hardy
[há:*r*di]

able to bear hard treatment; strong
adj. 내구력이 있는, 강건한
syn. robust
Only *hardy* plants will survive the severe cold in the Arctic area.

limber
[límbə*r*]

make flexible
v. 유연하게 하다
syn. supple
Baseball players do exercises at the beginning of the season in order to *limber* themselves up.

philanthropy
[filǽnθrəpi]

love of mankind; practical sympathy and benevolence
n. 박애, 자선, 인자
syn. charity
You must pay in humiliation of spirit for every benefit received at the hands of *philanthropy*.

recollect
[rekəlékt]

remember (something past); call to mind again
v. 생각해내다, 회상하다
syn. recall
Can you *recollect* the name of the author of *Ivanhoe*?

smite
[smait]

strike hard; have a powerful sudden effect on
v. 강타하다, 매혹하다
syn. affect
He was so *smitten* with the view that he stopped and took out his camera.

testimony
[téstiməni]

evidence; a solemn declaration, often one made by a witness in a lawcourt
n. (법정에서의) 증언, 증거
syn. proof
According to the *testimony* of the medical profession, the health of the nation is improving.

EXERCISE 1 Fill each blank with the most appropriate word given above. (Inflect the word if necessary.)

1. He is stiff when he begins to skate, but _____ up easily.
2. These x-marks on the drawing _____ all the possible entrances to the castle.
3. The teacher _____ the boys not to be late for the athletic meeting.
4. A few _____ men broke the ice on the pond and had a swim.
5. The sound of an explosion _____ our ears last night.

STUDY YOUR NEW WORDS-2

ale
[eil]

a kind of beer; an alcoholic drink similar to beer; lager; porter
n. 에일(맥주의 일종)
syn. ginger
He liked the bitter taste of the *ale*; beer is his favorite drink.

blend
[blend]

mix together; mix so thoroughly; mingle
v. 섞다, 혼합하다
syn. combine
Blend the butter and the sugar before adding other ingredients of the cake.

carnivorous
[kɑːrnívərəs]

flesh-eating
adj. 육식(성)의, 육식류의
syn. cannibal
The *carnivorous* animals are characterized especially by large, sharp canine teeth

denizen
[dénizn]

a person or animal that lives in a place; occupant
n. 서식자 (짐승), 주민, 거류자
syn. inhabitant
The common English sparrow is a *denizen* of America; it was first brought from Europe to America about 1850.

frenzy
[frénzi]

near madness; mental derangement; very great excitement
n. 광포, 열광
syn. ferment
She was in a *frenzy* of grief when she heard that her child was missing.

incapacitate
[inkəpǽsiteit]

limit in ability, power or fitness; paralyze
v. 무능력하게 하다, 무력화 시키다
syn. disable
The player's injury *incapacitated* him for participating in the football match.

massacre
[mǽsəkər]

slaughter of people or animals; pitilessly kill without mercy
n., v. 대량 학살(하다), 몰살(시키다)
syn. slaughter
The hunters came from the East to *massacre* the buffalos of the plains, killing several millions in a short time.

ponder
[pɑ́ndər]

think about deeply; consider seriously; muse
v. 숙고하다, 깊이 생각하다
syn. meditate
When I asked his advice, he *pondered* the matter and then told me not to go.

riddle
[rídl]

a puzzling question, statement or problem, usually as a game or pastime; puzzle; conundrum
n. 수수께끼, 알아맞추기
syn. enigma
To the *riddle* "What walks on four legs in the morning, two legs at noon, and three legs in the evening?" the answer is "man".

spank
[spæŋk]

strike with quick force; blow with the open hand; hit
v. 찰싹 때리다
syn. beat
The father *spanked* the naughty child for his bad manners.

totter
[tɑ́tər]

stand or walk with shaky, unsteady steps; falter
v. 비틀거리다, 비트적거리다
syn. stagger
The old man *tottered* across the room and sat sown on the sofa.

EXERCISE 2
Fill each blank with the most appropriate word given above.
(Inflect the word if necessary.)

1. The crowd was in a(n) _____ after the home team scored the winning goal.

2. The king ordered all the infants in the country to be _____.

3. Before casting his vote, a responsible and mature citizen should _____ his choice of candidates.

4. A bartender must know how to _____ different kinds of drinks.

5. The famous _____ of the Sphinx was an enigma that only Oedipus could interpret.

STUDY YOUR NEW WORDS-3

appease
[əpíːz]

make calm or quiet; tranquilize; pacify
v. 가라앉히다, 진정[완화]시키다
syn. placate
He tried to **appease** the crying child by giving him candy.

catastrophe
[kətǽstrəfi]

a sudden, unexpected, and terrible event that causes great suffering; disaster
n. 큰 재해, 대이변, 파멸
syn. calamity
The war was a terrible **catastrophe** in which many people died and many buildings were destroyed.

daunt
[dɔːnt]

cause to lose courage or the will to act; dishearten
v. 주춤하게 하다, 기죽게하다
syn. dismay
He felt completely **daunted** by the difficulties that faced him.

duration
[djuəréiʃən]

length of time; the time during which anything continues; term
n. 지속 기간, 기간
syn. period
He will be in the hospital for the **duration** of the school year.

gape
[ɡeip]

stare with the mouth open; yawn
v. 멍청히 입을 벌리고 보다, 입을 딱 벌리다
syn. stare, gawk
The crowd **gaped** at the daring tricks performed by the tightrope walker.

implore
[implɔ́:r]

beg something for; beseech
v. 애원하다, 탄원하다
syn. entreat
We *implored* him to act before it was too late.

muffle
[mʌ́fl]

wrap in something in order to soften or stop the sound; stifle
v. 싸다, 감아싸다
syn. wrap
She *muffled* her throat in a warm scarf not to catch a cold.

prank
[præŋk]

playful trick; a piece of mischief
n. 농담, 못된 장난
syn. trick
On April Fool's day people often play *pranks* on each other.

saunter
[sɔ́:ntər]

walk slowly and idly; amble;
v. 산책하다, 어슬렁어슬렁 걷다
syn. stroll
Soapy took the umbrella and *sauntered* off with it slowly.

trickle
[tríkl]

a thin flow or stream; ooze
n. 똑똑 떨어짐, 물방울
syn. drip
There was a *trickle* of blood from the wound on his face.

EXERCISE 3

Fill each blank with the most appropriate word given above.
(Inflect the word if necessary.)

1. A land reform program benefited the poor but it was a _____ for rich landowners.
2. She _____ the bell so that it would not awaken the family.
3. She _____ at the tall man, thinking that he might be her younger brother.
4. He served in the army for the _____ of World War I.
5. To _____ my angry neighbor, I offered to make good the damage.

STUDY YOUR NEW WORDS-4

astound
[əstáund]
shock with alarm or surprise; surprise very greatly
v. 놀라게 하다, 아연 실색케하다
syn. amaze
She was *astounded* by the news that she had won the speech contest.

clan
[klæn]
a group of families with a common ancestor
n. 씨족, 일문(一門), 벌족(閥族)
syn. tribe
The people living in that valley are all members of one *clan*.

distort
[distɔ́ːrt]
change from the truth; turn from the true meaning; misrepresent
v. 왜곡하다, 곱새기다
syn. falsify
Newspaper accounts of political and international affairs are often *distorted*.

entrust
[intrʌ́st]
charge with a trust; trust
v. 맡기다, 부탁하다, 위임하다
syn. commit
While travelling, they *entrusted* their children to the care of a baby sitter.

glutton
[glʌ́tn]
a greedy eater; a person who eats too much; gorger
n. 대식가, 폭식가, 탐식가
syn. gormandizer
Sometimes he gets hungry and eats like a *glutton*.

invalid
[ínvəlid]
1. not valid; without force or effect
adj. 무효의, 무가치한
syn. worthless
Unless a check is signed, it is *invalid*.

2. not well; weak and sick
adj. 병약한
syn. patient
He became *invalid* as the result of ill health and lack of exercises.

overtone
[óuvərtoun]
things that are suggested but not shown or stated clearly
n. 함축, 부대적 의미
syn. implication
His words were polite but there was an *overtone* of anger in his voice.

probe
[proub]
search into; examine thoroughly
v. 면밀히 조사하다

	syn. investigate They *probed* his past career to judge his qualifications.
shrine [ʃrain]	any sacred place, such as an altar, church, or temple; holy place *n.* 성당, 성지, 성소, 사당 syn. sanctuary There are many sacred *shrines* in the Near East.
statute [stǽtjuːt]	a law, especially one passed by a lawmaking body; act; measure *n.* 법령, 법규, 성문법 syn. bill The *statute* increased the taxes we must pay.
writhe [raið]	twist and turn; twist about; squirm *v.* (몸을) 비틀다, 몸부림치다 syn. wriggle The wounded soldier *writhed* uncomfortably in pain.

EXERCISE 4 Fill each blank with the most appropriate word given above.
(Inflect the word if necessary.)

1. He _____ the mud, searching for the ring he dropped.
2. His loud voice includes a(n) _____ of anger.
3. He _____ the account of his experiences to make a better story.
4. The _____ for the United States are made by Congress.
5. You have eaten the whole pie; you are really a(n) _____.

STUDY YOUR NEW WORDS-5

behold [bihóuld]	look at; see; witness *v.* 보다 syn. observe Watching the first man land on the moon we *beheld* a sight never seen before by man.
condescend [kɔndisénd]	come down willingly or graciously to the level of one's inferiors in rank *v.* 겸손하게 굴다, 으시대지 않고 ~해 주다

syn. deign

They should change this bad habit and **condescend** to be pleased what is pleasing.

dike
[daik]

1. a bank of earth or a dam built as a defense against flooding
n. 제방, 둑
syn. bank
More than 5,000 years ago the Chinese were controling the Yellow River floods with **dikes**.

2. a narrow passage dug to carry water away
n. 도랑, 개천
syn. ditch
The farmers dug a deep **dike** to carry water to the rice field.

flip
[flip]

toss or move with a snap of the finger
v. (손톱이나 손가락으로) 톡 치다, 튀기다
syn. toss
He **flipped** a coin on the counter to decide whether to go to theatre or not.

grisly
[grízli]

causing horror; frightful; ghastly; gruesome
adj. 섬뜩한, 소름끼치는, 무시무시한
syn. horrible
My uncle who had travelled many countries in the world told a **grisly** story about people who ate human flesh.

knave
[neiv]

a tricky or dishonest person; rascal; scoundrel
n. 악한, 무뢰한
syn. rogue
The **knaves** who set fire to the barn have been caught and sent to prison.

parley
[páːrli]

a talk held between leaders of opposing forces; talk; discussion
n. 회담, 협상, 교섭
syn. negotiation
The general held a **parley** with the enemy's leader about exchanging prisoners.

shred
[ʃred]

a small piece either cut off or torn off; scrap; bit
n. 조각, 파편, 약간, 소량
syn. fragment
There is not a **shred** of evidence that missing money was stolen.

surmise
[səːrmaiz]

form an idea or opinion with few supporting facts; suppose
v. 가정하다, 추측하다

syn. guess

The judge *surmised* his guilt; there was no proof that he killed the man.

vicissitude
[visísitjuːd]

regular change; a change of conditions or circumstances; a turn of fortune
n. 변화, 변천, 흥망성쇠
syn. variety

The future is so uncertain that we cannot know all the *vicissitudes* of our fortunes.

warden
[wɔ́ːrdn]

a person who looks after a place; head keeper; warder
n. 감시인, 문지기, 지키는 사람
syn. watchman

The fire *warden* told us not to light matches near the gas station.

EXERCISE 5 | **Fill each blank with the most appropriate word given above.**
(Inflect the word if necessary.)

1. I _____ open the pages of the magazine to find an interesting article.
2. Her new dress was torn into _____ by herself.
3. The _____ of life may suddenly make a rich man very poor.
4. The future is so uncertain that no one can _____ the course of his rest life.
5. Mrs. Smith has no servant but her husband will never _____ to help her with the housework.

해답

EXERCISE 1.	1. limbers	2. designate	3. admonished	4. hardy	5. smote
EXERCISE 2.	1. frenzy	2. massacred	3. ponder	4. blend	5. riddle
EXERCISE 3.	1. catastrophe	2. muffled	3. gaped	4. duration	5. appease
EXERCISE 4.	1. probed	2. overtone	3. distorted	4. statutes	5. glutton
EXERCISE 5.	1. flipped	2. shreds	3. vicissitudes	4. surmise	5. condescend

종합 연습 문제

1 In the space provided, write the *letter* of the word NOT RELATED to the other words on the line.

_____ 1. (A) investigate (B) prove (C) testify (D) scan

_____ 2. (A) scoundrel (B) bulwark (C) rascal (D) rogue

_____ 3. (A) weigh (B) ponder (C) signify (D) contemplate

_____ 4. (A) gruesome (B) ghastly (C) grisly (D) groove

_____ 5. (A) clan (B) fiend (C) party (D) fraternity

_____ 6. (A) reprove (B) reproach (C) admonish (D) advocate

_____ 7. (A) derision (B) riddle (C) enigma (D) conundrum

_____ 8. (A) pedlar (B) sentinel (C) warden (D) warder

_____ 9. (A) implore (B) fumble (C) beseech (D) entreat

_____ 10. (A) propensity (B) catastrophe (C) disaster (D) calamity

2 Read the following sentence and write the *letter* of the MEANING of the italicized word in the space provided.

_____ 1. The driver *distorted* the account of the fact to escape blame.
(A) illustrated (B) reported
(C) falsified (D) explained

_____ 2. The cat's happy expression bore *testimony* that it had eaten the cream.
(A) doubt (B) proof
(C) experience (D) revelation

_____ 3. We shall seek no terms and we shall tolerate no *parley*.
(A) persuaded (B) rescue
(C) larceny (D) fray

_____ 4. She *implored* her mother to give permission for her to go on the trip.
(A) persuaded (B) suggested
(C) beseeched (D) enforced

_____ 5. The Red Cross appealed to *philanthropy* to save the life of a prisoner.
(A) public (B) charity
(C) justice (D) attorney

_____ 6. The woman was *astounded* to learn that her dearest friend had been spreading bad gossip about her.
(A) surprised (B) irrigated
(C) disappointed (D) cumbered

_____ 7. Jack devoted himself to the protection of the *denizens* of the forest.
    (A) visitors   (B) customers
    (C) merchants   (D) inhabitants

_____ 8. We *surmised* that the traffic delay was caused by some accident on the highway.
    (A) assessed   (B) supposed
    (C) decided   (D) confessed

_____ 9. She tried to *probe* my mind and discover what I was thinking.
    (A) testify   (B) approve
    (C) investigate   (D) flatter

_____ 10. That man has been *designated* by the President as the next Secretary of State.
    (A) appointed   (B) decided
    (C) admitted   (D) recommended

3 In the space provided, write the *letter* of the word that has most nearly the SAME MEANING as the italicized word.

_____ 1. a *vicissitude* of life   (A) variation   (B) condition
                                                  (C) shortness   (D) process

_____ 2. the *ale* house   (A) gold   (B) drug
                                                  (C) beer   (D) log

_____ 3. a *shred* of evidence   (A) appearance   (B) security
                                                  (C) division   (D) bit

_____ 4. *hardy* sports   (A) difficult   (B) robust
                                                (C) important   (D) dangerous

_____ 5. the game *warden*   (A) manager   (B) observer
                                               (C) participant   (D) watchman

4 Fill each blank with the most appropriate word from the vocabulary list below.

VOCABULARY LIST

carnivorous	designate	duration
admonished	distort	implore
daunted	muffled	condescended
fend	testimony	bide

1. The examination questions were rather difficult, but the students were not _____ by them.

Lesson 21

2. He may get a good job if he can _____ his time.

3. We hope the war will be of short _____.

4. Now that his father is dead he must _____ for himself.

5. The colonel's wife finally _____ to visit the sergeant's sick wife.

6. Their guide _____ the mountain climbers to follow him carefully.

7. Sheep and cows are not _____ animals, but lions and tigers are.

8. The pupils presented their teacher with a gold watch in _____ of their respect and affection.

9. The sound of the bell was _____ by the curtains behind the door.

10. The committee will _____ him the winner of the contest tomorrow.

해답

1 1. C 2. B 3. C 4. D 5. B 6. D 7. A 8. A 9. B 10. A
2 1. C 2. B 3. A 4. C 5. B 6. A 7. D 8. B 9. C 10. A
3 1. A 2. C 3. D 4. B 5. D
4 1. daunted   2. bide   3. duration   4. fend   5. condescended
    6. admonished 7. carnivorous 8. testimony   9. muffled   10. designate

UNIT II

(Lessons 22~26)

- Enlarging Vocabulary

through ANTONYMS •

Lesson 22

PRETEST 22

Insert the *letter* of the best answer in the space provided.

1. Some people gather books *haphazard* and without _____.
   (A) consideration   (B) hastiness   (C) random

2. She *rued* very bitterly when she _____ her mother.
   (A) lost   (B) insulted   (C) met

3. Let us be exact in what we say so as to *preclude* any possibility of _____.
   (A) failure   (B) anomaly   (C) misunderstanding

4. The doctor *reproved* the nurse who had been _____ her patient.
   (A) examining   (B) neglecting   (C) caring

5. It was definite that he was to be a passenger on the boat, though he would not be *explicit* about his _____.
   (A) destination   (B) ability   (C) ticket

ANSWERS 1.A 2.A 3.C 4.B 5.A

STUDY YOUR NEW WORDS-1

abhor
[əbhɔ́ːr]

feel very great hatred and dislike for; hate very much; detest; loathe
v. 혐오하다, 몹시 싫어하다
ant. adore
Most people *abhor* the criminal of kidnapping the children.

boost
[buːst]

1. push up from below
v. 뒤에서 밀다, 밀어올리다
ant. lower
If you *boost* me up, I can reach the window easily.

2. an act of promoting or uplifting; encouragement
n. 후원, 응원, 성원
His friend's willingness to help him was a big *boost* to the morale.

detention
[diténʃən]

the act of holding back; detainment; delay
n. 구류, 유치, 저지
ant. release
The jail is used for ***detention*** of persons who have been arrested.

explicit
[iksplísit]

clearly or fully expressed or stated, leaving nothing to be imagined; definite;
adj. 명백한, 뚜렷이 말한
ant. implicit
He gave such ***explicit*** directions that everyone understood them.

invidious
[invídiəs]

likely to cause ill will or resentment
adj. 비위에 거슬리는, 불쾌한, 불공평한
ant. just
Wise teachers avoid ***invidious*** rules against the students.

malign
[məláin]

speak ill of; slander
v. 중상하다, 비방하다, 헐뜯다
ant. praise
You ***malign*** a generous person when you call him a stingy person.

potable
[póutəbl]

drinkable; fit for drinking
adj. 마실 수 있는, 마시기에 알맞은
ant. undrinkable
In place where the water is not ***potable***, they set up purifying system.

rue
[ru:]

be sorry for; regret; repent
v. 슬퍼하다, 한탄하다
ant. rejoice
I never went to school, and I've ***rued*** it bitterly all my life.

subsist
[səbsíst]

keep alive; live; exist
v. 살아가다, 생명을 보존하다, 생활해 가다
ant. decease
People in the far north ***subsist*** chiefly on fish and meat.

unruly
[ʌnrú:li]

hard to rule or control; ungovernable
adj. 다루기 어려운, 제멋대로 구는
ant. manageable
She was such an ***unruly*** child that nobody could get along with her.

> **EXERCISE 1** Fill each blank with the most appropriate word given above.
> (Inflect the word if necessary.)
>
> 1. He was quite _____ about the matter, leaving no doubt what he meant.
> 2. The mayor sued the television station because it _____ him by accusing him of dishonest use of city funds.
> 3. If I ask my sister to turn down the radio she makes it even louder; I can't understand why she is so _____.
> 4. He is in _____ in connection with the bribery affairs.
> 5. _____ me up the trees and I'll get some apples for you.

STUDY YOUR NEW WORDS-2

agile
[ǽdʒail]

active; able to move quickly and easily; lively; nimble
adj. 기민한, 몸이 재빠른, 경쾌한
ant. clumsy
The boy had *agile* mind, and could come up with excuses as quickly as his mother asked for them.

caprice
[kəprí:s]

a sudden change of mind without reason; whim
n. 변덕, 주책 없음
ant. steadfastness
His lack of money was the result of *caprice* in spending on unnecessary things.

disconsolate
[diskɔ́nsəlit]

hopelessly sad at the loss of something without comfort or hope
adj. 수심에 잠긴, 위안할 길이 없는
ant. jubilant
She is *disconsolate* about the death of her father.

fallacy
[fǽləsi]

a mistaken belief; a false idea; an error; delusion
n. 잘못된 생각, 궤변
ant. truth
It is a popular *fallacy* to suppose that riches always bring happiness.

ingenuous
[indʒénjuəs]

frank and open; candid; straightforward; naive
adj. 솔직한, 성실한, 순진한
ant. dissembling
She gave *ingenuous* answers to all of the strangers' questions.

solicitude
[səlísitjuːd]

anxious care; anxiety
n. 근심, 우려, 염려
ant. indifference
The ***solicitude*** shown to him by his neighbors after the robbery impressed him very deeply.

surplus
[sə́ːrpləs]

an amount over and above what is needed; excess
n. 나머지, 여분, 과잉, 초과
ant. deficit
The bank keeps a large ***surplus*** of money in reserve.

> **EXERCISE 3** **Fill each blank with the most appropriate word given above.**
> (Inflect the word if necessary.)
>
> 1. The children laughed with _____ at the circus man's humorous action.
> 2. She broke up her brother's marriage by spreading _____ rumors about his wife.
> 3. However many matches a team wins it should never be allowed to get _____.
> 4. Her silence gave _____ consent when I asked her to go to the dance party tonight.
> 5. They thanked for the _____ of the king over the well-being of their subjects.

STUDY YOUR NEW WORDS-4

abate
[əbéit]

become less strong; decrease; lessen
v. 약화되다, 줄다, 누그러뜨리다
ant. enhance
The doctor gave him some medicine to ***abate*** the pain.

consummate
[kɔ́nsʌmeit]

bring to completion; realize; fulfill
v. 성취하다, 완성하다
ant. baffle
His ambition was ***consummated*** when he won the prize.

dwindle
[dwíndəl]

become gradually fewer or smaller; shrink; diminish
v. 점점 작아지다, 감소되다
ant. increase
Our savings have ***dwindled*** since my wife was sent to hospital.

haphazard
[hǽphæzərd]

not to be planned; random; by chance
adv. 우연의, 되는 대로의, 함부로
ant. deliberate
It is a ***haphazard*** timetable; sometimes lessons happen and sometimes they don't.

obvious
[ɔ́bviəs]

easy to understand; clear; apparent; conspicuous
adj. 명백한, 명확한
ant. equivocal
It is ***obvious*** that a blind man ought not to drive an automobile.

overt
[óuvəːrt]

open or public; not hidden
adj. 표면에 나타난, 공공연한
ant. stealthy
I know only his ***overt*** reasons for refusing; he may have others.

rebuff
[ribʌ́f]

a rough or cruel answer when one is trying to be friendly or is asking for help
n. 거절, 퇴짜, (계획의) 좌절
ant. admission
We tried to be friendly, but his ***rebuff*** made us think he wanted to be left alone.

somber
[sɔ́mbər]

sad and gloomy; have deep shadows
adj. 우울한, 어둠침침한
ant. cheerful
He was sad, and his thought about the future was very ***somber***.

thwart
[θwɔːrt]

oppose and defeat; keep from doing something; frustrate; baffle
v. 훼방놓다, 방해하다
ant. encourage
The boy's lack of money ***thwarted*** his plans for college.

vehement
[víːhimənt]

having or showing strong feeling; caused by strong feeling; eager; passionate
adj. 격렬한, 맹렬한, 열렬한
ant. impassive
I have a ***vehement*** hatred of people who are cruel to animals.

EXERCISE 4 **Fill each blank with the most appropriate word given above.**
(Inflect the word if necessary.)

1. It was a(n) _____ room with dark furniture and heavy black hangings.

2. His happiness was _____ when she agreed to marry him.

3. When he did not drive the car home, it was _____ that he had an accident.

4. Although the rain has _____ somewhat, the wind is still blowing very hard.

5. I was _____ in my camping plans by the cold weather.

STUDY YOUR NEW WORDS-5

benign
[bináin]

having a kind disposition; benevolent; generous
adj. 자비로운, 친절한, 다정한
ant. malign
The *benign* old lady sent us a kind and warm smile.

degrade
[digréid]

reduce to a lower rank, often as a punishment; take away a position or an honor
v. 강등시키다, ~의 지위를 내리다
ant. promote
The sergeant was *degraded* to private for the reason of disobeying order.

ephemeral
[ifémərəl]

lasting for only a very short time; transitory
adj. 하루밖에 안가는, 하루살이의
ant. perpetual
My other writings are very *ephemeral*, but this book will be remembered forever.

illiterate
[ilítərit]

uneducated; unable to read and write; ignorant
adj. 문맹의, 무식한
ant. intelligent
People who have never gone to school are usually *illiterate*.

lavish
[lǽviʃ]

1. very free or too free in giving or spending; prodigal
adj. 아낌없는, 풍부한
ant. stingy
Not every rich man is *lavish* in spending money.

2. give or spend very freely or too freely
v. 아낌없이 주다, 아끼지 않다
It is a mistake to *lavish* kindness on ungrateful people.

peddle
[pédl]

go from place to place trying to sell small goods
v. 소매하다, 행상하다
ant. wholesale
He is the one who is *peddling* the drugs unlawfully.

Lesson 22

reprove
[riprú:v]

blame or find fault with in a gentle way; scold
v. 꾸짖다, 나무라다
ant. compliment
She *reproved* the maid in an angry voice for breaking the dish.

synthetic
[sinθétik]

artificially made; man-made; artificial
adj. 인조의, 인공의
ant. natural
Many kinds of fabrics, furs, and drugs are *synthetic* products.

unbounded
[ʌnbáundid]

boundless; without limits; tremendous
adj. 무한의, 한정되지 않은
ant. limited
His *unbounded* courage and compassion made him an excellent leader of the nation.

wretched
[rétʃid]

very unfortunate or unhappy; miserable; pitiful
adj. 불행한, 가엾은, 비참한
ant. fortunate
He was *wretched* when he failed the entrance examination again.

EXERCISE 5
Fill each blank with the most appropriate word given above.
(Inflect the word if necessary.)

1. Don't _____ yourself by answering such foolish charges against you.
2. The more important a man's position, the more _____ he is in his office job.
3. After the loss of their savings and their home they felt too _____ to see their old friends.
4. Giving money to help the red Cross is a(n) _____ act.
5. He writes in a very _____ way; there are many mistakes on every page.

해답

EXERCISE 1.	1. explict	2. maligned	3. unruly	4. detention	5. boost
EXERCISE 2.	1. ingenuous	2. precluded	3. sheer	4. disconsolate	5. mirage
EXERCISE 3.	1. glee	2. mischievous	3. complacent	4. implicit	5. solicitudes
EXERCISE 4.	1. somber	2. consummated	3. obvious	4. abated	5. thwarted
EXERCISE 5.	1. degrade	2. lavish	3. wretched	4. benign	5. illiterate

종합 연습 문제

1 In the blank space before each word in column I, write the *letter* of its closest ANTONYM in column II.

	COLUMN I	COLUMN II
_____	1. disconsolate	(A) clumsy
_____	2. consummate	(B) release
_____	3. malign	(C) natural
_____	4. illiterate	(D) opaque
_____	5. agile	(E) jubilant
_____	6. synthetic	(F) reality
_____	7. detention	(G) intelligent
_____	8. succinct	(H) praise
_____	9. sheer	(I) dissatisfy
_____	10. mirage	(J) verbose

2 Write the *letter* of the word that, if inserted in the sentence, would agree most with thought of the sentence.

1. They agreed to share in common any _____ of funds after all expenses were paid in full.
   (A) surplus   (B) surpass

2. He is _____ over the death of his favorite wife and weary of his life.
   (A) disconsolate   (B) invidious

3. The principal _____ the boy who had been smoking in the classroom.
   (A) satiated   (B) reproved

4. The boy gave a(n) _____ account of his acts, concealing nothing.
   (A) complacent   (B) ingenuous

5. My mother gave me _____ care and affection in my childhood.
   (A) lavish   (B) prudent

6. If your protest had been more _____, the dealer might have paid attention to it.
   (A) vehement   (B) agile

7. Her decision to wear only blue clothes was pure _____.
   (A) misdemeanor   (B) caprice

8. That politician didn't hesitate to eliminate his political enemies to fulfil his _____ ambition for power.
   (A) unbounded   (B) unruly

Lesson 22

9. The cheer group clapped their hands in _____ at the defeat of their opponent.
    (A) mirage   (B) glee

10. Cotton is natural fiber, but rayon and nylon are _____.
    (A) mandatory   (B) synthetic

3 In the blank space, write the *letter* of the word that most nearly menas the OPPOSITE of the italicized word.

_____ 1. *arable* (A) sterile (B) cruel
        (C) stingy (D) tedious

_____ 2. *ephemeral* (A) consequent (B) hardy
          (C) mute (D) perpetual

_____ 3. *fallacy* (A) success (B) truth
         (C) achievement (D) exploit

_____ 4. *abhor* (A) agree (B) approve
        (C) adore (D) assess

_____ 5. *preclude* (A) exclude (B) contend
         (C) permit (D) deplore

4 Fill each blank with the most appropriate word from the vocabulary list below.

VOCABULARY LIST

glee	ingenuous	abated
peddled	overt	edundant
maligned	wretched	implicit
dwindle	mischievous	lavish

1. The _____ boy went through the house hanging all the pictures upside down.

2. My mother didn't believe that Tom troubled me until she saw him in the _____ act of his pulling my hair.

3. The child shouted with _____ when the birthday cake was cut.

4. What a(n) _____ existence these poor people lead in the slums!

5. He _____ his innocent friend by calling him a robber.

6. The farmer _____ his fruit from house to house.

7. A teacher must give _____ praise to the pupils when they answer the questions correctly.

8. The ship waited till the storm _____ before sailing out to sea.

9. In "We two both ate an apple each." the word "two" is _____.

10. He agreed to give his _____ opinion if his name weren't mentioned in the news story.

해답

1 1. E   2. I   3. H   4. G   5. A   6. C   7. B   8. J   9. D   10. F
2 1. A   2. A   3. B   4. B   5. A   6. A   7. B   8. A   9. B   10. B
3 1. A   2. D   3. B   4. C   5. C
4 1. mischievous   2. overt   3. glee   4. wretched   5. maligned
   6. peddled   7. lavish   8. abated   9. redundant   10. ingenuous

Lesson 22   271

Lesson 23

PRETEST 23

Insert the *letter* of the best answer in the space provided.

1. If there is anything *amiss* in the house, it must be _____ immediately.
   (A) bought   (B) built   (C) repaired

2. There are more feelings of _____ in the *haughty* person than in common men.
   (A) pride   (B) anger   (C) horror

3. His gym shoes were *immaculate* in spite of the _____.
   (A) pavement   (B) rainy day   (C) burden

4. He tries to *dissemble* his _____ by talking repeatedly about how brave he was in the army.
   (A) courage   (B) cowardice   (C) guilty

5. His death was *retarded* several days by the _____ of his doctor.
   (A) negligence   (B) condition   (C) skill

ANSWERS 1. C 2. A 3. B 4. B 5. C

STUDY YOUR NEW WORDS-1

blithe | happy and cheerful; gay; joyful
[blaið] | *adj.* 즐거운, 유쾌한, 쾌활한
           | ant. miserable
           | She continued to work in a *blithe* spirit in spite of all difficulties.

dejected | in low spirits; sad; discouraged; depressed
[didʒéktid] | *adj.* 낙담한, 기운 없는, 풀없는
              | ant. exuberant
              | She was feeling *dejected* and unhappy until the good news cheered her up.

erratic | not steady; unconstant; irregular; uncertain
[irǽtik] | *adj.* 일정치 않은, 변덕스러운, 불규칙적인

ant. regular

He is an *erratic* fellow whose actions are usually completely unpredicatable.

immaculate
[imǽkjulit]

without a spot or stain; absolutely clean; pure
adj. 청순한, 맑고 깨끗한, 순결한
ant. filthy

When he was a child his life contained noble ambitions and *immaculate* thought.

loathe
[louð]

hate very much; feel strong dislike and disgust for; abhor
v. 몹시 싫어하다, 진저리내다
ant. admire

The little girl *loathed* to leave her mother for studying abroad.

pensive
[pénsiv]

thoughtful in a serious or sad way; meditative; reflective
adj. 생각에 잠긴, 시름에 잠긴 듯한
ant. airy

The woman in this painting has a *pensive* smile.

retard
[ritá:rd]

make slow; cause to happen later; delay
v. 늦어지게 하다, 지체시키다
ant. accelerate

I was *retarded* from keeping an appointment by a business conference that lasted most of the day.

shun
[ʃʌn]

avoid with determination; keep away from; eschew
v. 피하다, 비키다
ant. encounter

During his illness he *shunned* all society, and in particular those who had been his dearest friends.

stalwart
[stɔ́:lwərt]

strongly and stoutly built; sturdy; courageous; valient
adj. 튼튼한, 건장한
ant. feeble

She was proud of her *stalwart*, good-looking grandson.

EXERCISE 1   Fill each blank with the most appropriate word given above.
(Inflect the word if necessary.)

1. Her husband simply _____ whatever food she cooked for him without any reason.

2. Cold weather and insufficient rain have _____ the growth of the crops.

3. The teacher was _____ because one of his students failed to greet him on the street.

4. The coward soldier _____ hazardous duty by pretending to be sick.

5. He made up his mind to separate from the _____ girl who proved to be inconstant in human relations.

STUDY YOUR NEW WORDS-2

audible
[ɔ́:dəbl]

loud enough to be heard; hearable
adj. 들리는, 청취할 수 있는
ant. inaudible
They quarreled with such a loud noise that their voice was *audible* to the neighbors.

auspicious
[ɔ:spíʃəs]

with signs of success; favorable; propitious
adj. 길조의, 상서로운, 행운의
ant. unfavorable
The new boy had an *auspicious* first day in the elementary school.

elation
[iléiʃən]

high spirits; joy or pride; exultancy; gladness
n. 의기 양양
ant. depression
She was filled with *elation* at the news that she won the first prize in her class.

haughty
[hɔ́:ti]

having too much pride; arrogant; too proud of oneself and too scornful of others
adj. 오만한, 거만한, 도도한, 건방진
ant. modest
The *haughty* man thinks highly of himself while holding others in contempt.

jeopardy
[dʒépərdi]

danger; risk; peril
n. 위험, 위난(危難)
ant. safety
The officer's violation of a regulation is more *jeopardy* than the enlished man's offense.

mandatory
[mǽndətəri]

required by a command or order; compulsory; obligatory
adj. 의무적인, 강제적인, 명령의
ant. optional
It is *mandatory* to pay a debt within a certain period of time.

rebuke
[ribjú:k]

reprove; reproach; express disapproval of
v. 비난하다, 꾸짖다
ant. praise
The teacher ***rebuked*** the student for throwing the examination paper on the floor.

sparse
[spɑːrs]

scattered; with few members; scanty; occurring here and there.
adj. 성긴, 드문드문한, 희박한
ant. dense
Not many people came to see the game; the ***sparse*** crowd scattered thinly through the stadium.

undue
[ʌndjú:]

too much; excessive; not reasonable
adj. 지나친, 과도의, 부당한
ant. reasonable
A miser gives ***undue*** importance to making and saving money.

EXERCISE 2
Fill each blank with the most appropriate word given above.
(Inflect the word if necessary.)

1. They threw the dice on the ground; the letter "7" was a(n) _____ sign that the victory would be theirs.

2. A(n) _____ girl is always unpopular among her friends at school.

3. She spoke in such a low voice that her quiet remarks were barely _____.

4. It is a(n) _____ regulation that we must keep silence in the school library.

5. The man's life was in _____ when the tree fell suddenly.

STUDY YOUR NEW WORDS-3

allay
[əléi]

make (fear, anger, doubt) less; put at rest; quiet; pacify; alleviate
v. 가라앉히다, 누그러뜨리다, 완화시키다
ant. intensify
The doctor's friendly manner helped the patient ***allay*** his fears.

carnal
[kɑ́ːrnəl]

of the flesh; bodily; sensual
adj. 육체의, 육욕의
ant. spiritual
Gluttony and drunkenness have been called ***carnal*** vices.

defunct
[difʌ́ŋkt]

no longer in existence; dead; extinct; deceased
adj. 죽은, 소멸한, 현존하지 않는
ant. existent
A family name becomes *defunct* when the only heir dies without any son.

feasible
[fí:zəbl]

that can be done easily; practicable
adj. 실행할 수 있는, 가능한
ant. impractical
Of the many plans submitted, the committee selected the plan that seemed most *feasible*.

ingenuity
[indʒinjú(:)əti]

skill in planning or inventing; cleverness
n. 발명의 재주, 재간, 현명함
ant. stupidity
The boy showed *ingenuity* in making toys out of scraps of discarded wood.

mirth
[mə:rθ]

merriness and gaiety expressed by laughter
n. 명랑, 유쾌, 쾌락
ant. grief
My joke caused a great deal of *mirth* among the little children.

precarious
[prikɛ́əriəs]

unsafe; not firm or steady; full of danger; perilous; hazardous
adj. 위험한, 불안한
ant. safe
Soldiers on the battlefield lead a *precarious* life.

preordain
[prìːɔːrdéin]

predetermine; fix or decide before the beginning
v. 예정하다, 미리 정하다
ant. improvise
Some people believe that fate has *preordained* whether they will be happy or unhappy.

taciturn
[tǽsitəːrn]

saying very little; not fond of talking; uncommunicative; silent
adj. 말이 없는, 무언의, 입이 무거운
ant. loquacious
At the council board he was *taciturn* and never opened his lips.

venomous
[vénəməs]

poisonous; malicious; vindictive
adj. 독이 있는, 악의에 찬, 원한을 품고 있는
ant. benevolent
His eldest brother died after the *venomous* bite from the rattlesnake.

EXERCISE 3 Fill each blank with the most appropriate word given above.
(Inflect the word if necessary.)

1. The famous restaurant began to decline after the death of the host and now became _____.

2. Your explanation sounds _____, but I'm not sure I believe it.

3. His fears were _____ by the news that his family was safe in the storm.

4. His whole face was laughing; his face was full of _____.

5. You should be careful to drive on a(n) _____ path that winds its way along the mountainside.

STUDY YOUR NEW WORDS-4

amiss
[əmís]
improper; wrong; out of order
adj. 나쁜, 잘못된
ant. proper
The doctor said there was nothing *amiss* with her.

comprise
[kəmpráiz]
be made up of; consist of; include
v. 함유하다, 포함하다
ant. omit
This anthology *comprises* samples from the work of ten authors.

dissemble
[disémbl]
conceal one's real feelings, or thoughts; disguise; dissimulate
v. 숨기다, 감추다, 속이다
ant. disclose
Families that quarrel in the privacy of the home do well to *dissemble* when they go out to dinner.

glib
[glib]
speaking easily and smoothly; voluble; fluent; garrulous
adj. 입심 좋은, 그럴듯한
ant. terse
A *glib* door-to-door salesman sold her a set of books that she did not want.

invincible
[invínsəbl]
too strong to be conquered; indomitable; insuperable
adj. 정복할 수 없는, 난공불락의
ant. conquerable
Before World War II, the French thought their Maginot Line as an *invincible* bulwark against German invasion.

perfunctory
[pərfʌ́ŋktəri]

done hastily and without thought, interest, or care; mechanical; indifferent
adj. 형식적인, 마지못한, 기계적인
ant. meticulous
The lazy little boy gave his face a *perfunctory* washing.

replete
[riplíːt]

abundantly supplied; filled; full; abounding
adj. 가득찬, 충분한, 포식한
ant. vacuous
The Disney Land tour was *replete* with unexpected thrills and suspense.

solicit
[səlícit]

ask earnestly; try to get; beg; request
v. 간청하다, 졸라대다, 요구하다
ant. respond
We respectfully *solicit* your continuous friendship and patronage.

thraldom
[θrɔ́ːldəm]

bondage; slavery
n. 속박, 노역(奴役), 노예의 신분
ant. liberty
The nation will be soon liberated from the foulest *thraldom*.

wilt
[wílt]

cause to become less fresh and start to die; wither
v. 시들다, 이울다, 약해지다
ant. thrive
Give the flowers some water regularly, or they will *wilt*.

EXERCISE 4 Fill each blank with the most appropriate word given above.
(Inflect the word if necessary.)

1. Columbus had a(n) _____ belief that he would reach land by sailing west.

2. The United Kingdom _____ England, Wales, Scotland and Northern Ireland.

3. The hungry beggar felt _____ with food and drink, then sleepy.

4. The teacher _____ the earnest attention of his students to see the map on the blackboard.

5. From his angry looks, I knew something had gone _____ while I was away.

STUDY YOUR NEW WORDS-5

abominable
[əbɔ́mɪnəbl]

causing great dislike; hateful; detestable; disgusting; abhorrent
adj. 지긋지긋하게 싫은, 혐오할 만한
ant. admirable
That *abominable* place was so dirt and evil smelling that he turned away in disgust.

brainy
[bréini]

intelligent; clever
adj. 머리가 좋은
ant. silly
Brainy students could understand easily what the teacher explained to them.

deteriorate
[ditíəriəreit]

become worse; lessen in character
v. 악화되다, 나빠지다, 저하시키다
ant. ameliorate
As the morning progressed the weather *deteriorated* more and more.

exquisite
[ékskwizit]

very lovely; very finely made or done; delicate
adj. 절묘한, 우미한, 정교한
ant. common
In German he was an *exquisite* stylist, and he brought to that language a new sensitivity in the art of storytelling.

incurable
[inkjúərəbl]

cannot be cured or remedied
adj. 치료할 수 없는, 낫지 않는, 불치의
ant. remediable
Cancer is no more an *incurable* disease nowadays; it can be remedied by using radioactivity.

manual
[mǽnjuəl]

1. of or using the hands; done with hands
adj. 손의, 손으로 하는
ant. spiritual
Manual workers often earn more than office workers.

2. a book that helps its readers to understand or use something; handbook
n. 소책자, 편람, 입문서
This workbook has a teacher's *manual* in which examination problems and their answers are included.

potential
[pəténʃəl]

existing in possibility; latent; covert
adj. 가능성이 있는, 잠재적인
ant. exposed
He is a *potential* leader to control this large state.

Lesson 23

ruthless
[rúːθlis]

having no pity; showing no mercy; cruel; merciless; relentless
adj. 무정한, 인정머리 없는, 잔인한
ant. lenient
They are such *ruthless* parents that they never give presents to the children on Christmas Day.

vociferous
[vousífərəs]

shouting; loud and noisy; clamoring
adj. 소란한, 왁자지껄한, 시끄러운
ant. tranquil
Theatre lobbies were filled with a *vociferous* crowd during the intermission.

voluble
[vɔ́ljubl]

ready to talk much; having the habit of talking much; talkative
adj. 수다스러운, 변설좋은
ant. taciturn
Her explanations for failure to do the work were *voluble* but not easily believed.

EXERCISE 5
Fill each blank with the most appropriate word given above.
(Inflect the word if necessary.)

1. The _____ white fur coat that the lady has on is very expensive.
2. There is a(n) _____ danger of being bitten when one plays with a strange dog.
3. What a(n) _____ thing is this to treat the little boy so relentlessly!
4. Mother tried to control the unruly screaming and shouting of her _____ child.
5. Machine _____ rapidly in its function if it is not taken care of by the users.

해답

EXERCISE 1.	1. loathed	2. retarded	3. dejected	4. shuns	5. erratic
EXERCISE 2.	1. auspicious	2. haughty	3. audible	4. mandatory	5. jeopardy
EXERCISE 3.	1. defunct	2. feasible	3. allayed	4. mirth	5. precarious
EXERCISE 4.	1. invincible	2. comprises	3. replete	4. solicited	5. amiss
EXERCISE 5.	1. exquisite	2. potential	3. ruthless	4. vociferous	5. deteriorates

종합 연습 문제

1 In the blank space before each word in column I, write the *letter* of its closest ANTONYM in column II.

COLUMN I	COLUMN II
_____ 1. modest	(A) taciturn
_____ 2. elation	(B) filthy
_____ 3. voluble	(C) jeopardy
_____ 4. miserable	(D) preordain
_____ 5. ingenuity	(E) depression
_____ 6. stalwart	(F) stupidity
_____ 7. undue	(G) blithe
_____ 8. improvise	(H) reasonable
_____ 9. immaculate	(I) haughty
_____ 10. safety	(J) feeble

2 Write the *letter* of the word that, if inserted in the sentence, would agree most with thought of the sentence.

1. The new nurse was _____; she did not really care about her work.
   (A) perfunctory   (B) auspicious

2. The nobles used to treat the common people with _____ contempt.
   (A) undue   (B) sparse

3. All the flowers are _____ for lack of sunshine and water.
   (A) wilting   (B) wielding

4. In trying to solve the problem we seem to have exhausted all the _____ that the brain of man could suggest.
   (A) ingenuity   (B) ingenuousness

5. The queen's table was set with _____ dishes and silvers.
   (A) exquisite   (B) meticulous

6. He is a(n) _____ person who favored the baseball one day and opposed it the next.
   (A) erratic   (B) clumsy

7. Their cruel treatment of prisoners was so _____ that we couldn't see anymore.
   (A) invincible   (B) abominable

8. The manager _____ the clerk for the negligence of his duty.
   (A) rebuked   (B) rebuffed

Lesson 23

9. Christmas is a time of _____, especially for children.
   (A) misery (B) mirth

10. He _____ his hate by a false show of friendliness and reluctant smile.
    (A) disgusted (B) dissembled

3 In the blank space, write the *letter* of the word that most nearly menas the OPPOSITE of the italicized word.

_____ 1. *retard* the progress of   (A) detain   (B) hinder
                                          (C) abandon   (D) accelerate

_____ 2. *sparse* hair   (A) soft   (B) straight
                                          (C) dense   (D) curved

_____ 3. *invincible* courage   (A) visible   (B) cowardly
                                          (C) limited   (D) conquerable

_____ 4. *mandatory* order   (A) equivocal   (B) optional
                                          (C) compulsory   (D) inconsistent

_____ 5. *glib* answer   (A) uncertain   (B) loquacious
                                          (C) taciturn   (D) sincere

4 Fill each blank with the most appropriate word from the vocabulary list below.

VOCABULARY LIST		
jeopardies	replete	invincible
pensive	comprises	potential
voluble	amiss	precarious
ruthless	retarded	shun

1. A virtuous man will _____ evil companions and practices.

2. His course of graduate study _____ English, mathematics, and management.

3. She was in a(n) _____ mood, and sat down alone staring out the window.

4. The good and the evil are _____ character within each person.

5. Something must be _____ with a boy if he doesn't eat anything for days.

6. Ted is a(n) _____ speaker at meetings; he doesn't give much chance to others to say anthing.

7. The earliest pioneers in the West confronted a great many _____.

8. The climber had only a(n) _____ hold on the slipping rock.

9. The new apartment house is _____ with every modern furniture.

10. Economic progress in Latin America has been consistently _____ by a high birthrate.

해답

1	1. I	2. E	3. A	4. G	5. F	6. J	7. H	8. D	9. B	10. C
2	1. A	2. A	3. A	4. A	5. A	6. A	7. B	8. A	9. B	10. B
3	1. D	2. C	3. D	4. B	5. C					
4	1. shun	2. comprises	3. pensive	4. potential	5. amiss					
	6. voluble	7. jeopardies	8. precarious	9. replete	10. retarded					

Lesson 23

Lesson 24

PRETEST 24

Insert the *letter* of the best answer in the space provided.

1. The stranger's *derogatory* remarks about the town and its people made him _____.
   (A) stupid   (B) unpopular   (C) honest

2. The motorist was *acquitted* of _____; he was thereupon absolved from any claim for damages.
   (A) reckless driving   (B) witness   (C) suffering from the wound

3. One's childhood life seems happier in *retrospect* than in _____.
   (A) fancy   (B) reality   (C) adulthood life

4. A man may utter an *insolent* remark; he may be _____ of his associates.
   (A) cautious   (B) considerate   (C) contemptuous

5. The *acme* of the development of space ships probably lies in the _____.
   (A) future   (B) fortitude   (C) sagacity

ANSWERS 1. B 2. A 3. B 4. C 5. A

STUDY YOUR NEW WORDS-1

bleak
[bli:k]

cold and cheerless; without shelter from cold winds
adj. 황폐한, 쓸쓸한, 차가운
ant. cheerful
The weather in early December was *bleak* and unpleasant.

castigate
[kǽstigeit]

punish or scold severly in order to correct; rebuke; criticize
v. 징계하다, 혹평하다
ant. applaud
The electric inspector was *castigated* for having failed to check the wire as he was supposed to.

284 TOEFL·TOEIC·TEPS 중급 College Vocabulary

enmity
[énməti]

the state of feeling of being an enemy; hatred; hostility; animosity
n. 증오, 적의, 불화
ant. sympathy
We should overcome the worst that the tyrant's *enmity* can do.

impartial
[impá:rʃəl]

giving equal attention to all concerned; fair; not partial
adj. 편견 없는, 공평한
ant. prejudiced
In any case, parents should be *impartial* to their every child.

lucid
[lú:sid]

1. easy to follow or understand; plain
adj. 알기 쉬운, 간단 명료한
The teacher asked me to give a *lucid* explanation of my being late for class.

2. clear in intellect; same; rational
adj. 의식이 명료한, 제정신의
ant. obscure
The old man is confused most of the time but he does have *lucid* moments.

perpendicular
[pə:rpendíkjulər]

exactly upright; vertical; erect
adj. 수직의, 직각을 이루는
ant. horizontal
A square has 90-degree angles made by its four *perpendicular* sides.

retrospect
[rétrouspekt]

the act of looking back towards the past; thinking about the past
n. 회고, 회상
ant. prospect
My *retrospect* of life recalls to my view many good opportunities neglected.

sagacity
[səgǽsəti]

good judgment and understanding; wisdom; mental acuteness; shrewdness
n. 총명, 영민
ant. folly
The politician showed a good *sagacity* in avoiding the mistakes he'd made in the previous campaign.

urbane
[ə:rbéin]

having very good manners; refined; courteous
adj. 세련된, 품위있는
ant. vulgar
Urbane speech is educated speech, as distinguished from the speech of the ignorant.

EXERCISE 1 Fill each blank with the most appropriate word given above.
(Inflect the word if necessary.)

1. The _____ between Arabs and Israelis threatened to break into open war at any time.
2. The tree was leaning against the house and no longer _____.
3. A neutral observer, not a participant, asked for a(n) _____ account of how the fight started.
4. Lonely and ill, the old woman having no children faced a(n) _____ future.
5. Impartiality as well as _____ is required to be a good judge.

STUDY YOUR NEW WORDS-2

ardent
[á:rdənt]

full of zeal; very enthusiastic; eager
adj. 열심인, 격렬한
ant. impassive
After reading about the lives of several great Americans, John became an *ardent* student of American history.

derogatory
[diróɡətəri]

showing or causing lack of respect; disparaging; belittling
adj. 손상시키는, 가치를 떨어뜨리는
ant. enhancive
I can't bear his *derogatory* remarks about my brother's character.

discretion
[diskréʃən]

1. the quality of being discreet; good judgment
n. 신중, 사려, 분별력
ant. recklessness
I won't tell you what time to leave; you're old enough to use your own *discretion*.

2. freedom to judge or choice
n. 자유 재량, 판단의 자유
The house of the meetings will be fixed at the chairman's *discretion*.

hilarious
[hilέəriəs]

full of laughter; very merry; noisily gay; mirthful
adj. 들든, 명랑한, 들떠서 떠드는
ant. depressed
The party got quite *hilarious* after they brought more wine.

paramount [pǽrəmaunt]	supreme; predominant; chief in importance *adj.* 최고의, 지상(至上)의, 주요한 ant. mediocre It is a *paramount* responsibility of every officer to take care of his men before caring for himself.
recede [risíːd]	move back or away; retreat; retire *v.* (뒤로) 멀어지다, 퇴각하다, 물러나다 ant. approach Houses and trees seem to *recede* as we ride past in a train.
rife [raif]	widespread; common; numerous; prevalent *adj.* 매우 많은, 풍부한 ant. scanty The whole city was *rife* with rumors of political corruption and bribery.
spontaneous [spɔntéinjəs]	caused by natural impulse or desire; of one's own choice; voluntary *adj.* 자발적인, 자진해서 하는 ant. compulsive Both sides burst into *spontaneous* cheers at the magician's skillful tricks.
tenuous [ténjuəs]	very thin or slender; not dense; rare *adj.* 희박한, 엷은, 묽은 ant. thick The air ten miles above the earth is very *tenuous*.

EXERCISE 2 Fill each blank with the most appropriate word given above.
(Inflect the word if necessary.)

1. You must show more _____ in choosing your friends.
2. We consider lack of morale as the _____ cause for our defeat.
3. We thought his mistake was the most _____ joke we'd ever heard.
4. A pile of oily rags will sometimes breaks into a(n) _____ flame.
5. Superstition is still _____ in some underdeveloped countries.

STUDY YOUR NEW WORDS-3

acme
[ǽkmi]

the highest point; culmination; climax
n. 정상, 정점, 전성기
ant. bottom
A baseball player usually reaches the *acme* of his skill before he is thirty.

candor
[kǽndər]

fairness; impartiality; frankness and sincerity
n. 공정, 정직, 솔직
ant. feint
He spared no one's feelings and expressed his views with great *candor*.

dissuade
[diswéid]

persuade not to do something
v. 단념시키다, 못하게 말리다
ant. persuade
The father finally *dissuaded* his son from leaving school.

gratuitous
[grətjú(:)itəs]

not deserved or necessary; uncalled-for
adj. 그럴 필요 없는, 이유 없는, 무료의
ant. warranted
Her advice was quite *gratuitous*; I can think for myself.

impeach
[impíːtʃ]

accuse of wrong conduct
v. 탄핵하다, 고소하다
ant. exonerate
The House of Representatives has the sole power to *impeach* an officer of the United States Government.

ostensible
[ɔsténsəbl]

according to appearance; apparent
adj. 외면의, 표면의, 거죽만의
ant. substantial
Her *ostensible* purpose was to borrow some sugar, but she really want to see her neighbor's new furniture.

paltry
[pɔ́ːltri]

worthless; unimportant; worthlessly small; trivial
adj. 무가치한, 하찮은, 얼마 안 되는
ant. significant
The poor painter sold his paintings for a *paltry* sum of money.

sordid
[sɔ́ːrdid]

dirty; filthy
adj. 더러운, 지저분한
ant. clean
The poor family lived in a *sordid* long cabin in the valley.

tidy
[táidi]

neatly arranged; orderly
adj. 말쑥한, 정연한, 정돈된
ant. chaotic
She makes it a rule to keep her room neat and *tidy* after coming back from school.

EXERCISE 3 Fill each blank with the most appropriate word given above.
(Inflect the word if necessary.)

1. When he became prime minister, he reaches the _____ of his hopes.

2. The father _____ the boy from being a doctor, but persuaded him to be a politician.

3. The team felt cheat and challenged the umpire to prove his _____.

4. Were it not for your _____ interference, the children would have quickly settled their dispute.

5. My daughter is very _____ and never goes out without combing her hair.

STUDY YOUR NEW WORDS-4

aloof
[əlúːf]

at a distance but within view; apart
adv. 멀리 떨어져, 멀리서
ant. nearly
One tall boy stood *aloof* from all the small children.

cardinal
[káːrdinəl]

of highest importance; chief; principal
adj. 주요한, 기본적인
ant. insignificant
Regualr meal and exercise are of *cardinal* importance to our health.

drab
[dræb]

1. lacking brightness or color
adj. 우중충한
ant. bright
There are many *drab* houses in the smoky mining town.

2. not attractive; uninteresting; dull
adj. 멋없는, 재미없는
The life of a person who never does anything is dull and *drab*.

feud
[fjuːd]

a long and deadly quarrel
n. 불화, 숙원, 싸움, 반목
ant. intimacy
The two families had been at *feud* with each other for three generations.

insolent
[ínsələnt]

boldly rude; intentionally disregarding the feelings of others; insulting; impudent
adj. 건방진, 오만한
ant. humble
His *insolent* speech and behavior upset everyone in the room.

mitigate
[mítigeit]

make less in force or degree; make less severe; temper; moderate
v. 덜다, 경감시키다, 완화시키다
ant. aggravate
The judge said that nothing could *mitigate* the cruelty with which the man had treated the child.

pertinent
[pə́ːrtinənt]

connected directly to the point; relevant
adj. 타당한, 적절한
ant. irrelevant
A summary of the events leading up to this situation would be *pertinent* information.

predecessor
[prìdisésər]

a person holding a position or office before another
n. 전임자, 선임자
ant. successor
His *predecessor* quit because he was not least interested in this kind of job.

tardy
[táːrdi]

slow in acting or happening; delaying; dilatory
adj. 느린, 더딘, 완만한
ant. prompt
Let me apologize my being *tardy* in answering your letter.

whet
[hwet]

make someone wish for more; stimulate
v. 자극하다, (식욕을) 돋우다
ant. quell
You'd think she would never climb again, after falling down the mountain, but it just *whetted* her appetite.

EXERCISE 4 **Fill each blank with the most appropriate word given above.**
(Inflect the word if necessary.)

1. They did not speak when they met, for they were at deadly _____ with each other last week.

2. The teacher scolded the boy several times for being _____ for school.

3. Aspirin _____ the pain of his headache in about half an hour.

4. She held herself _____ from society, preferring to spend her days and nights dwelling on her memories.

5. Rumors of secret information on the actress' suicide _____ the curiosity of the public.

STUDY YOUR NEW WORDS-5

acquit
[əkwít]

say that a person is not guilty of wrong doing
v. 방면하다, 무죄로 하다, 면죄해 주다
ant. inculpate
The man accused of stealing the money was *acquitted* for lack of witness.

brittle
[brítl]

easily broken; fragile; frail
adj. 부서지기 쉬운, 깨지기 쉬운
ant. hard
Be careful not to break the box of glass; that thin glass is hard but *brittle*.

detract
[ditrǽkt]

remove some of the quality of worth; depreciate; derogate
v. 줄이다, (가치를) 떨어뜨리다
ant. exaggerate
The ugly frame *detracts* something from the beauty of the famous picture.

extirpate
[ékstə(:)rpeit]

pull up by the roots; destroy completely; eradicate; annihilate
v. 뿌리채 뽑아 버리다, 근절시키다, 박멸하다
ant. establish
To *extirpate* weeds is not only to destroy their visible parts but to pull them out by the roots.

indulgent
[indʌ́ldʒənt]

1. too kind or agreeable; giving in to another's wishes or whims
adj. 눈감아 주는, 마음대로 하게 하는
The *indulgent* mother bought her children everything they want.

2. not critical; lenient
adj. 엄하지 않은, 관대한
ant. stern
The *indulgent* teacher praised every poem we wrote.

mendacious
[mendéiʃəs]

lying; untruthful; dishonest
adj. 허위의, 사실이 아닌
ant. candid
The *mendacious* beggar told a different tale of woe at every house.

plausible
[plɔ́:zəbl]

appearing true; reasonable or fair
adj. 그럴듯한, 정말 같은
ant. incredible
For my own sake, I've told a *plausible* lie at the club meeting, but the members did not believe me at all.

sanction
[sǽŋkʃən]

permission with authority; support; approval
n. 인가, 재가(裁可)
ant. rejection
We have the *sanction* of the recreation department to play ball in this park.

shallow
[ʃǽlou]

not deep; lacking deep or serious thinking; superficial
adj. 얕은, 피상적인, 천박한
ant. profound
Youngsters usually rush into marriage with only the *shallow* notions of what love and responsibility mean.

verge
[və:rdʒ]

the edge or border; brim; the point at which something begins or happens
n. 가장자리, 변두리, 경계
ant. interior
We parked the car on the grass *verge* at the side of the highway.

EXERCISE 5 Fill each blank with the most appropriate word given above.
(Inflect the word if necessary.)

1. The scandal published in the newspaper _____ much from the mayor's reputation.
2. A(n) _____ explanation is the one that appears to be believable on the surface.
3. It is illegal to translate a book without the _____ of the author and the publisher.
4. She tried to hide her grief, but she was on the _____ of tears.
5. We look forward to the day when disease and poverty will be _____.

해답

EXERCISE 1.	1. enmity	2. perpendicular	3. impartial	4. bleak	5. sagacity
EXERCISE 2.	1. discretion	2. paramount	3. hilarious	4. spontaneous	5. rife
EXERCISE 3.	1. acme	2. dissuaded	3. candor	4. gratuitous	5. tidy
EXERCISE 4.	1. feud	2. tardy	3. mitigated	4. aloof	5. whetted
EXERCISE 5.	1. detracted	2. plausible	3. sanction	4. verge	5. extirpated

종합 연습 문제

1 In the blank space before each word in column I, write the *letter* of its closest ANTONYM in column II.

	COLUMN I	COLUMN II
_____	1. gratuitous	(A) depressed
_____	2. ardent	(B) significant
_____	3. paramount	(C) inculpate
_____	4. mendacious	(D) obscure
_____	5. enmity	(E) warranted
_____	6. paltry	(F) impassive
_____	7. hilarious	(G) substantial
_____	8. acquit	(H) mediocre
_____	9. ostensible	(I) candid
_____	10. lucid	(J) sympathy

2 Write the *letter* of the word that, if inserted in the sentence, would agree most with thought of the sentence.

1. The manager considered it _____ to his position to accept the demands of the trade union leaders.
       (A) derivative   (B) derogatory

2. My mother tried to _____ me from going to see the movie, for I had not finished my homework.
       (A) dissuade   (B) persuade

3. Discrimination and persecution have created an atmosphere of _____ between Negro and White.
       (A) amity   (B) enmity

4. The appetizer was delicious and _____ the hungry and tired man's palate.
       (A) whetted   (B) whipped

5. The spider hung from a _____ silky thread at the corner of the room.
       (A) tenuous   (B) tentative

6. People who are _____ in paying their bills are poor customers.
       (A) tedious   (B) tardy

7. After the severe storm the flag pole was no longer _____.
       (A) impartial   (B) perpendicular

Lesson 24

8. The rocky peaks of high mountains are always _____ and windy.
          (A) bleach   (B) bleak

9. The judge decided to _____ the man's sentence in the light of his previous record.
          (A) malign   (B) mitigate

10. The plan for the new building will be practised after all necessary _____ are obtained.
          (A) sanctities   (B) sanctions

3 In the blank space, write the *letter* of the word that most nearly menas the OPPOSITE of the italicized word.

_____ 1. *urbane*   (A) rural   (B) vulgar
                              (C) modern   (D) neglect

_____ 2. *castigate*   (A) agree   (B) preserve
                                (C) obey   (D) applaud

_____ 3. *shallow*   (A) profound   (B) relevant
                                (C) indifferent   (D) humble

_____ 4. *retrospect*   (A) antipathy   (B) prospect
                                (C) reality   (D) improvement

_____ 5. *impeach*   (A) castigate   (B) bestow
                                (C) exonerate   (D) recede

4 Fill each blank with the most appropriate word from the vocabulary list below.

VOCABULARY LIST

whet	predecessors	indulgent
discretion	tardy	cardinal
castigate	impartial	recede
spontaneous	tidy	acme

1. A judge cannot remain _____ without being free of all political pressure.

2. They're very _____ parents; they give their children presents all the time.

3. He is always _____ in paying back the borrowed money.

4. The laughter at his joke is never forced but always _____.

5. The _____ idea of the Labor Party's political thought is that all people should be equal.

6. It requires _____ to criticize someone without hurting his feelings.

7. This is the 5th plan we have made but it's no better than its _____.

8. I watched the coast of Korea slowly _____ into the distance.

9. Schubert reached the _____ of his skill while he was quite young.

10. Their living room was so _____ that it seemed doubtful that anyone actually lived in it.

해답

1	1. E	2. F	3. H	4. I	5. J	6. B	7. A	8. C	9. G	10. D
2	1. B	2. A	3. B	4. A	5. A	6. B	7. B	8. B	9. B	10. B
3	1. B	2. D	3. A	4. B	5. C					

4
1. impartial 2. indulgent 3. tardy 4. spontaneous 5. cardinal
6. discretion 7. predecessors 8. recede 9. acme 10. tidy

Lesson 25

PRETEST 25

Insert the *letter* of the best answer in the space provided.

1. Mr. Kim was a counsel for the *plaintiff*, and Mr. Park for the _____.
   (A) lawyer   (B) defendant   (C) jury

2. The _____ entered the harbor and began to *plunder* the town.
   (A) policemen   (B) pirates   (C) sailors

3. He is very *scrupulous* about the _____.
   (A) choice of his words   (B) manual labor   (C) water pollution

4. Their _____ were drawn *aslant* over their brows, and they were chewing gums leaning against the wall.
   (A) legs   (B) gloves   (C) caps

5. The crowd at the scene of the accident *impeded* the arrival of the _____.
   (A) jeopardy   (B) ambulance   (C) relish

ANSWERS 1.B 2.B 3.A 4.C 5.B

STUDY YOUR NEW WORDS-1

adjacent
[ədʒéisənt]

near or close; neighboring; next; bordering
adj. 인접의, 부근의, 접근한
ant. distant
No one in the *adjacent* apartments was awakened by their quarreling sounds.

calamity
[kəlǽməti]

a great misfortune; disaster; misfortune; misery
n. 재난, 참화, 불행, 비운
ant. bliss
The spring floods were great *calamity* to the farmers whose crops and houses were ruined.

devastate
[dévəsteit]

make waste; make unfit to live in; desolate; destroy
v. 유린하다, 황폐시키다
ant. fertilize
The floods and storms which have no precedent in the recorded history *devastated* the country.

exultant
[igzʌ́ltənt]

rejoicing greatly; triumphant
adj. 몹시 기뻐하는, 의기 양양한
ant. mournful
The *exultant* players were dancing in the ground over their team's victory.

inexhaustible
[inigzɔ́:stəbl]

cannot be exhausted; very abundant
adj. 지칠 줄 모르는 ; 무진장의
ant. limited
The wealth of our country seems *inexhaustible* to many people abroad.

maudlin
[mɔ́:dlin]

sentimental in a weak and silly way
adj. 눈물을 잘 흘리는, 감상적인
ant. unmoved
We saw a *maudlin* movie about an orphan who lost his parents in the war.

plunder
[plʌ́ndər]

rob; take by force; steal
v. 약탈하다, 빼앗다, 훔치다
ant. donate
The enemies *plundered* all the valuable things they could find in the village.

scrupulous
[skrú:pjuləs]

conscientious; exactly honest; very careful to do what is right
adj. 양심적인, 주의 깊은, 면밀한
ant. heedless
A *scrupulous* man never fails to give back the borrowed money to its owner.

sundry
[sʌ́ndri]

a number of; several; various
adj. 여러 가지의, 갖가지의, 잡다한
ant. unique
From *sundry* hints, I guessed I was to be given a bicycle for my birthday present.

zealous
[zéləs]

eager; earnest; actively enthusiastic
adj. 열심인, 열성적인, 열광적인
ant. neglectful
The children made *zealous* efforts to clean up the house for the Christmas party.

EXERCISE 1 Fill each blank with the most appropriate word given above. (Inflect the word if necessary.)

1. The troops in the besieged town gave a(n) _____ shout at the sight of new troops advancing to help them.
2. No one would think it _____ to weep at the death of a friend.
3. They were glad they had survived the _____ and had met with no disaster.
4. We are told that the potentialities of the human brain are _____.
5. In olden times soldiers _____ a conquered city and often gained great wealth.

STUDY YOUR NEW WORDS-2

altruistic
[æltruístik]

thoughtful of the welfare of others; unselfish
adj. 이타주의의, 애타주의적인
ant. selfish
We wonder if human beings are primarily *altruistic* or selfish.

clamor
[klǽmər]

a loud continuous, confused noise or shouting; uproar
n. 외치는 소리, (여론의) 아우성 소리
ant. silence
The public *clamor* for lower taxes continued year after year.

disintegrate
[disíntigreit]

break up into small pieces
v. 분해하다, 붕괴하다, 해체하다
ant. assemble
The old manuscripts had been *disintegrated* into a pile of fragments and dust.

forebear
[fɔ́:rbɛər]

an ancestor; forefather
n. 선조, 조상
ant. descendant
Although Napoleon was Corsican, he is considered by most modern Frenchmen to have been French as their own *forebears*.

intact
[intǽkt]

as if untouched; uninjured; whole
adj. 손대지 않은, 본래대로의, 완전한
ant. damaged
The money was returned *intact* by the boy who found it on the street.

molest
[moulést]

trouble or annoy intentionally; interfere with trouble
v. 괴롭히다, 성가시게 굴다
ant. soothe
We did not *molest* the big dog, because we were afraid of him.

profuse
[prəfjúːs]

very abundant; in plenty; generous
adj. 풍부한, 아낌없는, 마음이 후한
ant. sparing
The mourner's *profuse* tears at the burial were heartbreaking.

slack
[slæk]

careless; not tight or firm; sluggish
adj. 부주의한, 느슨한, 긴장이 풀린
ant. agile
He was *slack* in fulfilling his promises and responsibilities.

tart
[tɑːrt]

acid tasting; not sweet; sour; sarcastic
adj. 시큼한, 신랄한, 호된
ant. sweet
Tart apples taste sharp and are pleasantly acid in its taste.

viable
[váiəbl]

able to succeed in operation; able to keep alive; livable
adj. 실행 가능한, 생존할 수 있는, 자랄 수 있는
ant. impracticable
This plan looks all right in principle, but in practice it wouldn't be *viable*.

EXERCISE 2 **Fill each blank with the most appropriate word given above.**
(Inflect the word if necessary.)

1. The speaker could hardly be heard above the _____ of the uproaring crowd.

2. Don't be _____ in your efforts till the work is completely finished.

3. The dog that _____ sheep has to be driven out immediately.

4. A(n) _____ person is thoughtful of the welfare of the others.

5. Few buildings in the bombed city remained _____.

STUDY YOUR NEW WORDS-3

aslant
[əslǽnt]
not straight or level; sloping
adv. 비스듬히, 기울어져
ant. straight
The carpenter made the roof *aslant* to allow water to run down.

concede
[kənsíːd]
admit as true; acknowledge
v. 인정하다, 승인하다
ant. contradict
They *conceded* that victory was no longer attainable and agreed to a negotiated surrender.

distrust
[distrʌ́st]
have no confidence in; not trust; be suspicious of; doubt
n., v. 불신(하다), 의심(하다)
ant. confide
She could not allow the stranger to enter her house, for she *distrusted* him.

groggy
[grɔ́gi]
weak because of illness; unsteady
adj. 비틀거리는, 휘청거리는
ant. steady
The table is very *groggy*. I think the leg is going to fall off.

intrepid
[intrépid]
showing no fear; brave; fearless; courageous
adj. 용맹스러운, 두려움을 모르는
ant. timid
The *intrepid* fireman saved persons trapped in a burning building disregarding of his own safety.

overbearing
[ouvərbɛ́əriŋ]
arrogant; forcing others to one's own will; haughty
adj. 거만한, 오만한, 건방진
ant. humble
We found it hard to like the boy because of his *overbearing* manners.

rash
[ræʃ]
foolishly bold; not thinking enough of the results; reckless
adj. 분별없는, 경솔한
ant. deliberate
Only a *rash* person would have rushed into the burning house to save some clothes.

sporadic
[spərǽdik]
happening irregularly; scattered in time; occasional
adj. 산발적인, 때때로 일어나는

	ant. regular
	Though polio has been practically wiped out, there have been *sporadic* cases of the disease.
toxic [tɔ́ksik]	related to or caused by poisonous substance; poisonous *adj.* 유독한, 독(성)의 ant. harmless Fumes from automobiles and factory chimneys are *toxic*.

EXERCISE 3 Fill each blank with the most appropriate word given above.
(Inflect the word if necessary.)

1. When I left my bed after my long illness, I felt too _____ to stand.
2. The government _____ defeat as soon as the election results were known.
3. He keeps his money at home because he _____ banks.
4. It is _____ to cross the street without looking at both ways.
5. The _____ persons traveled west in spite of hardships and constant danger of Indian attack.

STUDY YOUR NEW WORDS-4

avert [əvə́ːrt]	turn aside or away; prevent happening; avoid; prevent *v.* 피하다, 비키다, (얼굴 따위를) 돌리다 ant. encounter The driver *averted* an accident by a quick turn of the steering wheel.
deduce [didjúːs]	reach a conclusion by reasoning; infer *v.* 추론하다, 연역하다 ant. induce Mother *deduced* from my loss of appetites what had happened to the cookies.
embark [imbáːrk]	1. go on board a ship, aircraft, or other vehicle *v.* (배나 비행기에) 태우다, 싣다 ant. disembark Our ship *embarked* passengers and wool at an Australian port. 2. set out; start *v.* 착수하다, 시작하다 After leaving college, the young man *embarked* on a new business career.

Lesson 25

humiliate
[hju(:)mílieit]

cause to feel humble; lower the pride or dignity; mortify
v. 욕보이다, 창피를 주다
ant. encourage
The boy *humiliated* his parents by behaving badly in front of the guests.

jovial
[dʒóuvjəl]

full of good humor; friendly; jolly; convivial
adj. 쾌활한, 명랑한, 유쾌한
ant. sorrowful
He enjoyed the companionship of a large number of *jovial* friends.

pastime
[pǽstaim]

a pleasant way of passing time; amusement; recreation as a game or sport
n. 오락, 소일거리, 기분 전환
ant. labor
Baseball has been called American's national *pastime* through four seasons.

renounce
[rináuns]

give up entirely; forego; relinquish
v. 포기하다, 단념하다
ant. claim
He *renounced* the task from the difficulties of deciding where to begin.

snug
[snʌg]

sheltered and warm; comfortable; cosy
adj. 안락한, 편안한, 아늑한
ant. uncomfortable
My grandmother likes to read a newspaper in a *snug* corner near the fireplace.

umpteen
[ʌmptíːn]

of a very large number
adj. 다수(多數)의
ant. few
She doesn't need to borrow a book because she's got *umpteen* books waiting to be read at home.

EXERCISE 4

Fill each blank with the most appropriate word given above.
(Inflect the word if necessary.)

1. Her instructions are so complicated that I cannot _____ from them what she wants.

2. The little cat has found a(n) _____ corner behind the stove.

3. Santa Claus is pictured as a(n) _____ old fellow with long beard on his face and a large bag on his back.

4. The shipwrecked sailors _____ all hope of rescue and were floating on the sea.

5. Hunting and fishing are _____ ardently followed by the devotees of those sports.

STUDY YOUR NEW WORDS-5

blur
[blə:r]

make less clear in form or outline
v. 희미하게 하다, 흐리게 하다
ant. purity
The boy *blurred* the picture by touching it before the paint was dry.

demolish
[dimɔ́liʃ]

destroy; pull or tear down
v. 부수다, 분쇄하다, 뒤엎다
ant. construct
The slums were *demolished* before the town was extended.

enslave
[insléiv]

make into a slave; take away freedom from
v. 노예로 하다, 예속시키다
ant. liberate
Education makes people easy to govern but impossible to *enslave*.

impede
[impí:d]

get in the way of; make something difficult to do; hinder; obstruct
v. 방해하다, 저지하다
ant. spur
Many a man is *impeded* in his career by a lack of belief in himself.

lull
[lʌl]

soothe with sounds or caresses; make calm; quiet
v. 달래다, 어르다, 진정시키다
ant. excite
The mother *lulled* the baby to sleep by singing a song.

plaintiff
[pléintif]

a person who begins a lawsuit
n. 원고, 고소인
ant. defendant
In the court the *plaintiff* asserted that the thief had stolen two hundred dollars from his store.

robust
[rəbʎst]

having or showing very good health; strong and healthy
adj. 튼튼한, 강건한
ant. weak
He was strong and healthy, but he's never been *robust* since his illness.

strenuous
[strénjuəs]

very active; full of energy; requiring much effort
adj. 분투적인, 열심인, 노력을 요하는
ant. idle
I wish to preach, not the doctrine of ignoble ease, but the doctrine of the *strenuous* life.

vitiate
[víʃieit]

1. weaken or spoil; harm the quality of
v. 손상하다, 해치다, 나쁘게 하다
Pollution from smoke and dust *vitiates* the air.

2. destroy the legal force or authority of; invalidate
v. 무효로 하다
ant. purge
All his attempts to improve were *vitiated* by his lack of willpower.

EXERCISE 5 Fill each blank with the most appropriate word given above.
(Inflect the word if necessary.)

1. The child's hysterical crying _____ the doctor from completing his examination.

2. They are going to _____ that old building to clear the road for a new highway.

3. Water spilled on the letter and _____ the writing.

4. He has a(n) _____ appearance though he is not actually well.

5. The contract was _____ because one person signed it under compulsion.

EXERCISE 1.	1. exultant	2. maudlin	3. calamity	4. inexhaustible	5. plundered
EXERCISE 2.	1. clamor	2. slack	3. molests	4. altruistic	5. intact
EXERCISE 3.	1. groggy	2. conceded	3. distrusts	4. rash	5. intrepid
EXERCISE 4.	1. deduce	2. snug	3. jovial	4. renounced	5. pastimes
EXERCISE 5.	1. impeded	2. demolish	3. blurred	4. robust	5. vitiated

종합 연습 문제

1 In the blank space before each word in column I, write the *letter* of its closest ANTONYM in column II.

COLUMN I	COLUMN II
_____ 1. tart	(A) steady
_____ 2. intrepid	(B) purge
_____ 3. sporadic	(C) unmoved
_____ 4. devastate	(D) build
_____ 5. vitiate	(E) heedless
_____ 6. groggy	(F) plaintiff
_____ 7. demolish	(G) fertilize
_____ 8. maudlin	(H) sweet
_____ 9. defendant	(I) cowardly
_____ 10. scrupulous	(J) regular

2 Write the *letter* of the word that, if inserted in the sentence, would agree most with thought of the sentence.

1. The decay of moral principles rapidly _____ the Roman society.
   (A) thwarted   (B) disintegrated

2. She has _____ all hope of going to Europe this year for lack of money.
   (A) embarked   (B) renounced

3. The whole town was _____ by the war flames.
   (A) devastated   (B) extorted

4. The _____ soldier carries out a dangerous mission, without letting fear prevent him from doing.
   (A) intrepid   (B) viable

5. We had a(n) _____ day moving into our new house.
   (A) overbearing   (B) strenuous

6. The nurse treated the wounded soldier with the most _____ care.
   (A) scrupulous   (B) venomous

7. We've _____ all her arguments and she has nothing more to say.
   (A) plundered   (B) demolished

8. It is _____ to cross the street without looking both ways.
   (A) indulgent   (B) rash

9. The fumes from furnaces and motor vehicles have _____ the air we breathe and shortened our life expectancy.
        (A) vitiated   (B) averted

10. He had no choice but to _____ that he had been guilty or bad judgment.
        (A) concede   (B) conceit

3 In the blank space, write the letter of the word that most nearly menas the OPPOSITE of the italicized word.

_____ 1. *altruistic* social animal   (A) critical   (B) gregarious
                                            (C) temporary   (D) selfish

_____ 2. *adjacent* farmhouse   (A) wealthy   (B) noisy
                                            (C) distant   (D) splendid

_____ 3. *sundry* articles   (A) fine   (B) opposed
                                            (C) gloomy   (D) unique

_____ 4. a *rash* promise   (A) deliberate (B) sluggish
                                            (C) rare   (D) reckless

_____ 5. *exultant* over success   (A) mournful   (B) lack
                                            (C) zealous   (D) indifferent

4 Fill each blank with the most appropriate word from the vocabulary list below.

VOCABULARY LIST		
scrupulous	rash	intrepid
calamity	zealous	deduced
inexhaustible	intact	impeded
viable	distrusted	concede

1. The salesman seems very _____ to persuade the housewife to buy the book.

2. When the fire broke out the party turned out to be a complete _____.

3. The deep snow and the extreme cold _____ our travel to Canada.

4. I'm willing to _____ that a large car would have cost more, but I still think we should have bought one.

5. A(n) _____ judge is careful to weight all the evidence and excludes all personal feelings.

6. From the fact that Socrates was a man and the principle that all men die. I _____ that Socrates would die.

7. The new president is a man of a(n) _____ energy.

8. They didn't believe him. In fact, they _____ him in all matters.

9. Only controlled disarmament can make a(n) _____ world in this nuclear age.

10. The second generation kept the family fortune entire; the heiress kept her father's art collection completely _____.

해답

1 1. H   2. I   3. J   4. G   5. B   6. A   7. D   8. C   9. F   10. E
2 1. B   2. B   3. A   4. A   5. B   6. A   7. B   8. B   9. A   10. A
3 1. D   2. C   3. D   4. A   5. A
4 1. zealous   2. calamity   3. impeded   4. concede   5. scrupulous
   6. deduced   7. inexhaustible 8. distrusted   9. viable   10. intact

Lesson 26

PRETEST 26

Insert the *letter* of the best answer in the space provided.

1. He was *suspended* from school for a week _____.
   (A) to help his father   (B) for bad conduct   (C) to study more

2. Though they *disapproved* of the details, they were in _____ agreement over the plan.
   (A) eccentric   (B) substantial   (C) nebulous

3. A coward soldier *eludes* hazardous duty by _____.
   (A) aggrieving   (B) wrangling   (C) malingering

4. The *offence* was such a minor _____ of manners that everyone overlooked it.
   (A) breach   (B) obstruction   (C) overdue

5. The Roman Empire rapidly *waned* in _____ in the 5th century.
   (A) victory   (B) power   (C) success

ANSWERS 1.B 2.B 3.C 4.A 5.B

STUDY YOUR NEW WORDS-1

aggrieve
[əgríːv]

cause grief or trouble to; injure unjustly
v. 괴롭히다, 학대하다
ant. console
The entire population was *aggrieved* by the tyranny of the king.

callous
[kǽləs]

1. unfeeling; not sensitive; insensible
adj. 무감각한, 멍청한, 냉정한
ant. sensitive
Only a *callous* person can see suffering without trying to relieve it.

2. hard and thick; hardened
adj. 굳은, 단단한
Walking barefoot on the asphalt pavement makes the bottom of your feet *callous*.

disapprove
[disəprúːv]

have an unfavorable or bad opinion of; express an opinion against
v. 찬성하지 않다, ~을 안 된다고 하다
ant. consent
She wants to continue her study in the United States, but her parents *disapprove* of her plan.

fabulous
[fæbjuləs]

nearly unbelievable; hard or impossible to believe
adj. 터무니없는, 믿을 수 없는, 엄청난
ant. true
Ten dollars is a *fabulous* price for an ordinary pencil.

infuriate
[infjúərieit]

make very angry; make furious
v. 격노시키다
ant. placate
He was *infuriated* by the policeman's rough treatment of his wife.

mordant
[mɔ́ːrdənt]

biting and cutting; severe; sarcastic
adj. 신랄한, 독설적인
ant. mild
His political opponents feared his *mordant* tongue, and even more his *mordant* pen.

prowess
[práuis]

great personal bravery; daring; courage; valor
n. 용기, 용감
ant. cowardice
The Indians sang a song of victory, describing their *prowess* in battle.

subversive
[səbvə́ːrsiv]

tending to overthrow; causing ruin; destructive
adj. 전복하는, 파괴하는
ant. constructive
He was arrested as a member of a *subversive* organization advocating the forceful overthrow of the present government.

temporary
[témpərəri]

lasting only a limited time; not permanent; transient
adj. 임시의, 일시의, 임시 변통의
ant. permanent
Many students find *temporary* jobs during their summer holidays.

EXERCISE 1
Fill each blank with the most appropriate word given above.
(Inflect the word if necessary.)

1. Do you think it is right for women to paint their lips or do you _____.
2. Two firemen showed great _____ by repeatedly rushing into the burning building to save many lives.
3. The parent was deeply _____ by his children's disobedience.
4. The teacher's _____ comment about the girl's essay made her cry.
5. The hunter made a(n) _____ shelter out of branches to avoid the heavy rain.

STUDY YOUR NEW WORDS-2

amass
[əmǽs]

heap together; gather; accumulate
v. 모으다, 축적하다
ant. dissipate
Through the years he *amassed* a large fortune to buy a farm after he retired.

colossal
[kəlɔ́sl]

of huge size; gigantic; vast; tremendous
adj. 거대한, 굉장한, 어마어마한
ant. trivial
The Empire State Building is a *colossal* structure.

dismal
[dízməl]

dark and gloomy; dreary; somber
adj. 우울한, 쓸쓸한
ant. joyous
Sickness or bad luck often makes a person feel *dismal*.

genial
[dʒíːnjəl]

cheerful and friendly; smiling and pleasant; kindly; jovial
adj. 다정한, 친절한, 상냥한
ant. sullen
She was glad to see us again and gave me a *genial* welcome.

inveterate
[invétərit]

confirmed in habit, practice, or feeling; habitual
adj. 버릇이 된, 상습적인, 뿌리 깊은
ant. occasional
It is hard for an *inveterate* smoker to give up tobacco.

offence
[əféns]

the act of breaking the law; sin; wrong; crime
n. 위반, 반칙, 범죄
ant. defence
The punishment for that *offence* is two years in prison.

sojourn
[sóudʒəːrn]

stay for a time; a brief stay
n., v. 체재(하다), 체류(하다)
ant. departure
During his *sojourn* in Africa he learned much about native customs.

suspend
[səspénd]

put off or stop for a period of time; postpone
v. 중지하다, 한때 멈추다, 연기하다
ant. schedule
A scientist *suspends* judgment and refrains from drawing conclusions until all the facts are in.

turmoil
[tə́ːrmɔil]

a state of confusion, excitement, and trouble; disturbance; tumult
n. 소란, 소동, 혼란
ant. tranquility
Six robberies in one night put our village in a *turmoil*.

| EXERCISE 2 | Fill each blank with the most appropriate word given above. (Inflect the word if necessary.) |

1. It is sometimes difficult to acknowledge that another person's lot may be more _____ than one's own.

2. Disturbing the place and breaking most traffic laws are _____ in this country.

3. My acquaintance made a(n) _____ fortune in the last ten years.

4. Train service will be _____ from midnight to 4 a.m. to permit repair.

5. The noise of cars passing along the road is a continual _____ to our quiet at home.

STUDY YOUR NEW WORDS-3

assent
[əsént]

agree to a suggestion; express agreement; agree
v. 동의하다, 찬성하다
ant. disagree
She **assented** to the doctor's assertion that her son was ill, but could not consent to having him hospitalized.

cosy
[kóuzi]

warm and comfortable; snug
adj. 아늑한, 포근한, 기분 좋은
ant. uncomfortable
The couple wish to live in a *cosy* little home rather than in a big mansion.

diversify
[daivə́:*r*sifai]

make different or various in form or quality; vary
v. 다양하게 하다, 각양각색으로 하다
ant. simplify
That factory is trying to *diversify* its products to sell in different markets.

haggard
[hǽgə*r*d]

looking worn from pain, fatigue, or hunger; gaunt
adj. 야윈, 수척한, 말라빠진
ant. fat
The *haggard* faces of the rescued miners showed that they had a great deal of sufferings.

irreparable
[iré*p*ərəbl]

cannot be repaired or made good
adj. 고칠〔돌이킬〕 수 없는, 불치의
ant. reparable
Careless drivers cause many *irreparable* accidents.

paternal
[pətə́:*r*nəl]

of or like a father; fatherly
adj. 아버지의, 아버지다운
ant. maternal
Everyone has two *paternal* grandparents and two maternal grandparents.

replica
[réplikə]

a copy of a work or art, especially one made by the original artist
n. 복사, 모사품(模寫品)
ant. original
The young artist made a *replica* of the famous painting.

seclusion
[siklú:ʒən]

the act of keeping away from others
n. 격리, 은둔, 한거

ant. publicity

His *seclusion* of the rabbit in the barn was kept secret from everyone else.

wrangle
[ræŋgl]

argue or dispute in a noisy or angry way; quarrel
v. 말다툼하다, 논쟁하다, 다투다
ant. coincide
The two friends *wrangled* and now they don't speak to each other.

EXERCISE 3   **Fill each blank with the most appropriate word given above.**
(Inflect the word if necessary.)

1. The little boy was a(n) _____ of his father in looks and voice.
2. To _____ one's reading is to read about a number of different subjects.
3. The house is not _____ tonight because our air conditioner is not working.
4. Hunger and suffering made the lost hikers _____.
5. She lives in _____ apart even from her closest friends.

STUDY YOUR NEW WORDS-4

bigoted
[bígətid]

holding fast to an opinion, belief, party, or other position; intolerant; prejudiced
adj. 고집 불통의, 편협한
ant. tolerant
Most *bigoted* people are intolerant of opposition.

deficient
[difíʃənt]

not complete; defective; imperfect
adj. ~이 모자라는, 부족한, 결함이 있는
ant. sufficient
Most of the food they eat is *deficient* in iron and protein.

elude
[iljú:d]

escape from by means of a trick
v. 교묘히 피하다, 회피하다
ant. encounter
The sly fox *eluded* the hunters by running back in the opposite direction.

ignoble
[ignóubl]

without honor; disgraceful; mean
adj. 비열한, 비천한, 천한
ant. noble
Some very great men have come from *ignoble* families.

kindred
[kíndrid]

related; belonging to the same group
adj. 관계가 있는, 유사한, 같은 성질의
ant. foreign
We are studying about dew, frost, mist, and other *kindred* facts or nature.

melancholy
[mélənkəli]

sad; gloomy; depressed in spirits; lamentable; deplorable
adj. 우울한, 울적한, 생각에 잠긴
ant. exhilerated
During the Romantic period it was fashionable in literature to have a *melancholy* outlook on the world.

poltroon
[pɔltrúːn]

a wretched coward
n. 비겁한 사람, 겁쟁이
ant. valor
No one likes to be regarded as a *poltroon*.

rout
[raut]

defeat completely and drive away
v. 패주시키다, 대파하다
ant. surrender
An army which has been overpowered may either surrender or be *routed*.

vulnerable
[vʌ́lnərəbl]

open to attack; can be easily wounded or injured
adj. 비난(공격) 받기 쉬운, 상처 입기 쉬운
ant. protected
The most massive defence system would still leave the nation *vulnerable* to nuclear attack.

EXERCISE 4   Fill each blank with the most appropriate word given above.
(Inflect the word if necessary.)

1. Weak teeth are usually caused by your diet in which calcium is _____.

2. Pollution of its drinking water left the city _____ to many diseases.

3. In the slums of some cities even small children learn _____ language.

4. The _____ news that the king is seriously ill made all of us pray God for his quick recovery.

5. The baseball team _____ its opponents by a score of ten to one.

STUDY YOUR NEW WORDS-5

abide
[əbáid]

remain; stay; wait
v. 머무르다, 묵다, 남다
ant. depart
The child *abided* with his grandparents for three years before being returned to his parents.

boisterous
[bɔ́istərəs]

noisily cheerful and rough; exuberant
adj. 시끄러운, 난폭한, 사나운
ant. silent
The audience in the theatre was irritated by the unruly screaming and *boisterous* children.

despicable
[déspikəbl]

deserving to be despised; contemptible
adj. 야비한, 비열한
ant. admirable
It is *despicable* to go away and leave a cat behind to starve.

exotic
[igzɔ́tik]

from a foreign country; not native; strange and unusual
adj. 외래의, 외국산의
ant. domestic
We saw many *exotic* plants at the flower exhibition, which we had never seen before.

imperative
[impérətiv]

1. urgent; essential; which must be done
adj. 절박한, 긴요한, 절대 필요한
ant. unnecessary
For the mountain climber, it is *imperative* to get food and water before sunset.

2. expressing a command, request, or warning
adj. 명령적인, 명령조의
My wife has such an *imperative* voice that everyone obeys her.

nonplus
[nɔnplʌ́s]

puzzle completely; make unable to say or do something; confuse
v. 할 바를 모르게 하다, 당혹시키다
ant. hearten
He was *nonplused* by the strange costumes he saw everywhere in the country.

pompous
[pɔ́mpəs]

foolishly solemn and self-important; pretentious
adj. 거만한, 건방진, 격식을 차리는
ant. informal
The leader of the band bowed in a *pompous* manner.

sever
[sévər]

break or cut apart; cut off; separate
v. 절단하다, 끊다, 끊어지다
ant. connect
The handle of the large cup *severed* when it hit the floor.

sultry
[sʌ́ltri]

hot and moist; oppressively hot
adj. 무더운, 찌는 듯이 더운
ant. cold
The day was so *sultry* that they had little energy left.

wane
[wein]

grow gradually smaller or less after being full or complete; diminish
v. 이지러지다, 약해지다, 작아지다
ant. wax
The moon was *waning*, and in such a *waning* light, it is very difficult to see the enemy.

EXERCISE 5   **Fill each blank with the most appropriate word given above.**
(Inflect the word if necessary.)

1. We were _____ to see two roads where we had expected only one.

2. The railway guard was a(n) _____ little official, who thought he controlled the whole railway system himself.

3. It is _____ that this very sick child should stay in bed at least for two weeks.

4. According to the Greek mythology, my wife had been _____ from my own body.

5. It is _____ of you to leave your wife and children without food and money.

해답

EXERCISE 1.	1. disapprove	2. prowess	3. aggrieved	4. mordant	5. temporary
EXERCISE 2.	1. dismal	2. offences	3. colossal	4. suspended	5. turmoil
EXERCISE 3.	1. replica	2. diversify	3. cosy	4. haggard	5. seclusion
EXERCISE 4.	1. deficient	2. vulnerable	3. ignoble	4. melancholy	5. routed
EXERCISE 5.	1. nonplused	2. pompous	3. imperative	4. severed	5. despicable

종합 연습 문제

1 In the blank space before each word in column I, write the *letter* of the closest ANTONYM in column II.

COLUMN I	COLUMN II
_____ 1. schedule	(A) constructive
_____ 2. melancholy	(B) occasional
_____ 3. callous	(C) publicity
_____ 4. exotic	(D) suspend
_____ 5. assent	(E) nonplus
_____ 6. seclusion	(F) exhilerated
_____ 7. subversive	(G) sensitive
_____ 8. hearten	(H) domestic
_____ 9. inveterate	(I) surrender
_____ 10. rout	(J) disagree

2 Write the *letter* of the word that, if inserted in the sentence, would agree most with thought of the sentence.

1. He had a(n) _____ habit of winking one eye.
    (A) mordant   (B) inveterate

2. Bus service will be _____ until the highway is repaired.
    (A) suspended   (B) mendacious

3. The constant noise from the machine _____ all the secretaries in the office.
    (A) infuriated   (B) placated

4. If a bill to be paid is ten dollars and you have only six dollars, four dollars is _____.
    (A) irreparable   (B) deficient

5. There are several _____ buildings in the business district of Seoul.
    (A) colossal   (B) pompous

6. Everyone _____ to the dance party at the Christmas Eve.
    (A) assented   (B) abided

7. Where to go, and what to do when we get there, are two _____ questions.
    (A) diversified   (B) kindred

8. The government dislikes this magazine because it prints _____ ideas.
    (A) subversive   (B) substantial

Lesson 26

9. I remember his name very well, but his name _____ me for the moment.
   (A) wrangles   (B) eludes

10. She _____ with some relatives in London for three months.
   (A) sojourned   (B) rambled

3 In the blank space, write the letter of the word that most nearly menas the OPPOSITE of the italicized word.

_____ 1. *elude*	(A) enlarge		(B) enclose
	(C) extend		(D) encounter
_____ 2. *dismal*	(A) joyous		(B) certain
	(C) easy		(D) stern
_____ 3. *wane*	(A) sane		(B) real
	(C) control		(D) wax
_____ 4. *seclusion*	(A) protection		(B) combination
	(C) publicity		(D) salvage
_____ 5. *ignoble*	(A) graceful		(B) calm
	(C) mordant		(D) genial

4 Fill each blank with the most appropriate word from the vocabulary list below.

> **VOCABULARY LIST**
>
> elude   seclusion   boisterous
> offence   infuriated   prowess
> turmoil   suspended   diversify
> wrangled   despicable   ignoble

1. The sailor's voice could not be heard above the _____ of the storm.

2. The man was highly praised for having the _____ to go into the burning house to save the little girl.

3. To steal from the collection plate in church or from a blind beggar is _____.

4. The hurricane _____ all ferry service for three days.

5. She was simply _____ by her husband's cold indifference about her new dress.

6. The children _____ about who should sit in the front seat of the car.

7. To _____ one's routine work is to break up one's day into segments devoted to various aspects of one's job.

8. That dirty old house is a(n) _____ to everyone who lives in the street.

9. He was amazed that no one else seemed to notice the _____ cruelty with which she treated her stepsons.

10. He rented a cottage in the woods for the summer, in which he could be in _____ while he was writing.

해답

1 1. D   2. F   3. G   4. H   5. J   6. C   7. A   8. E   9. B   10. I
2 1. B   2. A   3. A   4. B   5. A   6. A   7. B   8. A   9. B   10. A
3 1. D   2. A   3. D   4. C   5. A
4 1. turmoil   2. prowess   3. ignoble   4. suspended   5. infuriated
     6. wrangled   7. diversify   8. offence   9. despicable   10. seclusion

UNIT III

(Lessons 27~31)

- **Enlarging Vocabulary**
- **through DERIVATIVES**

Lesson 27

PRETEST 27

Insert the *letter* of the best answer in the space provided.

1. Department stores are often **congested** _____.
   (A) after 9 o'clock in the evening (B) before Christmas
   (C) on cold, windy days

2. A *judicious* parent _____ his children to decide many things for themselves.
   (A) forbids   (B) encourages   (C) dissuades

3. A(n) _____ person treats his work with *apathy*.
   (A) lazy   (B) wise   (C) old

4. _____ *simulate* flowers or leaves of a tree.
   (A) Most gardeners (B) Some people (C) Certain insects

5. Constant *vigilance* is necessary in order to _____ in driving.
   (A) avoid accidents (B) save gasoline (C) prevent engine trouble

ANSWERS 1.B 2.B 3.A 4.C 5.A

STUDY YOUR NEW WORDS-1

acclimate   get used to a new climate
[ǽklimeit]   *v.* 환경에 순응시키다, 순화시키다
                     n. acclimation
                     We are becoming *acclimated* to New York weather.

assail   attack with violence or continuous criticism; assault
[əséil]   *v.* 공격하다, 공박하다
                     n., adj. assailant
                     The senators *assailed* the President on the subject of the treaty between the two countries.

congest
[kəndʒést]

fill to full; overcrowd
v. 넘치게 하다, 충만시키다
n. congestion
His face was *congested* with anger as the argument grew more heated.

effusive
[ifjúːsiv]

showing too much feeling; too demonstrative and emotional
adj. 심정을 토로하는, 감정을 누르지 않는
n. effusion
Her *effusive* welcome made us feel most uncomfortable.

frugal
[frúːgəl]

without waste; not wasteful; saving; thrifty
adj. 검약한, 검소한
n. frugality
A good manager is *frugal* in the use of his funds.

insolvent
[insɔ́lvənt]

unable to pay one's debt; bankrupt
adj. 지불 불능의, 파산한
n. insolvency
The newspapers accused the government of being *insolvent* in its debts.

nausea
[nɔ́ziə]

the feeling that one is about to vomit; seasick
n. 메스꺼움, 욕지기, 배멀미
v. nauseate
Most passengers of the ship were seized with *nausea* during the storm at sea.

redeem
[ridíːm]

get back by payment; set free by payment; regain
v. 되찾다, 만회하다, 구제하다
n. redemption
She had no way to *redeem* her furniture out of pawn.

seep
[siːp]

leak slowly; ooze; trickle
v. 스며나오다, 새다
n. seepage
They used waterproof cement to prevent water from *seeping* through the roof of the tunnel.

symmetry
[símitri]

exact likeness in shape between the opposite sides of something
n. 좌우 대칭, 균형
adj. symmetrical
A swollen cheek spoiled the *symmetry* of his handsome face.

Lesson 27

> **EXERCISE 1** Fill each blank with the most appropriate word given above.
> (Inflect the word if necessary.)
>
> 1. John is not _____; he does not pour out his emotions.
> 2. After paying the money, he _____ his watch from the pawnshop.
> 3. My aunt is a (an) _____ housekeeper who buys and uses food carefully.
> 4. Main Street is _____ with the traffic of people driving to work each morning.
> 5. Country girls cannot easily _____ themselves to working in an office.

STUDY YOUR NEW WORDS-2

aggravate
[ǽgrəveit]

make worse or more severe
v. 악화시키다, 심화시키다
n. aggravation
New York's hot weather is often **aggravated** by its humidity.

balmy
[bá:mi]

soft and gentle; mild
adj. 향긋한, 부드러운
n. balm
A **balmy** breeze was blowing across the beautiful lake.

culmination
[kʌlminéiʃən]

the highest point; climax
n. 정점, 절정
v. culminate
The **culmination** of the doctor's life's work was his discovery of a cure for cancer.

endorse
[indɔ́:rs]

write one's name on the back of (a check, note, or other document)
v. 배서(背書)하다, 뒷면에 기재하다
n. endorsement
The storekeeper **endorsed** my bill when I paid the full amount.

hygiene
[háidʒi:n]

the science of keeping good health; rules of health
n. 위생학, 건강법
adj. hygienic
The main field of **hygiene** is concerned with healthy living and cleanliness.

intangible
[intǽndʒəbl]

not capable of being touched or felt; impalpable
adj. 만져서 알 수 없는, 무형의

n. intangibility
Sound is *intangible* and the same is true of light.

oblivious
[əblíviəs]

not mindful; forgetful
adj. 망각하고 있는, 잊고 있는
n. oblivion
Grandfather sat by the fireplace, *oblivious* of everything around him.

rite
[rait]

a solemn ceremony; formal procedure in a religious or other observance
n. 의례, 의식
adj. ritual
The funeral will be performed according to church *rites*.

simulate
[símjuleit]

put on a false appearance of; pretend; feign
v. 분장하다, 가장하다, ~인 체하다
adj. simulative
Her story was boring, but he *simulated* interest to please her.

transcribe
[trænskráib]

copy in writing or in typewriting
v. 복사하다, 베끼다
n. transcript
The account of the trial was *transcribed* from the stenographer's shorthand notes.

EXERCISE 2 Fill each blank with the most appropriate word given above.
(Inflect the word if necessary.)

1. The book was so interesting that I was completely _____ of my surroundings.
2. Sharon was the heroine of the play. She _____ the bewildered mother successfully.
3. His bad temper was _____ by a headache.
4. A priest administered the last _____ to the dying man.
5. The next day his speech was _____ in the newspapers, word for word.

STUDY YOUR NEW WORDS-3

annex
[ənéks]

join or add to something larger or more important
v. 병합하다, 부가하다
n. annexation
The United States *annexed* Texas in 1845.

brew
[bruː]

1. make (beer, ale, or mash) by soaking, boiling, and fermenting grain
v. (맥주, 소주 등을) 양조하다
n. brewage
Some people *brew* beer at home for home use.

2. bring about; plan; plot; contrive
v. (음모 등을) 야기하다, 꾸미다
n. brewage
The boys whispering in the corner are *brewing* some mischief.

deride
[diráid]

make fun of; laugh at in scorn
v. 조롱하다, 비웃다
adj. derisive
The boys *derided* him for his fear of the darkness.

evaluate
[ivǽljueit]

find out the value or the amount of; appraise
v. 평가하다, 가치를 검토하다
n. evaluation
She always *evaluates* people by their clothes.

imminent
[íminənt]

likely to happen soon; about to occur; impending; urgent
adj. 절박한, 급박한, 긴급한
n. imminence
Swept along by the swift current, he was in *imminent* danger of going over the waterfall.

judicious
[dʒudíʃəs]

having, using, or showing good judgment; wise; sensible; prudent; discreet
adj. 사려 깊은, 분별 있는, 현명한
n. judiciousness
A *judicious* historian selects and weighs facts carefully and critically.

preponderance
[pripɔ́ndərəns]

greater number; greater power or influence
n. 우세, 우위, 우월
adj. preponderant
There is a *preponderance* of hot days in July and August.

sage
[seidʒ]

showing wisdom or good judgment; wise
adj. 현명한, 명민한
n. sageness
Many *sage* staffs around the commander helped him win the battle.

specter
[spéktər]

a phantom or ghost, especially one of a terrifying nature or appearance; ghost; phantom
n. 유령, 요괴, 귀신
adj. spectral
The *specter* of the murdered man haunted the house.

tumult
[tjúmʌlt]

the confused noise and excitement of a big crowd; uproar
n. 소요, 소동, 혼잡
adj. tumultuous
The shout of "Fire" caused a great *tumult* in the theater.

EXERCISE 3
Fill each blank with the most appropriate word given above.
(Inflect the word if necessary.)

1. The defeated team was greeted by a(n) _____ of angry voices of the crowd.

2. There is a(n) _____ of tigers in the forest, and only a small number of monkeys and elephants.

3. The expedition has now returned, and its members are beginning to _____ and integrate the facts gathered in the field and at the base.

4. The old professor gave us _____ advice, which we have never forgotten.

5. Her little daughter cried in her bed, saying she had seen a dreadful _____ in her dream.

STUDY YOUR NEW WORDS-4

apathy
[ǽpəθi]

lack of interest or desire for activity; indifference; unconcern
n. 냉담, 무심, 무감각
adj. apathetic
Her *apathy* since her husband's death worries her children.

collide
[kəláid]

rush against each other; crush
v. 충동하다, 부딪치다
n. collision
If the aims of two countries *collide*, there may be a war.

drape
[dreip]

cover or hang with cloth falling loosely in folds as a decoration
v. (피륙·포장 따위로) 덮다, 장식하다
n. drapery
The buildings were *draped* with red, white, and blue bunting.

fatuous
[fǽtʃuəs]

stupid; foolish; ridiculous; silly
adj. 우둔한, 어리석은, 바보 같은
n. fatuity
After his boring speech for over an hour, the *fatuous* speaker waited for applause from the audience.

impudent
[ímpjudənt]

without shame or modesty; rudely bold; insolent; impertinent
adj. 뻔뻔스러운, 파렴치한, 건방진
n. impudence
The *impudent* boy made faces at the teacher.

meditate
[méditeit]

think quietly; consider carefully for a long time; reflect
v. 숙고하다, 묵상하다
adj. meditative
I could have given a much better answer if I had had enough time to *meditate*.

purify
[pjúərifai]

make pure; cleanse
v. 깨끗이 하다, 정화하다
n. purification
This music seems to *purify* one's spirit of evil thoughts.

suave
[swɑːv]

smoothly agreeable or polite; showing good manners
adj. 온화한, 상냥한
n. suavity
The secretary's beautiful figure and *suave* manners made the office bright.

vigilance
[vídʒiləns]

watchful care; watchfulness; alertness
n. 경계, 조심
adj. vigilant
The watchman who caught the thief was praised for his *vigilance*.

EXERCISE 4
Fill each blank with the most appropriate word given above.
(Inflect the word if necessary.)

1. After we had waited for about twenty minutes, a(n) _____ man came along and tried to get in at the head of our line.
2. The citizen's _____ to local affairs resulted in poor government.
3. This salt has been specially _____ for use in medicine.
4. The cat watched the mousehole with _____.
5. He _____ for two days before giving his final answer.

해답					
EXERCISE 1.	1. effusive	2. redeemed	3. frugal	4. congested	5. acclimate
EXERCISE 2.	1. oblivious	2. simulated	3. aggravated	4. rite	5. transcribed
EXERCISE 3.	1. tumult	2. preponderance	3. evaluate	4. sage	5. specter
EXERCISE 4.	1. impudent	2. apathy	3. purified	4. vigilance	5. meditated

종합 연습 문제

1 Complete the following table with the appropriate word forms.

ADJECTIVE	NOUN	VERB	ADVERB
1. _____	preponderance	_____	_____
2. _____	_____	deride	_____
3. _____	_____	redeem	XXXXX
4. _____	nausea	_____	_____
5. sagacious	_____	XXXXX	_____
6. _____	balm	XXXXX	_____
7. _____	_____	simulate	_____
8. effusive	_____	_____	_____
9. XXXXX	_____	seep	XXXXX
10. _____	_____	meditate	_____

2 Supply the correct form of the word in italics for the blank space in each sentence.

1. *endorse*   You have to sign the _____ on the back of a check, in evidence of its transfer or assuring its payment.

2. *oblivious*   Drug addicts like to use narcotic because it causes complete _____ of all sorrows.

3. *suave*   Before I asked her name, she introduced herself with perpect _____.

4. *symmetry*   Notice the _____ looks of human body; the right side is the counterpart of the left.

5. *drape*   The gay colors of the _____ made the living room bright and cheery.

6. *vigilance*   While she was out, the faithful dog kept _____ guard over the baby.

7. *frugal*   Riches are achieved with industry and kept by _____.

8. *apathy*   The lazy boy's _____ attitude toward schoolwork annoyed both his teacher and his parents.

9. *tumult*   I couldn't hear what she said because of the sailor's _____ voice.

10. *transcribe*   The college wanted a _____ of the student's high school record.

3 In the space provided, write the *letter* of the word NOT RELATED in meaning to the other words in each line.

_____ 1. (A) fatuous (B) grateful (C) ridiculous (D) stupid

_____ 2. (A) ghost (B) phantom (C) specter (D) perfume

_____ 3. (A) cynical (B) impending (C) imminent (D) urgent

_____ 4. (A) impalpable (B) insubstantial (C) intangible (D) indulgent

_____ 5. (A) elastic (B) judicious (C) prudent (D) discreet

_____ 6. (A) annex (B) subjoin (C) split (D) affix

_____ 7. (A) uproar (B) savor (C) riot (D) tumult

_____ 8. (A) insolent (B) impudent (C) impertinent (D) insane

_____ 9. (A) indifference (B) contour (C) apathy (D) unconcern

_____ 10. (A) ooze (B) seep (C) peep (D) trickle

4 Fill each blank with the most appropriate word from the vocabulary list below.

> **VOCABULARY LIST**
>
> collided   aggrabate   insolvent
> meditate   symmetry   imminent
> culmination   hygiene   endorse
> seeped   annexed   redeemed

1. He had to _____ the check before the bank would cash it.

2. Water had _____ into the house through the walls and roof.

3. The property on which the money was lent was _____ when the loan was paid back.

4. The black clouds, thunder, and lightning show that a storm is _____.

5. Telling a lie in the court will only _____ your guilt.

6. The Hawaiian Islands were _____ to the United States by act of Congress, July 7, 1898.

7. The _____ of the Christmas party was the appearance of Santa Claus.

8. The terrible earthquake killed thousands of people in the city, and it led me to _____ on the weakness of human beings.

9. The bump on the left side of her forehead spoiled the _____ of her face.

10. Two large ships _____ in the harbor and both sank.

해답

1

ADJECTIVE	NOUN	VERB	ADVERB
1. preponderant	(preponderance)	preponderate	preponderantly
2. derisive	derision	(deride)	deridingly
3. redemptive	redemption	(redeem)	XXXXX
4. nauseous	(nausea)	nauseate	nauseously
5. (sagacious)	sagacity	XXXXX	sagaciously
6. balmy	(balm)	XXXXX	balmily
7. simulative	simulation	(simulate)	simulatively
8. (effusive)	effusion	effuse	effusively
9. XXXXX	seepage	(seep)	XXXXX
10. meditative	meditation	(meditate)	meditatively

2
1. endorsement 2. oblivion 3. suavity 4. symmetrical 5. drapery
6. vigilant 7. frugality 8. apathetic 9. tumultuous 10. transcript

3
1. B 2. D 3. A 4. D 5. A 6. C 7. B 8. D 9. B 10. C

4
1. endorse 2. seeped 3. redeemed 4. imminent 5. aggravate
6. annexed 7. culmination 8. meditate 9. symmetry 10. collided

Lesson 28

PRETEST 28

Insert the *letter* of the best answer in the space provided.

1. A(n) _____ surgeon works with *dexterity*.
   (A) good   (B) unskilled

2. In _____ weather the air is very *humid*.
   (A) windy   (B) rainy

3. The little girl was in *ecstasy* over _____.
   (A) the pitiful beggar   (B) her new puppy

4. Work is *repugnant* to _____ people.
   (A) lazy   (B) diligent

5. The doctor said that _____ would *suffice* the patient.
   (A) smoking or drinking   (B) two meals a day

ANSWERS 1.A 2.B 3.B 4.A 5.B

STUDY YOUR NEW WORDS-1

accelerate
[æksélərèit]
cause to move faster; speed up
v. 가속하다, 촉진하다
n. acceleration
The engineer *accelerates* a train by turning on more power.

averse
[əvə́:rs]
turned away in mind or feeling; having a strong dislike; opposed
adj. 싫어하는, ~에 반대하는
n. aversion
I will keep it secret; I feel *averse* to telling it to someone.

corroborate
[kərɔ́bərèit]
make more certain; give support or certainty to; confirm
v. 확실히 하다, ~에 확증을 주다
adj. corroborative
Two persons who saw the road accident *corroborated* the driver's statement.

encamp
[inkǽmp]

make camp; settle in tents
v. 진을 치다, 야영하다
n. encampment
It took the soldiers only half an hour to *encamp* in the heavy rain.

humid
[hjú:mid]

slightly wet; moist; damp
adj. 습기 있는, 누기 찬
n. humidity
The air is very *humid* near the sea or large lake.

irrigation
[irigéiʃən]

the act of supplying water
n. 물을 댐, 관개(灌漑)
adj. irrigational
It is impossible to make plants grow in a desert without *irrigation*.

preeminent
[pri:émineənt]

standing out above all others; superior to others; outstanding
adj. 탁월한, 월등한, 현저한
n. preeminence
Every baseball player envies him; he is *preeminent* above all his rivals for pitching.

rudiment
[rú:dimənt]

the first steps or stages; a part to be learned first; beginning
n. 기본, 근본, 초보
adj. rudimentary
Everyone learns the *rudiments* of arithmetic at the elementary school.

stifle
[stáifl]

stop the breath of; cause difficulty in breathing; smother
v. 질식시키다, 숨막히게 하다
adj. stifling
When they got in the boiler room they were almost *stifled* by the heat.

versatile
[və́:rsətail]

able to do many things well; having many kinds of skill
adj. 다재다능한, 재주가 많은
n. versatility
He is a very *versatile* performer; he can act, sing, dance, and play the piano.

EXERCISE 1 Fill each blank with the most appropriate word given above.
(Inflect the word if necessary.)

1. _____ is needed to make crops grow in dry regions.

2. It is almost impossible to learn multiplication without knowing the _____ of addition.

3. Witnesses _____ her statement that there were two men in the room around that time.

4. Theodore Roosevelt was a(n) _____ man; he was successful as a statesman, soldier, sportsman, explorer, and author.

5. The black smoke filled the building and almost _____ the firemen in it.

STUDY YOUR NEW WORDS-2

anatomy
[ənǽtəmi]

the structure of animals and plants; structure
n. (동식물의) 구조, 조직, 해부학
adj. anatomical
The *anatomy* of an earthworm is much simpler than that of a man.

brawn
[brɔːn]

muscular strength; muscle
n. 근육, 힘
adj. brawny
Football requires brain as well as *brawn*.

dexterity
[dekstérəti]

skill in using the hands
n. 솜씨 좋음, 교묘함
adj. dexterous
Dexterity in questioning the witnesses helped the lawyer win many cases.

erupt
[irʌ́pt]

explode and pour fire; burst forth
v. 폭발하다, 분출하다
n. eruption
Mount Vesuvius hasn't *erupted* for a good many years.

hypothesis
[haipɔ́θisis]

an idea or suggestion put forward as a starting point for reasoning
n. 가설, 가정, 전제
adj. hypothetical
Let's discuss this topic on the *hypothesis* that it is true.

manipulate
[mənípjuleit]

handle or control with skill
v. 조종하다, 조작하다
n. manipulation
To drive an automobile, you must learn how to *manipulate* the steering wheel and pedals.

prowess
[práuis]

great personal bravery; daring
n. 용감, 용맹
adj. prowessful
The tribesmen sang a song of victory, describing their *prowess* in battle.

scrupulous
[skrú:pjuləs]

1. very careful to do what is right; conscientious
adj. 양심적인, 견실한
n. scrupulosity
A less *scrupulous* man wouldn't give the money back to its owner.

2. attending thoroughly to details; very cautious
adj. 세심한, 면밀한
n. scrupulosity
The nurse treated the wounded soldiers with the most *scrupulous* care.

suffice
[səfáis]

meet the desires, need, or requirement; satisfy
v. 충분하게 하다, 만족시키다
n. sufficiency
One hundred dollars a month will *suffice* for the old lady's need.

EXERCISE 2	**Fill each blank with the most appropriate word given above. (Inflect the word if necessary.)**

1. His new _____ gives a possible reason for the existence of life on the moon.

2. Mother told me that fifty dollars would _____ for my summer travel, but as it turned out, it was not enough.

3. His _____ and skill as a footballer makes it certain that he'll be chosen for the team.

4. A clever politician knows how to _____ his supporters.

5. Steve is _____ about returning books to the library on time; he has never paid a late fine.

STUDY YOUR NEW WORDS-3

antique
[ænti:k]
of a time long past; out of date; old-fashioned
adj. 오래된, 구식의, 시대에 뒤진
n. antiquity
He really likes *antique* art much more than modern art.

coherent
[kouhíərənt]
being naturally or reasonable connected; consistent; sticking together
adj. 조리가 서는, 시종 일관된
n. coherence
In *coherent* writing, every sentence is connected in thought to the previous sentence.

doze
[douz]
sleep lightly; be half asleep
v. 졸다, 겉잠 들다
adj. dozy
After dinner my father often *dozes* in his chair for a while.

fascinate
[fǽsineit]
attract very strongly; enchant by charming qualities
v. 매혹하다, 황홀케 하다
n. fascination
The actress's beauty and cleverness *fascinated* everyone in the room.

innovate
[ínouveit]
make change; bring in something new
v. 혁신하다, 쇄신하다
n. innovation
Some people like to *innovate* the old systems and traditions; others like to preserve them.

mystify
[místifai]
bewilder purposely; perplex; puzzle to make mysterious
v. 미혹시키다, 불가해하게 하다
n. mystification
The magician's tricks *mystified* the audience in the theater.

recur
[rikə́:r]
come up again; occur again; be repeated
v. 반복되다, 재발하다
n. recurrence
Leap year *recurs* every four years, and in the year February has 29 days.

shimmer
[ʃímər]
shine with a soft trembling light; gleam faintly
v. 희미하게 비치다, 가물거리다
adj. shimmery
The sky was clear, and moonlight was *shimmering* on the lake.

technicality
[teknikǽləti]

a technical matter, term, or expression
n. 전문 사항, 전문 용어
v. technicalize
The general explained the military *technicalities* of the matter to the newspaper reporters.

> **EXERCISE 3** Fill each blank with the most appropriate word given above.
> (Inflect the word if necessary.)
>
> 1. The children were _____ by all the marvellous toys in th shop window of the store.
> 2. He bought a(n) _____ chair at a high price, which had been made in 1860.
> 3. A(n) _____ sentence is easy to read and clear to understand.
> 4. The magician put an egg in an empty box, and in a few seconds a hen came out of it. I was completely _____ about what happened.
> 5. It is difficult to _____ when people prefer the old, familiar way of doing things.

STUDY YOUR NEW WORDS-4

articulate
[ɑːrtíkjulit]

1. spoken in distinct syllables or words; clear
adj. 분명한, 명료한
n. articulation
A baby cries and gurgles but does not use *articulate* speech.

[ɑːrtíkjuleit]

2. speak distinctly; express in clear sounds or words
v. 분명히 말하다, 또박또박 발음하다
n. articulation
The speaker was careful to *articulate* his words so that everyone in the hall could understand him.

confront
[kənfrʌ́nt]

meet face to face; face boldly; stand facing
v. 마주치다, 맞서다, 직면하다
n. confrontation
The soldiers were *confronted* by two terrorists as they left their camp.

ecstasy
[ékstəsi]

a condition of very great joy; rapture
n. 황홀경, 무아경
v. ecstasize
While she was waiting for her boyfriend in the tearoom, a sweet melody filled her with *ecstasy*.

foster
[fɔ́stər]

help the growth or development of; promote; help to grow
v. 육성하다, 조성하다, 양육하다
n. fosterage
The mother tried to *foster* her son's interest in music by taking him to concerts frequently.

irradiate
[iréidieit]

shine upon; light up; make bright; illuminate
v. 비추다, 빛나게 하다, 밝게 하다
n. irradiation
The hall is not dim; the four large lamps *irradiate* it.

obstinate
[ɔ́bstinit]

firmly holding to one's opinion or purpose; stubborn
adj. 완고한, 고집 센, 끈질긴
n. obstinacy
The *obstinate* man would go his own way, in spite of all warnings.

repugnant
[ripʌ́gnənt]

disagreeable or offensive; distasteful
adj. 비위에 거슬리는, 싫은, 불유쾌한
n. repugnance
Some people eat foods that are *repugnant* to others.

soporific
[soupərífik]

causing or tending to cause sleep; drowsy
adj. 졸음을 오게 하는, 졸린
adv. soporiferously
After his *soporific* speech for an hour, the speaker received no applause from the audience.

triumph
[tráiəmf]

a notable success or achievement; great victory
n. 승리, 대성공
adj. triumphant
The conquest of outer space is one of the greatest *triumphs* of modern science.

EXERCISE 4 **Fill each blank with the most appropriate word given above.**
(Inflect the word if necessary.)

1. We _____ the little girl while her mother was in hospital.

2. John was a really _____ man; we tried to get him to change his mind, but in vain.

3. The little band of settlers, with rifles on their hands, _____ the bandits.

4. The general achieved a glorious _____ over the enemy in the battle.

5. A(n) _____ sermon can not get the audience to pay attention to the speaker; it merely makes the hearers fall into sleep.

EXERCISE 1.	1. irrigation	2. rudiment	3. corroborated	4. versatile	5. stifled
EXERCISE 2.	1. hypothesis	2. suffice	3. prowess	4. manipulate	5. scrupulous
EXERCISE 3.	1. fascinated	2. antique	3. coherent	4. mystified	5. innovate
EXERCISE 4.	1. fostered	2. obstinate	3. confronted	4. triumph	5. soporific

종합 연습 문제

1 Complete the following table with the appropriate word forms.

	ADJECTIVE	NOUN	VERB	ADVERB
1.	_____	ecstasy	_____	_____
2.	__XXXXX__	_____	encamp	__XXXXX__
3.	_____	_____	cohere	_____
4.	_____	hypothesis	_____	_____
5.	_____	shimmer	shimmer	__XXXXX__
6.	_____	_____	recur	_____
7.	antique	_____	_____	__XXXXX__
8.	_____	_____	fascinate	_____
9.	_____	_____	_____	sufficiently
10.	_____	_____	erupt	_____

2 Supply the correct form of the word in italics for the blank space in each sentence.

1. *doze* — Most people feel unwilling to work in a _____ summer afternoon.
2. *dexterity* — A successful manager should be _____ in handling people as well as managing money.
3. *antique* — That vase is of such great _____ that nobody knows how old it is.
4. *brawn* — The muscles of his _____ arms are as strong as iron bands.
5. *foster* — The chairman stood at the head of _____ of community development.
6. *recur* — More care in the future will prevent _____ of the same mistake.
7. *suffice* — The ship had a _____ of provisions for a voyage of two months.
8. *articulate* — If you read slowly, your _____ will be much better.
9. *humid* — On a hot, sultry day it is very difficult to work because of the _____.
10. *averse* — She always put three spoons of sugar in her coffee; she has an _____ to the bitter taste of it.

3 In the space provided, write the *letter* of the word that has most nearly the SAME MEANING as the italicized word.

_____ 1. the final *triumph* over the enemy (A) warning (B) victory (C) attack (D) fire

Lesson 28

_____ 2. the *articulate* speech (A) boring   (B) amusing   (C) solemn   (D) clear

_____ 3. an *obstinate* man (A) stubborn   (B) soporific   (C) repugnant   (D) coherent

_____ 4. to *corroborate* his testimony (A) confirm   (B) confess   (C) conceal   (D) conclude

_____ 5. an *antique* gown (A) beautiful   (B) precious   (C) old-fashioned   (D) dirty

3 Fill each blank with the most appropriate word selected from the vocabulary list below.

VOCABULARY LIST

coherent	irradiated	recur
prowess	accelerate	erupt
averse	manipulated	confronted
hypothesis	foster	ecstasy

1. He likes to talk about political problems among his friends, but was _____ to discussing politics in public.

2. The clerk stole money from the firm and _____ the accounts to conceal his theft.

3. Sunshine, fresh air, and rest often _____ a person's recovery from sickness.

4. The driver was so upset that he could not give a(n) _____ account of the accident.

5. We hope his illness will not _____; no longer can he afford to pay his medical expenses.

6. Films and pictures about recent wars sometimes _____ angry memories and feelings of hatred between nations.

7. Mystics, religious prophets, and poets have been known to go into _____ when meditating or seeking inspiration.

8. The volcano suddenly began to _____ lava and ashes, and the inhabitants took refuge to a safe place.

9. When Columbus first presented his _____ that the earth is round, very few believed it.

10. Two firemen showed great _____ by repeatedly rushing into the burning building to save many lives.

해답

1

ADJECTIVE	NOUN	VERB	ADVERB
1. ecstatic	(ecstasy)	ecstasize	ecstatically
2. XXXXX	encampment	(encamp)	XXXXX
3. coherent	coherence	(cohere)	coherently
4. hypothetical	(hypothesis)	hypothesize	hypothetically
5. shimmery	(shimmer)	(shimmer)	XXXXX
6. recurrent	recurrence	(recur)	recurrently
7. (antique)	antiquity	antiquate	XXXXX
8. fascinating	fascination	(fascinate)	fascinatingly
9. sufficient	sufficiency	suffice	(sufficiently)
10. eruptive	eruption	(erupt)	eruptively

2 1. dozy   2. dexterous   3. antiquity   4. brawny   5. fosterage
   6. recurrence   7. sufficiency   8. articulation   9. humidity   10. aversion

3 1. B   2. D   3. A   4. A   5. C

4 1. averse   2. manipulated   3. accelerate   4. coherent   5. recur
   6. foster   7. ecstasy   8. erupt   9. hypothesis   10. prowess

Lesson 29

PRETEST 29

Insert the *letter* of the best answer in the space provided.

1. It takes years of hard work to *compile* _____.
   (A) a good dictionary (B) a foreign language

2. The early _____ lives were full of *tribulations*.
   (A) Christians' (B) emperors'

3. The soldier was _____ for *valor* in battle.
   (A) heavily punished (B) given a medal

4. The coach's *autocratic* manner made him _____ among the players of the team.
   (A) popular (B) unpopular

5. She was greatly *encumbered* on the trip by _____.
   (A) the big radio (B) a good companion

ANSWERS 1. A 2. A 3. B 4. B 5. A

STUDY YOUR NEW WORDS-1

abound
[əbáund]
be plentiful or numerous; exist in large numbers
v. 풍부하다, 많이 있다
adj. abundant
Our nation *abounds* in opportunities for well-educated young men and women.

arrogant
[ǽrəgənt]
in a proud, superior manner; showing too much pride
adj. 거만한, 건방진
n. arrogance
He behaved in such *arrogant* manners in his firm that he was at last fired out.

compile
[kəmpáil]
make or form a book or a list out of various materials
v. 편찬하다, 편집하다, 수집하다

n. compilation

It takes a long time as well as many experts working together to *compile* an encyclopedia.

entreat
[entríːt]

keep asking earnestly; beg and pray; implore
v. 간청하다, 간원하다
n. entreaty

The muderer *entreated* the judge to show mercy, but was sentenced to death.

filth
[filθ]

foul, disgusting dirt; obscenity
n. 오물, 불결물, 더러움
adj. filthy

The alley was filled with lots of garbage and other *filth*.

incumbent
[inkʌ́mbənt]

resting as a duty; being the moral duty of (someone)
adj. 의무로 지워지는, 도덕적 의무가 되는
n. incumbency

It is *incumbent* on you to give a father's advice before your son leaves home.

monotony
[mənɔ́təni]

sameness of tone or pitch; lack of variety
n. 단조로움, 무미 건조
adj. monotonous

At sea, everything that breaks the *monotony* of the surrounding expanse attracts attention.

reciprocate
[risíprəkeit]

give in return; give and receive
v. 보답하다, 주고받다
n. reciprocation

I hope I can *reciprocate* your hospitality sometime.

shaggy
[ʃǽgi]

covered with a mass of hair or wool
adj. 털복숭이의, 털이 많은
n. shagginess

The *shaggy* dog always sleeps in the bed with her.

tribulation
[tribjuléiʃən]

great trouble or misery; hardship; affliction
n. 고난, 고생, 시련
v. tribulate

Hunger, cold, and sickness were among the *tribulations* of pioneer life.

EXERCISE 1
Fill each blank with the most appropriate word given above.
(Inflect the word if necessary.)

1. She invited me to her birthday party, and I _____ by wishing her a happy Christmas.
2. The blue whale once _____ in the Antarctic, but is becoming more and more scarce.
3. She _____ her father to send her to the United States for her further study.
4. He _____ enough information on his tour of South Africa to write a book.
5. It is _____ upon you to warn the boy of the harm of smoking.

STUDY YOUR NEW WORDS-2

adolescent
[ædoulésnt]

1. growing up from childhood to adulthood
adj. 청춘의, 청춘기의
n. adolescence
He read many books in the *adolescent* stage of his life.

2. a person growing up from childhood to manhood or womanhood
n. 청년, 젊은이
One who is 15 years old is not an adult, but an *adolescent*.

autocratic
[ɔːtəkrǽtik]

of or like an autocrat; having absolute power or authority; dictatorial
adj. 독재자의, 독재적인
n. autocracy
Adolf Hitler demanded the *autocratic* power; no one could rigorously oppose his plans or decisions.

congenial
[kəndʒíːniəl]

having similar tastes and interests; agreeable
adj. 마음이 맞는, 마음이 내키는
n. congeniality
All the furniture of the room was very *congenial* to my taste.

encumber
[enkʌ́mbər]

make free action or movement difficult; hinder; obstruct; hamper
v. 방해하다, 막다, 거치적거리게 하다
n. encumbrance
The room was *encumbered* with heavy furniture.

horrify
[hɔ́rifai]

cause to feel horror; shock very much
v. 몸서리치게 하다, 무섭게 하다
n. horror
Every night the little girl was *horrified* by the tiger's cry.

manifest
[mǽnifest]

apparent to the eye or to the mind; obvious; evident
adj. 명백한, 분명한
n. manifestation
It is now *manifest* that, if you don't return the book to the library right now, you will have to pay a late fine.

nutrition
[nju:tríʃən]

the action of providing or state of being provided with food
n. 영양, 영양 섭취
adj. nutritious
Good health is not always obtained by good *nutrition*.

repress
[riprés]

keep down; hold back; prevent from acting; suppress
v. 억누르다, 억제하다, 진압하다
n. repression
They could *repress* the rising of people with the help of the army.

smuggle
[smʌ́gl]

bring into or take out of a country secretly and against the law
v. 밀수하다, 밀매하다
n. smuggler
They were accused of *smuggling* of diamonds from foreign countries.

tangible
[tǽndʒəbl]

can be touched or felt by touch; physical; material
adj. 만져서 알 수 있는, 실체적인, 유형의
n. tangibility
There has been a *tangible* improvement in his school work.

EXERCISE 2 **Fill each blank with the most appropriate word given above.**
(Inflect the word if necessary.)

1. I enjoyed the party last night; the _____ atmosphere of the party pleased me.
2. Milk, meat, fruits, and vegetables provide good _____.
3. It is a crime to _____ jewelry into Korea.
4. They are _____ by their parents, who prevent them from playing or shouting.
5. Rubbish and old boxes on the passage _____ the fire escape.

STUDY YOUR NEW WORDS-3

analogy
[ənǽlədʒi]

a degree of likeness or sameness; likeness in someways between things
n. 유사, 비슷함, 닮음
adj. analogous
The teacher drew an *analogy* between the human heart and a pump.

billow
[bílou]

a very large wave of water
n. (큰) 파도
adj. billowy
The ship was tossed by the ocean *billows* in the storm.

detonate
[détouneit]

(cause to) explode suddenly with loud noise
v. 폭발시키다, 폭발하다
n. detonation
The bomb was *detonated* from several miles away; it caused no damage to our town.

entangle
[entǽŋgl]

get twisted up and caught; tangle
v. 엉클어지게 하다, 얽히게 하다
n. entanglement
The fly became *entangled* in the spider's web.

hibernate
[háibərneit]

pass the winter in a state like sleep; spend the winter
v. 동면하다, 겨울을 지내다
n. hibernation
During long severe winters some animals, such as badgers, ground squirrels, and some insects, *hibernate*.

intuition
[intjuíʃən]

the immediate perception or understanding of truths or facts without reasoning.
n. 직관, 직관적 통찰
adj. intuitive
By experience with all kinds of people the doctor has developed great powers of *intuition*.

pollute
[pəljúːt]

make impure, foul, or dirty; destroy the purity of; contaminate
v. 오염시키다, 더럽히다
n. pollution
Many rivers in Korea are *polluted* with filthy waste from factories.

revere
[rivíər]

give great respect and admiration to; respect deeply
v. 존경하다, 숭배하다

	n. reverence She *reveres* her grandfather; he is strict in decision, but shows great affection to her.
solitary [sɔ́litəri]	alone or single; without compainons; lonely ***adj.*** 외톨의, 혼자의, 고독한 **n.** solitude The hermit led a *solitary* life in the deep mountains far away from the town.
valor [vǽlər]	courage; bravery ***n.*** 용기, 용맹 **adj.** valiant They owed their lives to the *valor* of the firemen.

EXERCISE 3 — **Fill each blank with the most appropriate word given above.**
(Inflect the word if necessary.)

1. The bird flew into the nets, and the more it struggled the more it _____ itself.

2. The company commander showed great _____ in leading his men despite a painful wound in his leg.

3. The water along the beach was _____ by refuse from those factories.

4. In February, my parents returned from Florida where he had _____ since Christmas.

5. The students _____ the old professor; he has wisdom as well as profound knowledge in his field.

STUDY YOUR NEW WORDS-4

antagonist [æntǽgənist]	one who is opposed to another; opponent; adversary ***n.*** 적수, 적대자, 적 **adj.** antagonistic The brave knight defeated each *antagonist* who came against him.
cognizant [kɔ́gnizənt]	having knowledge; being fully aware of; conscious ***adj.*** 인식하고 있는, 알고 있는 **n.** cognizance As the doctor was fully *cognizant* of the patient's serious condition, he acted swiftly to relieve it.

Lesson 29

doleful
[dóulfəl]

very sad or dreary; mournful; dismal
adj. 음울한, 슬픈, 쓸쓸한
n. dolefulness
His *doleful* expression showed that he had failed in the examination.

facility
[fəsíləti]

1. the quality of being able to be done easily
n. 용이성, 손쉬움
v. facilitate
The *facility* of communication is far greater now than it was a hundred years ago.

2. an advantage; convenience
n. 편익, 편의; 설비
v. facilitate
A free bus to the airport is a *facility* offered only by this hotel.

improvise
[ímprəvaiz]

make up on the spur of the moment; sing or speak without preparation
v. 즉석에서 만들다, 즉흥적으로 하다
n. improvisation
He *improvised* a new stanza for the school song at the football game.

inquisitive
[inkwízitiv]

asking many questions; prying into other people's affairs
adj. 캐묻기 좋아하는, 알고 싶어하는
n. inquiry
The old lady was very *inquisitive* about what her neighbors were doing.

protrude
[prətrú:d]

(cause to) stick out or stretch outwards from a place; thrust forth
v. 불쑥 내밀다, 불쑥 나오다
n. protrusion
The policeman stopped the man when he saw a gun *protruding* from his pocket.

savor
[séivər]

a taste or smell; flavor; relish
n. 맛, 풍미, 향기
adj. savory
He used to say that argument adds a *savor* to conversation.

subvert
[sʌbvə́:rt]

overthrow; cause the downfall of; ruin; destroy
v. 뒤엎다, 멸망시키다, 파괴하다
n. subversion
Much of the city was *subverted* by the earthquake and a great fire.

EXERCISE 4 Fill each blank with the most appropriate word given above.
(Inflect the word if necessary.)

1. A normal child is very _____ about what animals live on the moon or stars.

2. The soup had been boiled too long and lost its peculiar _____.

3. It is obvious that the aim of communists is to _____ the democratic systems.

4. Keep your feet under your desk; do not let them _____ into the aisle.

5. The boys _____ a tent out of two blankets and a long pole.

EXERCISE 1.	1. reciprocated	2. abounded	3. entreated	4. compiled	5. incumbent
EXERCISE 2.	1. congenial	2. nutrition	3. smuggle	4. repressed	5. encumbered
EXERCISE 3.	1. entangled	2. valor	3. polluted	4. hibernated	5. reverse
EXERCISE 4.	1. inquisitive	2. savor	3. subvert	4. protrude	5. improvised

종합 연습 문제

1 Complete the following table with the appropriate word forms.

ADJECTIVE	NOUN	VERB	ADVERB
1. _____	valor	___XXXXX___	_____
2. _____	facility	_____	_____
3. inquisitive	_____	_____	_____
4. _____	_____	reciprocate	_____
5. _____	_____	abound	_____
6. _____	_____	revere	_____
7. _____	horror	_____	_____
8. _____	_____	compile	___XXXXX___
9. _____	_____	subvert	_____
10. _____	_____	protrude	_____

2 Supply the correct form of the word in italics for the blank space in each sentence.

1. *nutrition*   Apples and oranges are very _____ food.
2. *savor*   The _____ smell of roasting turkey greeted us as we entered the house.
3. *solitary*   Both the prosector in the desert and the shy person in the city live in _____.
4. *analogy*   The wing of an airplane is _____ to the wing of a bird.
5. *cognizant*   The judge took _____ of the accused man's ill health in handing down the sentence.
6. *facility*   The broken lock _____ my entrance into the empty house.
7. *encumber*   Shoes or long hair must be an _____ to a swimmer.
8. *manifest*   Entering the burning building was a _____ of his courage.
9. *reciprocate*   Although I gave him many presents, I had no _____ gifts from him.
10. *entreat*   The savages paid no attention to their captive's _____ for mercy.

3 In the space provided, write the *letter* of the word NOT RELATED in meaning to the other words on the line.

_____ 1.   (A) encumber   (B) obstruct   (C) irradiate   (D) hamper

_____ 2. (A) cognizant (B) averse (C) aware (D) conscious

_____ 3. (A) pollute (B) restrain (C) suppress (D) repress

_____ 4. (A) savor (B) relish (C) flavor (D) billow

_____ 5. (A) kindred (B) congenial (C) shaggy (D) sympathetic

_____ 6. (A) affliction (B) hardship (C) tribulation (D) nutrition

_____ 7. (A) ecstasy (B) antagonist (C) opponent (D) adversary

_____ 8. (A) obvious (B) manifest (C) obstinate (D) evident

_____ 9. (A) doleful (B) dismal (C) mournful (D) autocratic

_____ 10. (A) upset (B) smuggle (C) overthrow (D) subvert

Fill each blank with the most appropriate word from the vocabulary list below.

VOCABULARY LIST

filth	detonate	incumbent
protruded	congenial	analogy
repress	improvise	tangible
adolescent	monotony	entangled

1. He _____ his feet in the coil of rope and fell down.

2. No one lives in the old house; it is full of _____.

3. The police need _____ proof of his guilt before they can act against him.

4. If an actor forgets his words on the stage, he has to _____ the scene.

5. He is not an adult; he is still in the _____ stage of growth.

6. He enjoyed his trip to Europe very much; some _____ companions made the trip successful.

7. It is a(n) _____ responsibility on all military officers to maintain the dignity of the uniform.

8. The saucy child _____ her tongue when her mother balmed her for her laziness.

9. When she was given a Christmas gift from her boyfriend, she could not _____ her desire to open it immediately.

10. There is a(n) _____ between the way water moves in waves and the way light travels.

1

ADJECTIVE	NOUN	VERB	ADVERB
1. valiant	(valor)	XXXXX	valiantly
2. facile	(facility)	facilitate	facilely
3. (inquisitive)	inquisition or inquiry	inquire	inquisitively
4. reciprocal	reciprocation	(reciprocate)	reciprocally
5. abundant	abundance	(abound)	abundantly
6. reverent	reverence	(revere)	reverently
7. horrible	(horror)	horrify	horribly
8. compilatory	compilation	(compile)	XXXXX
9. subversive	subversion	(subvert)	subversively
10. protrusive	protrusion	(protrude)	protrusively

2
1. nutritious 2. savory 3. solitude 4. analogous 5. cognizance
6. facilitated 7. encumbrance 8. manifestation 9. reciprocal 10. entreaty

3
1. C 2. B 3. A 4. D 5. C 6. D 7. A 8. C 9. D 10. B

4
1. entangled 2. filth 3. tangible 4. improvise 5. adolescent
6. congenial 7. incumbent 8. protruded 9. repress 10. analogy

Lesson 30

PRETEST 30

Insert the *letter* of the best answer in the space provided.

1. The young man took the vows of *chivalry* to become a _____.
   (A) scholar   (B) knight   (C) judge

2. *Diagnosis* is one of the most important parts of the _____.
   (A) doctor's work   (B) nuclear warfare   (C) mechanical engineering

3. It is difficult to _____ someone who is *elusive*.
   (A) marry   (B) teach   (C) find

4. The woman was often *persecuted* by the man, and she _____ him.
   (A) likes   (B) knows   (C) hates

5. He is so *vindictive* that he never _____ anybody.
   (A) dislikes   (B) forgives   (C) despises

ANSWERS 1. B 2. A 3. C 4. C 5. B

STUDY YOUR NEW WORDS-1

addict	1. give oneself up to a habit
[ədíkt]	*v.* 빠지게 하다, (습관이) 들게 하다
	n. addiction
	He is *addicted* to alcohol and drugs.
[ǽdikt]	2. a person who is a slave to a habit
	n. 상용자, 중독자
	Doctors and policemen disagree on how to control drug distribution and handle *addicts*.

assiduous	having or showing careful and continual attention
[əsídʒuəs]	*adj.* 근면한, 열심인, 성실한
	n. assiduity
	He is *assiduous* at his studies; he works hard and steadily, and pays continual attention to his teacher.

Lesson 30   355

conspire
[kənspáiər]

plan secretly with others to do something unlawful or wrong; plot
v. 공모하다, 작당하다, 음모를 꾸미다
n. conspiracy
The two men *conspired* to steal the jewels and then sell them to a jeweler in another country.

elusive
[iljúːsiv]

hard to catch or find; evasive; hard to understand
adj. 잘 빠져 나가는, 잡기 힘든
n. elusion
He is such an *elusive* person; you never know where he is when you want him.

gaudy
[gɔ́ːdi]

too bright and gay to be in good taste; cheap and showy
adj. 번쩍번쩍 빛나는, 번지르르한, 야한
n. gaudiness
A cheap, *gaudy* steamboat arrived at the wharf from St. Louis.

ignite
[ignáit]

set on fire; cause to start to burn; kindle
v. 점화시키다, 불을 붙이다
n. ignition
He *ignited* the match by scratching it on the desk.

negotiate
[nigóuʃieit]

talk with another person to settle disagreement; arrange by discussion
v. 협의하다, 협상하다, 교섭하다
n. negotiation
The trade union is *negotiating* with the employers to get a better contract.

respiration
[rèspəréiʃən]

the act of inhaling and exhaling; breathing
n. 호흡, 호흡작용
adj. respiratory
Respiration is difficult at great heights, and some mountaineers wear oxygen masks to overcome such difficulty.

spice
[spais]

a vegetable substance used to flavor foods
n. 양념, 조미료, 향료
n. spicery
The speaker made a few funny jokes to add *spice* to his speech.

unanimous
[junǽniməs]

in complete accord or agreement; mutually agreed; with no oppositon
adj. 만장일치의, 이의없는

n. unanimity

The proposal was accepted with *unanimous* approval by the commitee.

EXERCISE 1   **Fill each blank with the most appropriate word given above.**
(Inflect the word if necessary.)

1. She would be attractive if she did not wear such _____ jewelry.
2. The children were _____ in their wish to go to the beach in summer.
3. The government has to _____ with opposition party on the new law.
4. The criminals had _____ to rob the First National Bank, but their plot was detected in advance of their action.
5. A drug _____ finds it almost impossible to stop using drugs.

STUDY YOUR NEW WORDS-2

aggregate
[ǽgriɡeit]

1. cause to come together into a group or mass
v. 모으다, 집합하다
n. aggregation
The power of the allies *aggregated* together was great, though individually some were quite weak.

2. amount as a whole to; add up to
v. ~에 달하다, 총계 ~가 되다
His various wages for the year *aggregated* 22,000.

banal
[bənǽl]

not new or interesting; very common; trite
adj. 평범한, 흔히 있는, 진부한
n. banality
Their conversation was *banal*, full of uninteresting remarks, such as "nice weather" and "slow traffic today."

curative
[kjúərətiv]

having the power to cure; tending to cure; remedial
adj. 효험이 있는, 치료가 되는
n. curativeness
Taking a rest in the mountains is very *curative* for breathing difficulties.

enforce
[infɔ́ːrs]

urge with force; cause to be carried out; compel
v. 강요하다, 억지로 시키다, 집행하다

n. enforcement

The robbers *enforced* obedience to their demand by threats of violence.

hypocrite
[hípəkrit]

a person who pretends to be very good or religious
n. 위선자
adj. hypocritical

No one in the village likes the man because he is a shameless *hypocrite*.

intercept
[intərsépt]

stop or seize on the way from one place to another
v. 가로채다, 가로막다
n. interception

It is illegal to *intercept* a letter or parcel before it is delivered.

persecute
[pə́ːrsikjuːt]

treat badly; cause to suffer constantly; do harm to; oppress; harass
v. 박해하다, 학대하다
n. persecution

Some early religious leaders were *persecuted* by their enemies.

sarcasm
[sáːrkæzəm]

the act of making fun of a person to hurt his feelings; harsh or bitter irony
n. 빈정거림, 비꼼, 풍자
adj. sarcastic

"Don't hurry!" said her father in *sarcasm* as she slowly dressed.

superfluous
[sjupə́ːrfluəs]

more than is needed or desired; excessive; surplus
adj. 남는, 여분의, 불필요한
n. superfluity

We have enough food for the picnic; any more food would be *superfluous*.

vindicate
[víndikeit]

show or prove the truth and justice; exculpate
v. 정당성을 입증하다, 혐의를 풀다
n. vindication

The report of the committee of inquiry completely *vindicates* him and declares his action to have been right and proper.

EXERCISE 2 **Fill each blank with the most appropriate word given above.**
(Inflect the word if necessary.)

1. A person who says one thing and does another is called a(n) _____.

2. "How unselfish you are!" said the girl in _____ as her brother took the biggest piece of the cake.

3. The cruel boy _____ the kitten by throwing stones at it whenever it came near to him.

4. I have already stated quite clearly what I think about your idea; any further comment on the subject would be _____.

5. Do not drink so much; you might take away 50 percent from the _____ power of the medicine.

STUDY YOUR NEW WORDS-3

animate
[ǽnimeit]

1. make lively; arouse to action; inspire
v. 생기를 불어넣다, 활기를 띠게 하다
n. animation
A smile *animated* her face as she went to the gate to meet her husband.

[ǽnimit]

2. having life; alive
adj. 생명이 있는, 살아있는
Many scientists now believe that there are some worlds in outer space having *animate* beings.

chivalry
[ʃívəlri]

the qualities of an ideal knight; the rules or beliefs of knight
n. 기사도, 기사도 정신
adj. chivalrous
Chivalry includes bravery, loyalty, honor, courtesy, respect for women, protection of the weak, and generosity.

diagnosis
[daiəgnóusis]

the act or process of finding out diseases; a careful study of the facts
n. 진찰, 진단
adj. diagnostic
The engineers made a complete *diagnosis* of the plane crash by examining the parts for defective workmanship.

exemplify
[igzémplifai]

show or illustrate by example
v. 예증하다, 예시하다
n. exemplification
The teacher *exemplified* the use of the word for the students.

impend
[impénd]

be likely to happen soon; be about to happen
v. 임박하다, 절박하다

Lesson 30 359

adj. impending
When a war *impends*, wise men try to prevent it in advance.

modulate
[mɔ́djuleit]
regulate or adjust; alter the voice in pitch, tone, or volume
v. 조정하다, (음성을) 조절하다
n. modulation
The speaker had a really noble voice which he could *modulate* with great skill.

prophecy
[prɔ́fisi]
the act of telling what will happen in the future; foretelling future events
n. 예언, 예측
v. prophesy
The teacher's *prophecy* that the boy would become a great national leader was later fulfilled.

sensuous
[sénʃuəs]
of the senses; derived from the senses; perceived by the senses
adj. 감각적인, 감각에 의한
n. sensuousness
After hard work we could feel the *sensuous* delight in a hot bath.

tact
[tækt]
the ability to say or do the right things; skill in handling difficult situations
n. 재치, 솜씨, 요령
adj. tactful
A minister of foreign affairs who lacks *tact* is a dangerous man.

vindictive
[vindíktiv]
having or showing a desire for revenge; revengeful; unforgiving; spiteful
adj. 복수심이 강한, 앙심을 품은
adv. vindictively
The *vindictive* little girl tore up her sister's papers.

EXERCISE 3   Fill each blank with the most appropriate word given above.
(Inflect the word if necessary.)

1. The two doctors made different _____ of my disease.

2. Our teacher is able to _____ a lecture on a dull subject with witty remarks.

3. Black clouds and the flashes of lightning are signs that a storm _____.

4. The cat stretched itself with _____ pleasure in the warm sun.

5. Some people are able to _____ their voices according to the size of the room in which they speak.

STUDY YOUR NEW WORDS-4

append
[əpénd]

add to a large thing; attach as a supplement
v. 첨부하다, 추가하다, 덧붙이다
n. appendix
If you hand in your report late, *append* a note explaining the reason for the delay.

communal
[kɔ́mjunəl]

of or for a community; owned jointly by all; public
adj. 공동의, 공공의, 공유의
v. communalize
The Plains Indian has a plentiful and regular supply of meat and skins by the *communal* buffalo hunting.

ecology
[i:kɔ́lədʒi]

a branch of biology that deals with the habits of living things.
n. 생태학(生態學)
adj. ecological
After learning *ecology* I could see the relation of living things to their environment and to each other.

forbear
[fɔ:rbɛ́ər]

hold back; keep from doing; refrain
v. 억제하다, 삼가다, 참다
n. forbearance
He's deserved to be punished several times, but I've *forborne* from doing so.

indifference
[indífərəns]

lack of interest or attention; unconcern
n. 무관심, 무심
adj. indifferent
It was a matter of *indifference* to him whether his hands were clean or dirty.

mediocre
[mi:dióukər]

of average quality; neither bad nor good; ordinary
adj. 좋지도 나쁘지도 않은, 평범한
n. mediocrity
He was a *mediocre* student; his academic records were not excellent, but not bad, either.

rehearse
[rihə́:rs]

1. tell in detail; say over again
v. 상세히 이야기하다, 되풀이하다
He *rehearsed* the story of all his sufferings in prison.

2. learn and practice for later performance
v. 시연하다, 예행 연습하다
n. rehearsal
We *rehearsed* our parts for the school play.

singular
[síŋgjulər]

extraordinary; unusual; queer; odd
adj. 기이한, 기묘한, 희한한
n. singularity
It is unwise to make yourself so *singular* in your clothes.

transient
[trǽnsiənt]

passing quickly or soon; not lasting; transitory; momentary
adj. 일시적인, 순간적인
n. transiency
My mood is only *transient*; it will go away pretty soon.

EXERCISE 4 Fill each blank with the most appropriate word given above.
(Inflect the word if necessary.)

1. I decided to _____ telling her the truth because I knew it would upset her.
2. The children _____ all the happenings of the day to their parents in the evening.
3. The detectives and the policemen were greatly puzzled by the _____ nature of the crime.
4. The boy's _____ to his school work worried both his teacher and his parents.
5. The author _____ a list of troublesome words at the end of the book.

해답

EXERCISE 1.	1. gaudy	2. unanimous	3. negotiate	4. conspired	5. addict
EXERCISE 2.	1. hypocrite	2. sarcasm	3. persecuted	4. superfluous	5. curative
EXERCISE 3.	1. diagnoses	2. animate	3. impends	4. sensuous	5. modulate
EXERCISE 4.	1. forbear	2. rehearsed	3. singular	4. indifference	5. appended

종합 연습 문제

1 Complete the following table with the appropriate word forms.

	ADJECTIVE	NOUN	VERB	ADVERB
1.	_____	chivalry	XXXXX	XXXXX
2.	banal	_____	_____	_____
3.	_____	_____	respire	XXXXX
4.	XXXXX	_____	rehearse	XXXXX
5.	unanimous	_____	XXXXX	_____
6.	_____	_____	intercept	XXXXX
7.	_____	_____	elude	_____
8.	XXXXX	_____	forbear	XXXXX
9.	_____	diagnosis	_____	_____
10.	mediocre	_____	XXXXX	XXXXX

2 Supply the correct form of the word in italics for the blank space in each sentence.

1. *conspire*   The leaders of the _____ against the government were caught and punished.

2. *singular*   The _____ of the woman's appearance attracted much attention in the party.

3. *persecute*   Religious and political _____ drove many people to the United States.

4. *enforce*   Strict _____ of the laws against speeding will reduce automobile accidents.

5. *assiduous*   He plans everything with unfailing _____.

6. *indifference*   The boy was so excited to see snow that he was _____ to the cold.

7. *prophecy*   I wouldn't dare to try to _____ who will win the election.

8. *superfluous*   I have a _____ of pencils for the exam; you may borrow one if you want.

9. *append*   The history book has an _____ containing an account of what has happened since 1950.

10. *sarcasm*   The teacher's _____ comment about the girl's essay made her cry.

3 In the space provided, write the *letter* of the word that has most nearly the SAME MEANING as the italicized word.

_____ 1. artificial *respiration* (A) fiber (B) flower
 (C) light (D) breathing

_____ 2. *append* a word list (A) make (B) copy
 (C) submit (D) attach

_____ 3. a *gaudy* dress (A) old-fashioned (B) bright and showy
 (C) very precious (D) too long

_____ 4. a man of *singular* ability (A) common (B) imaginative
 (C) exceptional (D) creative

_____ 5. the *mediocre* student (A) ordinary (B) excellent
 (C) arrogant (D) diligent

4 Fill each blank with the most appropriate word from the vocabulary list below.

VOCABULARY LIST

ignites	negotiate	communal
tact	indifference	transient
addicted	unanimous	spices
prophecy	intercepted	exemplify

1. His _____ that a war between the two countries would soon break out turned out real.

2. It rained all day in Pusan, but here we had only a(n) _____ shower for minutes.

3. Our leaders found it very difficult to _____ with the communists on the political problems.

4. You will not become _____ to smoking if you refuse cigarettes when they are offered.

5. The town swimming pool is a(n) _____ property; every member of the community can swim in the pool freely.

6. A diligent person works very hard, but a lazy person usually treats his work with _____.

7. She used several kinds of _____ in cooking the meat.

8. A wise politician should have a great _____ in dealing with his supporters.

9. We gained possession of the ball when John _____ a forward pass.

10. He was elected president of the committee by a(n) _____ vote.

해답

1

	ADJECTIVE	NOUN	VERB	ADVERB
1.	chivalrous	(chivalry)	XXXXX	XXXXX
2.	(banal)	banality	banalize	banally
3.	respiratory	respiration	(respire)	XXXXX
4.	XXXXX	rehearsal	(rehearse)	XXXXX
5.	(unanimous)	unanimity	XXXXX	unanimously
6.	interceptive	interception	(intercept)	XXXXX
7.	elusive	elusion	(elude)	elusively
8.	XXXXX	forbearance	(forbear)	XXXXX
9.	diagnostic	(diagnosis)	diagnose	diagnostically
10.	(mediocre)	mediocrity	XXXXX	XXXXX

2
1. conspiracy 2. singularity 3. persecution 4. enforcement 5. assiduity
6. indifferent 7. prophesy 8. superfluity 9. appendix 10. sarcastic

3
1. D 2. D 3. B 4. C 5. A

4
1. prophecy 2. transient 3. negotiate 4. addicted 5. communal
6. indifference 7. spices 8. tact 9. intercepted 10. unanimous

Lesson 31

PRETEST 31

Insert the *letter* of the best answer in the space provided.

1. The _____ was *apprehended* as he tried to cross the river.
   (A) conscientious policeman (B) little girl   (C) escaped prisoner

2. _____ *diverted* the audience's attention from the play.
   (A) The luxurious furniture on the stage (B) The actor's mature performance
   (C) The siren of the fire engine

3. The _____ was made by *excavating* the side of a mountain.
   (A) road   (B) dam   (C) tunnel

4. If a man _____, he becomes *intoxicated*.
   (A) drinks too much whisky (B) makes a large fortune
   (C) fails in an important examination

5. Most people who live _____ are *urban* dwellers.
   (A) near the coast   (B) in apartments (C) in jungles

ANSWERS 1.C 2.C 3.C 4.A 5.B

STUDY YOUR NEW WORDS-1

adhere
[ədhíər]

stick firmly to another or each other; cling; hold closely
v. 달라붙다, 점착하다, 고수하다
n. adherence
The two surfaces *adhered* to each other, and we couldn't get them apart.

audacity
[ɔːdǽsəti]

too much boldness; impudence; reckless daring; boldness
n. 뻔뻔스러움, 넉살 좋음, 대담무쌍
adj. audacious
He had the *audacity* to go to the party without being invited.

contiguity
[kɑ̀ntigjúəti]

the state of being very close together; nearness; proximity; adjacency
n. 인접, 근접, 접근

adj. contiguous
The *contiguity* of the house and the garage was a convenience in bad weather.

enchant
[intʃǽnt]

use magic on; bewitch; delight greatly; charm
v. 마법을 쓰다, 매혹하다
n. enchantment
The witch had *enchanted* the princess so that she would sleep for a month.

grandeur
[grǽndʒər]

great beauty, power, or size; greatness; majesty
n. 웅대, 장엄
adj. grand
As he watched the Niagara Falls, he thought of the *grandeur* of nature.

infer
[infə́:r]

find out by reasoning; come to believe after thinking
v. 추리하다, 추론하다
n. inference
From her story we *inferred* that they went to the United States unwillingly.

numb
[nʌm]

without ability to feel or move; unable to feel anything
adj. 마비된, 감각이 없는
n. numbness
I cannot write a letter; my fingers are *numb* with cold.

remit
[rimít]

1. send money in payment to a person or place
v. (돈을) 보내다, 우송하다
n. remittance
Please *remit* the amount of your bill by check.

2. forgive all or a portion of a debt or punishment
v. 면제하다, 용서하다
n. remission
The girl was accused of stealing a pair of shoes, but because of her young age the judge *remitted* the prison sentence.

skeptical
[sképtikəl]

unwilling to believe a claim or promise; distrustful; incredulous
adj. 회의적인, 회의론적인
n. skepticism
His *skeptical* remark about the team's chances of winning made us gloomy.

urban
[ə́:rbən]

of or having to do with cities or towns
adj. 도시의, 도회지에 있는
v. urbanize
The *urban* population of Korea has greatly increased during the last ten years.

> **EXERCISE 1** Fill each blank with the most appropriate word given above.
> (Inflect the word if necessary.)
>
> 1. The _____ of the little girl and the policeman prevented her from being kidnapped.
> 2. The audience was _____ by the grace of the young dancer.
> 3. In the United States today, the _____ population far outnumbers the farm population.
> 4. Apply the sticker on the dry surface, or it will not _____ properly.
> 5. I _____ from your letter that you did not wish to see us.

STUDY YOUR NEW WORDS-2

amputate
[ǽmpjuteit]

remove a part of the body by cutting off for medical reasons
v. 절단하다, 끊다
n. amputation
This is serious; I am afraid we'll have to **amputate** his leg.

bawdy
[bɔ́:di]

not decent; indecent; unchaste; lewd; obscene
adj. 음란한, 음탕한
n. bawdry
All the people in the party were disgusted with his **bawdy** jokes.

deformity
[difɔ́:rməti]

an abnormal shape of a body; malformation; disfigurement
n. 불구, 기형
adj. deformed
She is very attractive in spite of her slight **deformity**.

excavate
[ékskəveit]

make a hole by digging; hollow out
v. 굴착하다, 뚫다, 파내다
n. excavation
It took a long time to **excavate** the ancient city of Troy.

harass
[hərǽs]

make worried by causing trouble; bother; vex
v. 괴롭히다, 애먹이다
n. harassment
In olden times the coasts of England were frequently **harassed** by the Vikings.

intoxicate
[intɔ́ksikeit]

make drunk; excite beyond self-control
v. 취하게 하다, 도취시키다
n. intoxication
He does not drink at all; a little wine may *intoxicate* him.

placid
[plǽsid]

pleasantly calm or peaceful; quiet; tranquil; serence
adj. 평온한, 조용한, 고요한
n. placidity
The *placid* lake reflected the image of the old castle.

retaliate
[ritǽlieit]

pay back a wrong or injury; return evil for evil
v. 보복하다, 복수하다
adj. retaliatory
Mary kicked Susan, and Susan *retaliated* against her by biting.

stealthy
[stélθi]

done in a secret manner; sly; secret; furtive
adj. 은밀한, 비밀의
adv. stealthily
The cat found a bird sitting on the branch and crept with *stealthy* movements toward it.

wary
[wɛ́əri]

on one's guard against danger, deception, etc.; cautious; vigilant
adj. 조심스런, 방심하지 않는, 주의 깊은
n. wariness
He lied to me about my friend, and I have been very *wary* of him ever since.

EXERCISE 2 Fill each blank with the most appropriate word given above.
(Inflect the word if necessary.)

1. Better food has reduced the number of children born with _____.

2. He has been _____ by business troubles and his nagging wife.

3. I like the small restaurant at the foot of the mountain; it has an intimate and _____ atmosphere.

4. If we insult them, they will probably _____ against us sometime.

5. The joy of victory so _____ the members of the team that they jumped and sang and behaved like crazy men.

Lesson 31

STUDY YOUR NEW WORDS-3

annihilate
[ənáiəleit]

destroy completely; wipe out of existence; obliterate; exterminate; abolish
v. 전멸시키다, 완전히 없애다
n. annihilation
Three survivors told us in detail how the regiment was *annihilated* by the enemy.

chronological
[krɔnəlɔ́dʒikəl]

arranged according to the order of time
adj. 발생 순서대로의, 연대순의
n. chronicle
In telling a story we usually follows *chronological* order.

divert
[daivə́:rt]

turn aside or in a different direction; turn the attention away
v. 방향을 돌리다, (주의를) 다른 데로 쏠리게 하다
n. diversion
They are planning to *divert* the river to supply water somewhere else.

enhance
[inhǽns]

add up; make greater; heighten
v. 신장하다, 드높이다, 늘리다
n. enhancement
The moonlight on the lake *enhanced* the beauty of the scene.

imprison
[imprízn]

put in prison; keep in prison
v. 투옥하다, 감금하다
n. imprisonment
The criminal has been *imprisoned* in a dark cell for almost 10 years.

malice
[mǽlis]

a wish to hurt or make suffer; active ill will; enmity; spitefulness
n. 악의, 적의, 원한
adj. malicious
Do not bear *malice* toward him; he is a good man in nature.

prosecute
[prɔ́sikju:t]

1. bring before a court of law
v. 기소하다, 소추하다
n. prosecution
The driver was *prosecuted* for exceeding the speed limit on the expressway.

2. carry out; carry on
v. 수행하다, 해내다
n. prosecution
He started an inquiry into the cause of the fire, and *prosecuted* it for several weeks.

satirical
[sətírikəl]

exhibiting something in a scornful light; sarcastic; sardonic
adj. 풍자적인, 비꼬는
v. satirize
We were all amused by the *satirical* comparison of life at college and in the army.

subscribe
[səbskráib]

1. pay money for the regular delivery of newspapers, magazine, etc.
v. 구독하다, 구독 예약하다
n. subscription
They *subscribe* to a monthly magazine in addition to several daily newspaper.

2. give or pay a sum of money
v. 기부하다, 기부금을 내다
n. subscription
He *subscribed* a large amount of money to the collection for the hospital.

weird
[wiərd]

unnatural; mysterious; queer; unearthly
adj. 이상한, 기묘한, 불가사의한
n. weirdness
We heard a *weird* shriek from the darkness of the ruined castle.

EXERCISE 3 **Fill each blank with the most appropriate word given above.**
(Inflect the word if necessary.)

1. The growth of a city often _____ the value of land close to it.

2. Bryan tripped me so that I couldn't be able to play tomorrow. He did it not as a joke but out of _____.

3. No one survived the great avalanche; it _____ the whole village.

4. The teacher gave the pupils a (an) _____ list of events which had caused the First World War.

5. A juggler magician _____ audience's attention from one hand by making feints with the other.

STUDY YOUR NEW WORDS-4

apprehend
[æprihénd]

1. look forward to with fear; expect anxiously; dread
   v. 염려하다, 우려하다
   n. apprehension
   The guilty man *apprehends* danger in every sound.

2. seize a person who breaks the law; arrest
   v. 체포하다, 붙잡다
   n. apprehension
   The thief who had stolen the jewels was *apprehended* by the police and was put in jail.

commute
[kəmjúːt]

travel regularly to and from work
v. 통근하다, 통학하다
n. commutation
She *commutes* from Cambridge to London everyday.

emit
[imít]

send out heat, light, or sound; discharge; exude; eject
v. (열·빛 따위를) 발하다, 방출하다
n. emission
Heat and smoke *emitted* by the fire made it difficult for the firemen to put it out.

fortify
[fɔ́ːrtifai]

build forts on; strengthen
v. 요새화 하다, 강하게 하다
n. fortification
The soldiers *fortified* the position on the hill by building earthworks and erecting log walls.

inflict
[inflíkt]

give a blow; cause to suffer; impose
v. (타격을) 가하다, (세금·벌 따위를) 과하다
n. inflication
The government *inflicted* too heavy income taxes on the people.

mimic
[mímik]

make fun of by imitating; copy closely; imitate
v. 흉내내다, 모사하다, 모방하다
n. mimicry
She cut and painted pieces of paper that *mimicked* flowers so well that some people thought they were real.

reassure
[riːəʃúər]

comfort and make free from fear
v. 안심시키다, 마음 놓이게 하다

serial
[síəriəl]

n. reassurance
Her calm voice *reassured* the frightened child, and he felt much better.

of a series; arranged in a series; making a series
adj. 연속의, 연속적인, 계속되는
v. serialize
An exciting new *serial* story will begin in our next week's issue.

tactics
[tǽktiks]

the art of organizing and using military forces in war; method to gain advantage or success
n. 병법, 전술, 작전, 책략
adj. tactical
The *tactics* of pretending to cross the river and of making a retreat fooled the enemy.

EXERCISE 4
Fill each blank with the most appropriate word given above.
(Inflect the word if necessary.)

1. Hundreds of thousands of suburban residents regularly _____ to the city.
2. He _____ his uncle's voice and gestures very cleverly.
3. The captain's confidence during the storm _____ all the passengers of the ship.
4. Place volumes one to five on the shelf in a(n) _____ order.
5. If you want to be a successful politician you must make yourself able in _____.

해답

EXERCISE 1.	1. contiguity	2. enchanted	3. urban	4. adhere	5. inferred
EXERCISE 2.	1. deformity	2. harassed	3. placid	4. retaliate	5. intoxicated
EXERCISE 3.	1. enhances	2. malice	3. annihilated	4. chronological	5. diverts
EXERCISE 4.	1. commute	2. mimicked	3. reassured	4. serial	5. tactics

종합 연습 문제

1 Complete the following table with the appropriate word forms.

ADJECTIVE	NOUN	VERB	ADVERB
1. XXXXX	_____	mimic	XXXXX
2. _____	_____	retaliate	_____
3. grand	_____	XXXXX	XXXXX
4. _____	_____	adhere	_____
5. _____	satire	_____	_____
6. _____	_____	emit	XXXXX
7. bawdy	_____	XXXXX	XXXXX
8. XXXXX	_____	enhance	XXXXX
9. _____	chronicle	_____	_____
10. numb	_____	XXXXX	XXXXX

2 Supply the correct form of the word in italics for the blank space in each sentence.

1. *malice*　　　I think that story is nothing more than a _____ gossip.

2. *infer*　　　He never arrives on time, and my _____ is that he feels the meetings are useless.

3. *apprehend*　　Her _____ about the dangers of the travelling were increased by the recent accident.

4. *chronological*　Columbus kept a careful and detailed _____ of his voyage.

5. *enchant*　　In the Greek story, Circe turned men into pigs by her _____.

6. *audacity*　　The _____ boy went to the party without being invited.

7. *prosecute*　　The _____ will be stopped if the stolen money is returned.

8. *contiguity*　　No one wants to buy the house even at considerablly low price, because it is _____ to a cemetery.

9. *subscribe*　　Your _____ to the newspaper expires next week.

10. *reassure*　　The doctor told her that she would soon recover her health, but she didn't believe it in spite of all his _____.

3 In the space provided, write the *letter* of the word NOT RELATED in meaning to the other words in each line.

_____ 1. (A) abolish (B) exterminate (C) annihilate (D) deride
_____ 2. (A) symmetry (B) contiguity (C) adjacency (D) proximity
_____ 3. (A) harass (B) bother (C) meditate (D) vex
_____ 4. (A) enmity (B) anatomy (C) malice (D) spitefulness
_____ 5. (A) vigilant (B) wary (C) cautious (D) coherent
_____ 6. (A) cling (B) stifle (C) stick (D) adhere
_____ 7. (A) satirical (B) sarcastic (C) sardonic (D) sagacious
_____ 8. (A) sly (B) furtive (C) arrogant (D) stealthy
_____ 9. (A) congenial (B) serene (C) tranquil (D) placid
_____ 10. (A) elusive (B) skeptical (C) incredulous (D) distrustful

4 Fill each blank with the most appropriate word from the vocabulary list below.

VOCABULARY LIST

inflict	prosecuting	chronological
diverted	inferred	adhere
amputated	audacity	intoxicated
tactics	apprehend	mimicking

1. The newspapers in this file are arranged in _____ order so that everyone can easily find the issue he wants.

2. The boy made all his friends laugh by _____ the teacher's slow and solemn way of talking.

3. When coaxing failed, she changed her _____ and began to cry.

4. Be careful when you use the keen ax; it can _____ a bad wound on your leg.

5. The doctor _____ the wounded soldier's leg in order to save his life.

6. Now I see how foolish I was to _____ the outcome of the test. I passed it easily.

7. A loud noise _____ my attention from cooking and everything was burnt.

8. A glass of whisky _____ him, and he could not drive his car.

9. Glue and paste are used to make one surface _____ to another.

10. I looked at his boots and _____ that he was a policeman.

1

	ADJECTIVE	NOUN	VERB	ADVERB
1.	XXXXX	mimicry	(mimic)	XXXXX
2.	retaliatory	retaliation	(retaliate)	retaliatorily
3.	(grand)	grandeur	XXXXX	XXXXX
4.	adherent	adherence	(adhere)	adherently
5.	satirical	(satire)	satirize	satirically
6.	emissive	emission	(emit)	XXXXX
7.	(bawdy)	bawdry	XXXXX	XXXXX
8.	XXXXX	enhancement	(enhance)	XXXXX
9.	chronological	(chronicle)	chronologize	chronologically
10.	(numb)	numbness	XXXXX	XXXXX

2 1. malicious 2. inference 3. apprehensions 4. chronicle 5. enchantment 6. audacious 7. prosecution 8. contiguous 9. subscription 10. reassurance

3 1. D 2. A 3. C 4. B 5. D 6. B 7. D 8. C 9. A 10. A

4 1. chronological 2. mimicking 3. tactics 4. inflict 5. amputated 6. apprehend 7. diverted 8. intoxicated 9. adhere 10. inferred

UNIT IV
(Lessons 32~35)

- **Enlarging Vocabulary**
- **through DEFINITIONS**

Lesson 32

PRETEST 32

Insert the *letter* of the best answer in the space provided.

1. *Barometers* are used for measuring the _____ of the atmosphere.
   (A) pressure   (B) humidity   (C) temperature

2. She found _____ quite a *chore*.
   (A) smoking   (B) fishing   (C) housekeeping

3. *Coral* is often used for making _____.
   (A) powerful weapon   (B) precious jewellery   (C) winter coat

4. We can _____ by *twining* strings.
   (A) make a rope   (B) pull a car   (C) climb the cliff

5. Most of _____ comes from this *reservoir*.
   (A) the passengers of this bus   (B) the city's water for drink
   (C) leather for making shoes

ANSWERS 1.A 2.C 3.B 4.A 5.B

STUDY YOUR NEW WORDS-1

adversity
[ədvə́ːrsəti]
a condition of unhappiness, misfortune, or distress
n. 역경, 고초, 불행
He that never was acquainted with *adversity* has seen the world but on one side.

blister
[blístər]
a little baglike place in the skin filled with water.
n. 수포, 물집
My new shoes have made *blisters* on my heels.

clatter
[klǽtər]
a number of rapid short knocking sounds
n. 딸그락딸그락(덜걱덜걱)하는 소리
The *clatter* of metal plates was heard from the kitchen.

digital [dídʒitl]	having to do with, or using digits ***adj.*** 숫자로 된, 숫자를 사용하는 Most of telephone dials use *digital* numbers.	
gash [gæʃ]	a long, deep cut or wound; incision ***n.*** 깊은 상처, 심한 상처 He cannot work today; he got a *gash* in his hand while axing.	
impunity [impjúnəti]	freedom from punishment, injury or other bad consequences ***n.*** 처벌되지 않음, 무사, 무난 Even militarily weak and small nations have defied U. N. decisions with *impunity*.	
manure [mənjúər]	a substance put on the soil as fertilizer ***n.*** 거름, 비료 Plants grow much faster and stronger when they are given *manure*.	
porous [pɔ́:rəs]	full of pores or tiny holes ***adj.*** 기공이 많은, 다공성의 Glass is not *porous*; it doesn't allow liquid to pass through.	
shack [ʃæk]	a roughly-built hut or cabin ***n.*** 오두막, 가건물 There are a lot of *shacks* in the run-down part of the town near the railroad.	
span [spæn]	a stretch between two limits; the distance between two supports ***n.*** 전장(全長), 지간(支間), 길이 The average life *span* of the people has increased considerably since the 19th century.	
twitch [twitʃ]	pull with a sudden jerk; give a sudden quick pull ***v.*** 잡아채다, 홱 잡아당기다 The strong wind *twitched* the paper out of her hand.	

EXERCISE 1 **Fill each blank with the most appropriate word given above.**
(Inflect the word if necessary.)

1. Sunburn has made a lot of _____ on my back.

2. The farmers spread _____ on the field to make it produce better crops.

3. The _____ in the cafeteria made it hard to hear one another talk.

4. A good friend will not desert you in time of _____.

Lesson 32

5. A(n) _____ clock shows the time by displaying it in numbers, such as 2:30, in stead of by hands moving around the dial.

STUDY YOUR NEW WORDS-2

armistice
[á:rmistis]

a stop in fighting; temporary peace; truce
n. 휴전, 정전
The French battleships were placed within the power of Nazi Germany in accordance with the *armistice* terms.

breach
[bri:tʃ]

an opening made by breaking down something solid; act of breaking
n. 불이행, 터진 곳, 절교
I would be a *breach* of duty for the guard to leave before his replacement comes.

comity
[kɔ́məti]

friendly, polite, and respectful behavior and manners; courtesy; civility
n. 예의, 우의, 예양(禮讓)
To help a new student get oriented furthers the *comity* of the school.

dungeon
[dʌ́ndʒən]

a dark underground room or cell to keep prisoners in
n. 지하 감옥, 토굴 감옥
Some prisoners in the *dungeon* will be released tomorrow.

gregarious
[grigɛ́əriəs]

living in groups; fond of living with others
adj. 군거하는, 집단을 좋아하는
He is a *gregarious* man; he enjoys the companionship of a large number of friends.

incur
[inkə́:r]

run into something unpleasant
v. (위험·빚을) 초래하다, (비난·벌을) 받다
The explorers *incurred* great dangers when they tried to cross the rapids.

mole
[moul]

1. a spot on the kin, usually brown
n. 사마귀, 점
She has a small *mole* on the left side of her nose.

2. a small animal that lives underground most of time
n. 두더지
The *mole* digs holes and passages underground and makes its home in them.

patent
[péitənt]

a government grant giving a person the sole right to make and use his invention
n. 특허, 특허권
He has applied for a *patent* upon his latest invention.

sip
[sip]

drink little by little; drink only a little at a time
v. 한 모금씩 마시다, 홀짝홀짝 마시다
This coffee is very hot. Do not drink it quickly, but *sip* it.

sulfur
[sʌ́lfər]

a light-yellow nonmetallic chemical element
n. 유황
Sulfur is found abundantly in volcanic regions.

upsurge
[ʌpsə́:rdʒ]

an upward turn or trend; rise; upturn
n. 증가, 고조, 솟구쳐 오름
This year's *upsurge* in rice production is due to the new method of cultivation.

EXERCISE 2 Fill each blank with the most appropriate word given above.
(Inflect the word if necessary.)

1. Strong disagreement produced a(n) _____ between the business partners.
2. During the _____, they developed a plan for ending the war.
3. _____ is used in making gunpowder, matches, or various kinds of medicine.
4. He _____ a great many debts during his illness.
5. Hundreds of prisoners are still confined in the _____.

STUDY YOUR NEW WORDS-3

austere
[ɔːstíər]

severe or stern in manner or appearance
adj. 엄한, 준엄한, 엄격한
Grandfather was an *austere* man; he used to be silent and very strict to us.

bouquet
[buːkéi]

a bunch of flowers
n. 꽃다발
When I was in hospital, she called on me with a *bouquet* of roses in her hand.

coral
[kɔ́rəl]

a stone-like substance formed from the bones of small sea animals.
n. 산호, 산호층
In the Pacific Oceans there are many *coral* atolls that are ringlike islands.

forum
[fɔ́:rəm]

the place for public discussion; public discussion
n. 공개 토론회, 공개 토론장
A group of schoolmasters are holding a *forum* on new ways of teaching history.

gym
[dʒim]

a building for physical training or indoor sports
n. 체육관
On rainy days the students play games in the *gym*.

interject
[intərdʒékt]

throw in between other things; insert; interpose
v. 사이에 끼우다, 중도에 언급하다
"Not like that!" he *interjected* while explaining how to take the machine into pieces.

mushroom
[mʌ́ʃrum]

a small fungus shaped like an umbrella; toadstool
n. 버섯
Some *mushrooms* are good to eat; some, such as toadstools, are poisonous.

raft
[ræft]

logs fastened together to make a floating platform
n. 뗏목
They escaped from the wrecked ship on a *raft*.

smear
[smiər]

cover or stain with anything sticky, greasy, or dirty
v. (기름을) 바르다, (칠 따위를) 묻히다
The children looked like negroes; their faces were *smeared* with soot.

taper
[téipər]

make gradually smaller toward one end
v. 뾰족하게 하다, 점점 가늘게 하다
One end of a pencil is *tapered* off to a point.

via
[vaiə]

by way of; by means of
prep. ~을 경유로, ~에 의하여
I have read this French play *via* an English translation.

EXERCISE 3
Fill each blank with the most appropriate word given above.
(Inflect the word if necessary.)

1. Every now and then the speaker _____ a joke or story to keep us interested.

2. In tropical areas _____ grows in shallow water.

3. We could find no boats around the ferry, and we had to cross the river on a(n) _____.

4. The judge had a(n) _____ look on his face as he spoke to the criminal.

5. The carpenter _____ the end of the fence post with an ax.

STUDY YOUR NEW WORDS-4

barometer
[bərɔ́mitər]

an instrument for measuring the atmospheric pressure
n. 기압계, 고도계
Newspapers are often called *barometers* of public opinion.

comply
[kəmplái]

act in agreement with a request or a command
v. 응하다, 따르다
He *complied* with the doctor's order that he should take a rest at home.

coxcomb
[kɔ́kskoum]

a vain, empty-headed man; conceited dandy; fop
n. 멋쟁이, 맵씨꾼
A *coxcomb* spends too much money and time on his clothes and appearance.

foliage
[fóulidʒ]

the leaves of a plant, especially growing leaves
n. 나뭇잎 (집합적 의미)
In summer the house next door is hidden by luxuriant *foliage*.

hegira
[hédʒirə]

the flight of Mohammed from Mecca to Medina; flight
n. 헤지라, 도피, 도주
She made her plan for her annual summer *hegira* to the Miami beach.

lair
[lɛər]

the den or resting place of a wild animal
n. 야수의 잠자리, 소굴, 보금자리
The hunters traced the footmarks of a tiger and at last they found him in his *lair*.

nightmare
[náitmɛər]

an unpleasant and terrible dream; dream causing fear
n. 악몽, 몽마(夢魔)
The child had a terrible *nightmare* and awoke crying.

reservoir
[rézərvwɔːr]

a place where water is collected and stored for use
n. 저수지, 저수조, 못
This *reservoir* is large enough to supply water to the entire city.

sod
[sɔd]

a piece or layer of the ground covered with grass; turf
n. 뗏장, 떼, 잔디
He bought some *sods* to put in the bare spots of his lawn yard.

trash [træʃ]	anything of little or no worth; worthless stuff; rubbish ***n.*** 쓰레기, 잡동사니 Rake up the ***trash*** in the yard and burn it. We will have some guests tonight.
warehouse [wέərhaus]	a place where goods are kept; depository; storehouse ***n.*** 창고, 저장소 The furniture will stay in the ***warehouse*** until they pay the storage cost.

EXERCISE 4   **Fill each blank with the most appropriate word given above.**
(Inflect the word if necessary.)

1. In spring these naked branches will put their graceful _____ on again.
2. The salmon makes a trip to the rivers or creeks for spawning. On the contrary the _____ of the eel is toward the sea.
3. We cut some _____ from a field and covered a bare spot in the lawn with them.
4. When the _____ indicates a rapid drop in air pressure, it means storm is coming.
5. Some people go fishing to rivers; others go to _____ or lakes.

STUDY YOUR NEW WORDS-5

belch [beltʃ]	throw out gas through mouth; eructate ***v.*** 트림하다, 분출하다 The volcano ***belched*** a staggering amount of fire, smoke, and ashes.
chore [tʃɔːr]	a difficult or disagreeable thing to do ***n.*** 귀찮은 일, 자질구레한 일 It's such a ***chore*** to do the shopping everyday!
crimson [krímzn]	deep slightly purplish color ***n., adj.*** 진홍색(의), 심홍색(의) When she was asked a sudden question, her face turned ***crimson*** in embarrassment.
fugitive [fjúːdʒitiv]	a person escaping from the law, the police, or danger ***n.*** 도망자, 탈주자, 망명자 The ***fugitive*** had already packed and bought his ticket.

horde
[hɔːrd]

a large number or crowd; swarm; multitude
n. 무리, 떼, 집단
Two women were quarrelling on the street, surrounded by a *horde* of people.

linguist
[líŋgwist]

a person who studies the science of language
n. 언어학자
Usually a *linguist* is skilled in a number of languages besides his own.

petroleum
[pitróuljəm]

a natural oil found in the earth in certain parts of the world
n. 석유, 원유
The price of *petroleum* has been raised too high during the last few years.

rumple
[rʌmpl]

crumple; crush; wrinkle
v. 구기다, 헝클어뜨리다
Mary *rumpled* her dress by sitting on the floor.

sneeze
[smíːz]

let out the breath through the nose and mouth
v. 재채기하다, 기침하다
A person *sneezes* when he has a cold.

twine
[twain]

wind or wrap around; twist together
v. 꼬다, 감다
She *twined* her arms around his neck and kissed him.

whirr
[hwəːr]

make a regular sound by something beating against the air.
v. 윙소리를 내다, 윙하고 돌다
When we got inside the factory, we couldn't hear the guide explain because of the *whirring* of the motors.

EXERCISE 5

Fill each blank with the most appropriate word given above.
(Inflect the word if necessary.)

1. Each morning she would get up, do the _____, then go next door for a talk with her neighbor.
2. The _____ crossed the border by night to escape arrest.
3. A(n) _____ collects and records utterances, and, comparing these one another, abstracts the way of speaking.
4. The boy _____ his arms around his mother's leg and teased her for money to buy the toy.
5. _____ of Mongolians and Turks invaded Europe in the Middle Ages.

EXERCISE 1.	1. blisters	2. manure	3. clatter	4. adversity	5. digital
EXERCISE 2.	1. breach	2. armistice	3. sulfur	4. incurred	5. dungeon
EXERCISE 3.	1. interjected	2. coral	3. raft	4. austere	5. tapered
EXERCISE 4.	1. foliage	2. hegira	3. sods	4. barometer	5. reservoirs
EXERCISE 5.	1. chores	2. fugitive	3. linguist	4. twined	5. hordes

종합 연습 문제

1 In the space before each word in column I, write the *letter* of its correct meaning in column II.

COLUMN I	COLUMN II
_____ 1. lair	(A) full of tiny holes
_____ 2. nightmare	(B) a spot on the skin
_____ 3. mole	(C) a bunch of flowers
_____ 4. belch	(D) to drink little by little
_____ 5. upsurge	(E) to throw out gas through mouth
_____ 6. porous	(F) an unpleasant and terrible dream
_____ 7. via	(G) a condition of misfortune or distress
_____ 8. bouquet	(H) the resting place of a wild animal
_____ 9. adversity	(I) an upward turn or trend; rise
_____ 10. sip	(J) by way of; means of

2 Fill in the missing letters of the incomplete word. When completed, the word should mean the same as the word or expression in italics.

1. Please take the basket of T____H to the garbage can.
   rubbish

2. Gasoline and other fuel oils are made from P_____M.
   natural oil found in the earth

3. Lions and elephants are G_____S; tigers are not.
   living in groups

4. When the knife slipped it made a G__H in his thumb.
   deep wound

5. An A_____E is arranged by agreement on all sides, often while a permanent peace is being arranged.
   temporary peace

6. With a B_____R we can determine height above sea level and predict probable changes in the weather.
   instrument for measuring the atmospheric pressure

7. Giving one's seat to a lady in a crowded bus is a sign of C____Y.
   courtesy

8. The boys made a small S___K out of old boards in the backyard.
   roughly-built hut

Lesson 32

9. Do not T____H the curtain aside; it may be torn off.
   pull with a sudden jerk

10. An open F___M on birth control was held in the hall last Tuesday evening.
    public discussion

3 In the space provided, write the *letter* of the word NOT RELATED in meaning to the other words on the line.

_____	1.	(A) horde	(B) swarm	(C) span	(D) multitude
_____	2.	(A) malice	(B) courtesy	(C) civility	(D) comity
_____	3.	(A) indulge	(B) insert	(C) interpose	(D) interject
_____	4.	(A) mushroom	(B) fungus	(C) coral	(D) toadstool
_____	5.	(A) austere	(B) placid	(C) severe	(D) stern
_____	6.	(A) dungeon	(B) limbo	(C) jail	(D) castle
_____	7.	(A) turf	(B) manure	(C) lawn	(D) sod
_____	8.	(A) coxcomb	(B) fop	(C) dandy	(D) mole
_____	9.	(A) trash	(B) litter	(C) rubbish	(D) breach
_____	10.	(A) rumple	(B) crumple	(C) scramble	(D) wrinkle

4 Fill each blank with the most appropriate word from the vocabulary list below.

> **VOCABULARY LIST**
>
> impunity   whirr   smear
> patent   crimson   incurred
> petroleum   gym   rafts
> clatter   twined   gregarious

1. The _____ came from the kitchen where pans were being washed.

2. They decided to build a large _____ for indoor athletic sports.

3. Be careful! If you touch the wall you will _____ the fresh paint.

4. The boatman _____ the rope around the post to prevent his boat from drifting down the river.

5. Before boasts were invented, man first began to use _____ to cross rivers or streams.

6. The high price of _____ has driven many countries to develop new source of energy.

7. A baby likes to play by himself, but as he grows older he becomes _____.

8. As what she said was proved to be a lie, her face turned _____ with shame.

9. If laws are not enforced, crimes are committed with _____.

10. She _____ great debts by buying a luxurious car which she cannot afford.

해답

1 1. H   2. F   3. B   4. E   5. I   6. A   7. J   8. C   9. G   10. D
2 1. trash   2. petroleum   3. gregarious   4. gash   5. armistice
   6. barometer   7. comity   8. shack   9. twitch   10. forum
3 1. C   2. A   3. A   4. C   5. B   6. D   7. B   8. D   9. D   10. C
4 1. clatter   2. gym   3. smear   4. twined   5. rafts
   6. petroleum   7. gregarious   8. crimson   9. impunity   10. incurred

Lesson 32   389

Lesson 33

PRETEST 33

Insert the *letter* of the best answer in the space provided.

1. We watched the *astronauts'* journey to the _____ on television.
   (A) moon   (B) Antarctic

2. Many criminals were _____ on the *gallows*.
   (A) hanged   (B) shot to death

3. You need a _____ to take part in the *masquerade*.
   (A) mask   (B) uniform

4. The *phoenix* often symbolizes _____.
   (A) great victory   (B) eternal life

5. He always felt that his father's _____ *stigmatized* both of them.
   (A) prison record   (B) glorious death

ANSWERS 1.A 2.A 3.A 4.B 5.A

STUDY YOUR NEW WORDS-1

alloy
[ǽlɔi]
substance consisting of two or more metals melted and mixed together
n. 합금(合金)
An **alloy** is often harder, lighter, and stronger than the pure metals of which it is composed.

blackout
[blǽkaut]
the action of turning off all lights as a protection against an air raid
n. 등화 관제
The streets were not lighted at night during the **blackout**.

cater
[kéitər]
provide food and supplies; provide what is needed
v. 음식을 조달하다, 요구에 응하다
Who is supposed to **cater** for your daughter's wedding next week?

cram
[kræm]

1. prepare oneself for an examination hastily
v. 벼락치기 공부를 하다
He is *cramming* facts and dates for his history examination tomorrow.

2. force or press into a small space; stuff
v. 처박아 넣다, 꽉 차게 하다
He *crammed* as many candy bars into his pockets as they would hold.

fleece
[fli:s]

rob by a trick or by charging too much money
v. 바가지 씌우다, 속임수로 빼앗다
If you paid $200 for the watch, you were *fleeced*. I saw it in a department store for $70.

habitat
[hǽbitæt]

the natural home of a plant or animal
n. 서식지, 번식지
The jungle is the natural *habitat* of wild animals and plants.

locksmith
[lɔ́ksmiθ]

a person who makes or repairs locks and keys
n. 자물쇠 제조공, 열쇠 수리공
I lost my key to the door, and I went to the *locksmith* to get a new one.

pant
[pænt]

breathe hard and quickly; speak with sort quick breaths
v. 헐떡거리다, 헐떡이며 말하다
He *panted* excitedly giving us the news as he had just heard it.

rickety
[rikiti]

likely to fall or break down; shaky or weak; tottering
adj. 쓰러질 듯한, 무너질 듯한, 흔들거리는
Don't use that old cart; it's *rickety*.

stigmatize
[stígmətaiz]

set some mark of disgrace on; reproach
v. 오명을 씌우다, 비난하다
He has been *stigmatized* as a coward and liar.

unquenchable
[ʌnkwéntʃəbl]

not capable of being satisfied; not quenchable
adj. 억누를 수 없는, 해갈될 수 없는
Having been in the desert without water for two days, his thirst was *unquenchable*.

EXERCISE 1 **Fill each blank with the most appropriate word given above.**
(Inflect the word if necessary.)

1. Many students _____ for the final examination in the library all through the night.

Lesson 33

2. The dog _____ along behind its master's horse.

3. A(n) _____ of gold and copper is harder and less costing than gold alone.

4. He runs a restaurant and also _____ for wedding and parties.

5. As to our white wine, they _____ it as a mere substitute for cider.

STUDY YOUR NEW WORDS-2

astronaut
[ǽstrənɔ̀ːt]

a pilot or member of the crew of a spacecraft; cosmonaut
n. 우주 비행사, 우주인
The *astronauts* of the United States are returning to the earth from the moon.

bequeath
[bikwíːð]

give or pass on to others after death
v. 유증하다, 유산을 남기다
One age *bequeaths* its knowledge to the next.

census
[sénsəs]

an official count of a country's total population
n. 인구 조사
In the United States there is a *census* every ten years.

crusade
[kruːséid]

the Christian expedition; a campaign of fight for a good cause
n. 십자군, 개혁 운동, 박멸 운동
Everyone of the city was asked to join the *crusade* for better housing.

ford
[fɔːrd]

cross a river or stream by walking through the water
v. 도섭하다, 걸어서 건너다
The stream was so deep that we could not *ford* it.

hover
[hóvər]

stay in or near one place
v. 배회하다, 머무르다
The dog *hovers* around the kitchen door every mealtime.

masquerade
[mæ̀skəréid]

1. a party or dance at which masks and fancy costumes are worn
n. 가장 무도회, 거짓 꾸밈
They were all dressed up to attend the *masquerade*.

2. disguise oneself; pretend to be
v. 가장하다, 변장하다
He got a free ticket to the play by *masquerading* as a friend of the actors.

phoenix
[fíːniks]

an imaginary bird symbolizing eternal life
n. 불사조(不死鳥)
The *phoenix* is believed to live for 500 years and then burn itself and be born again from the ashes.

rye
[rai]

a plant with grain for making flour and as food for cattle
n. 호밀
Some people prefer the dark bread made from *rye* to the white bread made from wheat.

stunt
[stʌnt]

a feat to attract attention; act showing boldness or skill
n. 곡예, 묘기
In the film he jumps off a running car and performs other dangerous *stunts*.

versus
[və́ːrsəs]

against
n. (소송·경기 등에서) ~대(對) (vs.로 흔히 씀)
The most exciting game in hockey was Havard *versus* Yale.

EXERCISE 2 Fill each blank with the most appropriate word given above.
(Inflect the word if necessary.)

1. The helicopter _____ over the spot where the lost men had been seen.

2. After the Second World War, many Japanese joined in the _____ for warless world.

3. The millionaire will _____ his colossal fortune to his only son.

4. The plane flew upside down, turned over twice, and did a few more _____ before landing.

5. The bridge is too far away from here. We'd better _____ the stream here.

STUDY YOUR NEW WORDS-3

artillery
[ɑːrtíləri]
large, heavy guns moved on wheel carriers; cannon
n. 포병, 대포 (집합적 의미)
Above all the *artillery* was the deciding factor in the battle.

bounty
[báunti]
money given by a government for some special act or service
n. 보상금, 장려금
In the early days of the West many states paid a *bounty* for captured criminals.

clench
[klentʃ]
close tightly together; grasp firmly
v. 꽉 다물다, 꽉 죄다, 꽉 쥐다
When he got a shot against typhus, the child *clenched* his teeth in pain.

dirk
[dəːrk]
a short, pointed, two-edged knife used as a weapon
n. 단검, 비수
I saw a burglar, with a *dirk* in his hand, getting into the room where she was sleeping.

gallows
[gǽlouz]
a wooden frame with a rope from which criminals are hanged; punishment by hanging
n. 교수대, 교수형
The murdered entreated the judge for mercy, but was sentenced to the *gallows*.

inedible
[inédəbl]
not suitable for eating; not edible
adj. 식용에 부적합한, 먹지 못하는
My steak, though delicious, was mostly fat and bones. Most of it was *inedible*.

morale
[mərǽl]
the state of mind with regard to pride or faith
n. 사기(士氣)
The *morale* of the football team was very low after its defeat.

prone
[proun]
1. inclined; liable; disposed; apt
adj. ~하기 쉬운, ~의 경향이 있는
We are more *prone* to make mistakes when we are tired.

2. lying face down; lying flat; incumbent; prostrate
adj. 수그린, 납작 엎드린
We fell *prone* on the ground and drank water from the spring.

scuttle
[skʌ́tl]
run with quick, hurried steps; scurry
v. 허둥지둥 도망치다, 급히 도망가다
The robbers grasped the peril of their position and *scuttled* away.

tack	s short nail or pin with a flat head
[tæk]	***n.*** 압정, 압핀
	The carpet was fastened to the floor with ***tacks***.

ward	a person who is under legal protection
[wɔːrd]	***n.*** 피보호자, 피후견인
	After his parents' death, the court made him a ***ward*** of his aunt.

EXERCISE 3 **Fill each blank with the most appropriate word given above.**
(Inflect the word if necessary.)

1. Some people hunts fugitives from the law or harmful animals to collect the _____ for their capture.
2. The children who had broken the window of the house _____ off when they saw a policeman.
3. We bought some _____ to fasten the small picture to the wall.
4. Trapped in the cave by a fall of rock, the men kept up their _____ by singing together.
5. While it was thundering, the little boy _____ his mother's arm in terror.

STUDY YOUR NEW WORDS-4

avalanche	a large mass of snow crashing down the side of mountain
[ǽvəlɑːnʃ]	***n.*** 눈사태
	The terrible ***avalanche*** buried the whole village, and very few people survived it.

briefcase	a flat bag for carrying loose papers or books
[bríːfkeis]	***n.*** 서류 가방
	I was so in a hurry that I left my ***briefcase*** at home.

commodious	having plenty of room; spacious; roomy
[kəmóudjəs]	***adj.*** 공간이 넓은, 널찍한
	The apartment is not ***commodious*** enough for his family to live in.

dynasty	a series of rulers who belong to the same family
[dáinəsti]	***n.*** 왕조(王朝)
	The Bourbon ***dynasty*** ruled France for more than two hundred years.

gibberish
[gíbəriʃ]

senseless chatter; confused meaningless talk; jargon; gabble
n. 횡설수설; 알 수 없는 말
After he got out of the bar, he suddenly began to yell drunken *gibberish* on the sidewalk.

invoke
[invóuk]

ask earnestly; request or beg for
v. 기원하다, 호소하다
I *invoked* his forgiveness many times, but failed to move him.

myriad
[míriəd]

a very great number; ten thousand
n. 무수(無數), 무수한 물건; 만(萬)
There are *myriads* of stars in the sky at night; we cannot count them.

quarry
[kwɔ́ːri]

a place from which stone, sand, etc. are dug out
n. 채석장(採石場)
Thousands of men and women are working in the *quarry* to get stones for use in building the castle.

slum
[slʌm]

a city area of poor living conditions and dirty buildings
n. 빈민굴, 빈민촌
Poverty and disease are common in the *slums*.

tinkle
[tíŋkl]

make short, light, ringing sounds
v. 딸랑딸랑거리다, 따르릉따르릉거리다
He *tinkled* his coins together in his pocket.

whirlpool
[hwɔ́ːrlpuːl]

a place with circular currents of water
n. 소용돌이
The swimmer caught in the *whirlpool* struggled to keep from drowning.

EXERCISE 4 Fill each blank with the most appropriate word given above.
(Inflect the word if necessary.)

1. The history shows that China was in a prosperous condition under the Ming _____.

2. The government is tearing down the _____ and building new houses.

3. When you swim do not get close to the _____; you may be drowned.

4. Even during change of classes there is no crowding because the halls and stairways are _____.

5. The country faced with famine is expected to _____ the help of its more fortunate neighbors.

STUDY YOUR NEW WORDS-5

blockade
[blɔkéid]

the shutting up of a place by police or soldiers
n. 봉쇄, 폐색, 저지
We ended our *blockade* of the enemy's port when peace was established.

burrow
[bʌ́rou]

a hole dug in the ground by an animal for refuge
n. (짐승이 파 놓은) 굴
The fox likes to live in a *burrow*; it's warm in winter and cool in summer.

corollary
[kɔ́rɔ́ləri]

natural consequence or result
n. 당연한 결과, 자연적인 결과
Destruction and suffering are *corollaries* of war.

fawn
[fɔ:n]

try to get favor by acting in flattering way
v. 아첨하다, 아양떨다
Many flattering relatives *fawned* on the rich old man.

grope
[group]

feel about with the hands
v. 손으로 더듬다, 더듬어 찾아보다
He *groped* for the light switch in the dark basement.

nostalgia
[nɔstǽldʒiə]

a painful yearning for one's home; yearning for something in the past
n. 향수(鄉愁), 과거에의 동경
The soldiers were filled with *nostalgia* by hearing my old favorite song.

resound
[rizáund]

be loudly and clearly heard; give back sound
n. 울려퍼지다, 반향하다
The notes of the hunting horn *resounded* through the forest.

splinter
[splíntər]

1. split or break into small pieces
v. 쪼개다, 찢다
The fireman *splintered* the locked door with an ax to save the boy in the room.

2. a sharp-pointed piece broken off hard material
n. 조각, 파편
No one in the plane survived the crash; it crashed down into *splinters*.

truce
[tru:s]

the act of stopping flighting; peace for a short time; armistice
n. 정전, 휴전
A *truce* was declared at Christmas between the two armies.

vernacular
[vərnǽkjulər]

the language spoken by the members of a certain country or place
n. 모국어, 지방어, 전문어
There is not a single grammar book on the *vernacular* of this African tribe.

EXERCISE 5   **Fill each blank with the most appropriate word given above.**
(Inflect the word if necessary.)

1. We raised our _____ of the enemy's port when peace was established.
2. He _____ on her only to borrow money; in fact he does not like her so much.
3. The blind man _____ his way to the door of the room.
4. A five-day _____ was declared between the two armies on the New Year's Day.
5. The name of the new champion _____ all over the world.

EXERCISE 1.	1. crammed	2. panted	3. alloy	4. caters	5. stigmatized
EXERCISE 2.	1. hovered	2. crusade	3. bequeath	4. stunts	5. ford
EXERCISE 3.	1. bounty	2. scuttled	3. tacks	4. morale	5. clenched
EXERCISE 4.	1. dynasty	2. slums	3. whirlpool	4. commodious	5. invoke
EXERCISE 5.	1. blockade	2. fawns	3. groped	4. truce	5. resounded

종합 연습 문제

1 In the space before each word in column I, write the *letter* of its correct meaning in column II.

	COLUMN I	COLUMN II
_____	1. clench	(A) the area of poor living conditions
_____	2. invoke	(B) to give to others after death
_____	3. slum	(C) a feat to attract attention
_____	4. artillery	(D) to rob by a trick
_____	5. latch	(E) to ask earnestly; beg for
_____	6. fleece	(F) large heavy guns
_____	7. stunt	(G) to grasp firmly
_____	8. bequeath	(H) a simple fastening for a door
_____	9. splinter	(I) to stay near one place
_____	10. hover	(J) to break into small pieces

2 Fill in the missing letters of the incomplete word. When completed, the word should mean the same as the word or expression in italics.

1. She could put all her clothes in one C_____S drawer.
   spacious

2. An A_____E often carries with it thousands of tons of rock, and sometimes destroys houses and roads.
   large mass of snow

3. Good health is a C_____Y of good nutrition.
   natural consequence

4. Terribly drunken men are apt to quarrel with others or yell G_____H on the street.
   confused meaningless talk

5. The poisonous mushrooms are not suitable for eating; they are I_____E.
   not eatable

6. One who has to spend so much of his life in foreign countries always feels N_____A.
   painful yearning for one's home

7. He hammered a T__K into the wall and hung the picture from it.
   short nail with a flat head

8. Two robbers sneaked into the room and one of them pointed his D__K toward the old man's neck.
   short knife as a weapon

Lesson 33 399

9. A M____D of thoughts passed through her mind.
   great number

10. We are P___E to think evil of people whom we do not like.
    apt

3 In the blank space, write the *letter* of the word that best completes the sentence.

1. Many teenagers have a(n) _____ thirst for adventure stories; they read one after another.
   (A) commodious   (B) unquenchable

2. A _____ of all the harbors would require thousands of warships.
   (A) blockade   (B) truce

3. I _____ my way to the seat in the dark theater.
   (A) groped   (B) scuttled

4. There are many strange words in the _____ of lawyers.
   (A) crusade   (B) vernacular

5. Don't take a seat on the _____ chair; it might be broken down.
   (A) rickety   (B) sturdy

4 Fill each blank with the most appropriate word selected from the vocabulary list below.

VOCABULARY LIST

habitat	blackout	locksmith
blockade	alloy	versus
fleeced	vernacular	stigmatized
resounded	forded	masqueraded

1. They _____ their political opponent as a liar so as to make him unpopular.

2. The prince who _____ as a peasant walked into the town, and no one reconizged him.

3. If you paid $1,000 for the used car, you were _____. The mechanic says it's worth no more than $500.

4. Brass is a(n) _____ of copper and zinc.

5. After the earthquake the police set up a(n) _____ into the town to prevent looting.

6. If you lose the key to your apartment, you can get a new one from the _____.

7. The noise of laughter and whistles _____ through the empty corridor.

8. The big cricket match is starting today; it's England _____ Australia.

9. During the enemy's air raid we have to turn off or conceal all the lights for a perfect _____.

10. Having lived in the United States for a long time, he had got used to speaking English. But when he returned home to Korea he soon lapsed into his _____.

해답

1 1. G   2. E   3. A   4. F   5. H   6. D   7. C   8. B   9. J   10. I
2 1. commodious   2. avalanche   3. corollary   4. gibberish   5. inedible
   6. nostalgia   7. tack   8. dirk   9. myriad   10. prone
3 1. B   2. A   3. A   4. B   5. A
4 1. stigmatized   2. masqueraded   3. fleeced   4. alloy   5. blockade
   6. locksmith   7. resounded   8. versus   9. blackout   10. vernacular

Lesson 34

PRETEST 34

Insert the *letter* of the best answer in the space provided.

1. Most of *anesthetics* put the patients to _____.
   (A) pain   (B) delight   (C) sleep

2. They found a *cavern* in the side of the _____.
   (A) mountain   (B) building   (C) cabinet

3. *Chisels* are used to _____ wood, stone, or metal.
   (A) cut   (B) melt   (C) decorate

4. *Gruel* is often given to those who are _____.
   (A) diligent, sincere, or excellent   (B) deserved to be punished
   (C) sick or very old

5. *Soot* usually collects _____.
   (A) in the shallow, warm stream   (B) under the branches of a tree
   (C) on the inside of chimneys

ANSWERS 1. C 2. A 3. A 4. C 5. C

STUDY YOUR NEW WORDS-1

anesthetic
[ænisθétik]

substance that produces inability to feel pain
n. 마취제
The use of *anesthetics* is less than a hundred years old.

beacon
[bí:kən]

a light or fire used as a signal to guide or warn
n. 봉화, 신호탑
The fire on the hill was a *beacon* to the villagers that the enemy was coming.

coroner
[kɔ́:rənər]

an official who investigates the cause of death
n. 검시관(檢屍官)
The *coroner* concluded that the death of the old woman was accidental.

duel
[djúːəl]

a formal fight to settle a quarrel or avenge an insult
n. 결투, 투쟁
They decided to settle their quarrel by a *duel*.

graft
[græft]

put a shoot from one tree into a slit in another tree
v. 접목하다, 이식하다
Peach trees can be *grafted* on plum trees.

impersonal
[impə́ːrsənəl]

not influenced by personal feeling
adj. 개인적 감정에 의하지 않은, 공정한
"First come, first served" is an *impersonal* remark.

loom
[luːm]

appear dimly or vaguely
v. 어렴풋이 보이다, 아련히 떠오르다
A large iceberg *loomed* through the thick, gray fog.

peal
[piːl]

a loud, long sound; the loud ringing of bells
n. 큰 소리, 울림 소리
As the speaker made a funny joke, *peals* of laughter rang through the auditorium.

roundup
[ráundʌp]

bringing cattle together; a gathering
n. (가축을) 몰아 모으기, 모집, 모임
The missing cattle are recovered in the annual *roundup*.

straggle
[strǽgl]

wander in a scattered fashion; roam; stray from the rest
v. 흩어져 거닐다, 무질서하게 늘어지다
The cowboys worked all night to gather the cattle that had *straggled* behind the rest of the herd.

ulterior
[ʌltíəriər]

beyond what is seen or expressed; hidden or kept secret
adj. 숨겨진, 표면에 나타나지 않는
He was suspected of having *ulterior* motives for making his generous offer, but in fact his offer was from the bottom of his heart.

EXERCISE 1 **Fill each blank with the most appropriate word given above.**
(Inflect the word if necessary.)

1. We _____ a branch of a tree on another tree so that it will grow there permanently.

2. He was very tired, and he fell asleep in spite of _____ of thunder.

3. As the children walked along the street, they _____ behind their parents.

4. The answers from a(n) _____ of scholars and business leaders helped the President set up his policies.

5. History should be written from a(n) _____ point of view.

STUDY YOUR NEW WORDS-2

auction
[ɔ́:kʃən]

public sale of goods to the person who offers the most money
n. 경매, 공매
The old Chippendale chair was sold at a good price at the *auction*.

calligraphy
[kəlígrəfi]

beautiful writing by hand
n. 서예, 서도
The old man is famous for superb *calligraphy*.

cope
[koup]

fight with some degree of success; get on successfully
v. 대처하다, 처리하다
Jean felt unable to *cope* with driving in heavy traffic after her accident.

cucumber
[kjú:kəmbər]

a long green vegetable with firm flesh seed inside
n. 오이
Please get some *cucumbers* in the vegetable section; I'll make pickles.

gruel
[gruəl]

a nearly liquid food
n. (노약자나 환자에게 주는) 죽
Her grandfather is 90 years old, and every mealtime she has to prepare *gruel* for him by boiling oatmeal in water.

hustle
[hʌ́sl]

push or shove roughly; bustle; jostle
v. 밀치다, 떠밀다, 밀어붙이다
She *hustled* off her children to school and started working.

maneuver
[mənú:vər]

1. planned movement of the armed forces; skillful plan or movement
n. 기동, 책동, 작전
Every year the army and the navy hold *maneuvers* for practice.

2. move skillfully, get by clear tricks
v. 기동하다, 책략을 쓰다
She *maneuvered* her car into a narrow parking space with ease.

plight [plait]	a bad or dangerous situation; predicament *n.* 곤경, 역경 He was in a terrible *plight*, trapped at the back of the cave.
scoff [skɔf]	speak or act disrespectfully; laugh at; sneer; jeer *n.* 비웃다, 코웃음치다 I came to the meeting to *scoff*, but the speaker persuaded me.
stun [stʌn]	knock unconscious; make senseless *v.* 기절시키다, 정신을 잃게 하다 She was *stunned* by the news of her mother's death.
vulture [vʌ́ltʃər]	a large bird related to the eagle *n.* 독수리 A *vulture* usually lives on the flesh of dead animals.

EXERCISE 2 — Fill each blank with the most appropriate word given above.
(Inflect the word if necessary.)

1. Many people at the _____ bid on the old furniture, but he was given the contract for it.

2. Mother could not _____ with all the housework and two sick children.

3. The policemen caught the thief on the street and _____ him into their van.

4. She was in a sad _____ when her husband got ill and she had quite inadequate money for his medical expenses.

5. When we refused to use his idea, he tried to force it on us by a series of _____.

STUDY YOUR NEW WORDS-3

bankrupt [bǽŋkrəpt]	a person who is unable to pay his debts *n.* 파산자, 지불 불능자 After his store burned, the storekeeper became a *bankrupt*.
cavern [kǽvərn]	a large deep cave *n.* 동굴, 굴 It suddenly began to shower, and we took refuge into the *cavern*.

chrysanthemum
[krisǽnθəməm]

any of various types of garden plant with round flower
n. 국화(菊花)
Chrysanthemum usually blooms in fall and shows great varieties in the size and color of its flower.

fishery
[fíʃəri]

the occupation of catching fish; a place for catching or breeding fish
n. 어업, 어장
The inhabitants of the port are occupied mainly with *fishery*.

gust
[gʌst]

a sudden, violent rush of wind; a short outflow of feeling
n. 일진의 바람, 돌풍, 격정
In a *gust* of uncontrollable anger he broke the picture in pieces.

ingratiate
[ingréiʃieit]

make (oneself) very pleasant to someone in order to gain favor
v. 마음에 들도록 하다, 환심을 사다
She tried to *ingratiate* herself with the teacher by some precious gifts.

munition
[mjuníʃən]

material used in war such as guns, shells, bombs, etc.
n. 군수품, 군용품, 전쟁 물자
The reason why we lost the war was not just because of a shortage of *munitions*.

prostrate
[prɔstréit]

lay down flat; cast down
v. 엎드리게 하다, 쓰러뜨리다
The wretched slaves *prostrated* themselves before their master.

smolder
[smóuldər]

burn and smoke without flame; continue in a suppressed condition
v. (불꽃 없이) 연기가 나다, (마음 속에서만) 끓다
The campfire *smoldered* for several hours after the blaze died down.

tattoo
[tətú:]

a series of taps or raps; beating of drums or bugles
n. 똑똑 (두드리는 소리), 탕탕 (치는 소리)
The hail beat a loud *tattoo* on the windowpane.

wield
[wi:ld]

use or control skillfully; manage; control
v. (도구나 힘을) 쓰다, 사용하다, 휘두르다
In a democratic system it is the people that *wield* the power.

EXERCISE 3 **Fill each blank with the most appropriate word given above.**
(Inflect the word if necessary.)

1. He was beating a(n) _____ on the table with his fingers while singing a pop song.

2. The people's discontent _____ for years before it broke out into open rebellion.

3. While he was walking down the street, a(n) _____ of chilly wind blew his hat off.

4. We have to save our _____ to meet the enemy's attack in the near future.

5. All the captives except him _____ themselves before the conqueror.

STUDY YOUR NEW WORDS-4

allude
[əlúːd]
refer indirectly; mention slightly; insinuate
v. 암시하다, 넌지시 비치다 (항상 to가 따름)
In his letter he *alluded* me to a matter which I had completely forgotten.

chisel
[tʃízl]
a tool with a sharp cutting edge at the end of a strong blade
n. 끌, 정 (조각용)
A *chisel* and a hammer are indispensable tools for a sculptor.

cricket
[kríkit]
a small brown insect related to the grasshopper
n. 귀뚜라미
Male *crickets* make a chirping noise by rubbing their front wings together.

flit
[flit]
fly or move lightly and swiftly; flutter
v. 홀쩍 날다, 훨훨 날다
As we stepped into the bush, birds *flitted* from tree to tree.

high-handed
[haihǽndid]
using one's power too forcefully; domineering; autocratic
adj. 횡포의, 고압적인
It was rather *high-handed* to punish the child for the accident.

lag
[læg]
fall behind; move too slowly
v. 처지다, 뒤떨어지다
The child *lagged* behind others because he was very tired.

naughty
[nɔ́ːti]
not obedient; bad in behavior; mischievous
adj. 말 안 듣는, 장난꾸러기의, 되지못한
You *naughty* boy! I told you not to play on the road.

rattle
[rǽtl]

a number of short, sharp scound
n. 덜거덕덜거덕, 덜걱덜걱
We used to hear the *rattle* of the milk bottles in the early morning.

soot
[suːt]

a black substance in the smoke
n. 검댕, 매연
Soot is caused by incomplete burning and makes smoke dark.

tributary
[tríbjutəri]

a stream or river that flows into a larger one; a nation that pays tribute to another
n. 지류(支流), 속국
The Ohio River is one of the *tributaries* of the Mississippi River.

undo
[ʌndúː]

1. cause to be as if never done; cancel or reverse; rescind
v. 원상태로 돌리다, 취소하다
The workmen mended the road, but a heavy storm *undid* their work.

2. unfasten, untie, or open
v. 풀다, 열다, 끄르다
The children began to *undo* the string round the parcel to see what was in it.

EXERCISE 4 **Fill each blank with the most appropriate word given above.**
(Inflect the word if necessary.)

1. We found it hard to like the new boy because of his _____ manners.
2. She did not say Mr. Smith's name, but it was clear she was _____ to him.
3. The Soviet Union still _____ far behind the United States in the exploration of the space.
4. The Roman Empire had many _____ around it at its golden age.
5. The teacher punished the _____ girl; she had been disobedient to her teacher.

STUDY YOUR NEW WORDS-5

belabor
[biléibər]

beat vigorously; thrash
v. 때리다, 세게 치다
The rider *belabored* his tired horse with a stick.

circumference
[sərkʌ́mfərəns]

the boundary line of a circle or of certain other surfaces
n. 원주, 둘레, 주위
After dinner they walked around the *circumference* of the lake.

devolve
[divɔ́lv]

be handed down to someone else; be transferred
v. (권리, 의무 등이) 위임되다, 넘어가다
In case of failure of direct descendants, the throne *devolves* upon the nearest prince.

fret
[fret]

(cause to) be continually worried an anxious
v. 마음을 졸이다, 조마조마해 하다
Don't *fret* too much ; everything will be all right.

honk
[hɔŋk]

make the cry of wild goose
v. (기러기 따위가) 울다, 경적을 울리다
The wild geese *honked* high in the autumn sky.

levy
[lévi]

collect by authority or force
v. 징수하다, 징발하다
The government decided to *levy* a tax on tobacco; it had been free from tax.

override
[ouvərráid]

prevail over; take no notice of
v. 무시하다, 무효로 하다
The new rule *overrides* all the previous ones.

rally
[rǽli]

bring together again; come together again
v. 다시 모으다, 다시 모이다
The scattered soldiers were *rallied* in the vale for the next attack.

sprawl
[sprɔːl]

stretch out oneself or one's limbs
v. 수족을 쭉 뻗다, 쭉 뻗고 눕다
Many people *sprawled* on the beach in their bathing suits.

trudge
[trʌdʒ]

walk heavily, wearily, or with effort
v. 터벅터벅 걷다, 터덜터덜 걷다
The old man *trudged* through the deep snow back towards home.

Lesson 34

EXERCISE 5 Fill each blank with the most appropriate word given above.
(Inflect the word if necessary.)

1. The girls at the camp _____ to get the meals when the cook was sick.

2. Every point on the _____ of a circle is at the same distance from the center.

3. You must not _____ other's happiness in pursuit of your own.

4. If the president is unable to handle his duties, they _____ upon the vice president.

5. The man concerned with his responsibilities will not be _____ about the matter of his privileges.

EXERCISE 1.	1. graft	2. peals	3. straggled	4. roundup	5. impersonal
EXERCISE 2.	1. auction	2. cope	3. hustle	4. plight	5. maneuvers
EXERCISE 3.	1. tattoo	2. smoldered	3. gust	4. munitions	5. prostrated
EXERCISE 4.	1. high-handed	2. alluding	3. lags	4. tributaries	5. naughty
EXERCISE 5.	1. rallied	2. circumference	3. override	4. devolve	5. fretted

종합 연습 문제

1 In the space before each word in column I, write the *letter* of its correct meaning in column II.

COLUMN I	COLUMN II
_____ 1. gruel	(A) to fall behind; move too slowly
_____ 2. levy	(B) a light or fire used as a signal
_____ 3. munition	(C) a nearly liquid food
_____ 4. lag	(D) to fight with some degree of success
_____ 5. beacon	(E) to prevail over
_____ 6. override	(F) the planned movement of the armed forces
_____ 7. cope	(G) material used in war
_____ 8. stun	(H) to bring together again
_____ 9. rally	(I) to make unconscious
_____ 10. maneuver	(J) to collect by authority or force.

2 Fill in the missing letters of the incomplete word. When completed, the word should mean the same as the word or expression in italics.

1. When the commander is unable to handle his duties, they D_____E upon the next ranking officer.
                                       are handed down

2. He is almost exhausted now; he had to T____E about 20 miles along the rugged road.
           walk heavily and wearily

3. In China, C_____Y is a higher accomplishment than painting.
      beautiful writing by hand

4. When a person is declared to be a B_____T by the court of law, his property is distributed among the people to whom he owes money.
           person unable to pay his debts

5. A C____N has three zones; the open area just inside the entrance, a twilight region and the perfectly dark interior.
   large deep cave

6. At the F_____Y we saw long trays of fish eggs under water that would turn into trouts later.
   a place for breeding fish

7. He is rather unfamiliar to me, but frequently calls on me with expensive gifts. I can't understand his U_____R purpose for doing so.
         hidden

Lesson 34

8. C_____R is eaten usually in thin slices in a salad, or used to make pickles.
long green vegetable

9. He insulted me in public, and I challenged him to a D__L.
formal fight

10. One of the old lady's eyes resembled that of V_____E.
large bird related to the eagle

3 In the space provided, write the *letter* of the word NOT RELATED in meaning to the other words in each line.

_____	1.	(A) hustle	(B) bustle	(C) jostle	(D) castle
_____	2.	(A) disobedient	(B) naughty	(C) tributary	(D) mischievous
_____	3.	(A) belabor	(B) thrash	(C) beat	(D) devolve
_____	4.	(A) tattoo	(B) plight	(C) adversity	(D) predicament
_____	5.	(A) scoff	(B) loom	(C) sneer	(D) jeer
_____	6.	(A) insinuate	(B) trudge	(C) allude	(D) imply
_____	7.	(A) levy	(B) straggle	(C) roam	(D) wander
_____	8.	(A) domineering	(B) autocratic	(C) ulterior	(D) high-handed
_____	9.	(A) undo	(B) stun	(C) cancel	(D) reverse
_____	10.	(A) fly	(B) flutter	(C) flit	(D) fret

4 Fill each blank with the most appropriate word selected from the vocabulary list below.

VOCABULARY LIST

gust	circumference	auction
anesthetics	rattle	ingratiate
graft	allude	fret
belabored	prostrated	scoffed

1. At a(n) _____ each thing is sold to the person who offers the most money for it.

2. The _____ of the earth is nearly 25,000 miles at the equator.

3. Some politicians tried to _____ with rich or influential people so as to get more supporters.

4. After the terrible hurricane, we saw many trees _____ on the sidewalk.

5. The girl _____ at his proposal of marriage, but she married him later.

6. No one has been able to _____ together trees belonging to quite distant families.

7. Do not _____ at the train's delay; it will arrive here soon.

8. As his poor donkey became exhausted under the heavy load, the man _____ him soundly.

9. Doctors often use _____ before performing surgical operations so that patients will not feel pain.

10. Do not ask him about his failure; do not even _____ to it.

해답

1 1. C   2. J   3. G   4. A   5. B   6. E   7. D   8. I   9. H   10. F
2 1. devolve   2. trudge   3. calligraphy   4. bankrupt   5. cavern
   6. fishery   7. ulterior   8. cucumber   9. duel   10. vulture
3 1. D   2. C   3. D   4. A   5. B   6. B   7. A   8. C   9. B   10. D
4 1. auction   2. circumference   3. ingratiate   4. prostrated   5. scoffed
   6. graft   7. fret   8. belabored   9. anesthetics   10. allude

Lesson 34

Lesson 35

PRETEST 35

Insert the *letter* of the best answer in the space provided.

1. We can seldom see the *cavalry* in modern battlefields. It has been replaced by the _____.
   (A) infantry   (B) armor   (C) artillery

2. He _____ three candles with a single *puff*.
   (A) picked up   (B) took away   (C) blew out

3. The *surname* of John W. Smith is _____.
   (A) John   (B) W.   (C) Smith

4. the actress wore a black *wig* _____.
   (A) over her blond hair   (B) around her slender waist
   (C) over her shoulders

5. The boys made *snares* to _____.
   (A) collect stamps   (B) catch rabbits   (C) cross the river

ANSWERS 1.B 2.C 3.C 4.A 5.B

STUDY YOUR NEW WORDS-1

ambush
[æmbuʃ]

1. a surprise attack from a place of hiding
   n. 잠복, 매복
   The soldiers lay in *ambush*, waiting for the signal to open fire.

2. put soldiers in hiding for a surprise attack
   v. 잠복시키다, 매복시키다
   The major *ambushed* his troops in the woods on both sides of the road.

brag
[bræg]

praise oneself or what one has; boast; vaunt
v. 뽐내다, 허풍떨다
He is always *bragging* about what he can do with a car.

cleanse
[klenz]

make clean by chemical or other technical processes
v. 깨끗이 하다, 청결하게 하다
Be sure that you *cleanse* the wound before bandaging it.

discourse
[dískɔːrs]

an orderly expression of ideas in speech or writing
n. 강연, 설교, ~론(論)
The professor will deliver a *discourse* on the poetic style of John Keats.

foxhole
[fɔ́kshoul]

a hole in the ground from which one or two soldiers fire at the enemy
n. 개인호
In World War Ⅱ, the general made it a point of pride to dig his own *foxhole*.

inflammation
[infləméiʃən]

a painful, hot, red swelling of some part of the body
n. 염증(炎症)
The *inflammation* of his knee made it difficult for him to walk.

lever
[lévər]

a bar used for lifting something heavy
n. 지레, 지렛대
The huge stone is so heavy that we cannot move it without a *lever*.

notation
[noutéiʃən]

a system of signs and symbols used in the sciences or arts
n. 기호법, 표기법
In arithmetic we use the Arabic *notation*(1, 2, 3, and so on) or sometimes the Roman *notation* (Ⅰ, Ⅱ, Ⅲ, and so on).

ransom
[rǽnsəm]

a price paid or demanded before a captive is set free
n. (포로나 인질을 되찾는 데 드는) 몸값
A large *ransom* was asked for the safe return of the child.

sop
[sɔp]

dip or soak
v. 담그다, 적시다
He *sopped* a piece of bread in milk; it was too crisp to eat.

tingle
[tiŋgl]

have a pricking, stinging feeling
v. 따끔따끔 아프다, 쑤시다
His cheek *tingled* from the slap she had given him.

EXERCISE 1 **Fill each blank with the most appropriate word given above.**
(Inflect the word if necessary.)

1. The priest delivered a long _____ upon the evils of untrustfulness.

2. The two scientists use different _____ for the same objects.

3. The room is too dirty. Please _____ the room with soap and water.

4. As th enemy's artillery began to fire, the soldiers jumped into their _____.

5. Her ears were _____ with cold after ice skating for an hour.

STUDY YOUR NEW WORDS-2

armament
[á:rməmənt]

war equipment and supplies; equipment of the armed forces
n. 군비, 장비, 병기
A large percentage of the budget is for *armaments*.

brunch
[brʌntʃ]

a combination of breakfast and lunch
n. 조반 겸 점심
On Sunday she gets up late in the morning and has a *brunch* around 10:30.

coffin
[kɔ́fin]

a box into which a dead person is put to be buried; casket
n. 관(棺), 널
His *coffin* was laid to rest in a deep grave.

envision
[invíʒən]

see in the mind as a future possibility; envisage
v. 상상하다, 마음 속에 그리다
The mother *envisioned* her little girl as a prima ballerina.

gangster
[gǽŋstər]

a member of a gang of criminals or rogues
n. 갱단의 일원, 악한
The *gangster* who had taken part in the robbery was arrested by the police.

illegible
[ilédʒəbl]

very hard or impossible to read; not legible
adj. 판독하기 어려운, 읽을 수 없는
The ink had faded so that many words were *illegible*.

malcontent
[mǽlkəntent]

a discontented or rebellious person
n. 불평분자, 불평가
The rebellion was started by some *malcontents* who had been dissatisfied with the policy.

pavilion
[pəvíljən]

a large tent or a light building used for shelter or pleasure
n. 간이 건물(대형 천막, 관람석 따위)
We will take a rest in the *pavilion* until the game starts.

shroud
[ʃraud]

something that covers or conceals; a cloth to be wrapped round a corpse
n. 장막, 가리개, 수의(壽衣)
The prisoners escaped out of the jail under the *shroud* of night.

spurt
[spəːrt]

flow out suddenly or violently; gush; spout; squirt
v. 분출하다, 뿜어 나오다
The room soon filled with the water *spurting* from the broken pipe.

varnish
[váːrniʃ]

liquid which gives a clear, hard, shinny surface
n. 니스, 바니시
He put *varnish* on the table top to protect it, but somebody has scratched it.

EXERCISE 2 **Fill each blank with the most appropriate word given above.**
(Inflect the word if necessary.)

1. The architect looked at the plans and _____ the finished house.

2. They prayed to God for the dead before lowering the _____ into the grave.

3. The strike was caused by a few _____ who felt they had been ignored when the promotions were made.

4. Do not put the hot plate on the table; it may spoil the _____ on it.

5. Blood will _____ out from the wound when the artery is cut off.

Lesson 35

STUDY YOUR NEW WORDS-3

ballad
[bǽləd]
a poem or song that tells a story; a popular love song
n. 민요, 속요
Many of old *ballads* are sung to new words.

butt
[bʌt]
1. the thicker end of anything; the end that is left
n. 굵은 쪽의 끝 부분, 개머리판, 담배 꽁초
The *butt* of pipe stuck out from the wall where the sink had been removed.

2. push or hit with the head or horns
v. 받다 (머리, 뿔 따위로)
The goat *butted* the boy and knocked him down.

consul
[kɑ́nsəl]
an official who protects or helps his citizen in a foreign country
n. 영사(領事)
You will have to call the *consul* before your passport is expired.

enshrine
[inʃráin]
enclose in a shrine; keep sacred; cherish
v. 안치하다, 간직하다, 소중히 모시다
Memories of happier days were *enshrined* in the old man's heart.

gobble
[gɑ́bl]
eat fast and greedily; gulp; devour
v. 게걸스레 먹다, 꿀떡 삼키다
He *gobbled* the ice cream so fast that he got a headache.

harangue
[hərǽŋ]
a loud or long speech; a noisy speech; tirade
n. 열변, 장광설
We had to listen to a long *harangue* about our own shortcomings.

mow
[mou]
cut down with a machine or scythe
v. 베다, 베어 쓰러뜨리다
He spent the whole afternoon *mowing* the grass in the backyard.

pilgrim
[pílgrim]
one who travels to a holy place for religious purposes
n. 순례자, 성지 참배자
In the Middle Ages, many people used to go as *pilgrims* to Jerusalem and to other holy places in Europe.

shear
[ʃiər]
remove from by cutting; cut off
v. (털을) 깎다
The farmers *sheared* the wool from the sheep.

strangle	kill by pressing the throat; choke; stifle
[stræŋgl]	*v.* 교살하다, 질식시키다
	He *strangled* her to death by a cord put around her neck.

walnut	a large, round, eatable nut
[wɔ́:lnət]	*n.* 호두
	The kernel of the *walnut* is eaten by itself or used in cakes or cookies.

EXERCISE 3 Fill each blank with the most appropriate word given above.
(Inflect the word if necessary.)

1. The _____ who came from various countries in Europe entered the church to pray.

2. Let me show you how to strike the enemy with the _____ of your rifle.

3. The old man sang _____ of the clan's heroes, often to the tune of a folk song.

4. He joined the army two months ago. When I met him yesterday he looked very strange with his closely _____ head.

5. His high, stiff collar was so tight that it was almost _____ his neck.

STUDY YOUR NEW WORDS-4

beaver	an animal with soft fur and feet adapted to swimming
[bí:vər]	*n.* 해리(海狸), 비버
	Beavers are noted for their skill in building dams across steams.

cavalry	soldiers who fight on horseback
[kǽvəlri]	*n.* 기병, 기병대
	The *cavalry* is much superior in mobility to the infantry.

creak	make a sharp, high sound; squeak; grate
[kri:k]	*v.* 삐걱삐걱 소리를 내다
	The floor *creaked* as he stepped on a loose board.

fir	an evergreen tree belonging to the pine family
[fə:r]	*n.* 전나무
	The *fir* remains green all year and its needles are distributed evenly around the branch.

hangar
[gǽŋgər]

a garage for airplanes
n. 격납고
During the heavy storm, airplanes should be kept in the *hangar*.

kernel
[kə́ːrnəl]

the soft part of a seed; core; nucleus
n. 핵심, 심수, (과일의) 인(仁)
The *kernel* of the argument is who discovered the islands first.

measles
[míːzlz]

a contagious disease of infants caused by virus
n. 홍역
What seems to be a cold often turns out to be the beginning of *measles*.

puff
[pʌf]

a short, quick blast of air, smoke, etc.
n. 한번 불기, 훅불기
With a huge *puff* the baloon was blown up and then suddenly burst.

sleet
[sliːt]

partly frozen rain; snow mixed with rain
n. 진눈깨비
Sleet forms when rain falls through a layer of cold air.

surname
[sə́ːrneim]

a last name; family name
n. 성(姓)
A woman, after marriage, usually drops her *surname* and take that of her husband.

wig
[wig]

head-covering of false hair
n. 가발
Women often wear *wigs* over their real hair for beauty or fashion.

EXERCISE 4

Fill each blank with the most appropriate word given above.
(Inflect the word if necessary.)

1. Would you please repair the door? It always _____ whenever I open it.
2. This beautiful Christmas tree was made of a small _____.
3. The _____ of his religious teaching is love for all men.
4. It is very dangerous to drive a car as the road is covered with _____.
5. _____ is much more common in children than in grown-ups.

STUDY YOUR NEW WORDS-5

bleach
[bliːtʃ]

make white by using chemicals or exposing to sunlight
v. 표백하다, 희게 하다
Bleached bones lay on the hot sands of the desert.

chariot
[tʃǽriət]

a two-wheeled carriage pulled by horses
n. 고대의 2륜 전차
Chariots were used in ancient times for fighting, racing, and in processions.

crutch
[krʌtʃ]

a support to help a lame person walk
n. 목각, 목발
He has been crippled since he broke his leg. Now he can't walk without a pair of *crutches*.

flirt
[fləːrt]

play at love; make love without meaning it
v. 농탕치다, (이성과) 시시덕거리다
She *flirted* with many men but loved only one.

gull
[gʌl]

a graceful seabird living on or near sea
n. 갈매기
They were very pleased to see some *gulls* flying in the sky, full of hope that they would soon get ashore.

kit
[kit]

a set of tools, instruments, supplies, etc.
n. (도구) 한 벌, 한 세트
When I bought a new car, a *kit* of tools came with it.

morsel
[mɔ́ːrsəl]

a small bite; a small quantity; fragment; bit
n. 한 조각, 소량, 한 입
The hungry children did not leave a *morsel* of food on their plates.

prototype
[próutətaip]

the first or primary type of anything; original or model
n. 원형(原型)
The strange mechanical device is the *prototype* of modern cars.

snare
[snɛər]

a trap for catching an animal
n. 덫, 올가미, 함정
They set a *snare* for rabbits on the hill, but unfortunately a wild cat was caught by it.

trigger
[trigər]

1. a device which, when pressed, starts an action
n. 방아쇠
When you squeeze the *trigger*, a round or rounds of ammunition are fired.

2. set off; start; initiate
v. ~을 야기하다, ~을 일으키다
When the burglar tripped the wire it *triggered* an alarm.

weir
[wiər]

a small dam or wall erected across a river
n. 둑, 댐
The *weir* across the river stops or controls the flow of the river above it.

EXERCISE 5   **Fill each blank with the most appropriate word given above.**
(Inflect the word if necessary.)

1. The hollowed log used by primitive people is the _____ of the modern ship.

2. The girl was very hungry, and consume the oatmeal to the last _____.

3. She doesn't like going to parties because her husband always _____ with every girl in the room.

4. The sun will _____ the cloth and make it whiter.

5. Hold your breath while squeezing the _____, or you cannot hit the target.

해답

EXERCISE 1.	1. discourse	2. notations	3. cleanse	4. foxholes	5. tingling
EXERCISE 2.	1. envisioned	2. coffin	3. malcontents	4. varnish	5. spurt
EXERCISE 3.	1. pilgrims	2. butt	3. ballads	4. sheared(shorn)	5. strangling
EXERCISE 4.	1. creaks	2. fir	3. kernel	4. sleet	5. measles
EXERCISE 5.	1. prototype	2. morsel	3. flirts	4. bleach	5. trigger

종합 연습 문제

1 In the space before each word in column I, write the letter of its correct meaning in column II.

COLUMN I   COLUMN II

_____ 1. consul   (A) a support to help a lame person walk

_____ 2. mow   (B) snow mixed with rain

_____ 3. chariot   (C) a combination of breakfast and lunch

_____ 4. hangar   (D) to eat fast and greedily

_____ 5. sleet   (E) a graceful seabird

_____ 6. armament   (F) a two-wheeled carriage pulled by horses

_____ 7. gull   (G) to cut down with a machine

_____ 8. crutch   (H) war equipment and supplies

_____ 9. brunch   (I) a garage for airplanes

_____ 10. gobble   (J) an official who protects or helps his citizens in a foreign country

2 Fill in the missing letters of the incomplete word. When completed, the word should mean the same as the word or expression in italics.

1. You can move the huge stone by using only a short L___R.
   bar used for lifting something heavy

2. It is unpleasant to hear one B__G about his own abilities, achievements, or possessions.
   praise oneself

3. The hinges on the door C___K; they need oiling.
   make a sharp, high sound

4. The angry senator arose and delivered a H_____E.
   long, loud speech

5. He wouldn't do such silly things if he had a M____L of sense.
   small quantity; bit

6. The detective used marked money as a S___E for the thief.
   trap

7. They built a W__R in order to convey the stream to the mill.
   small dam

8. The soldier slowly pressed the T_____R to shoot the riffle.
   device which, when pressed, causes firing

Lesson 35

9. The boy's handwriting was so bad that his letter to his mother was I_____E.
   impossible to read

10. The I_____N of her elbow made it impossible for her to swim.
    painful, hot, red swelling

3 In the space provided, write the *letter* of the word NOT RELATED in meaning to the other words in each line.

_____ 1.	(A) gobble	(B) bleach	(C) devour	(D) gulp
_____ 2.	(A) weir	(B) core	(C) nucleus	(D) kernel
_____ 3.	(A) clarify	(B) cleanse	(C) purify	(D) pledge
_____ 4.	(A) drag	(B) sop	(C) dip	(D) soak
_____ 5.	(A) stifle	(B) choke	(C) flirt	(D) strangle
_____ 6.	(A) brag	(B) vaunt	(C) fawn	(D) boast
_____ 7.	(A) tingle	(B) shear	(C) prick	(D) sting
_____ 8.	(A) creak	(B) aqueak	(C) grate	(D) allot
_____ 9.	(A) spout	(B) squat	(C) squirt	(D) squrt
_____ 10.	(A) rogue	(B) gangster	(C) villain	(D) ballad

4 Fill each blank with the most appropriate word from the vocabulary list below.

VOCABULARY LIST

ransom	measles	butt
ambush	prototype	notation
shroud	enshrined	levied
strangled	honked	envisioned

1. The crude craft which the Wright brothers made in 1903 was the _____ of the modern airplane.

2. The basic human rights are _____ in the constitution.

3. Many people went to America because they _____ a better future there for themselves and their children.

4. Indians often trapped their enemies by _____, instead of meeting them in open battle.

5. After smoking, do not throw away the _____ on the street; you will be heavily fined.

6. Music has a special system of _____, and so does chemistry.

7. The sufferer of _____ usually has a high fever and small red sports on the skin.

8. She was almost _____ on a piece of meat that caught in her throat.

9. The kidnappers asked a large _____ for the return of the little girl.

10. The enemy seems to attack our defense positions tonight under the _____ of darkness.

해답

1 1. J 2. G 3. F 4. I 5. B 6. H 7. E 8. A 9. C 10. D
2 1. lever 2. brag 3. creak 4. harangue 5. morsel
    1. snare 7. weir 8. trigger 9. illegible 10. inflammation
3 1. B 2. A 3. D 4. A 5. C 6. C 7. B 9. D 9. B 10. D
4 1. prototype 2. enshrined 3. envisioned 4. ambush 5. butt
    6. notation 7. measles 8. strangled 9. ransom 10. shroud

Lesson 35

UNIT V

(Lessons 36~40)

- **Discriminating**

TROUBLESOME WORDS •

Lesson 36

PRETEST 36

Insert the *letter* of the best answer in the space provided.

1. The court *annulled* the marriage because it was _____.
   (A) legitimate   (B) illegal   (C) incomplete

2. The *excess* of imports over exports will _____ national economy.
   (A) harm   (B) stablize   (C) boost

3. It is considered to be _____ to read somebody else's *diary*.
   (A) generous   (B) impolite   (C) dangerous

4. He *augmented* his wages by _____ his free time.
   (A) wasting   (B) enlarging   (C) working in

5. _____ persons are *averse* to punishing people.
   (A) Critical   (B) Indifferent   (C) Generous

ANSWERS 1. B 2. A 3. B 4. C 5. C

STUDY YOUR NEW WORDS-1

access
[ǽkses]

the right or privilege to approach, enter, or use; entrance; approach
n. 가까이 할 권리, 출입, 접근
The students have *access* to the library only in the afternoon.

excess
[iksés, ékses]

more than enough; surplus; overabundance
n. 과잉, 과다, 초과
Last year we had several floods; we had an *excess* of rain.

adapt
[ədǽpt]

make suitable; adjust; fit
v. 적응하다, 적응시키다, 개조하다
Long ago Eskimos learned how to *adapt* to the cold to live in the Arctic Region.

adopt
[ədápt]

take as one's own; accept formally
v. 채택하다, 양자로 삼다
The club *adopted* a new set of rule concerning its membership.

adverse
[ǽdvəːrs, ædvə́ːrs]

unfriendly in purpose; hostile; injurious
adj. 불리한, 해로운, 거꾸로의, 역의
His *adverse* criticism didn't upset me, but encouraged me.

averse
[əvə́ːrs]

not liking; opposed; unwilling
adj. 싫어하는, 반대하여
My parents are *averse* to our picnic plan; they don't approve of it.

affect
[əfékt]

have an effect upon; influence; change
v. ~에 영향을 미치다, (병이) 침범하다
The government decision whether to continue the project will *affect* the future of our national economy.

effect
[ifékt]

something made to happen by a person or thing; result; consequence
n. 결과, 효과, 영향
I have warned him to drive slowly several times, but it doesn't have any *effect* at all.

affectation
[æfektéiʃən]

an artificial way of talking or acting; show; pretense
n. 꾸밈, 꾸미는 태도
The new secretary is sincere and quite without *affectation*.

affection
[əfékʃən]

gentle, lasting love as of a parent of its child; fondness
n. 애정, 애착
The insane man felt no affection for his child.

EXERCISE 1   In the blank space, insert the *letter* of the word that best completes the sentence.

1. The _____ of losses over profits will ruin the business.
   (A) access   (B) excess

2. The man _____ an old car engine to drive his boat.
   (A) adapted   (B) adopted

3. An unbalanced diet has an _____ effect upon health.
   (A) adverse   (B) averse

4. This medicine will have a miraculous _____ on you.
   (A) affect   (B) effect

5. Nothing is greater than mothers' _____ for their children.
   (A) affectation   (B) affection

Lesson 36

STUDY YOUR NEW WORDS-2

allusion
[əlúːʒən]
indirect reference; hint; suggestion; insinuation
n. 암시, 언급, 넌지시 비추기〔비꼬기〕
The preacher likes to make an *allusion* to Homer while preaching.

illusion
[ilúːʒən]
a false impression; misleading appearance
n. 환상, 환영, 환각
The white walls create the *illusion* that the roon is very large.

annual
[ǽnjuəl]
coming once a year; living only one year or season
adj. 일년(마다)의, 일년생의
My birthday party is the biggest *annual* event of my family.

annul
[ənʌ́l]
make void; cancel; nullify
v. 무효로 하다, 취소하다
The judge *annulled* the contract because one of the signers was too young.

appraise
[əpréiz]
estimate the value, amount, quality, or merit of; judge; rate
v. 평가하다, 견적하다
The couple *appraised* the house carefully before offering to buy it.

apprise
[əpráiz]
give notice to; inform; notify
v. ~에 알리다, ~에 통고하다
The club members were immediately *apprised* of his change of plans.

argument
[ɑ́ːrɡjumənt]
a discussion by persons who disagree; dispute; debate
n. 논쟁, 논거
We should try to settle the matter by *argument*, not by fighting.

augment
[ɔːɡmént]
make greater in size, number, amount, or degree; enlarge; increase
v. 증대시키다, 증가시키다
The king *augmented* his power by taking over rights that had belonged to the nobles.

assure
[əʃúər]
tell positively or confidently; guarantee; convince
v. 안심시키다, ~에게 보증하다
The man *assured* himself that the bridge was safe before crossing it.

insure
[inʃúər]
1. guard against loss or harm
v. 보험에 들다
He *insured* his car against accident. theft, and fire.

2. make sure; ensure

v. 확실하게 하다

Don't forget to check your work to *insure* its accuracy.

EXERCISE 2

In the blank space, insert the *letter* of the word that best completes the sentence.

1. It was an _____ caused by the dim lights that made me think I saw a man in the shadows.
   (A) allusion (B) illusion

2. An _____ plant lives only one year or season.
   (A) annual (B) annul

3. We were _____ that they would arrive before noon.
   (A) appraised (B) apprised

4. His strong _____ persuaded us to accept his conclusion.
   (A) arguments (B) augments

5. After the fire, the captain of the ship _____ the passengers that there was no more danger.
   (A) assured (B) insured

STUDY YOUR NEW WORDS-3

bandage
[bǽndidʒ]

a strip of cloth used in binding up and dressing a wound
n. 붕대
The doctor tied up the patient's broken ankle with a *bandage*.

bondage
[bɔ́ndidʒ]

lack of freedom; slavery; servitude
n. 속박, 굴종, 노예의 신세
They seem to love *bondage* more than liberty.

carton
[káːrtən]

a box made of cardboard or pasteboard
n. 상자, 마분지
Pack the books in a small *carton* to carry it easily.

cartoon
[kaːrtúːn]

a drawing of persons, things, or events in an amusing way
n. 만화
Political *cartoons* often represent the U. S. as a tall man with chin whiskers, called Uncle Sam.

censor
[sénsər]

1. a person who examines books, plays, letters, etc., to prohibit what seems objectionable
n. 검열관
The novel was banned by the ***censor*** as likely to stir up suspicion of the government among the readers.

2. prohibit, suppress, or remove allegedly objectional material
v. 검열하다
Every dictator ***censors*** the newspapers in his country.

censure
[sénʃər]

reprimand; blame; denounce
v. 비난하다, 질책하다
The principal of the school ***censured*** the students for their rude behavior.

collision
[kəlíʒən]

a violent rushing against; clash; conflict
n. 충돌, 불일치
Many people were killed in the ***collision*** between the bus and the car.

collusion
[kəlú:ʒən]

a secret agreement for some wrong or harmful purpose; conspiracy
n. 공모, 음모
The leaders of the ***collusion*** against the government were caught and punished.

confidant
[kɔnfidǽnt]

a close friend
n. 막역한 친구
I have only one ***confidant*** to whom I can tell my secrets.

confident
[kɔ́nfidənt]

firmly believing; certain; sure
adj. 확신하는, 자신 있는
The doctor felt ***confident*** that his patient would recover from pneumonia.

EXERCISE 3
In the blank space, insert the *letter* of the word that best completes the sentence.

1. According to the Bible, Moses led Israelites out of _____ from Egypt.
   (A) bandage   (B) bondage

2. Sir Max Beerborn made _____ of many prominent politicians, artists, and writers.
   (A) cartons   (B) cartoons

3. The employer _____ him for neglecting his work.
   (A) censored   (B) censured

4. There was a _____ of interests on how to spend the club's money.
   (A) collision   (B) collusion

5. The politician spoke the voters in a _____ voice.
   (A) confidant   (B) confident

STUDY YOUR NEW WORDS-4

consul
[kánsəl]

a foreign-based government official below the rank of ambassador
n. 영사
I am a Swedish. Is there a Swedish *consul* in Omaha?

council
[káunsəl]

a group of people organized to deliberate or rule; meeting; conference; assembly
n. 회의, 평의회, 협의회
The *council* of ministers advised the king to dismiss the general.

counsel
[káunsəl]

1. advice; recommendation; opinion
n. 권고, 조언
The young man refused to listen to the old man's *counsel*.

2. a lawyer or adviser
n. 변호사, 변호인
The murder suspect refused to answer the questions on the advice of his *counsel*.

dairy
[dɛ́əri]

a farm or barn where milk cows are kept; a place where milk and milk products are prepared and sold
n. 젖 짜는 곳, 우유 판매점
The Hopkinses run the biggest *dairy* farm in the State of Arizona.

diary
[dáiəri]

a daily record or journal
n. 일기(장), 일지
It is very rewarding to keep a *diary* of daily happenings.

decease
[disíːs]

an act or fact of dying; death
n. 사망
Upon his *decease* all his properties passed to his wife.

disease
[dizíːz]

sickness; illness
n. 병, 질병
Measles and chicken pox are two *diseases* of childhood.

decent
[díːsnt]

suitable; respectable; socially acceptable.
adj. 예절바른, 점잖은, 상당한
It is not *decent* to laugh at a crippled person.

descent
[disént]

coming down from a higher to a lower place
n. 강하, 전락, 폭락
The road makes a sharp *descent* just around the corner.

dissent
[disént]

1. differ; disagree
v. 의견을 달리하다
The three justices *dissented* from the Supreme Court's decision.

2. difference of opinion; disagreement
n. 불찬성, 의견 차이
Dissent among the senior members was the main cause of the disintegration of the club.

EXERCISE 4 In the blank space, insert the *letter* of the word that best completes the sentence.

1. A _____ looks after the business interests of his own country and protects citizens of his country who are traveling or living there.
   (A) counsel (B) consul (C) council

2. My family buys milk and ice cream at a local _____.
   (A) dairy (B) diary

3. Many _____ are caused by bacteria; cleanliness helps prevent them.
   (A) deceases (B) diseases

4. The _____ of the balloon was more rapid than its rise had been.
   (A) decent (B) descent (C) dissent

해답					
EXERCISE 1.	1. B	2. A	3. A	4. B	5. B
EXERCISE 2.	1. B	2. A	3. B	4. A	5. A
EXERCISE 3.	1. B	2. B .	3 B	4. A	5. B
EXERCISE 4.	1. B	2. A	3. B	4. B	

종합 연습 문제

1 In the space before each word in column I, write the *letter* of its correct meaning in column II.

	COLUMN I	COLUMN II
_____	1. access	(A) coming down from a higher to a lower place
_____	2. excess	(B) the right to enter
_____	3. adverse	(C) prohibit allegedly objectionable material
_____	4. averse	(D) more than enough
_____	5. appraise	(E) estimate the value of
_____	6. apprise	(F) not liking
_____	7. censor	(G) unfriendly in purpose; injurious
_____	8. censure	(H) reprimand; blame
_____	9. descent	(I) difference of opinion
_____	10. dissent	(J) give notice to

2 In the space before each sentence, write the *letter* of the word which has the SAME MEANING as the italicized expression.

_____ 1. Most animals easily *adjust* themselves to the weather and surroundings.
    (A) adapt   (B) adopt

_____ 2. The disease *influenced* his mind so that he lost his memory completely.
    (A) affected   (B) effected

_____ 3. It's not good to make a personal *insinuation* to anyone.
    (A) allusion   (B) illusion

_____ 4. A teacher should be able to *estimate* ability and achievement in students.
    (A) appraise   (B) apprise

_____ 5. It is quite certain that a *clash* with Congress will ruin the government's plans.
    (A) collision   (B) collusion

3 In the space provided, write the letter of the word or expression that has most nearly the SAME MEANING as the italicized word.

_____ 1. cause and *effect*   (A) reason   (B) consequence
    (C) condition   (D) influence

_____ 2. *decent* suit   (A) respectable   (B) tight
    (C) loose   (D) untidy

Lesson 36

_____ 3. the Korean *consul* (A) resident (B) close friend
                                    (C) lawyer   (D) foreign-based official

_____ 4. plaintiff's *counsel* (A) witness   (B) lawyer
                                    (C) judge   (D) prosecutor

_____ 5. *confident* voice   (A) faint   (B) loud
                                    (C) certain   (D) clear

_____ 6. candy *carton*   (A) box   (B) drawing
                                    (C) taste   (D) sweetness

_____ 7. *adopt* children   (A) educate   (B) take as one's own
                                    (C) adjust   (D) control the number of

_____ 8. *adverse* conditions (A) unfavorable (B) suitable
                                    (C) acceptable (D) regretful

_____ 9. mother's *affection* (A) prejudice (B) fondness
                                    (C) chore   (D) understanding

_____ 10. optical *illusion*   (A) indirect suggestion (B) distant view
                                    (C) sudden disturbance (D) false impression

4 Fill each blank with the most appropriate word from the vocabulary list below.

VOCABULARY LIST

collusion	adapt	argument
illusion	access	decease
consul	affectation	insure
confidant	adverse	apprised

1. The general's sudden _____ left the army without a leader.

2. It's not easy to approach to the building. The only _____ to that building is along that muddy track.

3. One of the striking facts of nature is the ability of living things to _____ themselves to any environment on earth.

4. I believe the judge is biased against us. He gave us a(n) _____ decision on the case.

5. Her roughness is but a(n) _____; she is really a quiet, gentle girl.

6. John told me that the teacher had _____ us there would be a test on Monday.

7. He won the _____ against the other members of the association by producing figures to prove his point.

436 TOEFL · TOEIC · TEPS 중급 College Vocabulary

8. When you mail a package with valuable items, it is safe to _____ it against theft and damage.

9. The two men made the _____ to steal the jewels and sell them to a jeweler in another country.

10. John talked about his personal matters with his _____.

해답

1 1. B   2. D   3. G   4. F   5. E   6. J   7. C   8. H   9. A   10. I
2 1. A   2. A   3. A   4. A   5. A
3 1. B   2. A   3. D   4. B   5. C   6. A   7. B   8. A   9. B   10. D
4 1. decease   2. access   3. adapt   4. adverse   5. affectation
     6. apprised   7. argument   8. insure   9. collusion   10. confidant

Lesson 36

Lesson 37

PRETEST 37

Insert the *letter* of the best answer in the space provided.

1. The mechanic *disassembled* the car to _____ it.
   (A) buy   (B) sell   (C) repair

2. A *drought* of three months _____ the wheat.
   (A) ruined   (B) helped   (C) ripened

3. The boy gave an *ingenuous* account of his acts, _____ nothing.
   (A) discarding   (B) telling   (C) concealing

4. The abolitionists felt a *moral* responsibility to _____ the slaves.
   (A) capture   (B) free   (C) trade

5. The driver was *prosecuted* for his _____ driving.
   (A) skillful   (B) careful   (C) reckless

ANSWERS 1.C 2.A 3.C 4.B 5.C

STUDY YOUR NEW WORDS-1

desert
[dézərt]
n. 사막

[dizə́:rt]
v. 버리다, 돌보지 않다

1. an arid area
   Lawrence rode a camel across the *desert* on an exploring expedition.

2. abandon; forsake
   He had intended to *desert* his wife and children, but changed his mind.

dessert
[dizə́:rt]
n. 후식(後食), 디저트

a sweet course at the end of a meal
Strawberry pie is one of my most favorite *desserts*.

438 TOEFL·TOEIC·TEPS 중급 College Vocabulary

disassemble
[dìsəsémbl]

take apart; take to pieces
v. 해체하다
Many students know how to *disassemble* the radio, but few know how to put it together.

dissemble
[disémbl]

hide (one's true feelings, intentions, etc.); disguise
v. 숨기다, 감추다
She tried to *dissemble* her anger with a smile on her face.

draught, draft
[drɑft]

the first rough written form of anything; a rough plan
n. 도안, 초안
I've made a first *draught* of my speech for Friday, but it still needs a lot of work.

drought
[draut]

a long period of dry weather; continued lack of rain; dryness
n. 가뭄, 한발
The long *drought* has killed most of the crops in the fields.

eligible
[élidʒəbl]

suitable to be chosen; desirable; qualified
adj. 적임의, 뽑힐 수 있는
She knows a lot of *eligible* young men who are all rich and attractive.

illegible
[ilédʒəbl]

very hard or impossible to read; not legible
adj. 읽기 어려운, 불명료한
The ink had faded so that many words were *illegible*.

eminent
[émənənt]

highly respected; well-known; distinguished; outstanding
adj. 뛰어난, 탁월한, 저명한
Washington was *eminent* both as general and as President.

imminent
[ímənənt]

about to happen; impending
adj. 임박한, 절박한
The scientist predicted that an earthquake was *imminent* in Tokyo area.

EXERCISE 1 In the blank space, insert the *letter* of the word that best completes the sentence.

1. Great sections of _____ in Arizona and California have been made into farmland by irrigation.
   (A) desert   (B) dessert

2. Somehow he was able to _____ the radio but failed to reassemble it.
   (A) disassemble   (B) dissemble

Lesson 37

3. He made three different _____ of his report before he handed it in final form.
    (A) draughts   (B) droughts

4. The old professor was looking for an _____ young man for his daughter.
    (A) eligible   (B) illegible

5. Censure is the tax a man pays to the public for being _____.
    (A) eminent   (B) imminent

STUDY YOUR NEW WORDS-2

exalt
[igzɔ́:lt]

raise a person to a high position; elevate; promote
v. 높이다, 올리다, 승진시키다
The members *exalted* Mr. Smith when they elected him president of the association.

exult
[igzʌ́lt]

rejoice greatly; show delight; be very glad
v. 무척 기뻐하다, 기뻐 날뛰다
All the people *exulted* to find that our national team won the gold medal in the International Basketball Tournament.

ingenious
[indʒí:njəs]

skillful; clever; inventive; cleverly made
adj. 교묘한, 영리한, 재간 있는
The trap made of an old tin can and some wire is an *ingenious* device.

ingenuous
[indʒénjuəs]

frank and open; sincere; simple
adj. 솔직한, 순진한
The *ingenuous* person had never thought of being suspicious of what others told him.

jealous
[dʒéləs]

fearful that a person one loves may love someone else; possessive; envious
adj. 질투가 많은, 시샘하는
When my little brother sees mother holding the new baby, he becomes *jealous*.

zealous
[zéləs]

actively enthusiastic; eager; earnest; ardent; fervent
adj. 열심인, 열광적인
The clerk in the toy section of the department seems very *zealous* in pleasing the customers.

material [mətíəriəl]	anything of which something can be made ***n.*** 재료, 원료 The dress that Miss Kim was wearing at the party was made of synthetic *material*.
materiel [mətiəriél]	supplies; military supplies; equipment ***n.*** 장비, 군수품 The statesman said the Iron Curtain countries had vast resources in manpower and *materiel*.
moral [mɔ́(:)rəl]	good in character or conduct; right; just ***adj.*** 도덕적인, 윤리적인 George Washington is known to be a *moral* and just man.
morale [mɔrǽ:l]	a state of mind in terms of confidence and courage ***n.*** 사기(士氣), 풍기 I am sure that we will win the battle; the *morale* of our troops is very high.

EXERCISE 2 In the blank space, insert the *letter* of the word that best completes the sentence.

1. He was _____ to the most eminent position in the government.
   (A) exalted (B) exulted
2. The _____ boy made a radio set for himself after reading the manual.
   (A) ingenious (B) ingenuous
3. The boys and girls made _____ efforts to clean up the house for the party.
   (A) jealous (B) zealous
4. The general needs more troops and _____ to win the victory.
   (A) material (B) materiel
5. The _____ of the team is low after its seven consecutive defeats.
   (A) moral (B) morale

STUDY YOUR NEW WORDS-3

ordinance
[ɔ́ːrdinəns]

a rule or law made by authority; regulation; canon
n. 법령, 포고, 조례
Freedom of religious worship was guaranteed to all settlers in the Northewst Territory by the *Ordinance* of 1787.

ordnance
[ɔ́ːrdnəns]

cannon or artillery; arms; armament
n. 포, 병기, 군수품
The pirate ships in the West Indies were armed with heavy *ordnance*.

parish
[pǽriʃ]

a district that has its own church and clergyman
n. 교구(敎區)
The minister worked very hard to make the rounds of his *parish* and visit the homes of the sick.

perish
[périʃ]

be destroyed; die
v. 멸망하다, 죽다
They said that this flower would not *perish* even when frost comes.

perpetrate
[pə́ːrpitreit]

do or commit (crime, fraud, trick, or anything bad)
v. (나쁜 짓, 과오를) 범하다, 저지르다
The police still don't know who *perpetrated* the murder of the housewife.

perpetuate
[pərpétjueit]

make perpetual; keep from being forgotten; preserve
v. 영속시키다, 영존시키다, 불멸하게 하다
This monument was built to *perpetuate* the memory of the national hero.

personality
[pərsənǽləti]

the quality that makes one person be different and act differently from another; character; disposition
n. 개성, 성격
Many psychologists are inclined to attribute the formation of *personality* entirely to the operation of the cultural and physical environment.

personalty
[pə́ːrsnəlti]

personal property
n. 동산
That car is his *personalty*; using it without his permission is illegal.

persecute
[pə́ːrsikjuːt]

harass persistently; oppress; torment; wrong
v. 박해하다, 학대하다
Blessed are those who are *persecuted* for righteousness' sake.

prosecute
[prɔ́sikjuːt]

1. try by law; bring a case before a law court
v. 입건하다, 기소하다
The engineer of the wrecked train was *prosecuted* for criminal negligence.

2. carry out; follow up; pursue
v. 수행하다, 추구하다
He *prosecuted* an inquiry into reasons for the company's failure.

EXERCISE 3 In the blank space, insert the *letter* of the word that best completes the sentence.

1. Some countries have _____ forbidding the use of soft coal for heating.
   (A) ordinances   (B) ordnances

2. A countless number of young soldiers _____ to win the war against North Korea.
   (A) parished   (B) perished

3. The country _____ in postage stamps the centenary of her political independence.
   (A) perpetrated   (B) perpetuated

4. The job is very difficult; it requires a man of strong _____.
   (A) personality   (B) personalty

5. The old man _____ the dog by whipping it cruelly whenever it came near.
   (A) persecuted   (B) prosecuted

STUDY YOUR NEW WORDS-4

portable
[pɔ́ːrtəbl]

capable of being carried or moved; easily carried
adj. 휴대용의, 운반할 수 있는
The author takes his *portable* typewriter wherever he goes.

potable
[póutəbl]

fit for drinking; drinkable
adj. 마시기에 알맞는, 마실 수 있는
They set up purifying systems in dozens of places where the water was not *potable*.

prescribe
[priskráib]

1. recommend a rule to be followed; order; direct
v. 규정하다, 명하다
Good citizens always do what the laws *prescribe*.

2. order as a remedy or treatment
v. 처방하다
The doctor *prescribed* a new medicine for the pain in my joints.

proscribe
[prouskráib]

forbid by law; prohibit as wrong; condemn
v. 금지하다, 배척하다
In earlier days, the church *proscribed* dancing and cardplaying.

reality
[ri(:)æləti]

the quality or state of being real; real existence; a real thing
n. 사실, 진실, 실체
Slaughter and destruction are terrible *realities* of war.

realty
[ríəlti]

real estate
n. 부동산
His *realty* includes a big mansion and several buildings in Incheon.

statue
[stǽtju:]

an image of a person or animal carved or cast in solid material; sculpture
n. 상(像), 조상(彫像)
Nearly every city in the United States has a *statue* of some famous man.

stature
[stǽtʃər]

the height of a person or thing; tallness
n. 키, 신장
A man six feet tall is above average *stature* in this part of the world.

vacation
[vəkéiʃən]

a time of rest and freedom from work; holiday
n. 휴가
My family is going to have a short *vacation* at the east coast.

vocation
[voukéiʃən]

a particular occupation; business; profession; trade
n. 직업, 천직
You will not make a good teacher, unless you feel teaching is your *vocation*.

EXERCISE 4

In the blank space, insert the *letter* of the word that best completes the sentence.

1. A _____ radio is popular because we can take it wherever we go.
   (A) portable   (B) potable

2. What punishment does the law _____ for this kind of crime?
   (A) prescribe   (B) proscribe

3. Her dream of marrying a prince became a _____.
   (A) reality   (B) realty

4. I watched him nearly for an hour; he sat rigid, immovable, like a _____.
   (A) statue   (B) stature

5. She chose teaching as her _____ because she thought she has a special fitness for it.
    (A) vacation   (B) vocation

해답	EXERCISE 1.	1. A	2. A	3. A	4. A	5. A
	EXERCISE 2.	1. A	2. A	3. B	4. B	5. B
	EXERCISE 3.	1. A	2. B	3. B	4. A	5. A
	EXERCISE 4.	1. A	2. A	3. A	4. A	5. B

종합 연습 문제

1 In the space before each word in column I, write the *letter* of its correct meaning in column II.

COLUMN I	COLUMN II
_____ 1. draught	(A) raise a person to a higher rank
_____ 2. drought	(B) easily carried
_____ 3. exalt	(C) harass persistently
_____ 4. exult	(D) lack of rain
_____ 5. personality	(E) a rough written form of anything
_____ 6. personalty	(F) rejoice greatly
_____ 7. persecute	(G) character
_____ 8. prosecute	(H) fit for drinking
_____ 9. portable	(I) personal property
_____ 10. potable	(J) try by law

2 In the space before each sentence, write the *letter* of the word which has the SAME MEANING as the italicized expression.

_____ 1. The regiment assembled troops and *supplies* to prepare for the attack.
    (A) material   (B) materiel

_____ 2. She is very short-tempered; she never *hides* her anger on any occasion.
    (A) disassembles   (B) dissembles

_____ 3. Where are you planning to go for your *holiday* this summer?
    (A) vacation   (B) vocation

_____ 4. The scientist *abandoned* his country and helped the enemy.
    (A) deserted   (B) desserted

_____ 5. It is difficult to *forbid* a party without infringing on the right of the individual to dissent.
    (A) prescribe   (B) proscribe

3 In the space provided, write the *letter* of the word or expression that has most nearly the SAME MEANING as the italicized word.

_____ 1. delicious *dessert*   (A) meal   (B) sweet food
    (C) smell   (D) exotic music

_____ 2. *eligible* bachelor   (A) qualified   (B) handsome
    (C) educated   (D) engaged

_____ 3. bronze *statue*   (A) metal   (B) vase
                                (C) sculpture   (D) era

_____ 4. heavy *ordnance*   (A) punishment   (B) artillery
                                (C) tax   (D) rain

_____ 5. *eminent* biologist (A) mediocre   (B) outstanding
                                (C) ehthusiastic (D) diligent

_____ 6. *zealous* for fame (A) indifferent (B) envious
                                (C) ready   (D) eager

_____ 7. *ingenuous* report (A) sincere   (B) wise
                                (C) carefully written (D) short

_____ 8. traffic *ordinance* (A) violation   (B) accident
                                (C) regulation   (D) jam

_____ 9. dress *material*   (A) fabric   (B) style
                                (C) manual   (D) supplier

_____ 10. *portable* television (A) automatic (B) capable of being carried
                                (C) easy to set up (D) educational

Fill each blank with the most appropriate word from the vocabulary list below.

VOCABULARY LIST

prosecuted	jealous	reality
ingenious	perpetrated	illegible
potable	imminent	ordiance
perished	stature	morale

1. The girl was _____ when she discovered that the boy loved someone else.

2. My sister is so _____ that she will think of a way to do the work more easily.

3. The black clouds, thunder, and lightning show that a storm is _____.

4. I doubted the _____ of what he had seen; I thought he must have dreamed it.

5. He started an inquiry into the causes of the fire, and _____ it for several weeks.

6. Hundreds of settlers _____ that year because of drought, famine, and epidemic diseases.

7. Trapped in the cave by a fall of rock, the men kept up their _____ by singing together.

Lesson 37

8. The boy's band writing was so bad that his letter to his mother was _____.

9. It usually takes a year for a dog to grow to its full _____.

10. The two thieves _____ the robbery of the jewelry store, and stole jewelries worth 2 million dollars.

해답

1 1. E   2. D   3. A   4. F   5. G   6. I   7. C   8. J   9. B   10. H
2 1. B   2. B   3. A   4. A   5. B
3 1. B   2. A   3. C   4. B   5. B   6. D   7. A   8. C   9. A   10. B
4 1. jealous   2. ingenious   3. imminent   4. reality   5. prosecuted
    6. perished   7. morale   8. illegible   9. stature   10. perpetrated

Lesson 38

PRETEST 38

Insert the *letter* of the best answer in the space provided.

1. _____ is an *alumna* of a small local college in Illinois.
   (A) He   (B) She   (C) It

2. The boy was so angry that he *clenched* his _____.
   (A) room   (B) anger   (C) fists

3. The soldier gave _____ a *contemptuous* look.
   (A) his lovely daughter   (B) the deserter   (C) his pal

4. An *egoist* loves only for _____ pleasure.
   (A) his own   (B) somebody else's   (C) everyone's

5. It is *immoral* to _____ another man's property.
   (A) buy   (B) protect   (C) steal

ANSWERS 1.B 2.C 3.B 4.A 5.C

STUDY YOUR NEW WORDS-1

alumna
[əlʌ́mnə]
a female graduate of a school
n. alumnus의 여성형
pl. alumnae
My wife is an *alumna* of Ehwa Women's University.

alumnus
[əlʌ́mnəs]
a male graduate of a school
n. 졸업생, 동창생
pl. alumni
President Kennedy was an *alumnus* of Harvard University.

alumni (*pl.*)
[əlʌ́mnai]
graduates of a school
n. alumnus의 복수형
My son and my daughter are both *alumni* of Ohio State University.

amoral
[æmɔ́rəl]

not subject to moral judgement; lacking a knowledge of right and wrong; non-moral
adj. 도덕적 판단력이 없는
Cats are *amoral*; they can't be censured for killing birds.

immoral
[imɔ́rəl]

violating morality; sinful; wicked
adj. 부도덕한, 행실이 나쁜
Lying and stealing are considered *immoral* conducts in every human society.

unmoral
[ʌ́nmɔrəl]

not pertaining to morality; neither moral nor immoral
adj. 초도덕적인, 도덕에는 관심이 없는
Most scientists believe their research to be *unmoral*, no matter what the results will be.

avocation
[ævoukéiʃən]

something that a person does besides his regular business; hobby
n. 취미, 도락
Stamp collecting as well as fishing is Mr. Evan's favorite *avocation*.

vocation
[voukéiʃən]

main job; occupation; profession
n. 직업
Bookkeeping is Mr. Jones' *vocation*, and photography is his avocation.

biannual
[baiǽnjuəl]

occurring twice a year
adj. 연 2회의, 반년마다의
Our school doctor recommends a *biannual* visit to the dentist; I am going to the dentist's second time this year.

biennial
[baiénjəl]

occurring once every two years; living for two years
adj. 2년에 한 번의, 2년마다의
The sophomores and seniors are taking the *biennial* exam this afternoon.

EXERCISE 1   In the blank space, insert the *letter* of the word that best completes the sentence.

1. Do you and your wife belong to the same _____ association?
    (A) alumna   (B) alumnus   (C) alumni

2. You can't blame the baby for breaking the antique vase because he is _____.
    (A) amoral   (B) immoral   (C) unmoral

3. Golf is a hobby of most people, but it is the _____ of a professional golfer.
    (A) avocation   (B) vocation

4. The _____ examinations for the college applicants will be given in May and October this year.
   (A) biannual   (B) biennial

STUDY YOUR NEW WORDS-2

chord
[kɔːrd]

a string of a stringed musical instrument
n. (악기의) 현, 줄
He is replacing the broken *chord* of his violin.

cord
[kɔrd]

a thick string; a very thin rope
n. 새끼줄, 끈
He had tied the package with a *cord* before he took it to the post office.

clench
[klentʃ]

close tightly together; grasp firmly
v. (이를) 악물다, 꽉 다물다, (주먹을) 꽉 쥐다
He *clenched* his teeth to endure the pain of the wound suffered from the accident.

clinch
[klintʃ]

secure firmly by bending down a protruding point, as of a nail or slope
v. (박은 못 따위의) 끝을 꼬부리다
By *clinching* nails over the canvas, they held the torn sail to the mast.

climate
[kláimit]

the weather conditions of a place over a period of years
n. 기후
For fifty years or more the *climate* of the Arctic has been warming up gradually.

weather
[wéðər]

condition of the air with respect to temperature, moisture, cloudiness, etc. around a certain place
n. 일기, 기상, 날씨
The *weather* will be very hot and humid in Seoul today.

compare
[kəmpɛ́ər]

point out how persons or things are alike and how they differ
v. 비교하다, 비유하다
We *compared* two books to see which one had the better illustrations.

contrast
[kəntrǽst]

compare persons or things (of different kinds) to show their differences
v. 대조하다, 대조되다
She *contrasted* her present life of luxury with the poverty of her childhood.

Lesson 38 | 451

connotation
[kɔnoutéiʃən]

the added meaning that a word suggests or implies
n. 함축, 내포
The words "snake" and "red" have unpleasant **connotations** for many people.

denotation
[di:noutéiʃən]

the exact, literal meaning of a word
n. 의미, 외연
The **denotation** of the word "home" is "place where one lives," but it has many connotations.

> **EXERCISE 2**   In the blank space, insert the *letter* of the word that best completes the sentence.
>
> 1. The porter tied the bundle of clothes with a _____ to carry it easily.
>   (A) chord   (B) cord
> 2. The carpenter _____ the nails of the bookcase he was building.
>   (A) clenched   (B) clinched
> 3. We have to cancel our picnic because of bad _____.
>   (A) climate   (B) weather
> 4. Before you buy meat, you should _____ its price at several stores.
>   (A) compare   (B) contrast
> 5. The _____ of the word "snake" is a legless reptile with a long, thin body.
>   (A) connotation   (B) dennotation

STUDY YOUR NEW WORDS-3

contemptible
[kəntémptəbl]

deserving contempt or scorn; mean; low; worthless
adj. 경멸할 만한, 천시할 만한
Cheating on a test is considered one of the most **contemptible** acts in the Military Academy.

contemptuous
[kəntémptjuəs]

showing or feeling contempt; scornful; disdainful
adj. 경멸적인, 경멸하는
The rich man is **contemptuous** of my humble home and poor surroundings.

continual
[kəntínjuəl]

over and over again; regular but interrupted; frequent
adj. 잇따른, 되풀이되는
We experienced a **continual** series of hot spells last summer.

continuous
[kəntínjuəs]
continuing without stopping; ceaseless; unbroken; incessant
adj. 연속적인, 끊이지 않는
On holidays, we can see a *continuous* line of cars on highways.

credible
[krédəbl]
deserving or worthy of belief; believable; trustworthy; reliable
adj. 신용할 수 있는, 믿을 수 있는
It hardly seems *credible* that your son has grown so tall in one year.

credulous
[krédjuləs]
too much inclined to believe; easily deceived; gullible
adj. 쉽사리 믿는, 속아 넘어가기 쉬운
Only a *credulous* person would fall for that old trick.

disinterested
[disíntərəstid]
free from selfish motives; impartial; unbiased; fair
adj. 사욕이 없는, 공평한
An umpire must be an entirely *disinterested* but keen observer.

uninterested
[ʌníntərəstid]
not interested; uncaring
adj. 흥미 없는, 무관심한
The audience yawned and seemed *uninterested* in the politician's speech.

disorganized
[disɔ́:rɡənaizd]
thrown into confusion and disorder; disarranged
adj. 혼란된, 엉망진창의
The office, where everything had worked so smoothly, became completely *disorganized* after Mr. Levine resigned.

unorganized
[ʌnɔ́:rɡənaizd]
not formed into a systematized whole
adj. 조직되어 있지 않은, 조직이 없는
Form a union; an *unorganized* mob can accomplish nothing but chaos.

EXERCISE 3   In the blank space, insert the *letter* of the word that best completes the sentence.

1. Every employer has a _____ attitude toward sloppy work.
    (A) contemptible   (B) contemptuous

2. No one likes _____ interruptions while he is reading a book.
    (A) continual   (B) continuous

3. What he had said about the fire, though unusual, is _____.
    (A) credible   (B) credulous

4. His action cannot be considered to be _____ because he hoped to make money out of the affair.
    (A) disinterested   (B) uninterested

5. It's better to be _____ than not organized at all.
   (A) disorganized   (B) unorganized

STUDY YOUR NEW WORDS-4

divers
[dáivə(:)rz]

more than one; several; different
adj. 몇몇의, 약간의
A well-balanced diet is made up of *divers* foods.

diverse
[dáivə:rs]

various; unlike; varied
adj. 다양한, 각양각색의
A great many *diverse* opinions were expressed at the meeting, but none was worthwhile.

dual
[djú(:)əl]

composed or consisting of two parts; double; twofold
adj. 둘의, 이중의
The training airplane has *dual* controls, one set for the learner and one for the teacher.

duel
[djú(:)əl]

a formal fight to settle a quarrel or avenge an insult
n. 결투, 싸움, 투쟁
The opposing two lawyers fought a *duel* to settle their difference.

egoist
[égouist]

a person who seeks the welfare of himself; a self-centered, selfish person
n. 이기주의자, 자기만을 위하는 사람
John is such an *egoist* that he only cares about himself.

egotist
[égoutist]

a person who boasts too much about himself; a conceited person
n. 자기중심의 사람, 독선적인 사람
Marian is such an *egotist* that she talks about herself all the time.

emerge
[imə́:rdʒ]

come out; come up; come into view
v. 떠오르다, 나오다, 알려지다
After the shower, the sun *emerged* from behind the clouds.

immerge
[imə́:rdʒ]

put under water; dip; submerge; immerse
v. 담그다, 가라앉히다
He *immerged* his aching feet in a bucket of hot water.

emigrant
[émigrənt]

a person who leaves one country to move to another
n. (타국으로의) 이민, 이주민
It is expected that the total number of *emigrants* from this country will reach 20,000 this year.

immigrant
[ímigrənt]

a person who enters one country from another
n. (타국으로부터의) 이주자, 이주민
California has several thousands of *immigrants* from other states.

| EXERCISE 4 | In the blank space, insert the *letter* of the word that best completes the sentence. |

1. A person of _____ interests can talk about many subjects.
   (A) divers   (B) diverse

2. _____ are fought with guns or swords in the presence of witness called seconds.
   (A) Duals   (B) Duels

3. Perhaps the most eminent _____ that appeared in the world was Montaigne; he wrote too much about himself.
   (A) egoist   (B) egotist

4. A considerable number of new facts _____ as a result of the careful investigation.
   (A) emerged   (B) immerged

5. Canada has many _____ from Europe and Asia.
   (A) emigrants   (B) immigrants

해답					
EXERCISE 1.	1. C	2. A	3. B	4. A	
EXERCISE 2.	1. B	2. B	3. B	4. A	5. B
EXERCISE 3.	1. B	2. A	3. A	4. A	5. A
EXERCISE 4.	1. B	2. B	3. B	4. A	5. B

종합 연습 문제

1 In the space before each word in column I, write the *letter* of its correct meaning in column II.

COLUMN I	COLUMN II
____ 1. immoral	(A) a self-centered, selfish person
____ 2. unmoral	(B) the added meaning that a word implies
____ 3. chord	(C) showing contempt
____ 4. cord	(D) deserving contempt
____ 5. denotation	(E) a person who boasts too much about himself
____ 6. connotation	(F) the exact, literal meaning of a word
____ 7. egoist	(G) a very thin rope
____ 8. egotist	(H) violating morality
____ 9. contemptible	(I) not pertaining to morality
____ 10. contemtuous	(J) a string of a musical instrument

2 In the space before each sentence, write the *letter* of the word which has the SAME MEANING as the italicized expression.

____ 1. The *people who enter the U. S.* from Europe used to get off the boat in New York.
   (A) emigrants to the U. S.   (B) immigrants to the U. S.

____ 2. Both my daughters are *graduates* of Pembroke Women's College in Rhode Island.
   (A) alumnae   (B) alumni

____ 3. After his latest scandal, he hardly seems *trustworthy* as a politician.
   (A) credible   (B) credulous

____ 4. It seems that most Germans do not consider Hitler a *mean* person.
   (A) contemptible   (B) contemptuous

____ 5. The brain needs a *constant and uninterrupted* supply of blood to function properly.
   (A) continual   (B) continuous

3 In the space provided, write the *letter* of the word or expression that has most nearly the SAME MEANING as the italicized word.

____ 1. *biannual* publication   (A) once every two years   (B) twice a year
                                  (C) lasting for a year   (D) lasting for two years

____ 2. tropical *climate*   (A) weather conditions   (B) storm
                                (C) region   (D) crops and fruit

_____ 3. *continual* hammering   (A) perpetual   (B) unbroken
                                               (C) over and over again   (D) violent

_____ 4. *disinterested* umpire   (A) bored   (B) impartial
                                               (C) disguised   (D) wise

_____ 5. *dual* purposes   (A) fighting   (B) wicked
                                               (C) appropriate   (D) double

_____ 6. *clinched* nails   (A) secured firmly   (B) broken apart
                                               (C) put together   (D) fixed loosely

_____ 7. *immoral* acts   (A) wicked   (B) nonmoral
                                               (C) delayed   (D) impolite

_____ 8. *contemptuous* look   (A) showing contempt   (B) concealed
                                               (C) mean   (D) deserving contempt

_____ 9. *credulous* person   (A) reliable   (B) self-centered
                                               (C) sincere   (D) gullible

_____ 10. *clenched* fists   (A) fixed firmly   (B) closed tightly
                                               (C) opened widely   (D) trembled violently

Fill each blank with the most appropriate word from the vocabulary list below.

VOCABULARY LIST

immerged	duel	emigrants
uninterested	contemptible	credulous
connotations	contrasts	avocation
clenched	biennial	compared

1. It is very difficult to entertain anyone so _____ in everything.

2. I _____ my answers with the teacher's and found that I had made a mistake.

3. She was so _____ that the other children could fool her easily.

4. The reporter _____ his pencil in his teeth while he was wiping his glasses.

5. The _____ art shows were held in our city in 1970, 1972, 1974 and 1976.

6. "Skinny" and "slim" are two words for the same denotation, but their _____ are different.

7. Mr. Brown is a lawyer, but writing stories for children is his _____.

8. She _____ her right foot into the pool to see how cold the water was.

9. To avenge the insult, the man proposed a (an) _____ with handguns to the colonel.

Lesson 38

10. The strained language of his speeches _____ oddly with the ease and naturalness of his letters.

1 1. H	2. I	3. J	4. G	5. F	6. B	7. A	8. E	9. D	10. C
2 1. B	2. A	3. A	4. A	5. B					
3 1. B	2. A	3. C	4. B	5. D	6. A	7. A	8. A	9. D	10. B
4 1. uninterested	2. compared		3. credulous		4. clenched		5. biennial		
6. connotations	7. avocation		8. immerged		9. duel		10. contrasts		

Lesson 39

PRETEST 39

Insert the *letter* of the best answer in the space provided.

1. _____ people believe in *humane* treatment of prisoners.
   (A) Diligent   (B) Civilized   (C) Primitive

2. The _____ is an *imaginary* circle around the earth.
   (A) moon   (B) sun   (C) equator

3. Because he _____, he is *liable* to fail.
   (A) is getting along well   (B) is doing his best
   (C) wasn't working hard

4. He sat alone after the battle, *mourning* over the _____ of his best friend.
   (A) loss   (B) achievement   (C) help

5. A _____ can help some people to understand their *subconscious* urges.
   (A) physician   (B) phychiatrist   (C) surgeon

ANSWERS   1.B 2.C 3.C 4.A 5.B

STUDY YOUR NEW WORDS-1

farther [fá:rðər]	at a greater distance ***adv.*** 더 멀리, 더 앞으로 He has to leave now; he lives *farther* from here than I do.
further [fá:rðər]	to a greater extent; more; additional ***adv.*** 더욱 깊이, 더 나아가서, 더욱더 All the members of the committee agreed to inquire *further* into the matter.
hanged [hæŋd]	put to death by hanging ***v.*** hang(교살하다, 교수형에 처하다)의 과거 및 과거분사 The man living nextdoor *hanged* himself in sorrow after his wife died.

Lesson 39

hung
[hʌŋ]

suspended or caused to be suspended from a wall, ceiling, etc.
v. hang(걸다, 매달다)의 과거 및 과거분사
We *hung* our reproduction of "Mona Liza" above the fireplace.

historic
[histɔ́rik]

famous or important in history; noted; celebrated; renowned
adj. 역사적으로 유명한
Pulguksa is one of the *historic* spots that you should visit.

historical
[histɔ́rikəl]

concerned with history
adj. 역사의, 역사상의
Upon retiring from the office, the President gave all the *historical* papers to the library.

human
[hjúːmən]

of or concerning man
adj. 인간의, 인간적인
The philosopher claims that kindness is a *human* trait, but I don't believe it.

humane
[hjuː(ː)méin]

kind; tender; compassionate; merciful
adj. 자비로운, 인정 있는
Humane people are considerate of not only other people but also animals.

imaginary
[imǽdʒinəri]

existing only in the imagination; not real
adj. 상상의, 상상적인
Some people do not believe that ghosts are not real but *imaginary* beings.

imaginative
[imǽdʒinətiv]

having a good imagination; inventive
adj. 상상력이 풍부한
The *imaginative* child always likes to make up fairy tales.

EXERCISE 1   In the blank space, insert the *letter* of the word that best completes the sentence.

1. The crew pushed the boat _____ into the water to make it float.
   (A) farther   (B) further

2. Upon entering he took off his coat and _____ it on the hook.
   (A) hanged   (B) hung

3. It is a _____ fact that George Washington was the first President of the United States.
   (A) human   (B) humane

4. No life that breathes with _____ breath has ever truly longed for death.
   (A) human   (B) humane

5. The mind of storytellers must have great _____ powers.
   (A) imaginary   (B) imaginative

STUDY YOUR NEW WORDS-2

incomparable
[inkɔ́mpərəbl]

without equal; matchless; unique
adj. 견줄 데 없는, 타의 추종을 불허하는
Bessie Smith was an *incomparable* singer in her days.

uncomparable
[ʌnkɔ́mpərəbl]

so different that comparison is impossible; not open to comparison
adj. 비교가 불가능한, 비교할 수 없는
It is foolish to compare horses with airplanes; they are *uncomparable*.

incredible
[inkrédəbl]

hard to believe; unbelievable
adj. 믿을 수 없는
Some old superstitions seem *incredible* to most educated people.

incredulous
[inkrédʒuləs]

not ready to believe; doubting; skeptical
adj. 쉽사리 믿지 않는, 회의적인
People nowadays are *incredulous* about ghosts and witches.

lay
[lei]

put something down; place; put
v. 두다, 놓다, 쌓다
The gentleman *laid* his hand on his son's shoulder.

lie
[lai]

have one's body in a flat position along the ground or other surface; recline
v. 눕다
The wounded soldier was *lying* on the battlefield.

apt
[æpt]

1. having a natural or habitual tendency to do something; usually expected to
adj. ~하기 쉬운 (자연적인 또는 습관적인 경향)
This kind of shoe is *apt* to slip on wet ground.

2. quick to learn
adj. 영민한, 재능이 있는
Henry is an *apt* student of the practical science.

liable
[láiəbl]

1. in danger of having or doing
adj. 자칫하면 ~하는, ~의 위험이 있는
The children under the age of 10 are all *liable* to diseases.

2. responsible for the consequences
adj. ~의 책임이 있는, ~의 의무가 있는
He declared that he was not *liable* for his wife's debts.

likely
[láikli]

probable; expected but not as a matter of course
adj. ~할 것 같은, ~함직한 (가능성 강조)
The weather forecast says that it's *likely* to be hot tomorrow.

luxuriant
[lʌgzjúəriənt]

growing thick and green; producing abundantly; abundant
adj. 번성한, 울창한
The backyard of our house has a *luxuriant* growth of weeds.

luxurious
[lʌgzjúəriəs]

fond of luxury; self-indulgent; giving luxury
adj. 사치스러운, 호화스러운
She is too proud, too *luxurious*, to marry an average man like you.

EXERCISE 2 In the blank space, write the letter of the word that best completes the sentence.

1. According to *Iliad* written by Homer, Helen of Troy had _____ beauty.
   (A) imcomparable   (B) uncomparable

2. It is _____ that a perfect man like you could have made such a mistake.
   (A) incredible   (B) incredulous

3. A skillful workman is able to _____ bricks very accurately and quickly.
   (A) lay   (B) lie

4. Children are _____ to be noisy while they are playing.
   (A) apt   (B) liable   (C) likely

5. The governor of the state lives in a _____ mansion.
   (A) luxuriant   (B) luxurious

STUDY YOUR NEW WORDS-3

moan
[moun]

a long, low sound of suffering
n. 신음 소리, 슬퍼함
From time to time, during the night, there was a *moan* of pain from the sick man.

mourn
[mɔːrn]

feel or show sorrow over; grieve; lament
v. 슬퍼하다, 애통해 하다
The whole nation *mourned* the death of the much-loved President.

oral
[ɔ́ːrəl]

using speech; not written; spoken
adj. 구두의, 구술의
The company will give only *oral* tests to the applicants.

verbal
[vɔ́ːrbəl]

in or of words, as distinguished from other means of description
adj. 말의, 말에 관한
This written report contains both a *verbal* description and a sketch of the building.

personal
[pɔ́ːrsnəl]

of, for, or belonging to a particular person; individual; private
adj. 개인의, 자기만의, 사적인
The minister made a *personal* visit to the scene of the fighting.

personnel
[pəːrsənél]

the people employed in any work, business, or service
n. 인원, 직원
The general issued an order to capture the hill to all *personnel*.

respectably
[rispéktəbli]

in a worthy or proper manner; moderately; very well
adv. 훌륭하게, 썩 잘
The man seemed poor, but he was *respectably* dressed.

respectfully
[rispéktfəli]

in a respectful or polite manner; politely
adv. 공손히, 삼가서
Children should speak *respectfully* to their elders.

respectively
[rispéktivli]

in a specified order
adv. 각각, 각기
"Auf Wiedersehen," "au revoir," and "good-bye" are, *respectively*, German, French, and English farewells.

raise
[reiz]

1. lift something
v. 올리다, 게양하다
She *raised* her finger to her lips as a sign for silence.

Lesson 39 463

	2. grow or breed something *v.* 기르다, 사육하다 The farmer *raises* cattle and crops.
rise [raiz]	get up; arise; stand *v.* 오르다, 일어서다 The sun will *rise* at 5:45 tomorrow morning.

> **EXERCISE 3** — In the blank space, insert the *letter* of the word that best completes the sentence.
>
> 1. The sick man made a _____ in his sleep during the night.
>   (A) moan   (B) mourn
> 2. A (An) _____ agreement is not enough; we must have a written promise.
>   (A) oral   (B) verbal
> 3. You must apply for a job in the company's _____ office.
>   (A) personal   (B) personnel
> 4. The woman struggled to bring up her children _____.
>   (A) respectably   (B) respectfully   (C) respectively
> 5. When the snow melts, the river will _____ to its banks.
>   (A) raise   (B) rise

STUDY YOUR NEW WORDS-4

register [rédʒistər]	1. write in a list or record; write one's name in a list *v.* 등록하다, 기록하다 We have to go to the government patent office to *register* the new trademark. 2. have a letter recorded in a post office *v.* 등기 우편으로 보내다 It is safe to *register* the letter containing the check.
registrar [redʒistrá:r]	a keeper of official records; official recorder *n.* 등록계, 등기관 Go to the *registrar* of the University to know your grades.
sailer [séilər]	a ship with reference to its sailing power; a sailing vessel *n.* 돛단배, 범선 The boat we are on is the best *sailer* in the fleet.

sailor
[séilər]

a person with a job on a ship, especially one who is not a ship's officer.
n. 선원, 갑판원, 수병
The men in our navy are called *sailors* if they are not officers.

salon
[səlán]

a large room for receiving or entertaining guests
n. 객실, 응접실
A group of college professors were waiting in the main *salon* to see the Minister of Education.

saloon
[səlúːn]

a place where alcoholic drinks are sold and drunk; tavern; bar
n. 큰 홀, 식당
The ship's passengers have their dinners in the dining *saloon*.

subconscious
[sʌbkɔ́nʃəs]

present in the mind but not fully perceived; existing but not felt
adj. 잠재 의식의, 어렴풋이 의식하고 있는
It was certain that Oswald might have a *subconscious* desire to injure his father.

unconscious
[ʌnkɔ́nʃəs]

1. not conscious, as a person who has fainted
adj. 무의식의, 의식이 없는
Edna was *unconscious* for two hours after the accident.

2. not aware
adj. 모르는, 모르고 있는
The general was *unconscious* of being followed by the spy.

transcript
[trǽnskript]

a written or typewritten copy; a copy
n. 사본, 등본
The club's secretary prepared several *transcripts* of minutes of the meeting.

transcription
[trænskrípʃən]

the act or process of transcribing; copying
n. 필사, 전사, 고쳐 쓰기
The *transcription* of words into phonetic symbols requires special training.

EXERCISE 4

In the blank space, insert the *letter* of the word that best completes the sentence.

1. Write to the _____ of the university to get the application form.
   (A) register   (B) registrar

2. He got a job as a _____ of the ship to travel around the world.
   (A) sailer   (B) sailor

3. The majority of the citizens of this village are tired of the _____ and want it to be closed.
   (A) salon   (B) saloon

4. He was knocked completely _____ for several hours when the car struck him.
   (A) subconscious   (B) unconscious

5. The college wanted a _____ of the student's high school record.
   (A) transcript   (B) transcription

해답					
EXERCISE 1.	1. A	2. B	3. B	4. A	5. B
EXERCISE 2.	1. A	2. A	3. A	4. A	5. B
EXERCISE 3.	1. A	2. A	3. B	4. A	5. B
EXERCISE 4.	1. B	2. B	3. B	4. B	5. A

종합 연습 문제

1 In the space before each word in column I, write the *letter* of its correct meaning in column II.

COLUMN I	COLUMN II
_____ 1. incomparable	(A) totally unaware
_____ 2. uncomparable	(B) spoken
_____ 3. historic	(C) without equal; matchless
_____ 4. historical	(D) in or of words
_____ 5. liable	(E) not open to comparison
_____ 6. likely	(F) important in history
_____ 7. oral	(G) concerned with history
_____ 8. verbal	(H) in danger of having or doing
_____ 9. subconscious	(I) existing but not felt
_____ 10. unconscious	(J) probable

2 In the space before each sentence, write the *letter* of the word which has the SAME MEANING as the italicized expression.

_____ 1. As she came in, she *placed* the plate on the table.
    (A) laid   (B) lied

_____ 2. You should always treat older people *politely*.
    (A) respectfully   (B) respectively

_____ 3. Children in school usually *lift* their hands to answer a question.
    (A) raise   (B) rise

_____ 4. She told him to clean his room and said *more* that he must make his bed.
    (A) farther   (B) further

_____ 5. The mind of storyteller has great *creative* powers.
    (A) imaginary   (B) imaginative

3 In the space provided, write the *letter* of the word or expression that has most nearly the SAME MEANING as the italicized word.

_____ 1. *raise* cattle   (A) arise   (B) lift
                            (C) grow   (D) raze

_____ 2. *oral* examination   (A) listening   (B) spoken
                                       (C) verbal   (D) written

Lesson 39

_____ 3. *incomparable* beauty (A) matchless   (B) not comparable
                                     (C) uncontrastive   (D) equal

_____ 4. *historic* occasion   (A) concerned with history (B) resultant
                                     (C) important in history   (D) subsequent

_____ 5. *humane* treatment   (A) personal   (B) human
                                     (C) compassionate   (D) cruel

_____ 6. an *apt* pupil   (A) liable   (B) appropriate
                                     (C) responsible   (D) clever

_____ 7. *imaginative* story   (A) imagined   (B) not real
                                     (C) showing imagination (D) existing in mind

_____ 8. school *registrar*   (A) official recorder (B) list of names
                                     (C) registration   (D) records

_____ 9. *personal* matter   (A) of human being   (B) private
                                     (C) belonging to every one (D) not individual

_____ 10. beauty *salon*   (A) shop   (B) place
                                     (C) maker   (D) tavern

4 Fill each blank with the most appropriate word from the vocabulary list below.

VOCABULARY LIST

hanged	human	imaginary
incredible	imaginative	incredulous
moan	verbal	mourns
respectively	personnel	luxurious

1. All the characters in this book are _____ but not real.
2. The criminal was sentenced to be _____ by the neck until dead.
3. The _____ of the company are unhappy about the recent changes.
4. She gave a glass of beer to the man and a toy rabbit to the baby, _____.
5. His story of having seen a ghost seemed _____ to his family.
6. The lady couldn't bear this kind of humble life because she was accustomed to _____ life.
7. I heard the _____ of the patient all night; it wasn't a cheerful sound.
8. The old woman still _____ for her son, 30 years after his death.
9. To know what will happen in the future is beyond _____ power.

10. I was _____ when I heard that you had made such a mistake.

해답

1 1. C   2. E   3. F   4. G   5. H   6. J   7. B   8. D   9. I   10. A
2 1. A   2. A   3. A   4. B   5. B
3 1. C   2. B   3. A   4. C   5. C   6. D   7. C   8. A   9. B   10. A
4 1. imaginary   2. hanged   3. personnel   4. respectively   5. incredible
   6. luxurious   7. moan   8. mourns   9. human   10. incredulous

Lesson 40

PRETEST 40

Insert the *letter* of the best answer in the space provided.

1. The *altar* must be placed in the most _____ part of the church.
   (A) sacred   (B) hidden   (C) open

2. The officer argued that we had to use *cannon* against the _____.
   (A) pollution   (B) crime   (C) enemy

3. The _____ will not be in *session* again until after Christmas.
   (A) market   (B) train   (C) National Assembly

4. A *stationary* object is _____ to aim at than a moving object.
   (A) nearer   (B) easier   (C) more accurate

5. The sudden *ascent* of the elevator made most of the passengers _____.
   (A) dizzy   (B) happy   (C) sleepy

ANSWERS 1.A 2.C 3.C 4.B 5.A

STUDY YOUR NEW WORDS-1

altar
[ɔ́:ltər]
a table or raised level surface on which things are offered to a god
n. (교회의) 제단, 제대(祭臺)
The woman knelt before the *altar* to pray to God for her son's safe return.

alter
[ɔ́:ltər]
change; make different; vary; modify
v. 변경하다, 바꾸다
If it rains, we have to *alter* our plan to have a picnic on Sunday.

ascent
[əsént]
an act of going up; a rising; a climbing
n. 상승, 오름
Korean mountain climbers made a successful *ascent* of Mt. Mckinley in North America.

assent
[əsént]

acceptance of a proposal; agreement
n. 동의, 찬성
I won't give my *assent* to her plan because it is not well prepared.

cannon
[kǽnən]

a large gun, often mounted on wheels
n. 대포
There are several old *cannons* on the wall of the castle.

canon
[kǽnən]

a rule or law, especially of religious faith
n. 규범, 표준, 법규
This *canon* has been enacted by the church council very recently.

canvas
[kǽnvəs]

strong rough cloth used for tents, sails, bags, etc.; sailcloth; tarpaulin
n. 천막, 돛베, 화포, 베
The tops of my sneakers are made of *canvas*.

canvass
[kǽnvəs]

ask for political support or sales of one's goods, especially going from house to house
v. 주문〔권유〕하러 돌아다니다, 선거 운동을 하다
The salesman *canvassed* the whole city for subscriptions of the magazine.

cession
[séʃən]

a handing over to another; ceding; giving up
n. 할양(割讓), 양여
The *cession* of the territory could not be avoided because they lost the war.

session
[séʃən]

a formal meeting of an organization
n. 개회중, 회기
Be seated! The court is now in *session*.

EXERCISE 1 In the blank space, insert the *letter* of the word that best completes the sentence.

1. If the coat is too large, a tailor can _____ it to fit you.
   (A) altar   (B) alter

2. The teacher gave his _____ to the students' plan to have a dancing party.
   (A) ascent   (B) assent

3. His behavior offends against the _____ of good manners.
   (A) cannons   (B) canons

4. The Labor Party _____ all of this town but it won't win the election.
   (A) canvased   (B) canvassed

5. This year's _____ of the National Assembly has been unsusually long.
   (A) cession   (B) session

Lesson 40

STUDY YOUR NEW WORDS-2

faint
[feint]

1. lose consciousness briefly
v. 실신하다, 졸도하다
The soldier *fainted* at the sight of his own blood.

2. not clear; plain; dim
adj. 희미한, 약한
The color became *faint* as the sun set.

feint
[feint]

feign an attack; make a pretended blow
v. 치는 시늉을 하다, 견제 공격을 하다
He *feinted* with his left hand and hit me with his right.

intension
[inténʃən]

increase in degree; intensification; augmentation
n. 세기, 강도, 노력
In recent years there has been an *intension* of the struggle for political power in the country.

intention
[inténʃən]

a determination to act in a certain way; purpose; design; plan
n. 의도, 의향
She felt offended at my remarks, but it wasn't my *intention* to hurt her.

pray
[prei]

speak to God in worship; offer worship; ask earnestly
v. 기도하다, 간구하다
There is nothing that we can do now but *pray* God to help in our troubles.

prey
[prei]

an animal that is hunted and eaten by another animal
n. 먹이
The lion seized its *prey* and ate it.

principal
[prínsəpl]

1. most important; chief; main
adj. 주요한, 중요한
Chicago is the *principal* city in the Midwest of the United States.

2. the head of an elementary or secondary school
n. 교장
The *principal* told the teachers to dismiss school during the heavy snowstrom.

principle
[prínsəpl]

a general rule or truth that is a foundation for other truths
n. 원리, 원칙
This country was founded on the *principle* of individual freedom for all.

stationary	in a fixed position; standing still; not moving
[stéiʃənəri]	*adj.* 정지된
	The population of France remained *stationary* almost for a century.

stationery	writing materials such as paper, cards, etc.
[stéiʃənəri]	*n.* 문방구
	Herbert bought a notebook at the *stationery* store.

> **EXERCISE 2**   In the blank space, insert the *letter* of the word that best completes the sentence.
>
> 1. Some girls often _____ at the sight of a mouse.
>   (A) faint   (B) feint
> 2. Her _____ to help us was good, but she was only in our way.
>   (A) intension   (B) intention
> 3. The entire congregation bowed their heads to _____ to God.
>   (A) pray   (B) prey
> 4. Carelessness is a _____ cause of highway accident.
>   (A) principal   (B) principle
> 5. The man gave his son a box of _____ for Christmas.
>   (A) stationary   (B) stationery

STUDY YOUR NEW WORDS-3

address	the place to which one's mail is directed
[ǽdres]	*n.* 주소
	Please write your name and *address* on this paper.
[ədrés]	make a speech to
	v. 연설하다, 말을 걸다
	The President *addressed* the nation on the subject of war and peace.

attribute	a quality belonging to the nature of a person or thing; characteristic
[ǽtribjuːt]	*n.* 속성, 특질
	Darkness is an *attribute* of night, as brightness is that of day.
[ətríbju(ː)t]	believe something to be the result of
	v. ~에 돌리다, ~의 탓으로 하다
	We *attribute* Edison's success to intelligence and hard work.

Lesson 40

committee
[kəmíti]

a group of people chosen to do a particular job
n. 위원회
The teachers appointed a *committee* of five members to plan the class picnic.

[kɔmitíː]

a person entrusted by a court with the care of a person or estate
n. 후견인
The court appointed Mr. Lansing as the *committee* that would take care of the boy's property.

concert
[kɔ́nsərt]

a musical performance in which several musicians take part
n. 연주회, 음악회
She likes music very much; she never misses a *concert*.

[kənsə́ːrt]

arrange a matter or act by agreement with someone
v. 협조하다, 협정하다
We *concerted* on the most proper methods for speedily executing the manager's instructions.

content
[kɔ́ntent]

what is contained in anything; all things inside
n. 내용, 속에 담긴 것
I tried but couldn't understand the *content* of his speech.

[kəntént]

make a person satisfied or happy; gratify; appease
v. 만족시키다
John *contented* himself with two glasses of beer even though he could have had more.

EXERCISE 3   In the space provided, write the *letter* of the correct pronunciation of the italicized word.

1. He *addressed* me as though we were old friends. ( )
   (A) ǽdrest   (B) ədrést

2. Above all, patience is the most important *attribute* of a good teacher. ( )
   (A) ǽtribjuːt   (B) ətríbju(ː)t

3. The *committee* will meet today at four to discuss the matter. ( )
   (A) kəmíti   (B) kɔmitíː

4. The orchestra gave a *concert* that lasted two hours. ( )
   (A) kɔ́nsərt   (B) kənsə́ːrt

5. Will it *content* you if I let you have the candy tomorrow? ( )
   (A) kɔ́ntent   (B) kəntént

STUDY YOUR NEW WORDS-4

converse
[kɔ́nvəːrs]
the opposite of something
n. 역(逆), 전환
"Honest but poor" is the *converse* of "poor but honest."

[kənvə́ːrs]
talk together in an informal way; chat
v. 담화하다, 이야기를 나누다
He *conversed* with his wife about the summer vacation.

desert
[dézərt]
a sandy region with very little rain and few trees
n. 사막
The Sahara is a greate *desert* in the northern part of Africa.

[dizə́ːrt]
go away and leave; abandon
v. 버리다
After the family *deserted* the farm, its building fell to ruin.

digest
[dáidʒest]
a short, condensed account; summary
n. 적요, 요약
The publisher decided to publish a *digest* of international law.

[daidʒést, didʒést]
be changed into a form the body can absorb
v. 소화하다
I like milk very much, but I can't *digest* it very well.

instinct
[ínstiŋkt]
inborn tendency to act in a certain way
n. 본능
Most animals have an *instinct* to protect their young.

[instíŋkt]
charged or filled (with something)
adj. 가득 찬
Her face was *instinct* with benevolence and kindness.

intimate
[íntimit]
very familiar; known very well; close and familiar
adj. 친밀한, 절친한
Although the governor knew many people, he had few *intimate* friends.

[íntimeit]
suggest indirectly; hint; imply
v. 암시하다
He *intimated* that he was dissatisfied with his job.

Lesson 40   475

> **EXERCISE 4** In the space provided, write the *letter* of the correct pronunciation of the italicized word.

1. I disagree with your opinion; in fact, I believe the *converse* to be true. (　)
   (A) kɔ́nvəːrs　　　　(B) kənvə́ːrs
2. The government would build dams to harness electrical power and irrigate the *desert*. (　)
   (A) dézərt　　　　(B) dizə́ːrt
3. It takes a long time to *digest* heavy food. (　)
   (A) dáidʒest　　　　(B) didʒést
4. The very essence of an *instinct* is that it is followed independently of reason. (　)
   (A) ínstiŋkt　　　　(B) instíŋkt
5. Her smile *intimated* that she was very pleased. (　)
   (A) íntimitid　　　　(B) íntimeitid

STUDY YOUR NEW WORDS-5

minute [mínit]		one sixtieth of an hour; sixty seconds *n.* 분(分) The train arrived at exactly four *minutes* past eight.
[mainjúːt]		very small in size or degree, tiny; diminutive *adj.* 아주 작은, 사소한, 미소한 There has been a *minute* improvement in the working conditions of the factory.
object [ɔ́bdʒikt]		something that can be seen or felt; thing *n.* 물체, 대상 A dark *object* moved between me and the door.
[əbdʒékt]		give as a reason against something purpose *v.* 반대하다, 반대 이유를 대다 Do you *object* to my smoking in this room?
refuse [rifjúːz]		say no; decline to accept; reject *v.* 거절하다 He asked her to marry him but she *refused*.
[réfjuːs]		useless stuff; waste; rubbish; trash *n.* 폐물, 찌꺼기, 쓰레기 The street-cleaning department took away all *refuse* from the street.

tear
[tiər]

a drop of salty liquid that flows from the eye during pain or sadness
n. 눈물
The little girl was in *tears* because she'd lost her mother.

[tɛər]

pull apart or into pieces by force
v. 찢다, 째다
Don't *tear* up paper; put it in the waste basket.

used
[juːzd]

not new; second-hand
adj. 중고의, 낡은
The janitor removed *used* towels from the rack.

[juːst]

accustomed; usual
adj. ~에 익숙한
It took long to get *used* to foreign food.

EXERCISE 5   In the space provided, write the *letter* of the correct pronunciation of the italicized word.

1. His writing is so *minute* that it's difficult to read
    (A) mínit   (B) mainjúːt

2. The national museum in Seoul is full of interesting *objects*.
    (A) ɔ́bdʒikts   (B) əbdʒékts

3. She *refused* him when he asked her to marry him.
    (A) rifjúːzd   (B) réfjuːst

4. Why did you *tear* the cloth when I'd advised you to cut it with scissors?
    (A) tiər   (B) tɛər

5. John's uncle sells *used* cars at Chongro.
    (A) juːzd   (B) juːst

해답					
EXERCISE 1.	1. B	2. B	3. B	4. B	5. B
EXERCISE 2.	1. A	2. B	3. A	4. A	5. B
EXERCISE 3.	1. B	2. A	3. A	4. A	5. B
EXERCISE 4.	1. A	2. A	3. B	4. A	5. B
EXERCISE 5.	1. B	2. A	3. A	4. B	5. A

종합 연습 문제

1 In the space before each word in column I, write the *letter* of the expression which has the SAME MEANING in column II.

	COLUMN I	COLUMN II
_____	1. ascent	(A) a large gun
_____	2. assent	(B) a formal meeting
_____	3. cannon	(C) handing over to another
_____	4. canon	(D) purpose
_____	5. cession	(E) agreement
_____	6. session	(F) intensity
_____	7. intension	(G) a rule or law
_____	8. intention	(I) climbing
_____	9. stationary	(J) writing materials
_____	10. stationery	(K) not moving

2 In the blank space, write the *letter* of the expression which has the SAME MEANING as the italicized word.

1. He had a chance to *address* to a large audience for the first time in his life.
   (A) deliver a speech   (B) show his ability

2. A responsible man never *deserts* his wife and family.
   (A) forget   (B) abandon

3. He *intimated* a wish to go by saying that it was late.
   (A) implied   (B) mentioned

4. Mother *objected* that the weather is too bad to play outdoors.
   (A) opposed   (B) doubted

5. The picture on the wall is *instinct* with life and beauty.
   (A) lacking   (B) filled

3 In the space before each word, write the *letter* of the expression that CANNOT be the meaning of the italicized word.

_____	1. *attribute*	(A) trait	(B) lead to	(C) believe to be the result of
_____	2. *content*	(A) fortune	(B) gratify	(C) what is contained in anything
_____	3. *converse*	(A) chat	(B) the opposite of something	(C) preserve

_____ 4. *instinct*   (A) natural tendency   (B) charged   (C) extinguished

_____ 5. *intimate*   (A) threaten   (B) familiar   (C) hint

_____ 6. *object*   (A) thing   (B) oppose   (C) obligation

_____ 7. *refuse*   (A) diffuse   (B) reject   (C) waste

_____ 8. *used*   (A) not new   (B) accustomed   (C) not working

4 Fill each blank with the most appropriate word selected from the vocabulary list below.

VOCABULARY LIST

minutes'	attributed	principles
committee	ascent	address
pray	instinct	feinted
tears	alter	stationary

1. The success of the present project can be _____ to Mr. Johnson.

2. The _____ of Mount Everest requires superhuman strength and endurance.

3. The population of this town has been _____ for ten years at about 12,000 people.

4. If the coat is too large, a tailor can _____ it to fit you.

5. A single regiment _____ on the front of the fortress while the rest of the division prepared to attack from the rear.

6. One of the _____ of this book is that explanations of words should be in simple language.

7. Don't forget to write the return _____ on the parcel.

8. Birds do not learn to build nests but build them by _____.

9. My wife burst into _____ when she heard the bad news.

10. It's only a few _____ walk from here to the station.

해답
1 1. I   2. E   3. A   4. G   5. C   6. B   7. F   8. D   9. K   10. J
2 1. A   2. B   3. A   4. A   5. B
3 1. B   2. A   3. C   4. C   5. A   6. C   7. A   8. C
4 1. attributed   2. ascent   3. stationary   4. alter   5. feinted
   6. principles   7. address   8. instinct   9. tears   10. minutes'

Lesson 40   479

찾아보기

A

abandon	35
abate	265
abdicate	233
abdomen	194
abhor	260
abide	82, 315
abnormal	92
abode	54
abolish	22
abominable	279
abound	344
abrupt	20
absolve	207
absorb	47
abundance	92
accelerate	333
access	220, 428
acclimate	322
accrue	233
accurate	115
accuse	47
acknowledge	20
acme	288
acquire	138
acquit	291
adapt	187, 428
addict	355
address	473
adequate	68
adhere	366
adjacent	296
adjourn	181
adjust	47
administer	128
admonish	246
adolescent	346
adopt	429
adore	43
adorn	136
adverse	429
adversity	378
advocate	150
affect	429
affectation	429
affirmative	126
afflict	198
aggravate	324
aggregate	357
aggression	163
aggrieve	308
aghast	209
agile	262
agitate	163
agony	103
ailment	222
aisle	176
ale	248
allay	275
allege	58
allegiance	82
alley	37
allocate	224
allot	101
all-out	154
alloy	390
allude	407
allure	170
allusion	430
ally	12
aloof	289
altar	130, 470
alter	470
altruistic	298
alumna	449
alumni	449
alumnus	449
amass	310
amaze	90
ambush	414
amenable	161
amend	105
amiable	183
amicable	199
amid	126
amiss	277
ammunition	210
amoral	450
amputate	368
analogy	348
analyze	83
anatomy	335
ancestor	115
anesthetic	402
anew	170
anguish	22
animate	359
annex	326
annihilate	370

anniversary ... 14	associate ... 142	banquet ... 170
annual ... 430	assume ... 140	barbarian ... 35
annul ... 54, 430	assure ... 430	bargain ... 90
anomaly ... 237	astonish ... 181	barometer ... 383
antagonist ... 349	astound ... 252	barracks ... 14
antique ... 337	astronaut ... 392	barrier ... 31, 160
apathy ... 328	astronomy ... 70	batter ... 8
apologize ... 37	athlete ... 13	bawdy ... 368
apparel ... 226	attain ... 113	bayonet ... 214
appeal ... 78	attic ... 56	beacon ... 402
appease ... 127, 250	attire ... 181	bearable ... 92
append ... 361	attribute ... 159, 473	beaver ... 419
appetite ... 140	auction ... 404	beckon ... 220
applause ... 185	audacity ... 366	behalf ... 96
appraise ... 430	audible ... 274	behold ... 253
apprehend ... 372	augment ... 430	belabor ... 409
apprentice ... 92	auspicious ... 274	belch ... 384
apprise ... 430	austere ... 381	bellow ... 240
appropriate ... 66	autocratic ... 346	belongings ... 91
approximate ... 12	automatic ... 94	benevolent ... 138
apt ... 461	avalanche ... 395	benign ... 267
aptitude ... 154	averse ... 333, 429	bequeath ... 392
arable ... 264	avert ... 301	bereave ... 194
architect ... 163	avocation ... 450	besiege ... 91
architecture ... 105	awe ... 113	beware ... 21
arctic ... 56	awkward ... 22	biannual ... 450
ardent ... 286	axis ... 154	bias ... 207
argument ... 430		bicker ... 222
armament ... 416		bide ... 246
armistice ... 380	# B	biennial ... 450
armor ... 60		bigoted ... 313
array ... 174		billow ... 348
arrogant ... 344	badger ... 233	blackout ... 390
articulate ... 338	baffle ... 234	bleach ... 421
artillery ... 394	baggage ... 136	bleak ... 119, 284
ascent ... 470	bald ... 174	blend ... 43, 248
ascribe ... 201	ballad ... 418	bliss ... 23
aslant ... 300	balmy ... 324	blister ... 378
assail ... 31, 322	banal ... 357	blithe ... 272
assault ... 80	bandage ... 431	blizzard ... 199
assent ... 312, 471	bandit ... 196	blockade ... 397
assess ... 212	banish ... 159	blot ... 72
asset ... 227	bankrupt ... 405	blunder ... 124
assiduous ... 355	banner ... 101	blur ... 303

찾아보기 **481**

boisterous 315	cajole 226	choir 49
bond 163	calamity 296	chord 451
bondage 431	calligraphy 404	chore 384
boost 260	callous 308	chronological 370
booth 176	cancer 60	chrysanthemum 406
botch 238	candidate 182	chuckle 72
bounce 130	candor 288	circumference 409
bounty 394	cannon 471	cite 148
bouquet 381	canon 471	clamor 298
bout 49	canvas 471	clan 252
brag 414	canvass 471	clap 137
brainy 279	caprice 262	clarify 106
brawl 224	capture 183	clash 187
brawn 335	cardinal 289	classify 174
breach 380	careless 68	clatter 378
breadth 44	caress 72	claw 72
breed 96	cargo 154	cleanse 415
brew 326	carnal 275	clench 394, 451
briefcase 395	carnivorous 248	clergy 154
brink 124	carton 431	cliff 101
brisk 119	cartoon 431	climate 451
bristle 26	cast 125	clinch 451
brittle 291	castigate 284	cloak 240
broil 165	casual 161	clue 85
broth 235	catastrophe 250	clumsy 33
brunch 416	category 49	cluster 85
brutal 185	cater 390	clutch 8
budget 154	cavalry 419	coarse 66
bugle 130	cavern 405	coax 54
bullet 107	censor 432	code 160
bulletin 176	censure 198, 432	coffin 416
bulwark 201	census 392	cognizant 349
bunch 136	certify 13	coherent 337
burglar 31	cession 471	coincide 13
burrow 397	chafe 238	collapse 61
bustle 78	chamber 212	colleague 55
butt 418	chaos 69	collide 328
buzz 60	charcoal 130	collision 432
	chariot 421	collusion 432
	chasm 227	colossal 310
C	chauffeur 142	comity 380
	chip 119	commemorate 196
	chisel 407	commence 113
cab 124	chivalry 359	commend 44

committee 474	consummate 265	crimson 384
commodious 395	contemplate 8	cripple 154
commodity 26	contemporary 61	crisis 130
communal 361	contemptible 452	crook 102
communism 10	contemptuous 452	crouch 171
commute 372	contend 207	cruise 200
compact 49	content 474	crusade 392
compare 451	context 174	crutch 421
compassion 214	contiguity 366	cucumber 404
compile 344	continual 452	culmination 324
complacent 264	continuous 453	cumber 209
compliment 138	contrast 451	curative 357
comply 383	contrive 222	current 58
component 125	controversy 70	cynical 224
comprehend 94	convention 125	
comprise 277	converge 237	
compromise 187	converse 475	# D
concede 300	convey 13	
conceit 114	convict 152	
concentrate 49	coordinate 128	dainty 73
concept 106	cope 404	dairy 37, 433
concert 474	coral 381	daunt 250
concession 24	cord 451	dazzle 223
concrete 172	cordial 94	debate 117
concur 221	corollary 397	decease 433
condense 161	coroner 402	deceit 24
condescend 253	corpse 176	decent 434
condone 246	corroborate 333	decree 209
confidant 432	cosy 312	dedicate 24
confident 432	council 433	deduce 301
conform 140	counsel 433	defer 140
confront 338	courtesy 139	defiance 185
congenial 346	cowardly 184	deficient 313
congest 323	coxcomb 383	defile 196
congregate 183	cradle 45	deformity 368
congressman 107	craft 72	defunct 276
conjecture 234	cram 391	degrade 267
connotation 452	crave 79	dejected 272
consecrate 194	creak 419	deliberate 137
conservative 33	credible 453	delusion 44
conspicuous 44	credulous 453	demean 235
conspire 356	creed 14	demolish 303
consul 418, 433	crevice 235	demonstrate 185
consume 83	cricket 407	denial 150

denizen 248	discern 37	dreary 32
denotation 452	discipline 182	drill 79
denounce 221	disconsolate 262	drip 15
deny 45	discord 79	drought 439
depart 150	discourse 415	drunken 57
deplore 208	discreet 13	dual 403, 454
deprive 128	discretion 286	dubious 201
deputy 130	disdain 212	duel 454
derange 234	disease 433	dump 142
deride 326	disguise 96	dungeon 380
derogatory 286	dishonest 57	duplicate 237
descent 434	disintegrate 298	duration 250
desert 438, 475	disinterested 453	dwarf 115
designate 247	dismal 310	dwell 21
desolate 103, 165	dismember 264	dwindle 265
despicable 315	dismiss 114	dye 142
despoil 228	disorganized 453	dynasty 395
dessert 438	dispatch 26	
destine 174	dispense 55	
detach 161	disperse 45	# E
detain 214	dissemble 277, 439	
detention 261	dissent 434	
deteriorate 279	dissimulation 198	ecology 361
detonate 348	dissipate 238	economical 24
detract 291	dissuade 288	ecstasy 338
devastate 297	distort 252	edit 106
deviation 196	distract 141	efface 239
devolve 409	distrust 300	effect 429
devour 32	divers 454	effete 226
devout 240	diverse 454	effusive 323
dexterity 335	diversify 312	egoist 454
diagnosis 359	divert 370	egotist 454
diary 433	dizzy 24	elaborate 94
dictate 83	dodge 154	elation 274
digest 475	doleful 350	eligible 439
digital 379	domain 96	eloquence 186
dignify 10	dominant 106	elude 313
dike 254	dominate 163	elusive 356
diminish 56	doting 211	embark 301
dirk 394	doze 337	embellish 224
disapprove 309	drab 289	emerge 115, 454
disassemble 439	draft 439	emigrant 455
disaster 10	drape 328	emigrate 49
discard 226	draught 439	eminent 69, 439

emit 372	exclusive 186	filth 345
employee 152	exemplify 359	fir 419
encamp 334	exhale 33	fishery 406
enchant 367	exile 61	flake 107
enclose 137	exotic 315	flank 171
encumber 346	expand 59	fleece 391
endanger 45	expel 125	flexible 151
endorse 324	expend 47	fling 32
endow 21	expenditure 23	flip 254
enforce 357	expire 94	flirt 421
engross 211	explicit 261	flit 407
enhance 370	exquisite 279	flog 198
enlarge 69	external 95	fluent 83
enmity 285	extirpate 291	flush 85
enshrine 418	extract 117	foe 57
enslave 303	extracurricular 176	foliage 383
ensue 102	exult 440	forbear 361
entangle 348	exultant 297	ford 392
entreat 345		forebear 298
entrust 252		foresee 57
envision 416	# F	formal 26
envy 152		formidable 151
ephemeral 267		formulate 174
epoch 237	fabulous 309	fortify 372
equivalent 139	facet 201	fortitude 196
era 187	facetious 228	forum 382
eradicate 200	facilitate 117	foster 235, 339
erratic 272	facility 350	fowl 91
erroneous 47	faction 214	foxhole 415
erupt 335	faint 472	fracture 208
espy 213	fallacy 262	frail 117
essence 35	farther 459	frantic 26
esteem 148	fascinate 337	fray 221
eternal 127	fatuous 328	frenzy 249
evaluate 326	fawn 397	fret 409
eventually 79	feasible 276	friction 83
everlasting 104	feat 142	frolic 209
evoke 195	feeble 184	frontier 137
evolve 13	feint 472	frugal 323
exaggerate 162	fend 247	fugitive 384
exalt 58, 440	fertile 69	fumble 223
excavate 368	feud 289	fury 48
excess 104, 428	fiction 46	further 459
exclude 172	fiend 234	futile 69, 79

G

gale	151
gallant	127, 224
gallows	394
gamble	165
gangster	416
gap	102
gape	250
garage	176
garbage	9
gash	379
gaudy	356
gaunt	237
genial	310
germ	85
gibberish	396
gingerly	55
glee	264
glib	277
glimmer	200
glint	239
glisten	114
gloom	11
glorify	95
glossy	213
glutton	252
gobble	418
grab	114
graft	403
grandeur	367
gratify	127
gratuitous	288
gregarious	380
grim	69
grin	154
grind	130
grisly	254
groggy	300
groove	195
grope	397
gross	104
grudge	226
gruel	404
grumble	148
grunt	85
guise	241
gull	421
gulp	187
gush	211
gust	406
gym	382

H

habitat	391
haggard	312
hamper	221
hangar	420
hanged	459
haphazard	266
harangue	418
harass	368
hardy	247
harmony	35
harsh	91
haughty	274
hazard	70
headquarters	154
hearth	119
hearty	114
heave	26
heed	201
hegira	383
hemisphere	26
heritage	128
hermit	73
hibernate	348
hideous	149
high-handed	407
hilarious	286
hinder	160
historic	460
historical	460
hoard	102
hoarse	174
homage	32
homely	33
honk	409
horde	385
horrify	347
hospitable	11
hostile	80
hound	15
hover	392
huddle	202
hue	215
hug	55
human	460
humane	461
humid	334
humiliate	55, 302
hung	460
hurtle	228
hustle	404
hygiene	324
hypocrite	358
hypothesis	335

I

identical	184
identify	13
idiot	104
ignite	356
ignoble	313
illegible	416, 439
illiterate	267
illusion	115, 430
imaginary	460
imaginative	460
immaculate	273
immerge	454
immerse	225
immigrant	455

imminent 326, 439	inescapable 32	intimate 475
immoral 450	inevitable 81	intolerant 25
immortal 93	inexhaustible 297	intoxicate 369
impair...................................223	infant 11	intrepid................................300
impartial..............................285	infantry..................................61	intrude...................................36
impatient 44	infect 24	intuition...............................348
impeach 288	infer......................................367	invade...................................46
impede 303	infinite.................................104	invalid 252
impend 359	inflammation 415	invest...................................152
imperative 315	inflict...................................372	inveterate 310
impersonal 403	infuriate...............................309	invidious 261
implement 137	ingenious 139, 440	invincible 277
implicit................................264	ingenuity.............................276	invoke 396
implore................................251	ingenuous 262, 440	irradiate...............................339
impolite..................................69	ingratiate.............................406	irreparable...........................312
impose.................................152	ingredient............................79	irresponsible 139
imprison..............................370	initial 46	irrigation 334
improve...............................165	initiative..............................186	irritate..................................129
improvise............................350	injustice...............................115	isolate..................................160
impudent.............................328	innovate...............................337	iterate 239
impunity 379	innumerable.........................93	
inadequate 162	inquisitive 350	
inaugurate 175	inscription...........................198	**J**
incapacitate.........................249	insert 128	
incense 165	insignificant........................117	
incentive 235	insolent 290	janitor..................................213
incessant 237	insolvent 323	jaw...37
incomparable......................461	inspect.................................117	jealous.................................440
incomplete..........................172	install...................................26	jeopardy..............................274
inconsolable 197	instinct 475	jerk..15
incredible 461	insuperable 211	jolly......................................57
incredulous 461	insure 430	jolt..195
incumbent...........................345	intact 298	jovial 302
incur....................................380	intangible............................324	judicious 326
incurable 279	integrate......................104, 163	junction 85
indefinite...............................34	intellectual 172	justify....................................59
independent..........................81	intension.............................472	
index 107	intention..............................472	
indifference.........................361	intercept..............................358	**K**
indignant.............................171	intercourse..........................209	
indulge..................................35	interject...............................382	
indulgent.............................291	internal................................139	kernel 420
industrialize..........................59	interpret...............................182	kidnap 226
inedible 394	intimacy................................46	kin..114

kindred 314
kit 421
knave 254
knob 176

L

lag 407
lair 383
larceny 228
lash 26
latent 241
laundry 119
lavish 267
lay 461
leap 137
legend 67
legislate 152
legitimate 129
lever 415
levy 409
liable 104, 462
liberate 48
license 176
lie 461
likely 462
limber 247
limp 38
linguist 385
link 81
literate 162
loathe 273
locksmith 391
loiter 149
loom 403
lounge 182
lucid 285
lull 303
lump 200
luster 138, 215
luxuriant 462
luxurious 462

M

magnify 70
magnitude 208
maintain 153
malady 221
malcontent 416
malice 370
malign 261
mandatory 274
maneuver 404
manifest 347
manipulate 335
mansion 162
manual 279
manure 379
margin 129
marine 165
marsh 102
masquerade 392
massacre 249
material 441
materiel 441
mature 11
maudlin 297
maximum 57
maze 235
meadow 171
measles 420
meddle 198
mediocre 361
meditate 328
meek 162
melancholy 314
menace 91, 209
mendacious 291
mimic 372
minute 476
miracle 44
mirage 263
mirth 276
miscellaneous 105

mischief 67
mischievous 264
miser 83
miserable 139
missionary 131
mist 160
mistress 57
mitigate 290
moan 102, 463
mobile 171
modify 36
modulate 360
mold 15
mole 380
molest 299
monarch 83
monk 61
monotony 345
moral 441
morale 394, 441
mordant 309
morsel 96, 421
mortify 223
mourn 463
mow 418
muffle 251
multitude 116
mumble 202
munition 406
mushroom 382
mute 237
mutual 141
myriad 396
mystify 337

N

nasty 142
naughty 407
nausea 323
navigate 49
negotiate 356

nibble 197
nightmare 383
nominate 70
nonplus 315
nostalgia 397
notable 125
notation 415
notorious 103
nourish 165
nuisance 107
numb 367
nutrition 347

O

obedient 34
object 476
oblivious 325
obscure 81
obsolete 195
obstacle 9
obstinate 339
obstruct 55
obvious 266
offence 311
onerous 239
oppress 36
optimism 81
oral 463
orchard 61
ordeal 211
ordinance 442
ordnance 442
ostensible 288
ostentatious 225
overbearing 300
override 409
overt 266
overthrow 55
overtone 252
overwhelm 119

P

pacify 141
packet 213
pact 226
pageant 197
paltry 288
pane 49
panel 73
panic 108
pant 391
parallel 176
paramount 287
parish 442
parley 254
partisan 237
partition 84
paste 15
pastime 302
patent 381
paternal 312
pathetic 21
patron 15
pavilion 417
pawn 241
peal 403
peddle 267
peep 114
pension 27
pensive 273
perfume 138
perfunctory 278
perish 442
perpendicular 285
perpetrate 442
perpetual 184
perpetuate 442
perplex 48
persecute 358, 442
persevere 215
persist 67
personal 463

personality 442
personalty 442
personnel 463
pertinent 290
pervade 228
pest 49
petition 153
petroleum 385
petty 127
phase 166
phenomenon 73
philanthropy 247
phoenix 393
pilgrim 418
pillar 38
pinch 85
pine 234
pious 9
pirate 61
pith 208
placid 369
plaintiff 303
plausible 292
plight 405
plod 221
plunder 143, 297
plural 172
pollute 348
poltroon 314
pompous 315
ponder 249
pore 236
porous 379
portable 443
porter 160
portrait 106
posture 198
potable 261, 443
potential 38, 279
pouch 211
prairie 85
prank 251
pray 472
precarious 276

precaution 106	pry 226	recapture 55
precede 287	psychology 175	receipt 141
precipice 210	publicity 164	reciprocate 345
precise 34	puff 420	recite 71
preclude 263	pulpit 213	recollect 247
predecessor 290	pulse 106	reconcile 153
predict 79	punctual 129	recruit 131
predominant 223	purify 328	recur 337
preeminent 334		redeem 323
prefix 57		redundant 264
prejudice 11	# Q	refine 175
preliminary 93		refrigerator 38
premier 131		refuse 476
preordain 276	quaint 173	registrar 464
preponderance 326	quake 241	register 464
prescribe 59, 443	qualify 84	regulate 9
presentiment 225	quarry 396	rehearse 361
presume 59		relax 58
prevalent 119		reliable 95
prey 472	# R	relic 202
primitive 23		relish 208
principal 472		reluctant 186
principle 472	radiate 13	rely 164
priority 95	radical 32	remit 367
probe 252	raft 382	remnant 221
proficient 36	raid 79	remote 93
profuse 299	raise 463	renew 106
prohibit 117	rally 409	renounce 302
prolong 23	ransack 200	renowned 91
prominent 141	ransom 415	repel 79
prone 394	rapture 91	repent 118
propensity 239	rash 300	repetition 95
prophecy 360	rational 34	replete 278
proprietor 188	rattle 408	replica 312
proscribe 444	rave 215	repose 93
prosecute 370, 443	razor 15	repress 347
prostrate 406	reality 444	reproach 21
prototype 421	realm 114	reprove 268
protrude 350	realty 444	repugnant 339
provisional 44	reap 21	reservoir 383
provoke 71	reassure 372	resolute 118
prowess 309, 336	rebuff 266	resound 397
prowl 195	rebuke 275	respectably 463
prudent 67	recant 228	respectfully 463

respective 25		sequence 36
respectively 463		serene 81
respiration 356	# S	serial 373
respond 139		sermon 103
restore 71	sagacity 285	session 471
restrain 44, 129	sage 327	sever 316
retaliate 369	sailer 464	severe 50
retard 273	sailor 465	shack 379
retort 155	salon 465	shaggy 345
retract 164	saloon 465	shallow 292
retrospect 285	salute 50	shambles 228
revenue 105	salvage 241	shear 418
revere 348	salvation 131	sheer 263
reverse 171	sanction 292	shimmer 337
revise 188	sanctuary 210	shiver 32
rickety 391	sane 151	shove 86
riddle 249	sanitary 223	shovel 9
rife 287	sarcasm 358	shred 254
rigid 34	satiate 225	shrewd 93
rigorous 21	satirical 371	shrine 253
rim 85	saunter 251	shroud 417
riot 9	savor 350	shrug 120
rip 149	savory 173	shun 273
rise 464	scan 238	siege 182
risky 186	scholar 25	significant 129
rite 325	scoff 405	simplify 11
roam 171	scold 119	simulate 325
robust 303	scoop 195	simultaneous 67
roundup 403	scope 27	singe 239
rouse 80	scorch 213	singular 362
rout 314	scour 227	sip 381
routine 96	scourge 197	site 103
rubbish 236	scramble 108	skeleton 176
rudiment 334	screech 211	skeptical 367
rue 261	scrupulous 297, 336	skull 38
rummage 198	scuttle 394	slack 299
rumor 119	seclusion 312	slap 15
rumple 385	secure 182	slash 200
rural 23	seep 323	slaughter 59
ruthless 280	selfish 46	slay 215
rye 393	sensation 153	sleet 420
	sensitive 129	slim 56
	sensuous 360	slum 396
	sequel 241	slump 200

sly 32	spurt 417	subvert 350
smear 382	squeeze 108	succession 84
smite 247	stab 238	succinct 263
smog 202	stall 33	sue 195
smolder 406	stalwart 273	suffice 336
smother 234	stammer 86	suicide 15
smuggle 347	standstill 131	sulfur 381
snare 421	stately 9	sullen 61
sneak 208	stationary 473	sultry 316
sneeze 385	stationery 473	summary 36
snore 222	statistics 59	summit 81
snug 302	statue 444	sundry 297
sociable 153	stature 211, 444	superficial 58
sod 383	status 195	superfluous 358
sojourn 311	statute 253	superstition 188
solicit 278	stealthy 369	supervise 14
solicitude 265	stifle 334	supplement 59
solitary 349	stigmatize 391	suppress 103
somber 266	stool 91	surge 213
soot 408	straggle 403	surmise 254
soothe 116	strait 108	surname 420
sop 415	strangle 419	surplus 265
soporific 339	strategy 38	survive 95
sordid 288	streak 120	suspend 23, 118, 311
sovereign 48	strenuous 304	sustain 22
span 379	strife 143	swagger 227
spank 249	strip 143	swear 138
sparse 275	strive 183	symmetry 323
species 27	stroll 45	symptom 68
speck 143	strut 239	synthetic 268
specs 149	stubborn 67	
spectacle 125	stun 405	
spectator 73	stunt 393	# T
specter 327	sturdy 127	
speculate 236	suave 328	
spice 356	subconscious 465	tablet 215
splash 67	subdue 160	taboo 228
splinter 397	submarine 108	taciturn 276
spontaneous 287	submerge 173	tack 395
sporadic 300	submit 81	tackle 125
spout 199	subscribe 371	tact 360
sprawl 409	subsist 261	tactics 373
sprout 210	suburb 36	tangible 347
spur 166	subversive 309	taper 382

tardy 290	toxic 301	**U**
tariff 177	tract 188	
tart 299	trait 68	
tattoo 406	traitor 149	
tear 477	trample 131	ulterior 403
technical 86	tranquil 11	ultimate 97, 173
technicality 338	transcribe 325	umpteen 302
technique 25	transcript 465	unanimous 356
tedious 25	transcription 465	unbounded 268
telegraph 16	transfix 236	uncomparable 461
telescope 61	transform 96, 161	unconscious 465
temperate 48	transient 362	undermine 212
tempest 160	transit 97	undertake 38
temporary 93, 309	transparent 106	underworld 151
tension 71	trappings 229	undistinguished 23
tentative 139	trash 384	undo 408
tenuous 287	traverse 199	undue 275
terminate 186	tray 177	undulate 225
testimony 248	tread 210	unfair 184
textile 155	trench 38	unify 164
thaw 166	tribulation 345	uninterested 453
thigh 155	tributary 408	unique 81
thraldom 278	tribute 84	universal 107
thrash 73	trickle 251	unmoral 450
threshold 149	trifle 60	unorganized 453
thrifty 46	trifling 105	unquenchable 391
throb 234	trigger 422	unravel 240
throng 126	triumph 339	unruly 261
thwart 266	tropical 127	unworthy 11
tickle 177	truce 397	uphold 149
tidings 208	trudge 409	upset 10
tidy 289	tug 120	upsurge 381
timid 34	tumble 197	urban 367
tinge 222	tumult 327	urbane 285
tingle 415	turmoil 311	used 477
tinkle 396	tutor 143	usher 62
tint 86	twilight 184	utensil 214
toilet 155	twine 385	utmost 80
token 149	twinkle 143	
tolerate 80	twitch 379	**V**
torment 22	typify 186	
torrent 14	tyrant 71	
totter 249		
tow 9		vacancy 37

찾아보기 **493**

vacant 184	voluntary 46	
vacation 444	voluptuous 215	
vacuum 82	vulnerable 314	**Y**
vagary 227	vulture 405	
vague 70		yawn 150
valid 12		yoke 131
valor 349		
vanity 151	**W**	
vanquish 33		**Z**
variable 141	wail 188	
varnish 417	wallet 223	zeal 162
vehement 266	walnut 419	zealous 297, 440
vehicle 108	wane 316	zinc 108
vengeance 175	ward 395	zoology 127
venomous 276	warden 255	
veracity 185	warehouse 384	
verbal 463	warily 97	
verge 292	warrant 223	
verify 92	wary 369	
vernacular 398	waver 126	
versatile 334	wayfarer 202	
versus 393	weather 451	
vertical 34	weave 108	
veteran 82	weir 422	
vex 10	weird 371	
via 382	whet 290	
viable 299	whirlpool 396	
vicinity 56	whirr 385	
vicious 116	wholesome 34	
vicissitude 255	wield 406	
vigilance 329	wig 420	
vigor 72	wilt 278	
vile 68	wistful 199	
vindicate 358	withdraw 60	
vindictive 360	wither 188	
violate 173	withstand 172	
virtual 241	wizard 241	
vitiate 304	wont 202	
vocation 183, 444, 450	wrangle 313	
vociferous 280	wretched 268	
vogue 200	writhe 253	
void 116		
voluble 280		

무조건 따라하면 통하는
일상생활 영어 여행회화 365
이원준 저 | 128*188mm | 368쪽 |
12,000원(mp3 파일 무료 제공)

무조건 따라하면 통하는
일상생활 일본 여행회화 365
이원준 저 | 128*188mm | 368쪽 |
12,000원(mp3 파일 무료 제공)

무조건 따라하면 통하는
일상생활 중국 여행회화 365
이원준 저 | 128*188mm | 368쪽 |
12,000원(mp3 파일 무료 제공)

무조건 따라하면 통하는
일상생활 유럽 여행회화 375
양혜영 저 | 128*188mm | 360쪽 |
14,000원(mp3 파일 무료 제공)

미국을 뒤흔든 감동의 순간을 영어로 만나다
미국 명연설문 베스트 50
김정우 저 | 170*220mm | 448쪽
15,000원(mp3 CD 포함)

영국식 영어발음, 청취력 강화 + IELTS 리스닝 & 스피킹 완벽대비
영국 명연설문 베스트 30
강홍식 저 | 170*220mm | 336쪽
15,000원(mp3 CD 포함)

영어발음, 청취력 강화 + TOEIC 리스닝 & 스피킹 완벽대비
리더들의 명연설문 베스트 30
강홍식 저 | 170*220mm | 328쪽
15,000원(mp3 CD 포함)

[저자 직강 동영상 제공] 영어발음, 청취력 강화 + 리스닝 & 스피킹 30일 완전정복, 테드)
유명 인사들의 명연설문 듣고 말하기 베스트 30
박기령 저 | 170*220mm | 272쪽
15,000원(저자 직강 동영상 + mp3 DVD 포함)